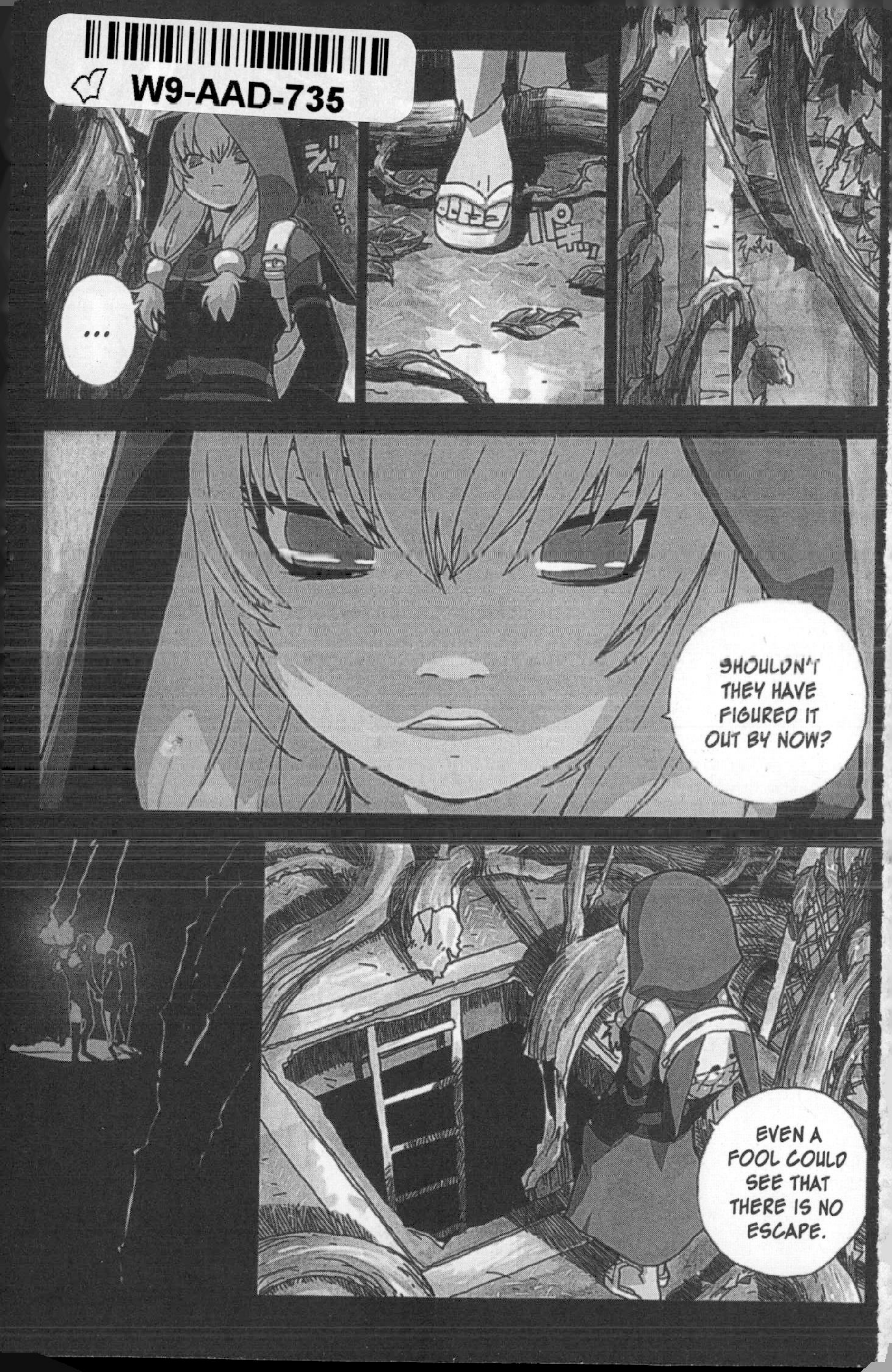
...
SHOULDN'T THEY HAVE FIGURED IT OUT BY NOW?
EVEN A FOOL COULD SEE THAT THERE IS NO ESCAPE.

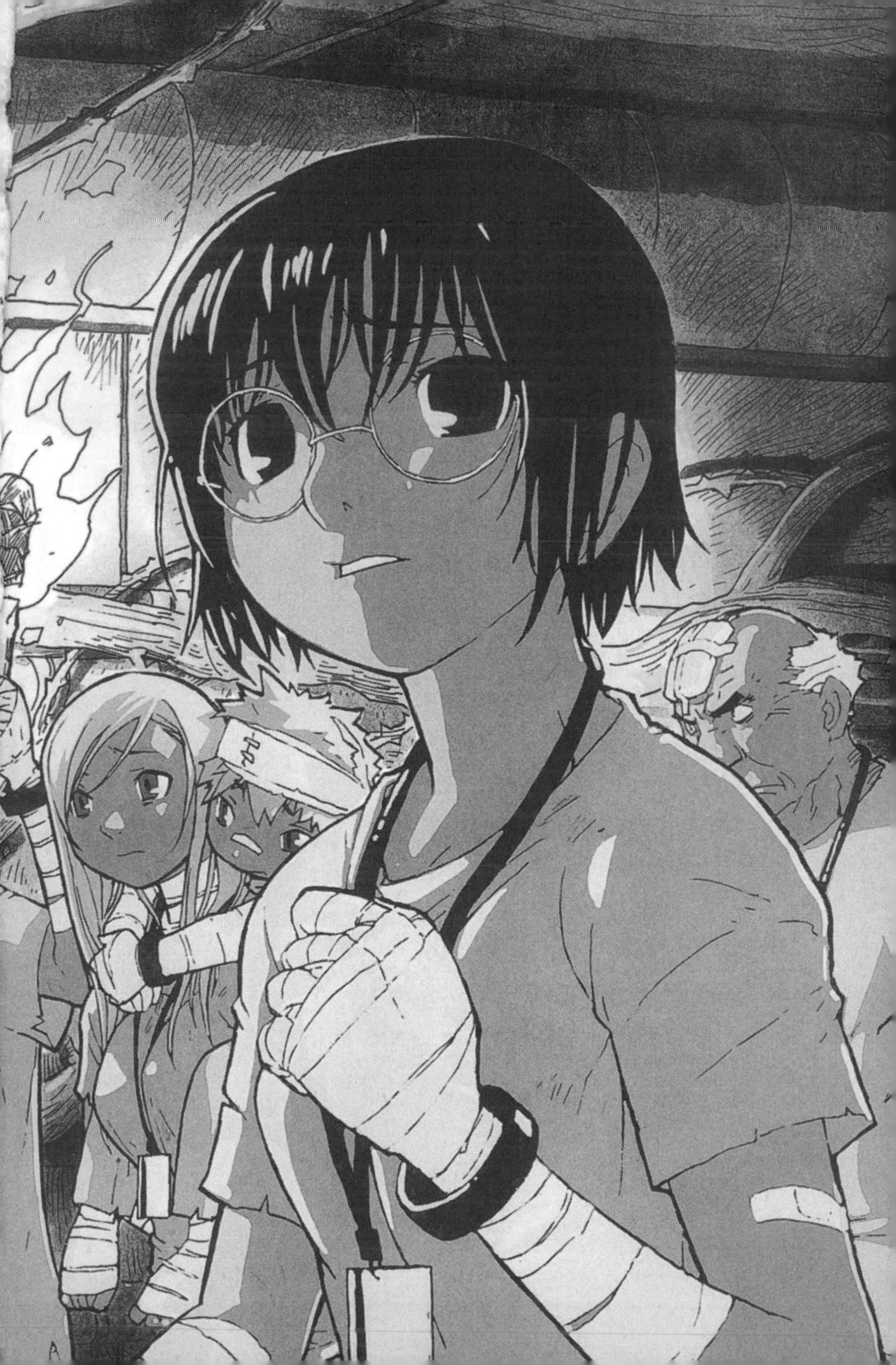

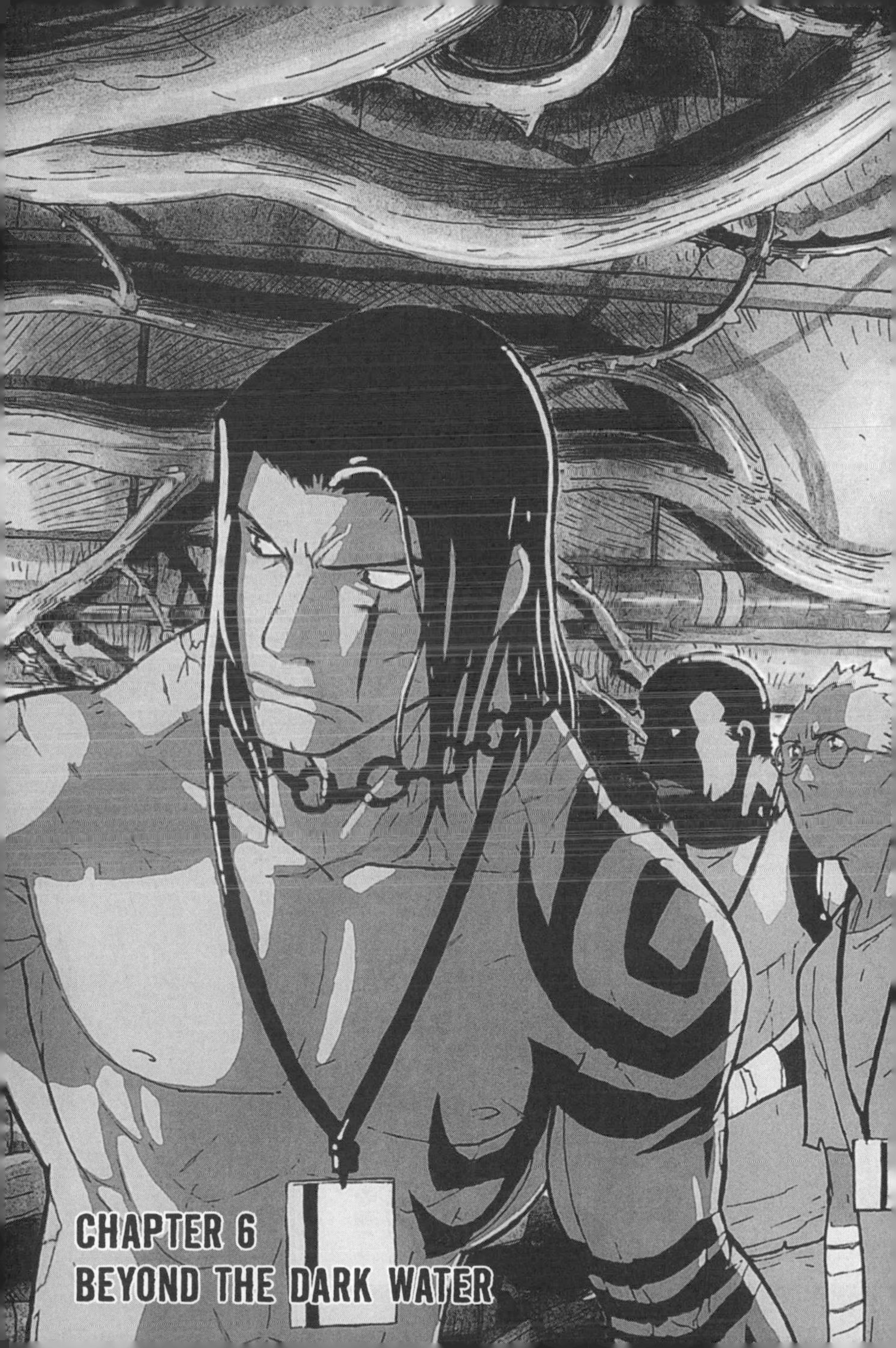
CHAPTER 6
BEYOND THE DARK WATER

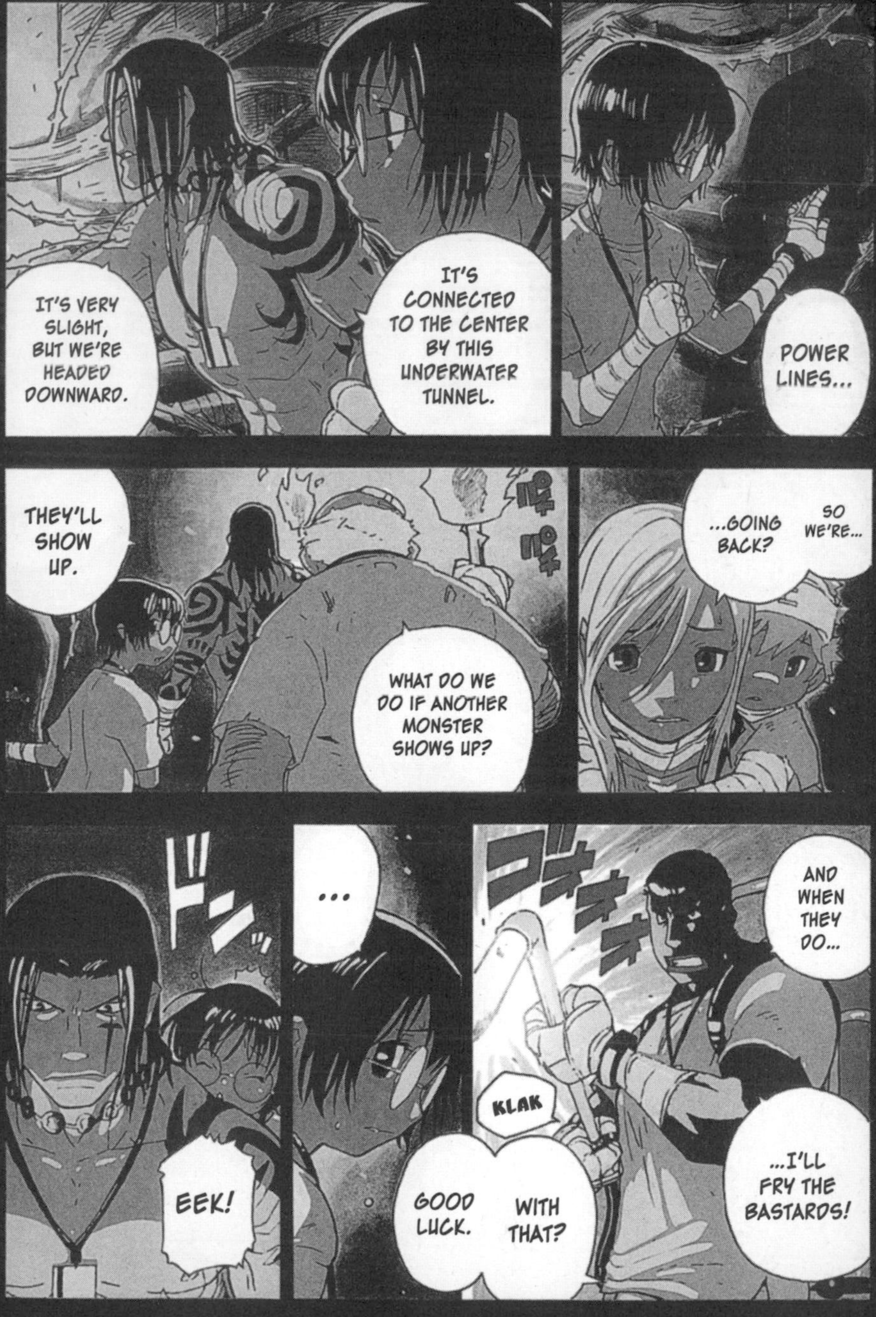
POWER LINES...
IT'S CONNECTED TO THE CENTER BY THIS UNDERWATER TUNNEL.
IT'S VERY SLIGHT, BUT WE'RE HEADED DOWNWARD.
SO WE'RE...
...GOING BACK?
WHAT DO WE DO IF ANOTHER MONSTER SHOWS UP?
THEY'LL SHOW UP.
AND WHEN THEY DO...
...I'LL FRY THE BASTARDS!
KLAK
WITH THAT?
GOOD LUCK.
...
EEK!

いばらの王

King of Thorn.

②

岩原裕二
Yuji Iwahara

King of Thorn Volume 2
Created by Yuji Iwahara

Translation - Alexis Kirsch
English Adaptation - Aaron Sparrow
Copy Editor - Stephanie Duchin
Retouch and Lettering - Star Print Brokers
Production Artist - Michael Paolilli
Graphic Designer - James Lee

Editor - Tim Beedle
Digital Imaging Manager - Chris Buford
Pre-Production Supervisor - Erika Terriquez
Production Manager - Elisabeth Brizzi
Managing Editor - Vy Nguyen
Creative Director - Anne Marie Horne
Editor-in-Chief - Rob Tokar
Publisher - Mike Kiley
President and C.O.O. - John Parker
C.E.O. and Chief Creative Officer - Stuart Levy

A  Manga

TOKYOPOP and  are trademarks or registered trademarks of TOKYOPOP Inc.

TOKYOPOP Inc.
5900 Wilshire Blvd. Suite 2000
Los Angeles, CA 90036

E-mail: info@TOKYOPOP.com
Come visit us online at www.TOKYOPOP.com

ISBN: 978-1-59816-236-3

First TOKYOPOP printing: October 2007
10 9 8 7 6 5 4 3 2
Printed in the USA

KING of THORN ™

Volume 2

Created by
Yuji Iwahara

KING of THORN ™

Contents

KING of THORN™

Volume 2

Created by
Yuji Iwahara

HAMBURG // LONDON // LOS ANGELES // TOKYO

Story So Far

It wasn't supposed to be like this. Kasumi had all the interests and dreams of a typical teenage girl—listening to music, finding a cute boyfriend, getting into a good college. She was happy and optimistic, looking forward to navigating the corridors of adolescent life with her twin sister Shizuku at her side. And then Medusa struck.

Like many epidemics, this one started quietly—a rumor here and there, a story told to you by a neighbor about someone he knew, an article buried in the back of the evening paper. But pretty soon, it exploded. A disease that slowly turns the victim to stone, the Medusa Virus was deadly and untreatable, and it didn't take long to get out of control.

Chosen as part of a small group of individuals who were to be cryogenically frozen until a cure could be found, Kasumi was one of the lucky ones, but she didn't feel like celebrating. Shizuku, who was also afflicted with the disease, wasn't chosen. As she entered the cryo-pod and drifted off to sleep, Kasumi's thoughts lay with her sister and the near certainty that she would never see her again.

But something went wrong. Her cryo-sleep cut short, Kasumi finds herself awakened uncured and in a world she barely recognizes. The once urban cryogenics center is now overgrown with hostile vines and thorns, and violent beasts prowl the countryside. If Kasumi is to have any chance at survival, she must now band together with her fellow survivors to piece together what went wrong, and determine if there's any way to fix it. It won't be an easy task, however, for this new world is a deadly one, with new dangers awaiting around every corner...

WHAT'S WRONG?
TAKE A LOOK.
?
ポチャン
?!
ポチャン
ポチャン
IT'S FLOODED!
A DEAD END?
NO.
LOOK.
THERE'S A DRAFT.

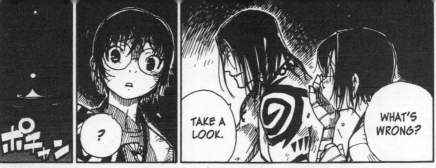

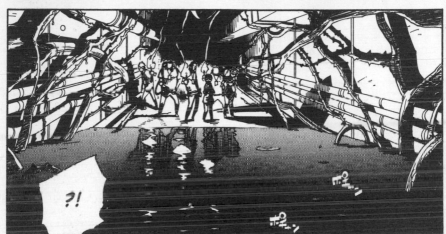

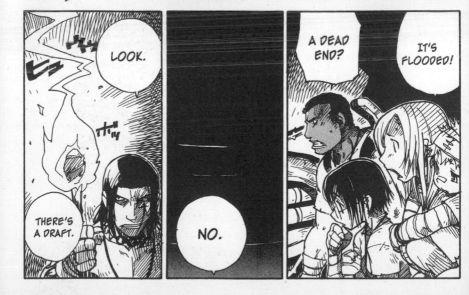

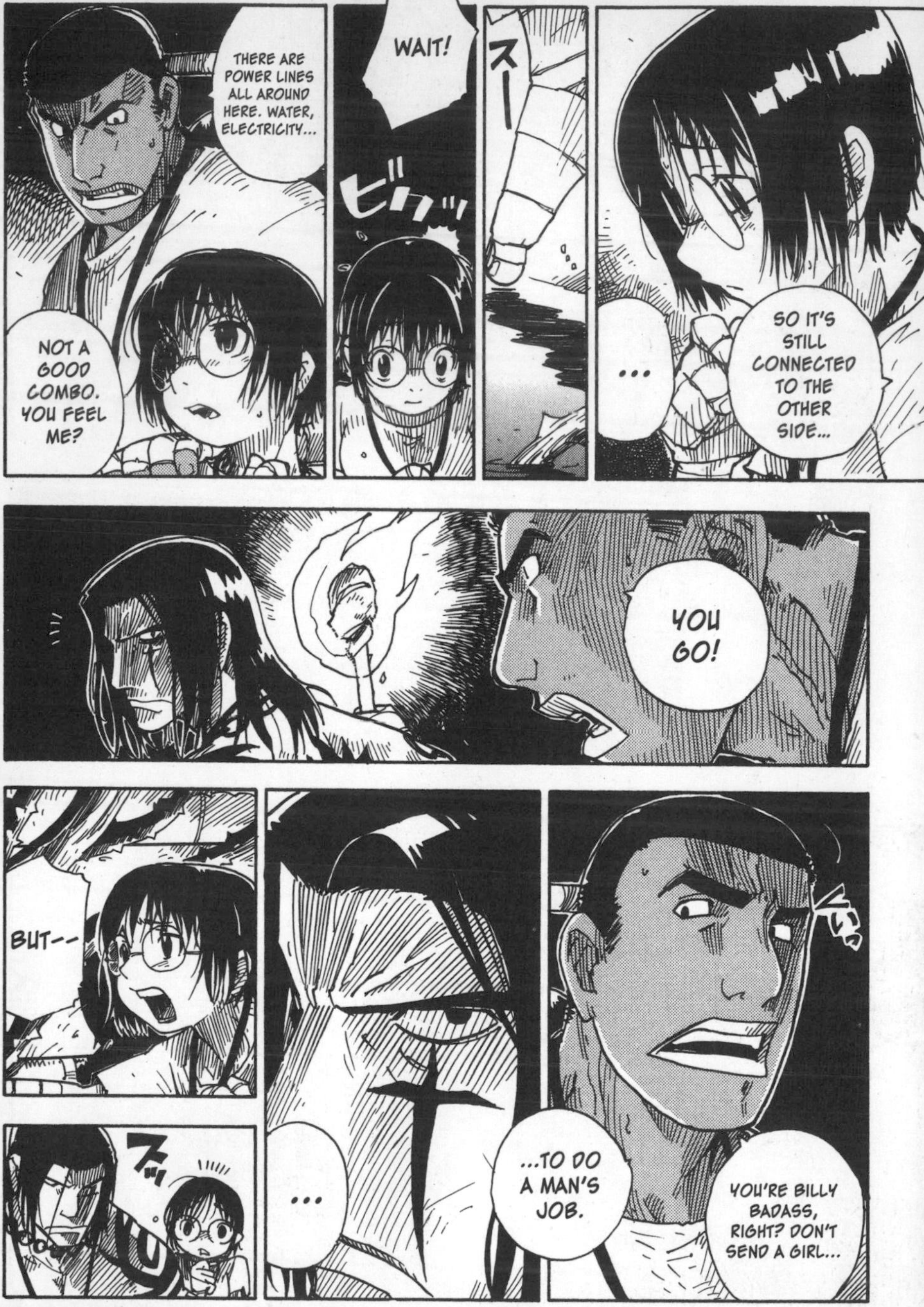

SO IT'S STILL CONNECTED TO THE OTHER SIDE...
...
WAIT!
THERE ARE POWER LINES ALL AROUND HERE. WATER, ELECTRICITY...
NOT A GOOD COMBO. YOU FEEL ME?
YOU GO!
YOU'RE BILLY BADASS, RIGHT? DON'T SEND A GIRL...
...TO DO A MAN'S JOB.
...
BUT--

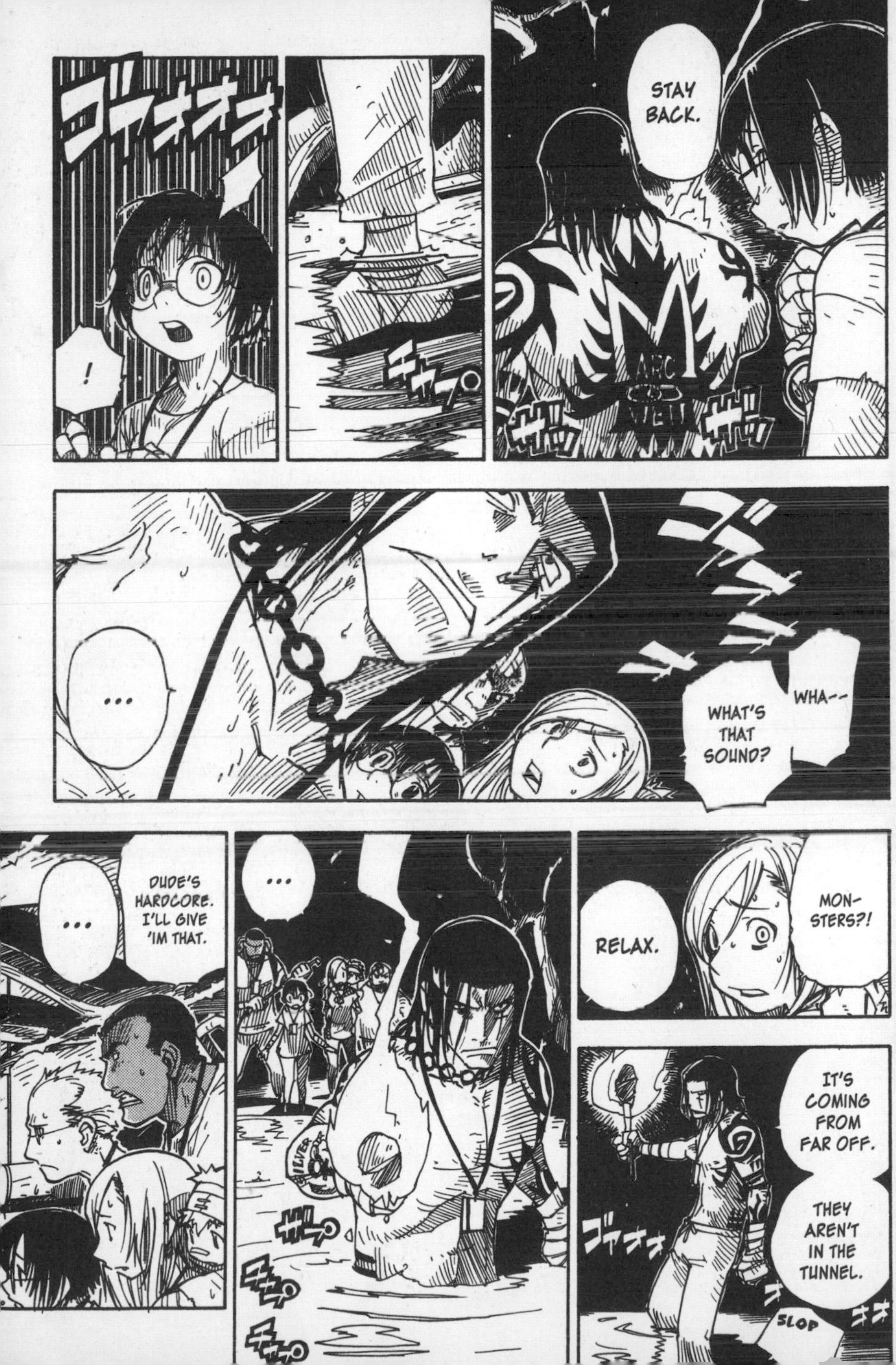
STAY BACK.
ゴァオオオ
!
WHA--
WHAT'S THAT SOUND?
...
MON-STERS?!
RELAX.
IT'S COMING FROM FAR OFF.
THEY AREN'T IN THE TUNNEL.
SLOP
...
DUDE'S HARDCORE. I'LL GIVE 'IM THAT.
...

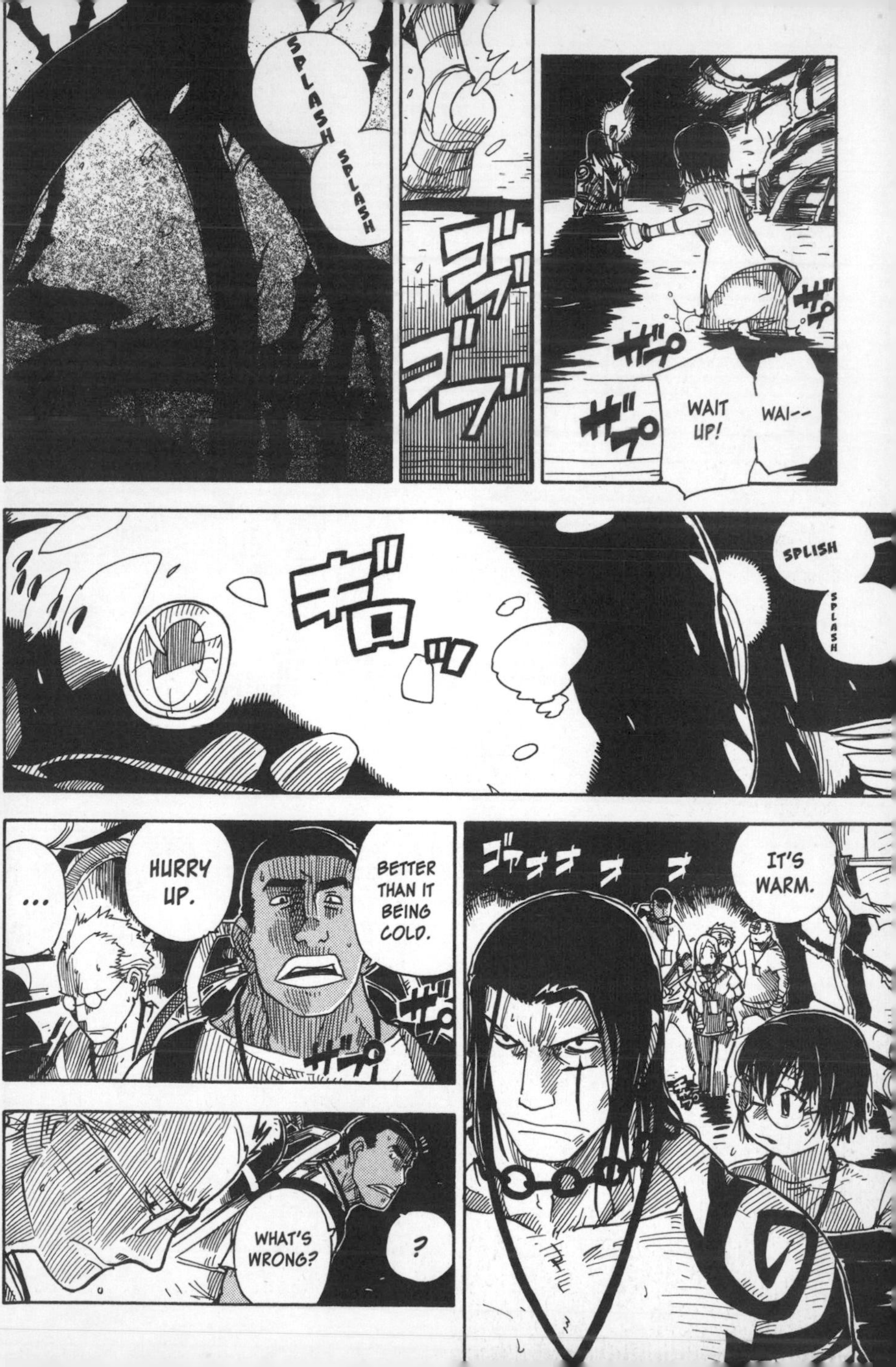
ザプ
ザプ
ザプ
WAIT UP!
WAI--
ゴブ
ゴブ
SPLASH
SPLASH
SPLASH
SPLISH
SPLASH
ギロ
ゴァオオオオ
IT'S WARM.
BETTER THAN IT BEING COLD.
HURRY UP.
...
ザプ
ザプ
?
WHAT'S WRONG?

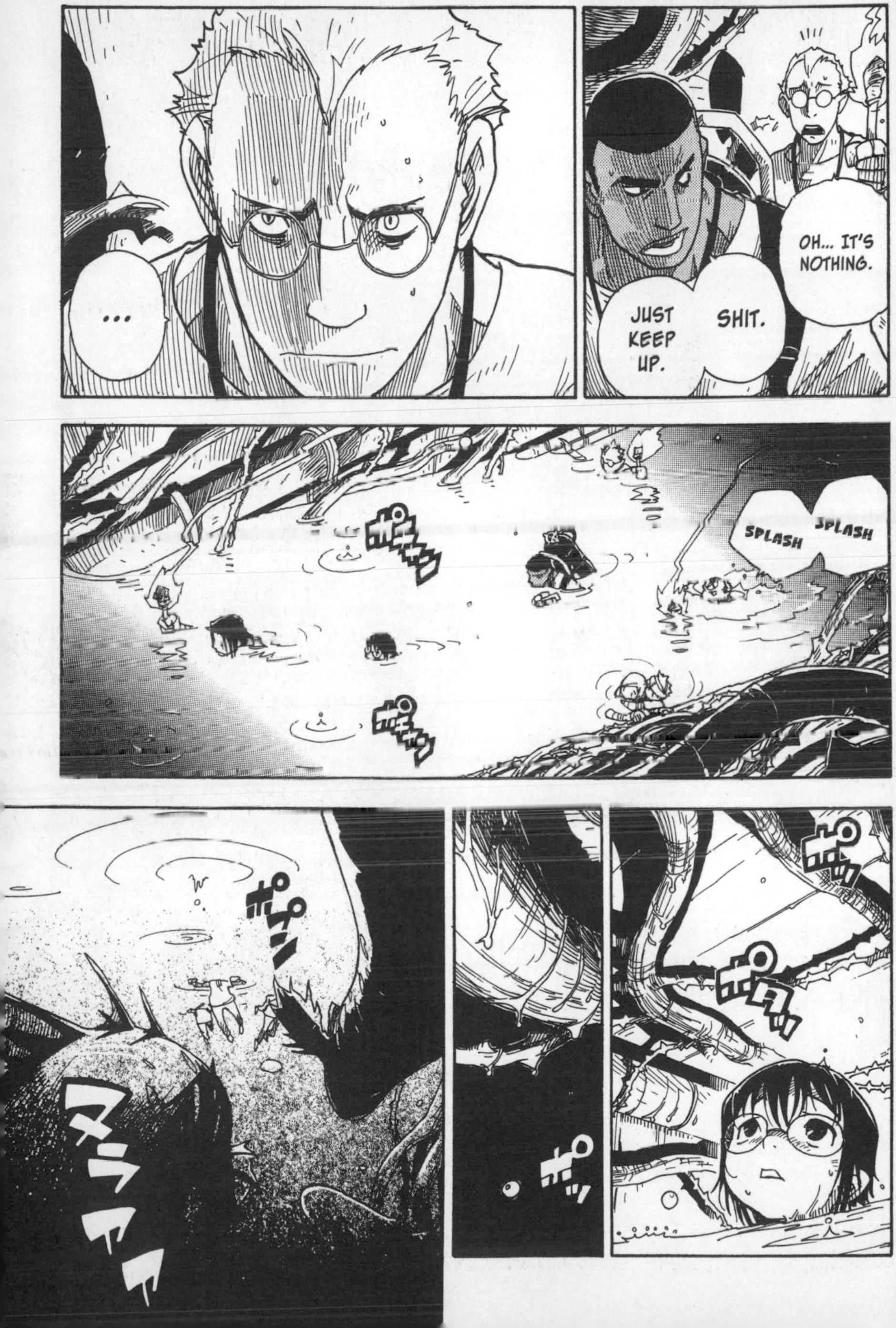
OH... IT'S NOTHING.
SHIT.
JUST KEEP UP.
...
SPLASH
SPLASH

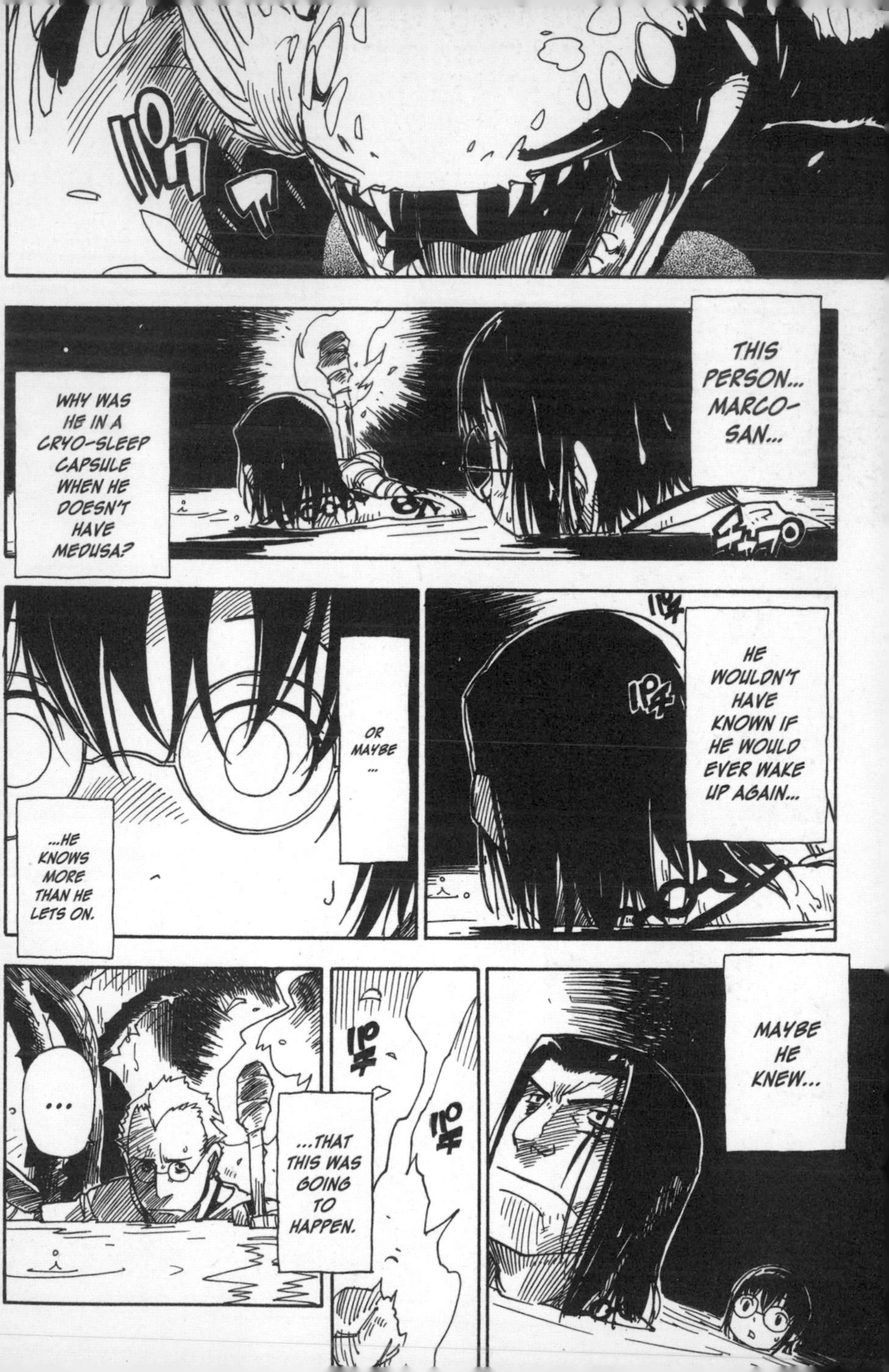
THIS PERSON... MARCO-SAN...
WHY WAS HE IN A CRYO-SLEEP CAPSULE WHEN HE DOESN'T HAVE MEDUSA?
HE WOULDN'T HAVE KNOWN IF HE WOULD EVER WAKE UP AGAIN...
OR MAYBE ...
...HE KNOWS MORE THAN HE LETS ON.
MAYBE HE KNEW...
...THAT THIS WAS GOING TO HAPPEN.
...

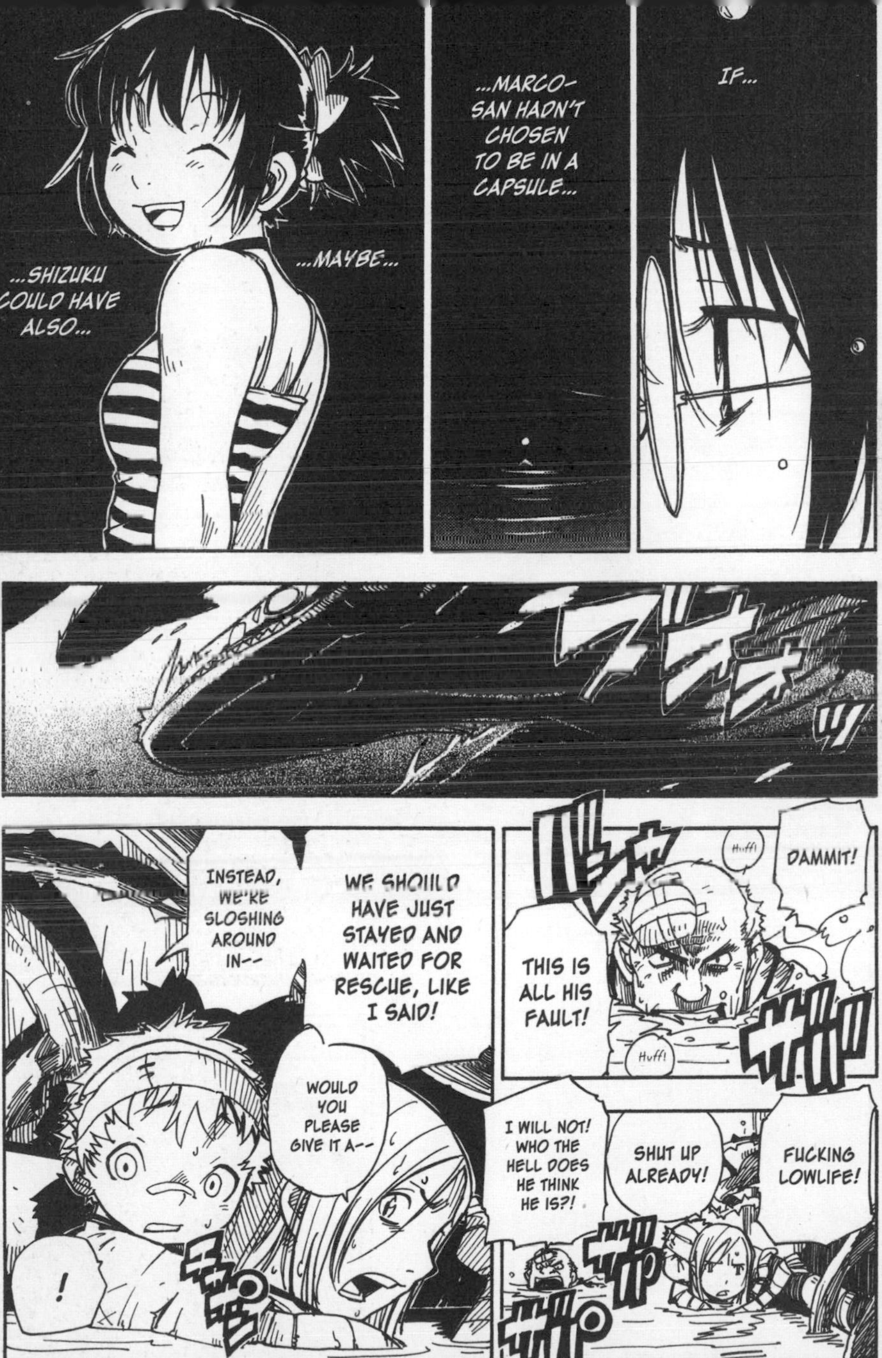
IF...
...MARCO-SAN HADN'T CHOSEN TO BE IN A CAPSULE...
...MAYBE...
...SHIZUKU COULD HAVE ALSO...
DAMMIT!
Huff!
THIS IS ALL HIS FAULT!
Huff!
WE SHOULD HAVE JUST STAYED AND WAITED FOR RESCUE, LIKE I SAID!
INSTEAD, WE'RE SLOSHING AROUND IN--
FUCKING LOWLIFE!
SHUT UP ALREADY!
I WILL NOT! WHO THE HELL DOES HE THINK HE IS?!
WOULD YOU PLEASE GIVE IT A--
!

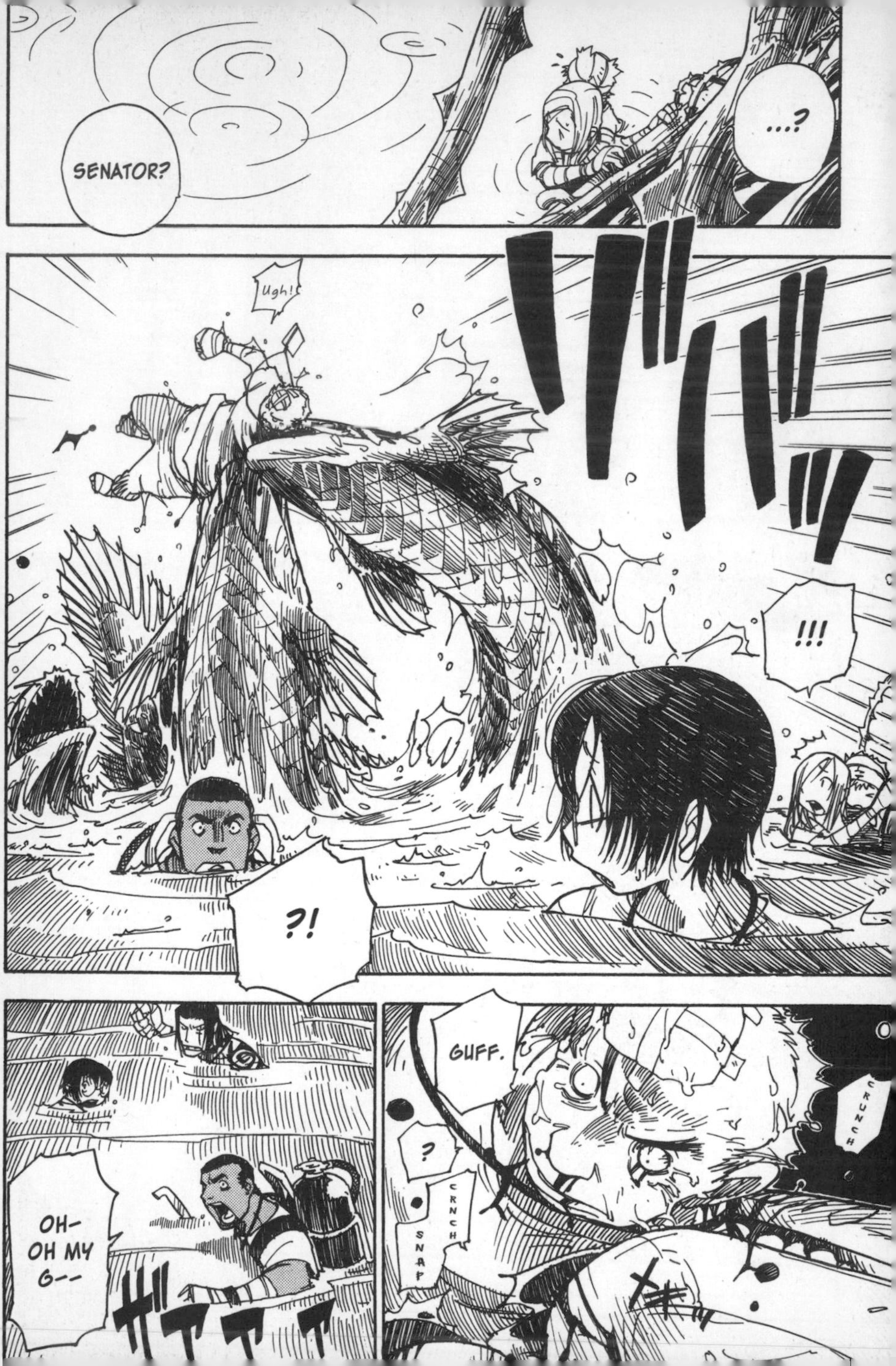
...?
SENATOR?
Ugh!
!!!
?!
OH-
OH MY
G--
GUFF.
?
CRNCH
SNAP
CRUNCH

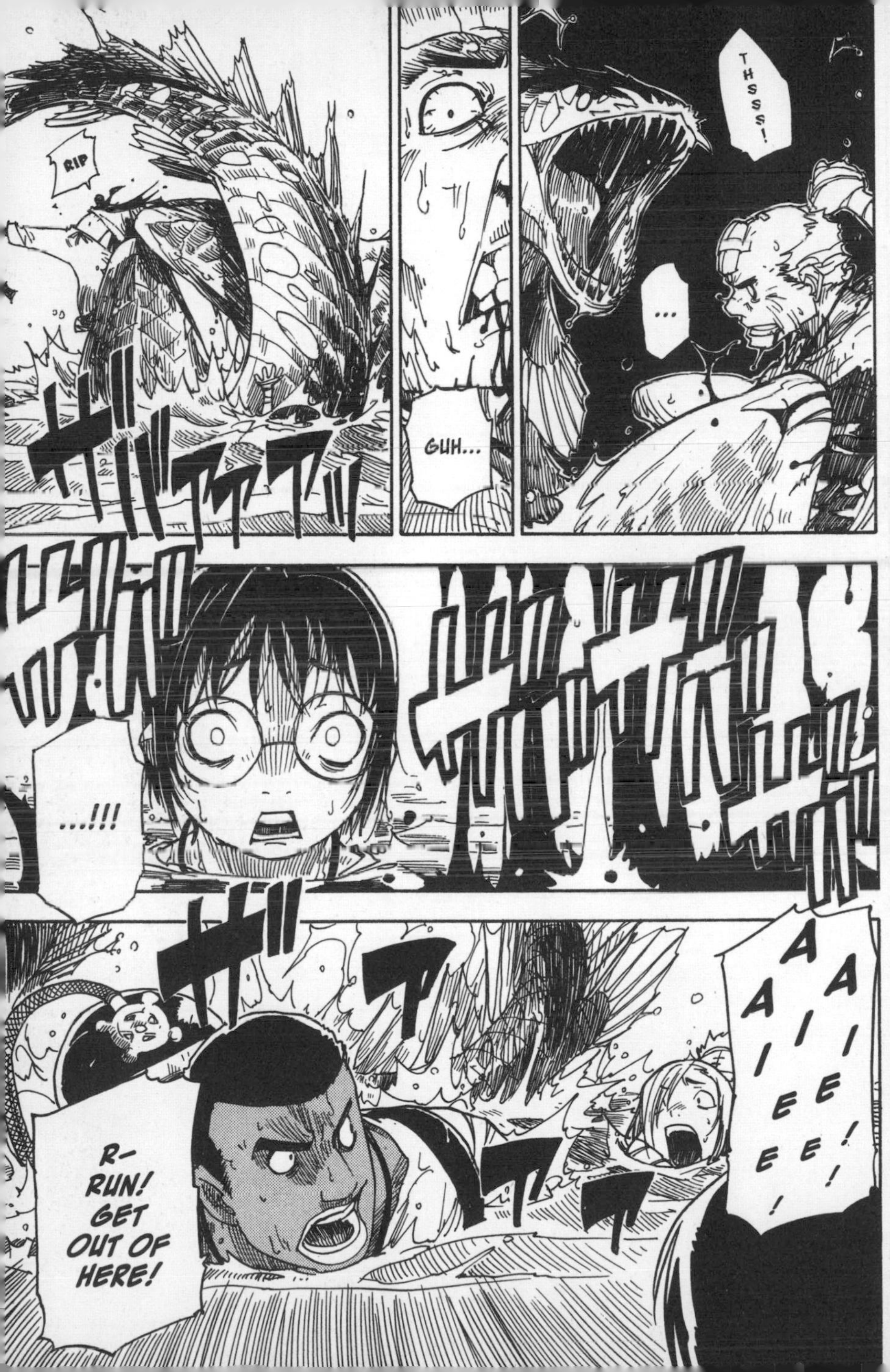
THSSS!
...
GUH...
RIP
...!!!
AAIIEEE!
AIIEEE!
R-RUN! GET OUT OF HERE!

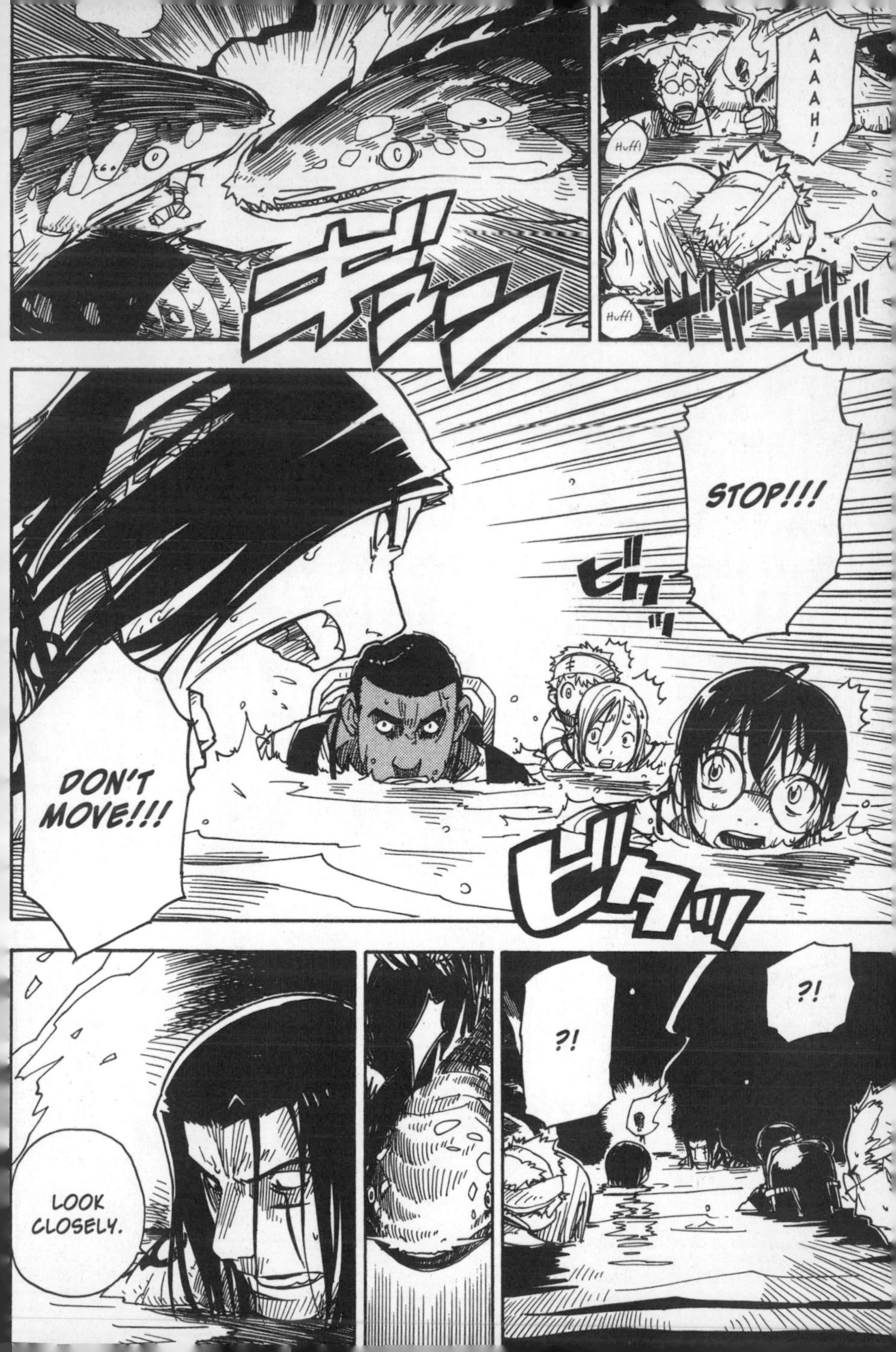

AAAAH!
Huff!
Huff!
STOP!!!
DON'T MOVE!!!
?!
?!
LOOK CLOSELY.

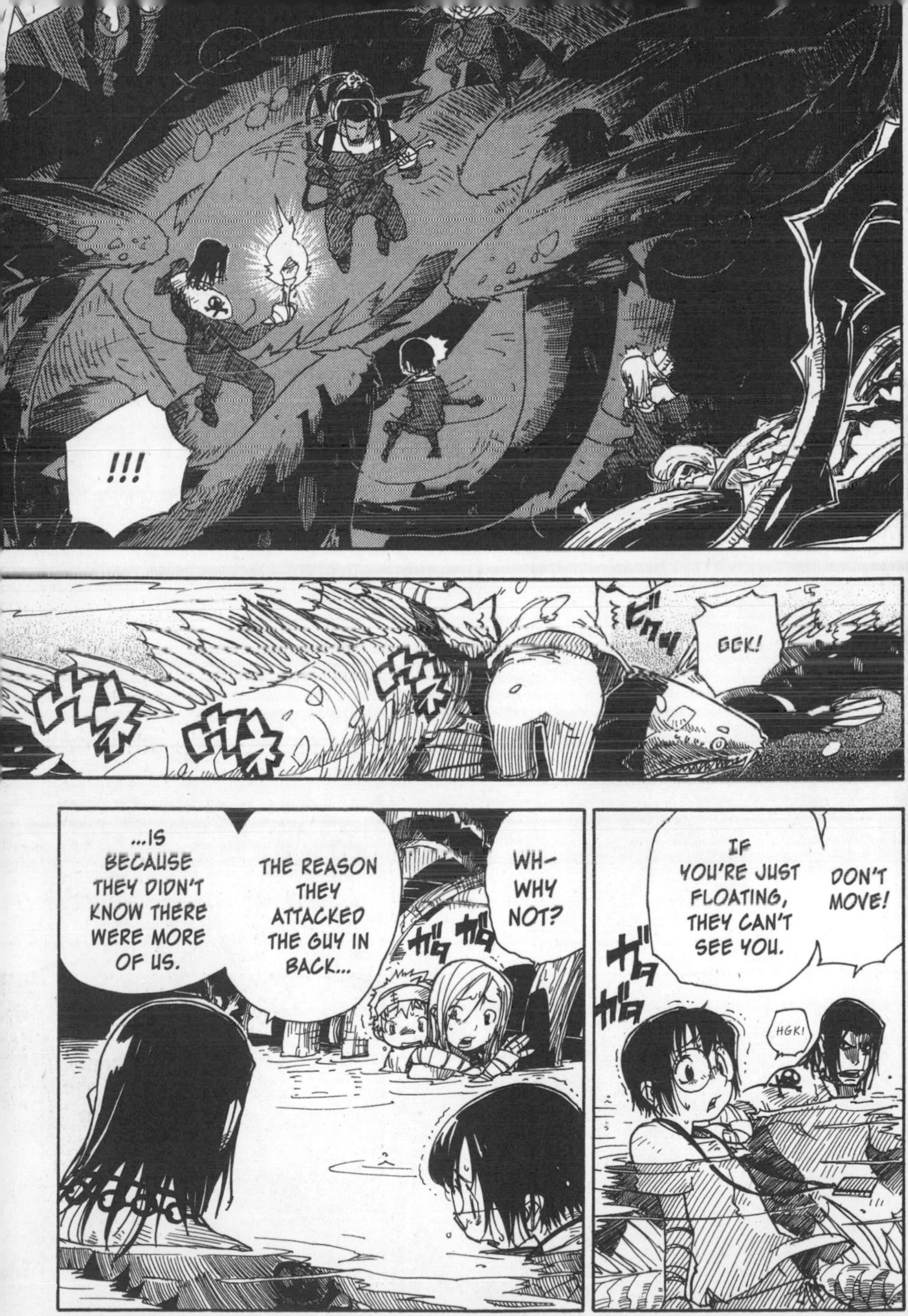
!!!
GCK!
DON'T MOVE!
IF YOU'RE JUST FLOATING, THEY CAN'T SEE YOU.
HGK!
WH- WHY NOT?
THE REASON THEY ATTACKED THE GUY IN BACK...
...IS BECAUSE THEY DIDN'T KNOW THERE WERE MORE OF US.

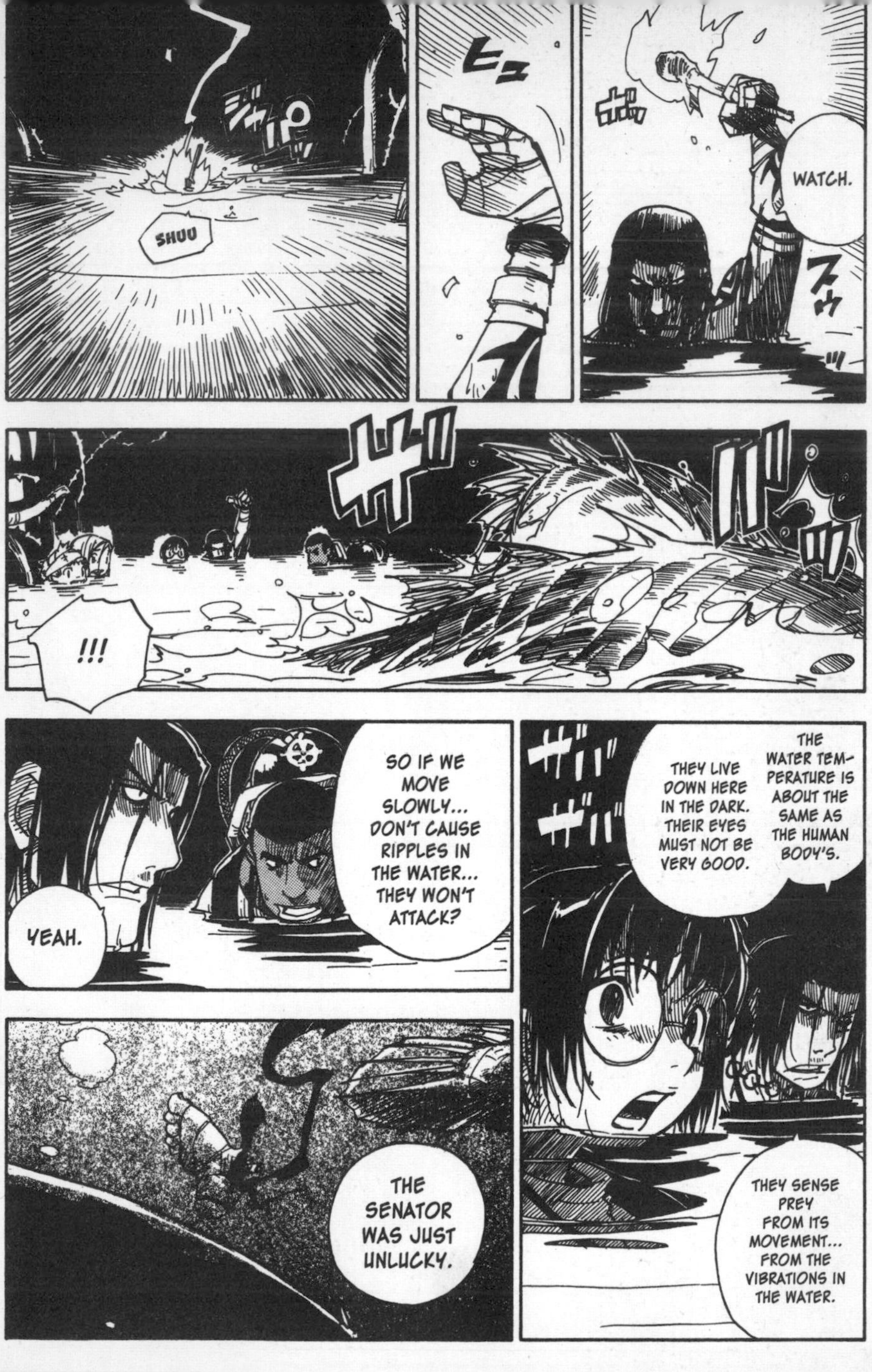
WATCH.
SHUU
!!!
THE WATER TEM-PERATURE IS ABOUT THE SAME AS THE HUMAN BODY'S.
THEY LIVE DOWN HERE IN THE DARK. THEIR EYES MUST NOT BE VERY GOOD.
THEY SENSE PREY FROM ITS MOVEMENT... FROM THE VIBRATIONS IN THE WATER.
SO IF WE MOVE SLOWLY... DON'T CAUSE RIPPLES IN THE WATER... THEY WON'T ATTACK?
YEAH.
THE SENATOR WAS JUST UNLUCKY.

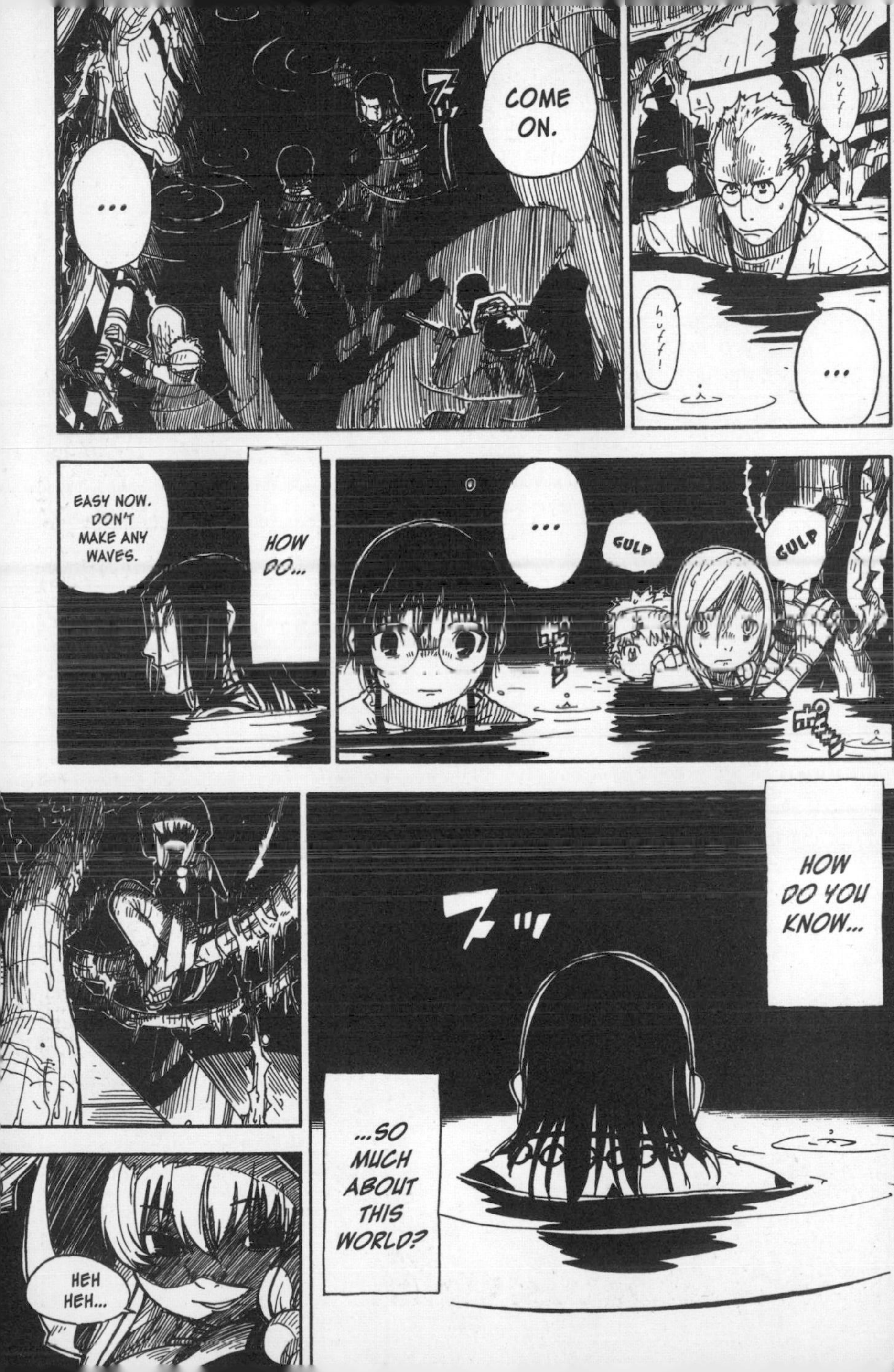
huff!
huff!
...
COME ON.
...
...
GULP
GULP
HOW DO...
EASY NOW. DON'T MAKE ANY WAVES.
HOW DO YOU KNOW...
フッ
...SO MUCH ABOUT THIS WORLD?
HEH HEH...

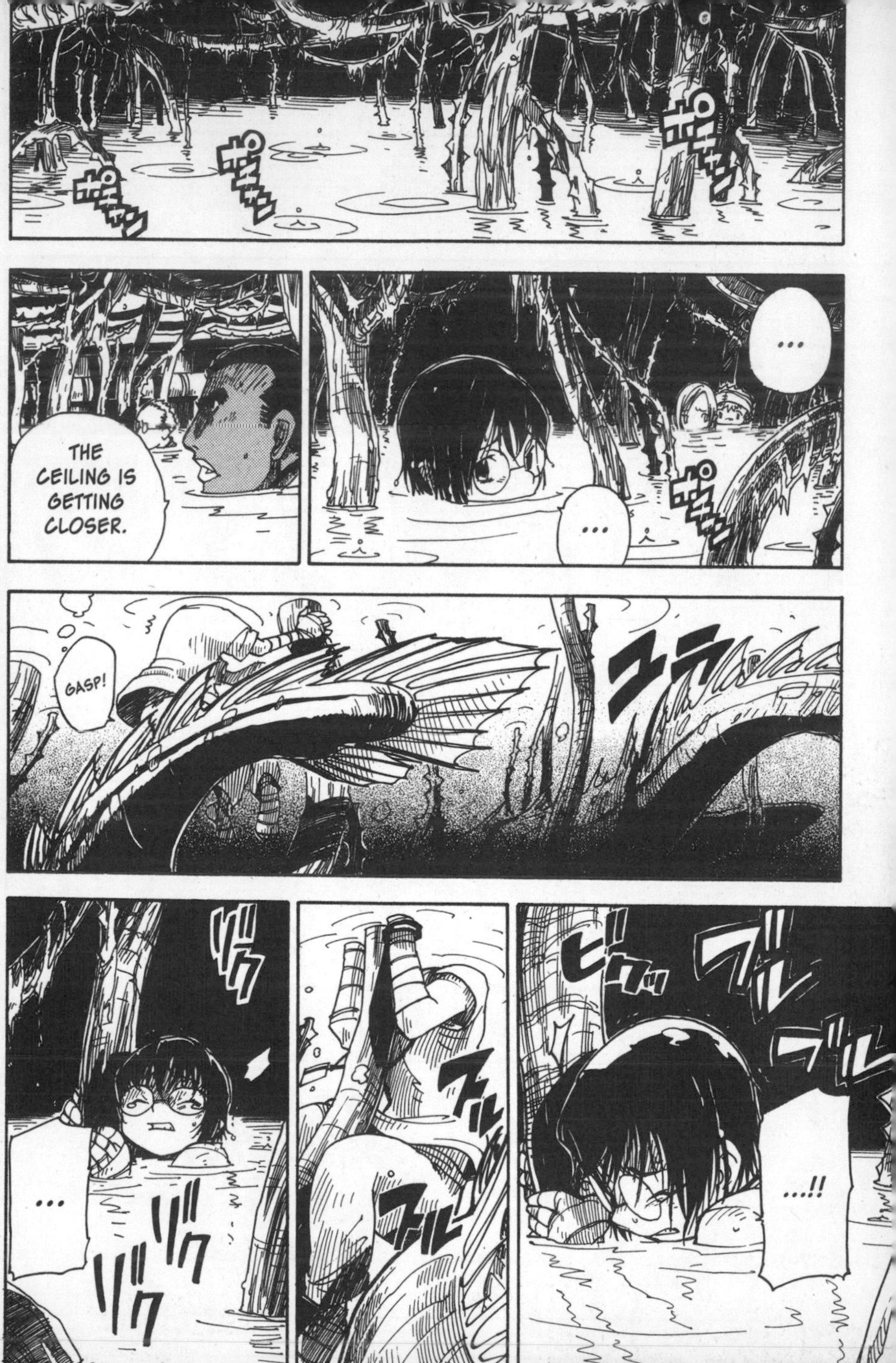
ポチャン
ポチャン
ポチャン
...
...
ポチャン
THE CEILING IS GETTING CLOSER.
ユラ
GASP!
ビクッ
ブル
ブル
...!!
フル
フル
ゾク
ゾク
ゾク
...

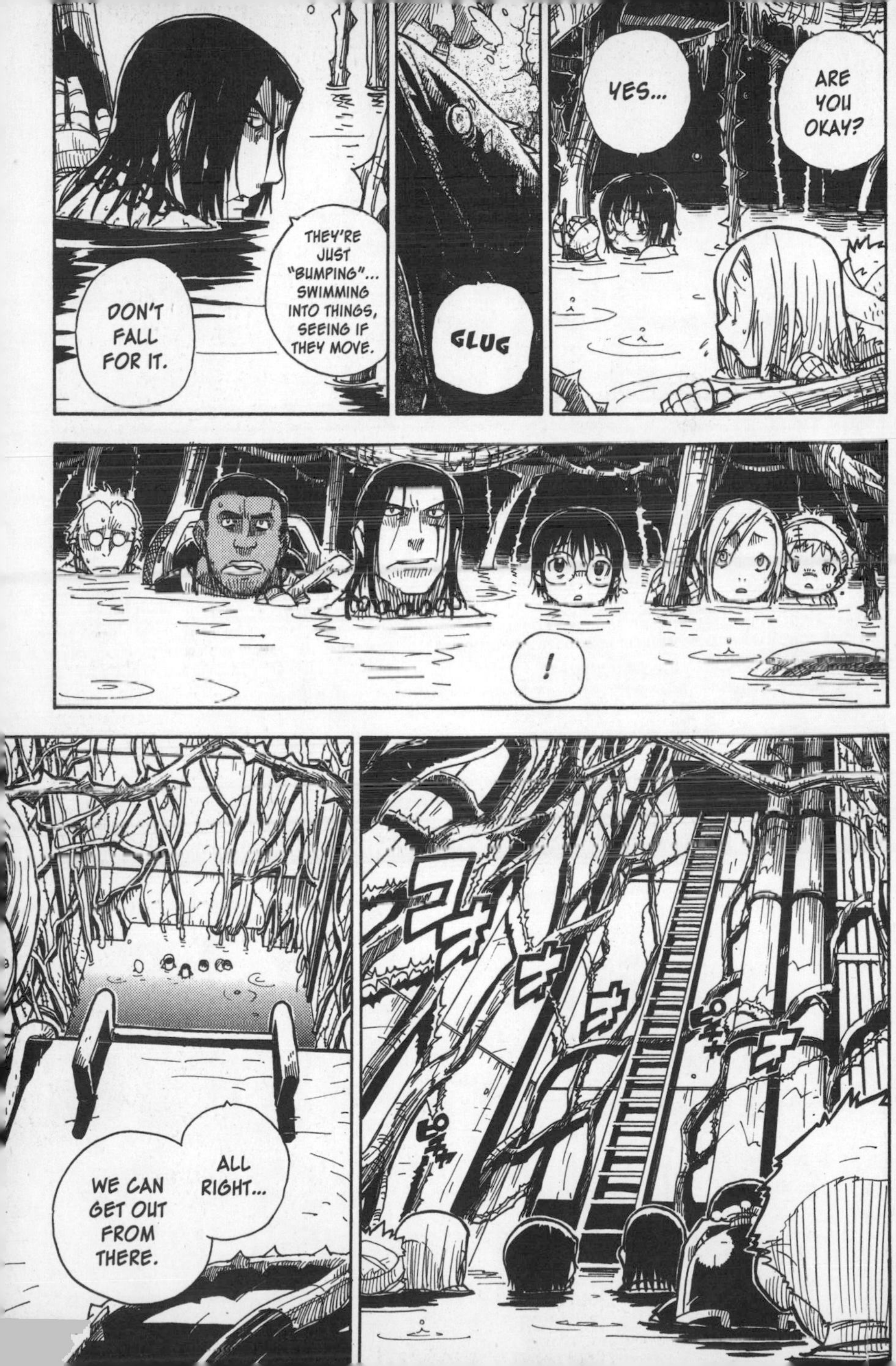
ARE YOU OKAY?
YES...
GLUG
THEY'RE JUST "BUMPING"... SWIMMING INTO THINGS, SEEING IF THEY MOVE.
DON'T FALL FOR IT.
!
ALL RIGHT...
WE CAN GET OUT FROM THERE.

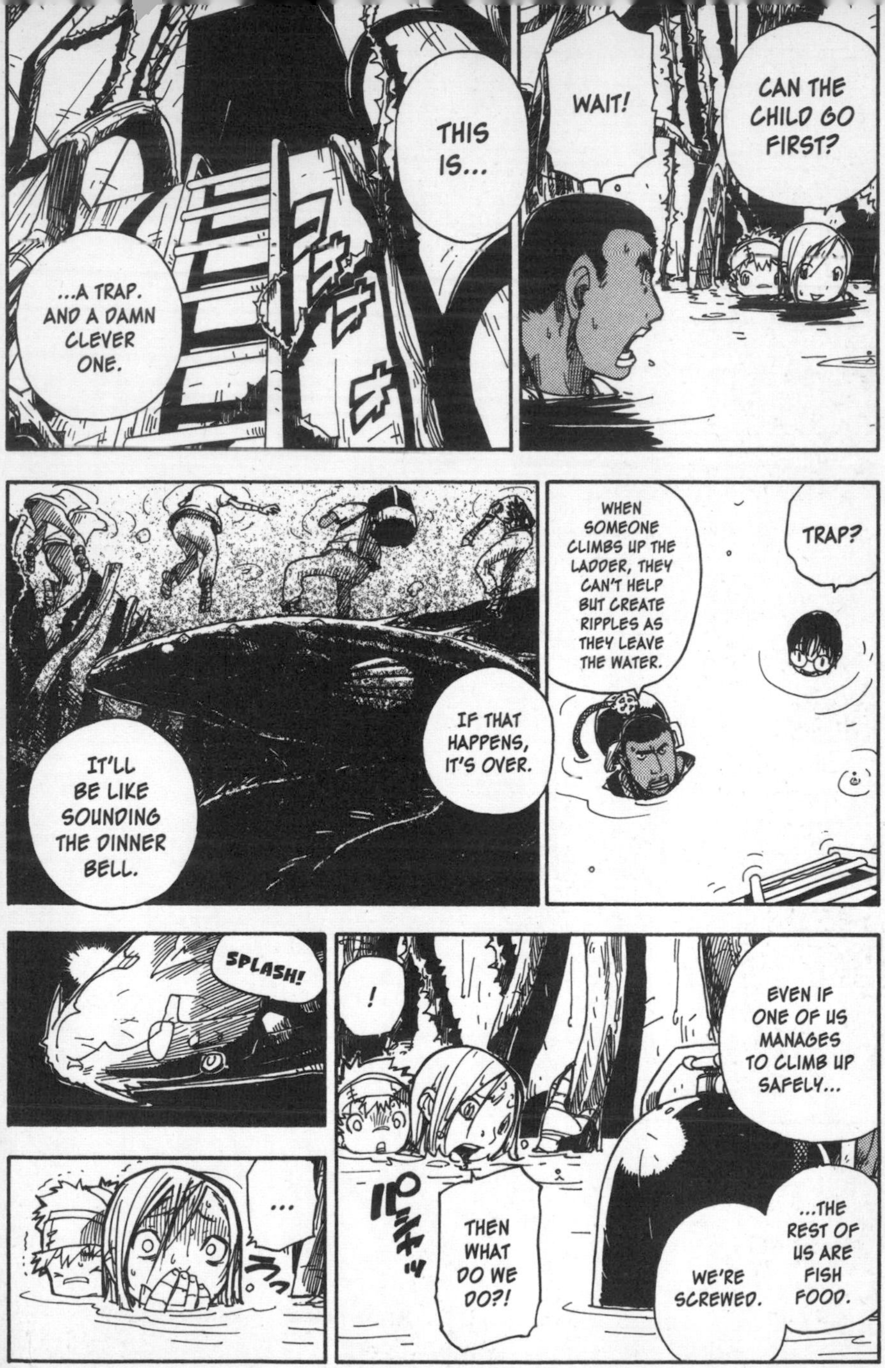
CAN THE CHILD GO FIRST?
WAIT!
THIS IS...
...A TRAP. AND A DAMN CLEVER ONE.
TRAP?
WHEN SOMEONE CLIMBS UP THE LADDER, THEY CAN'T HELP BUT CREATE RIPPLES AS THEY LEAVE THE WATER.
IF THAT HAPPENS, IT'S OVER.
IT'LL BE LIKE SOUNDING THE DINNER BELL.
EVEN IF ONE OF US MANAGES TO CLIMB UP SAFELY...
...THE REST OF US ARE FISH FOOD.
WE'RE SCREWED.
THEN WHAT DO WE DO?!
!
SPLASH!
...

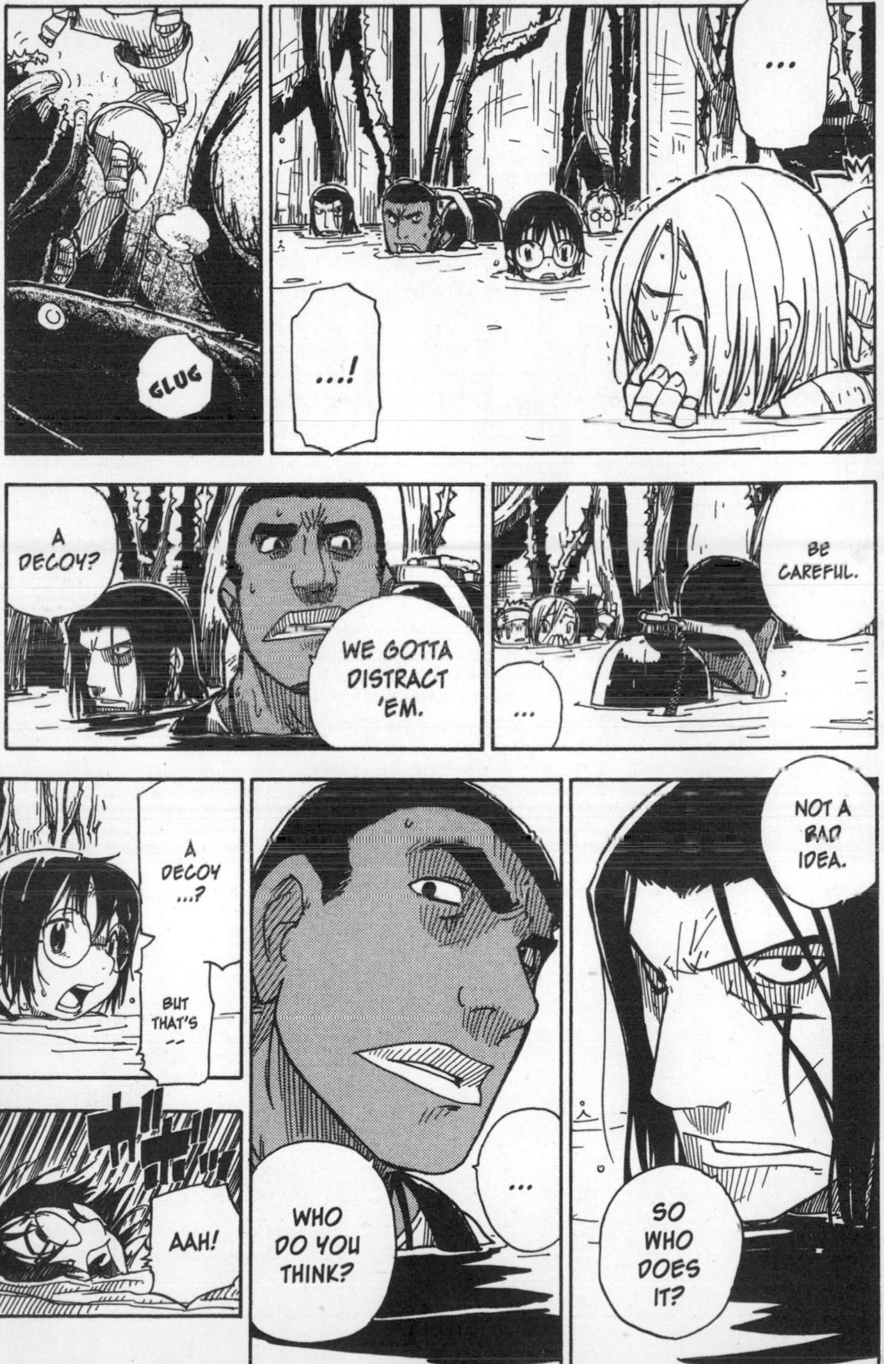
...
...!
GLUG
BE CAREFUL.
...
WE GOTTA DISTRACT 'EM.
A DECOY?
NOT A BAD IDEA.
SO WHO DOES IT?
...
WHO DO YOU THINK?
A DECOY ...?
BUT THAT'S --
AAH!

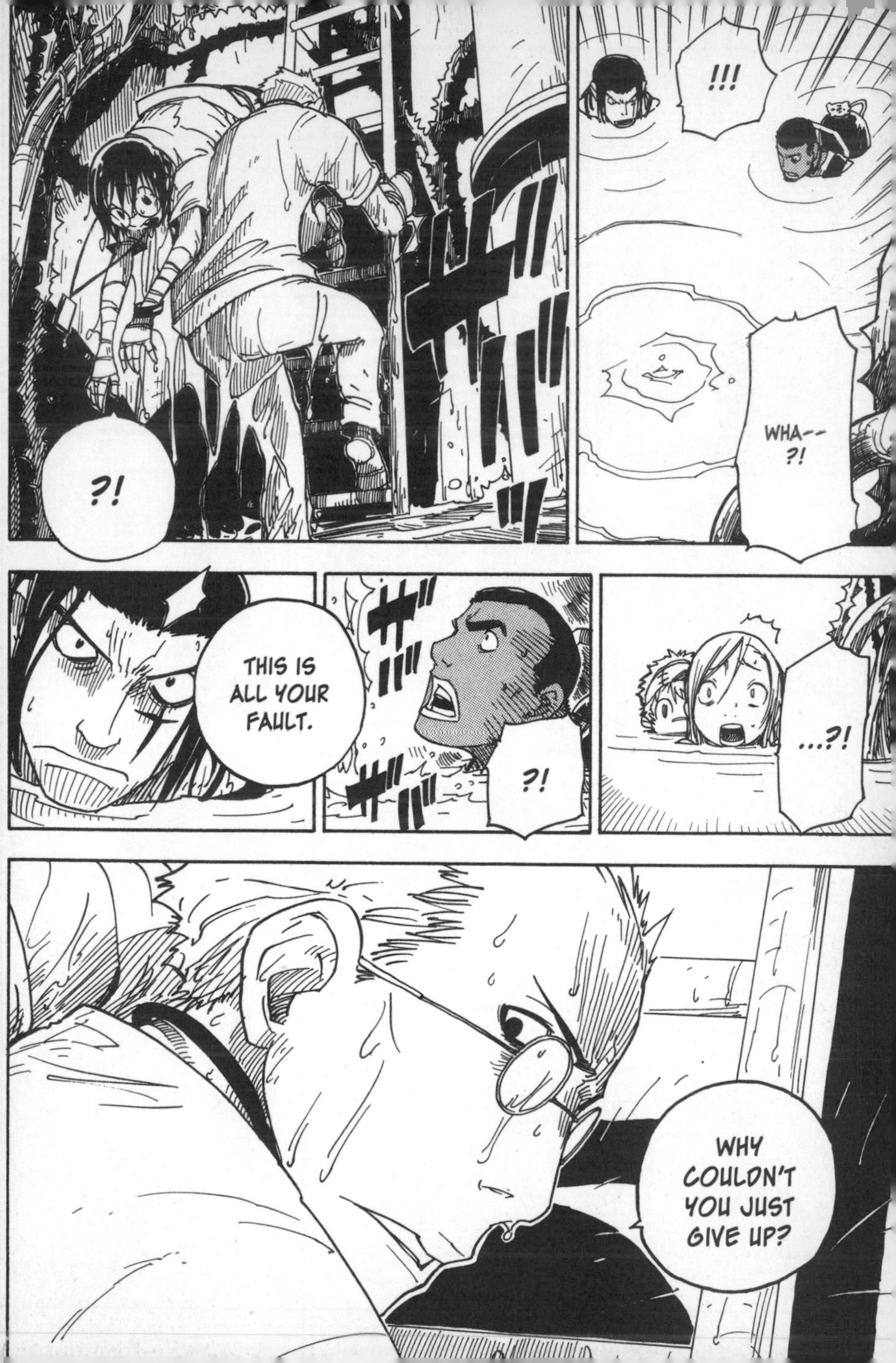
!!!
WHA-- ?!
?!
...?!
?!
THIS IS ALL YOUR FAULT.
WHY COULDN'T YOU JUST GIVE UP?

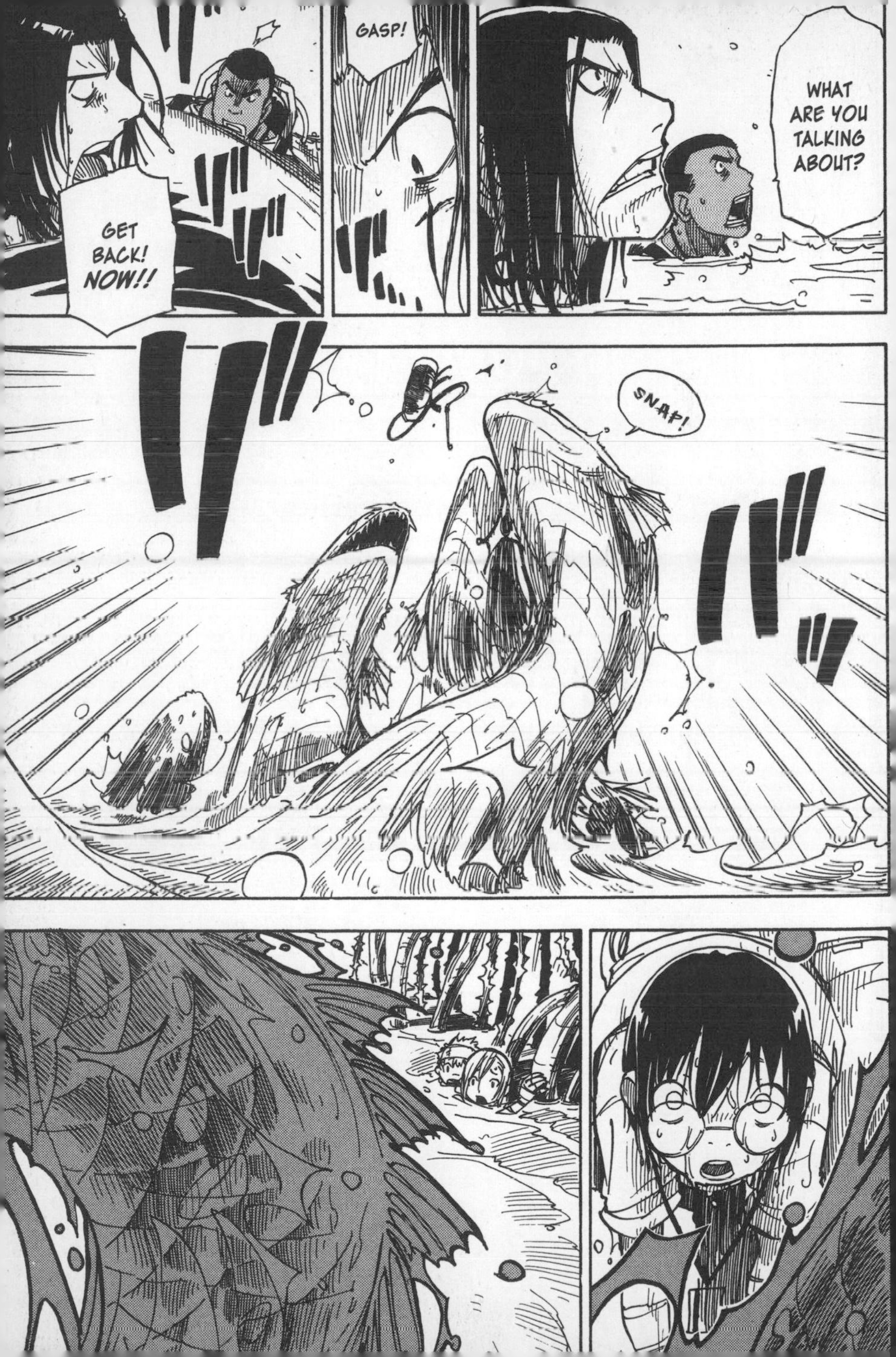
GET BACK! NOW!!
GASP!
WHAT ARE YOU TALKING ABOUT?
SNAP!

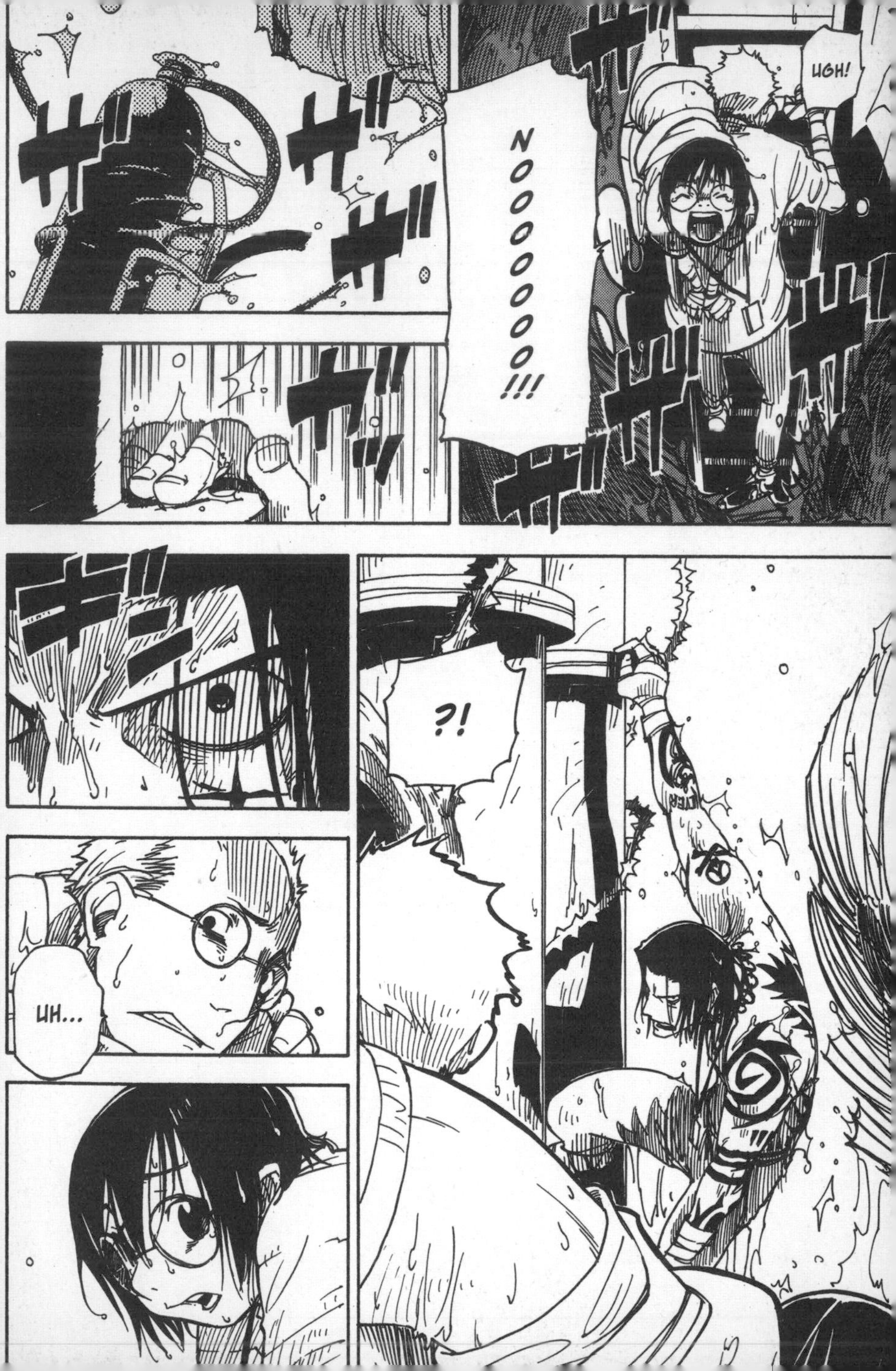
UGH!
NOOOOOOOOO!!!
?!
UH...

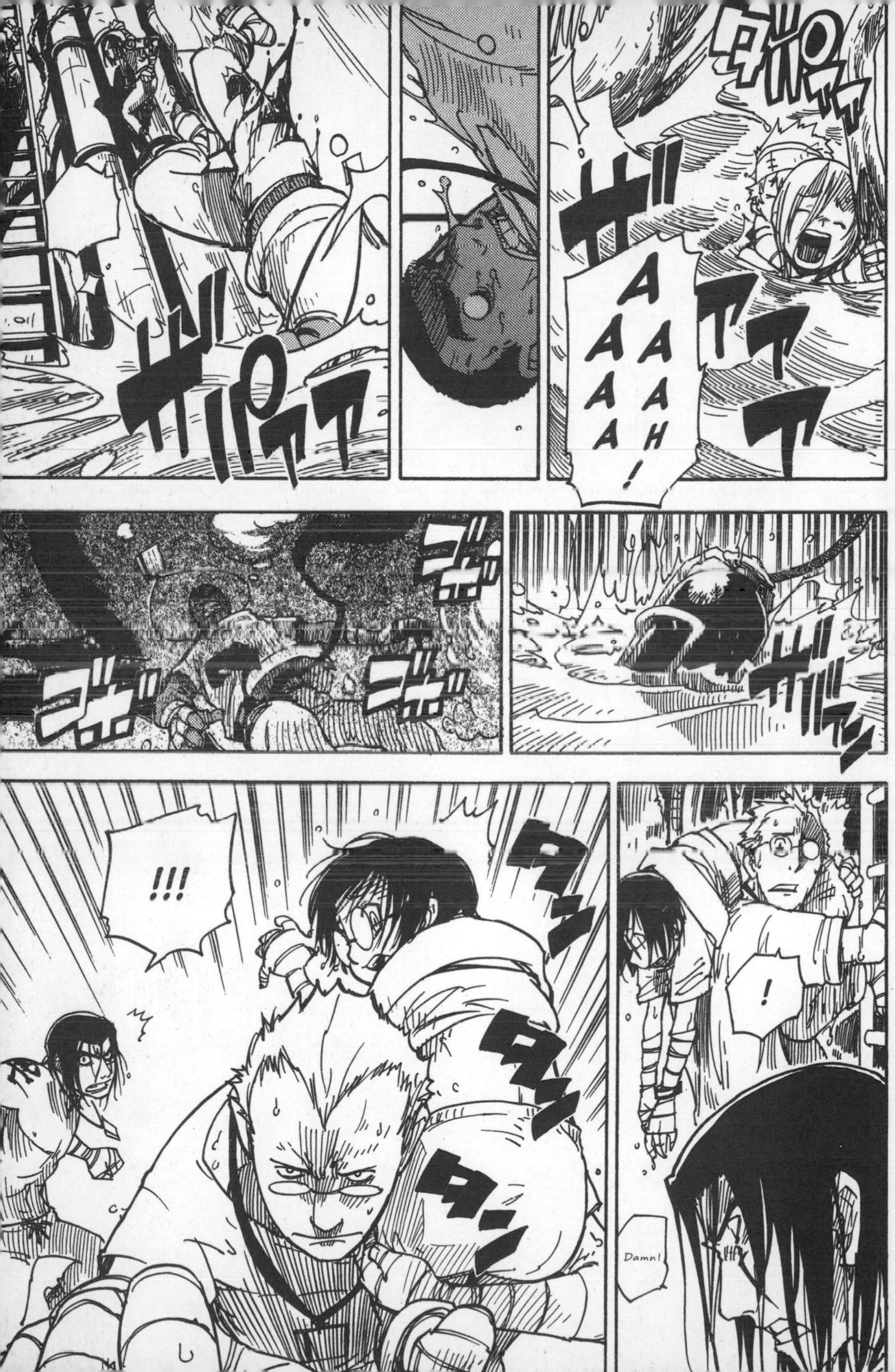

AAAAAAAAH!
!
Damn!
!!!

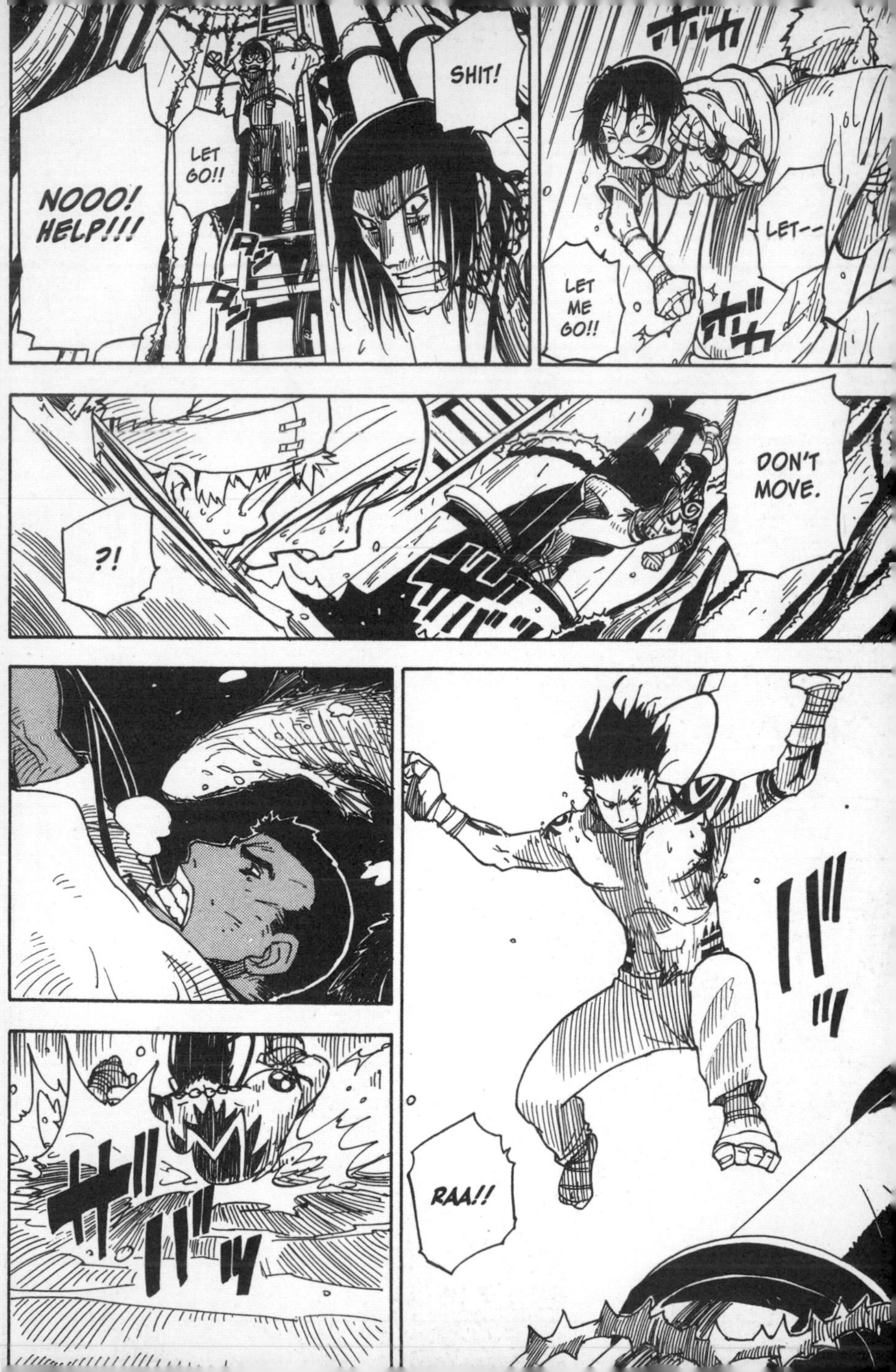
LET--
LET ME GO!!
SHIT!
LET GO!!
NOOO! HELP!!!
DON'T MOVE.
?!
RAA!!

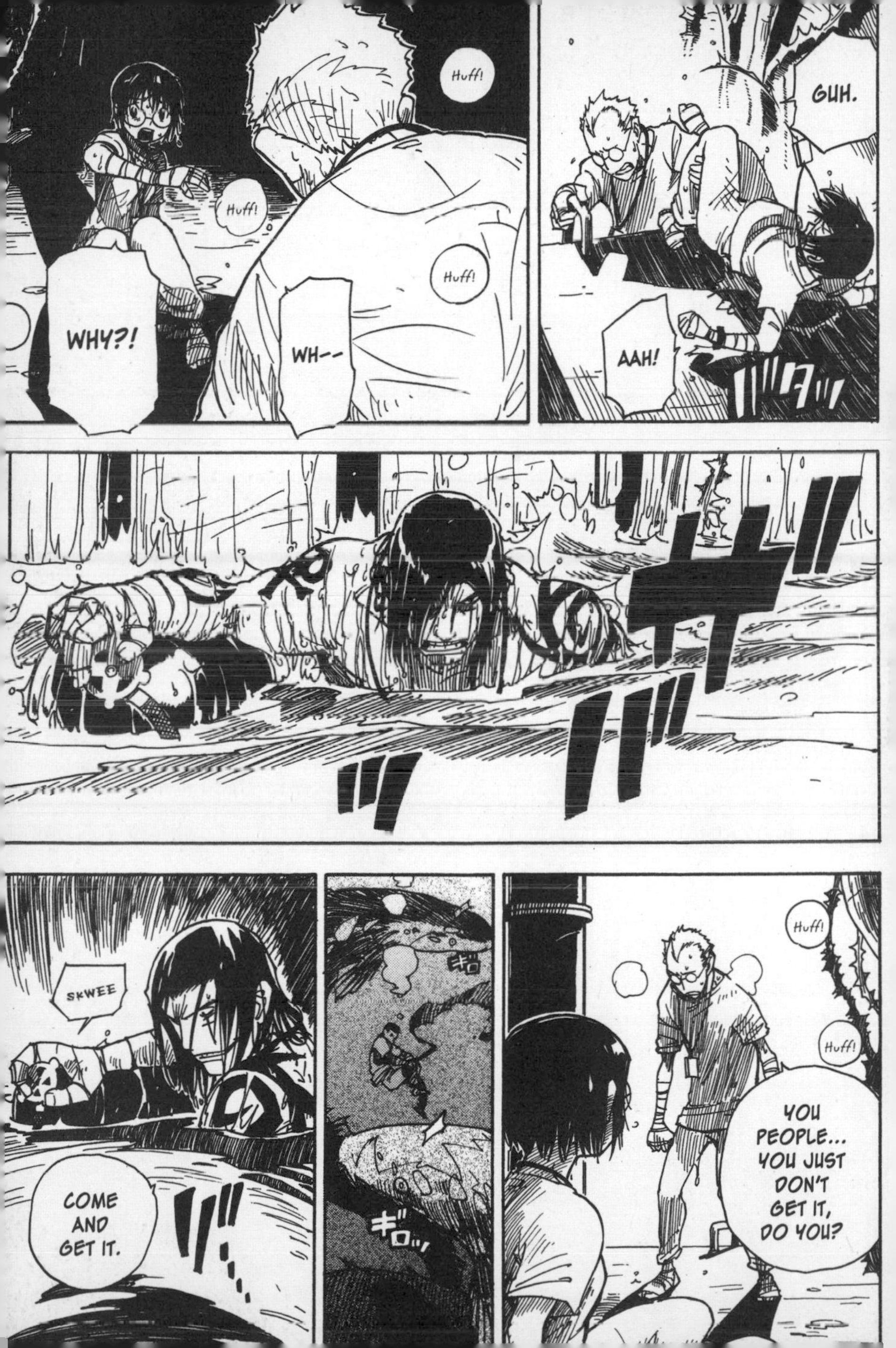
Huff!
Huff!
Huff!
WHY?!
WH--
GUH.
AAH!
SKWEE
COME AND GET IT.
Huff!
Huff!
YOU PEOPLE... YOU JUST DON'T GET IT, DO YOU?

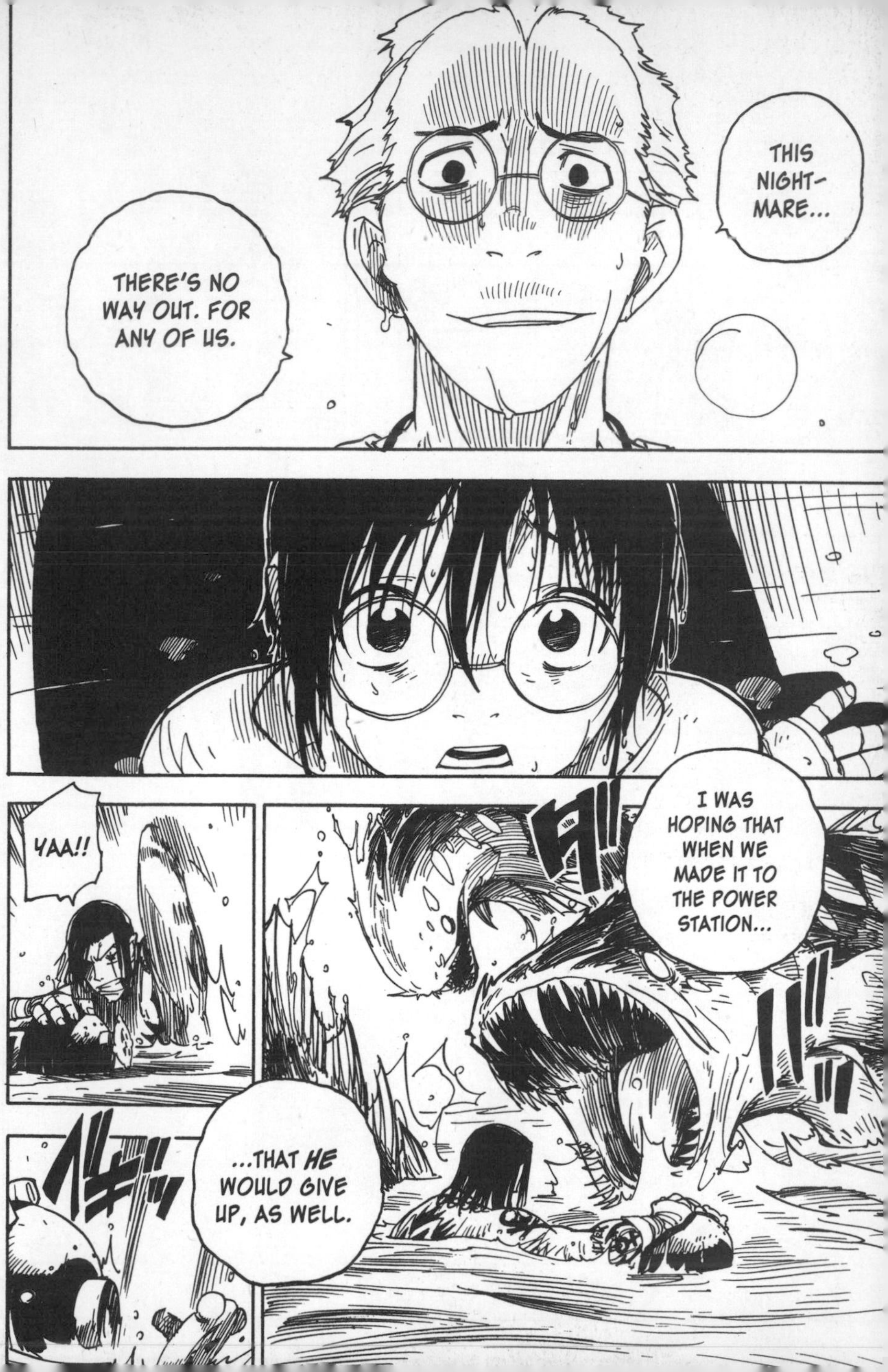
THIS NIGHT-MARE...
THERE'S NO WAY OUT. FOR ANY OF US.
I WAS HOPING THAT WHEN WE MADE IT TO THE POWER STATION...
YAA!!
...THAT HE WOULD GIVE UP, AS WELL.

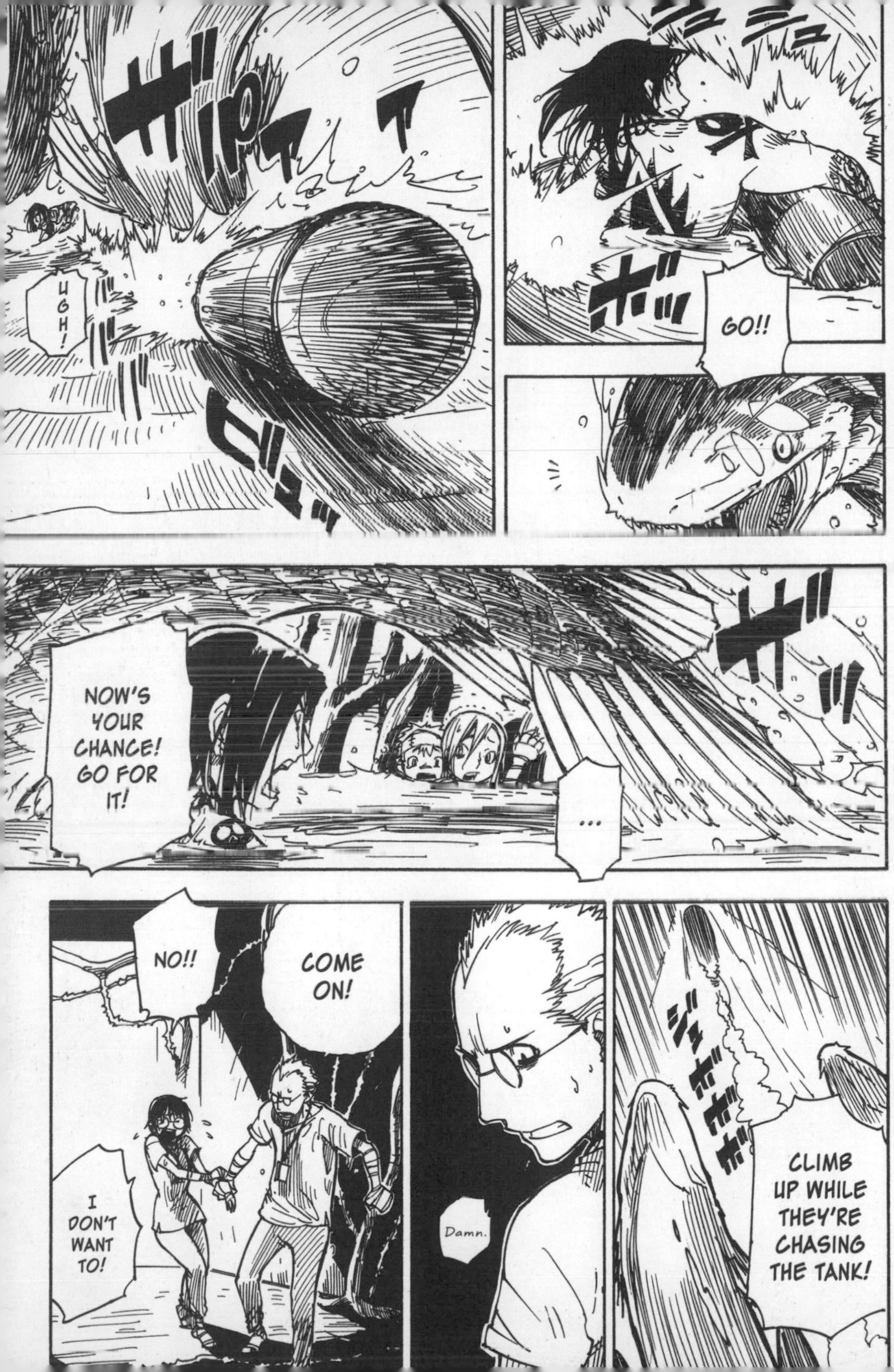
GO!!
UGH!
...
NOW'S YOUR CHANCE! GO FOR IT!
CLIMB UP WHILE THEY'RE CHASING THE TANK!
Damn.
COME ON!
NO!!
I DON'T WANT TO!

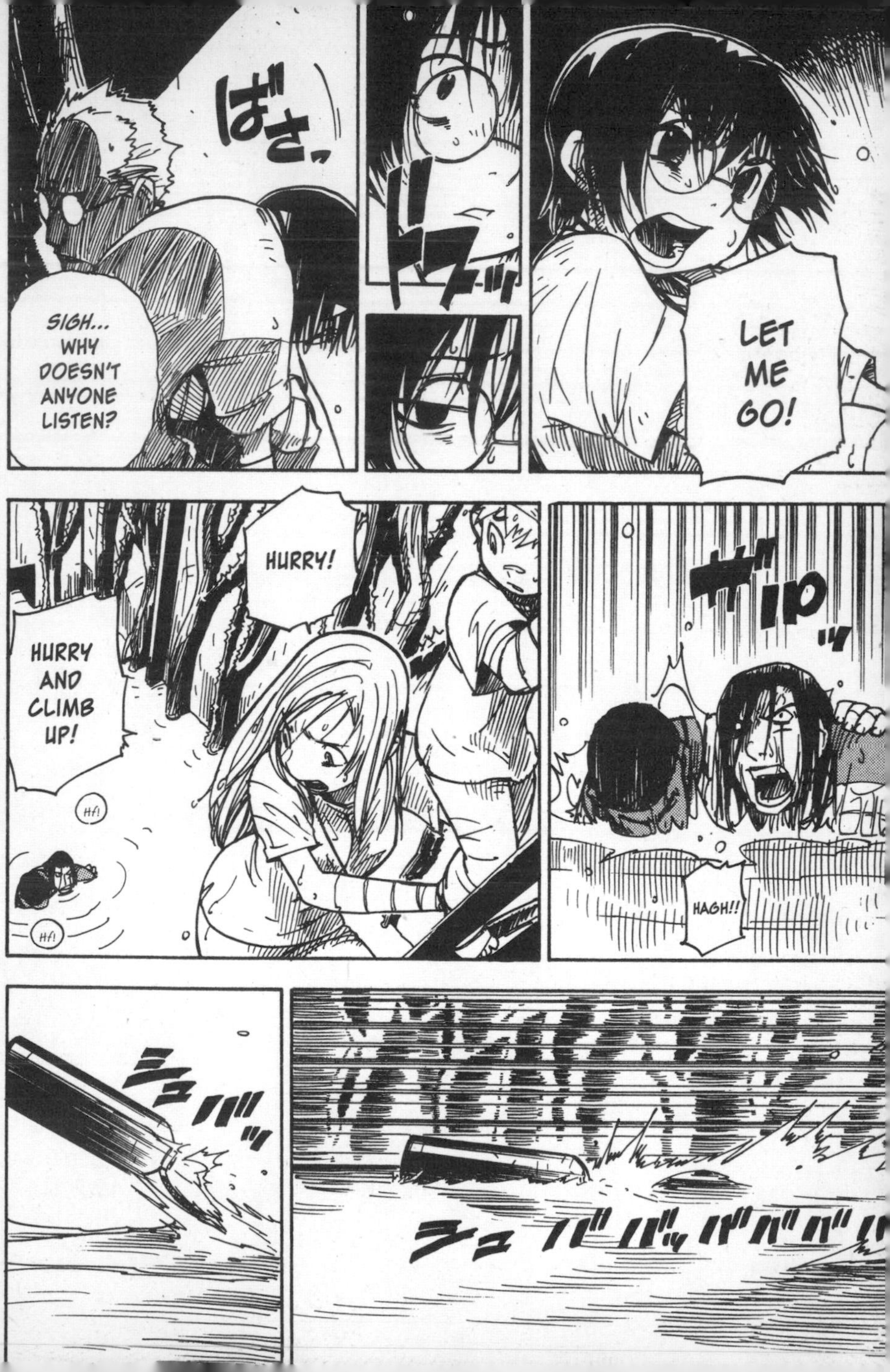
LET ME GO!
ばさっ
SIGH... WHY DOESN'T ANYONE LISTEN?
HAGH!!
HURRY!
HURRY AND CLIMB UP!
Hf!
Hf!
シュバッ

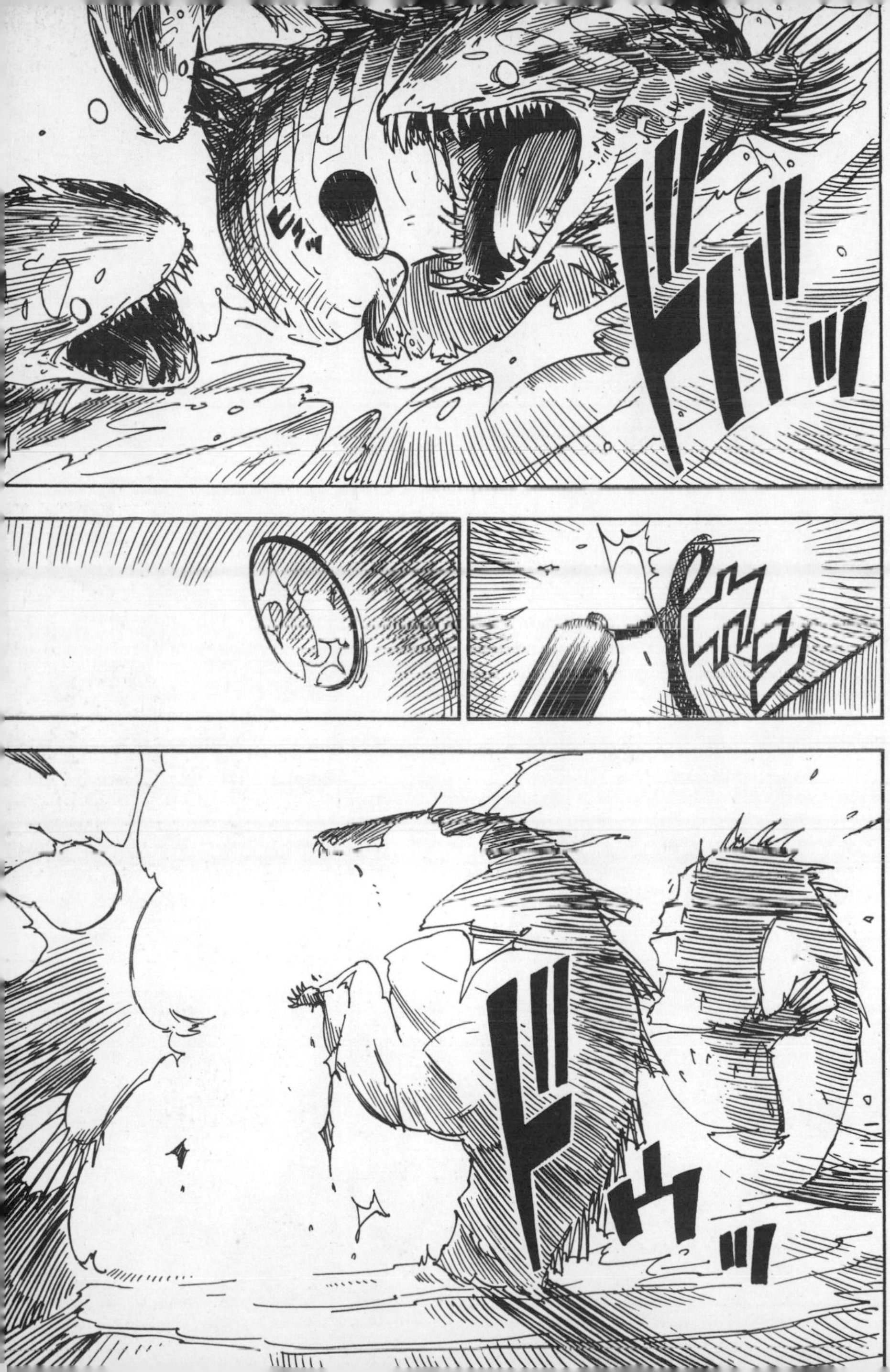
ドドドッ
ヒュッ
ドゥッ

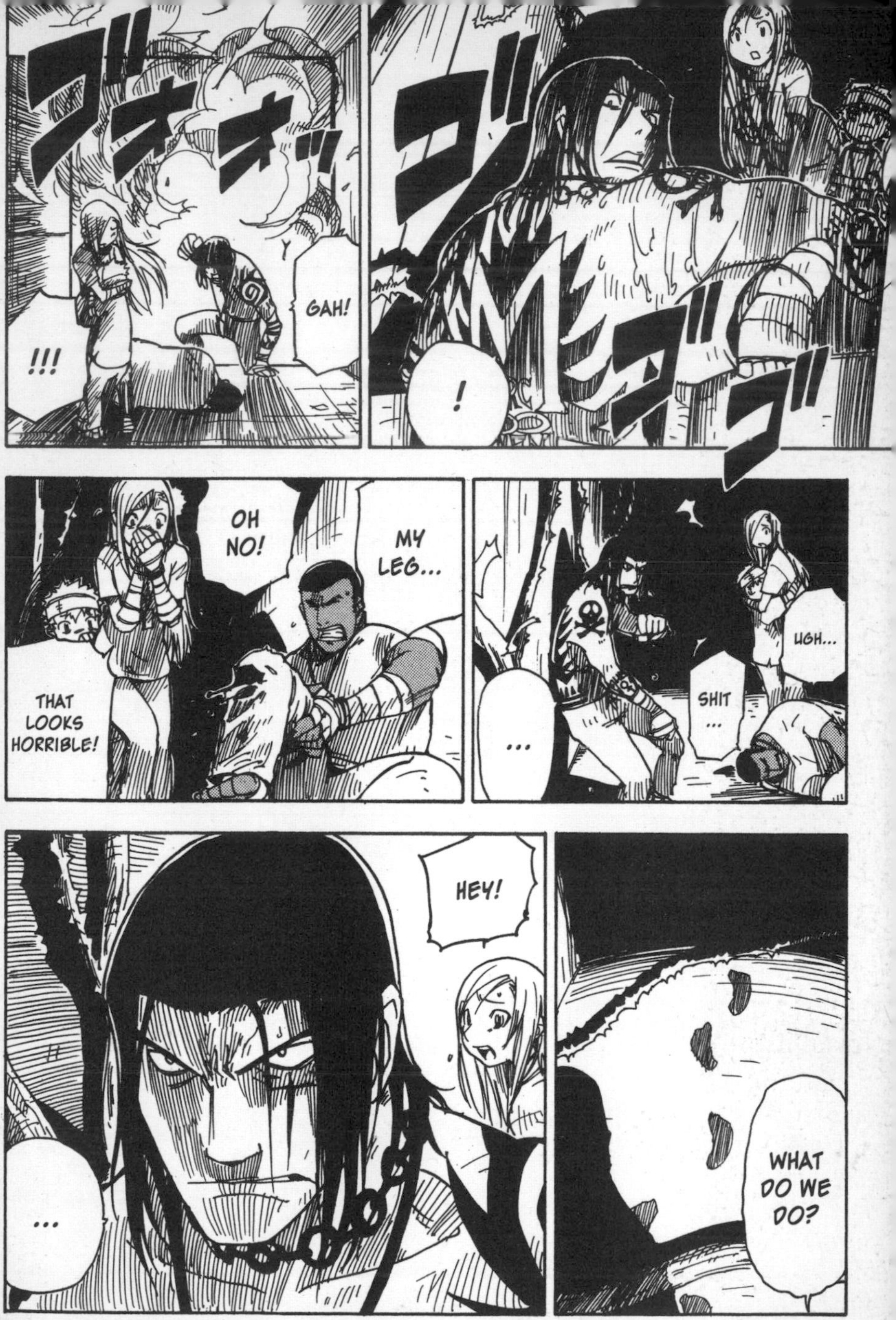
!
GAH!
!!!
UGH...
SHIT ...
...
MY LEG...
OH NO!
THAT LOOKS HORRIBLE!
WHAT DO WE DO?
HEY!
...

CHAPTER 7
ONE DOWN

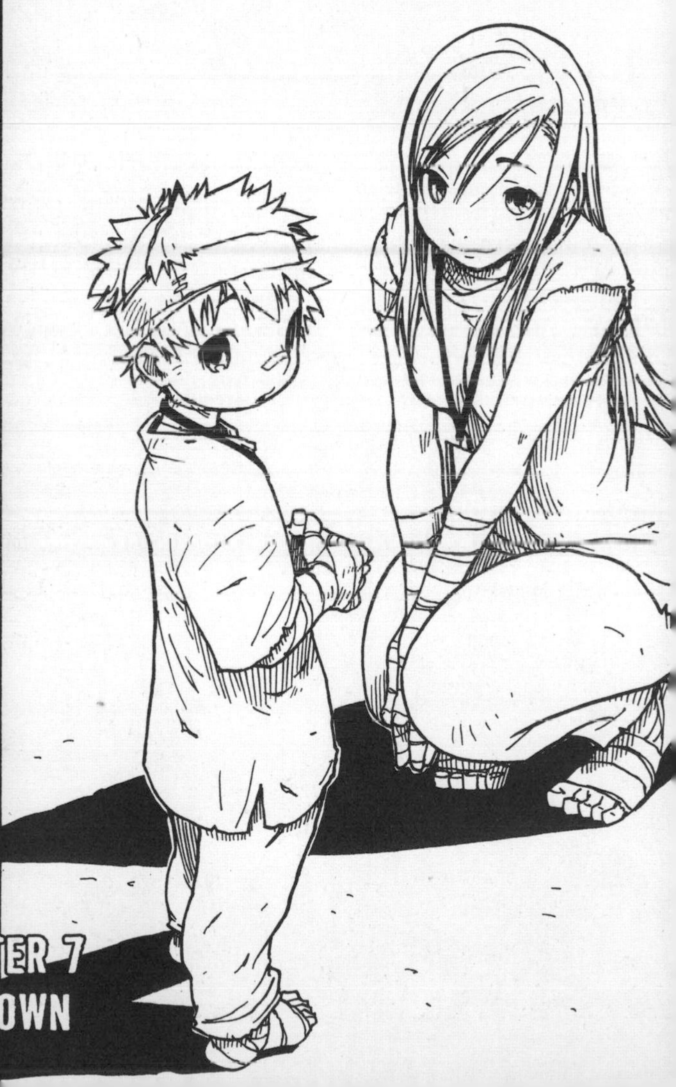

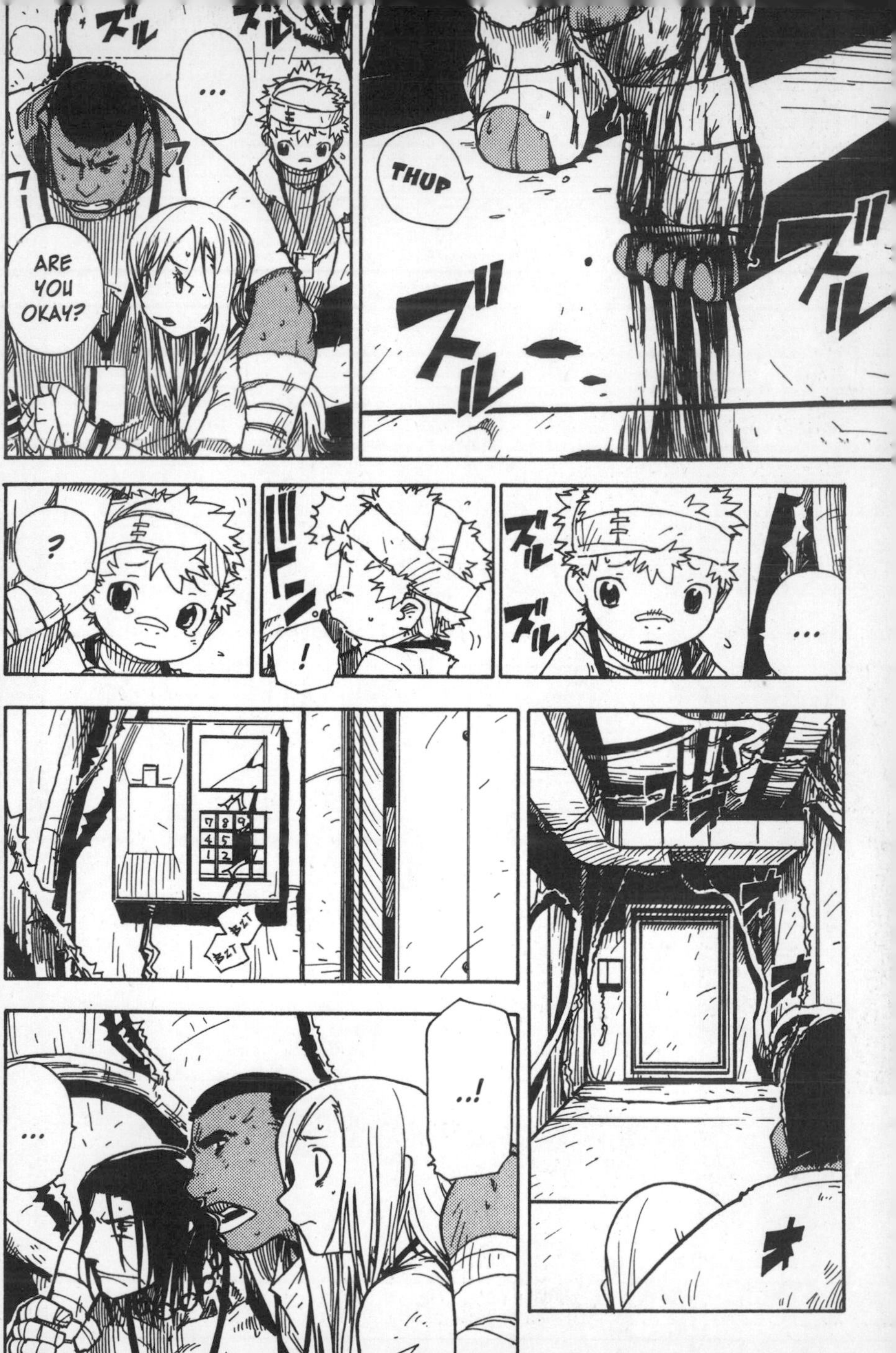
THUP
...
ARE YOU OKAY?
...
!
?
BZT BZT
..!
...

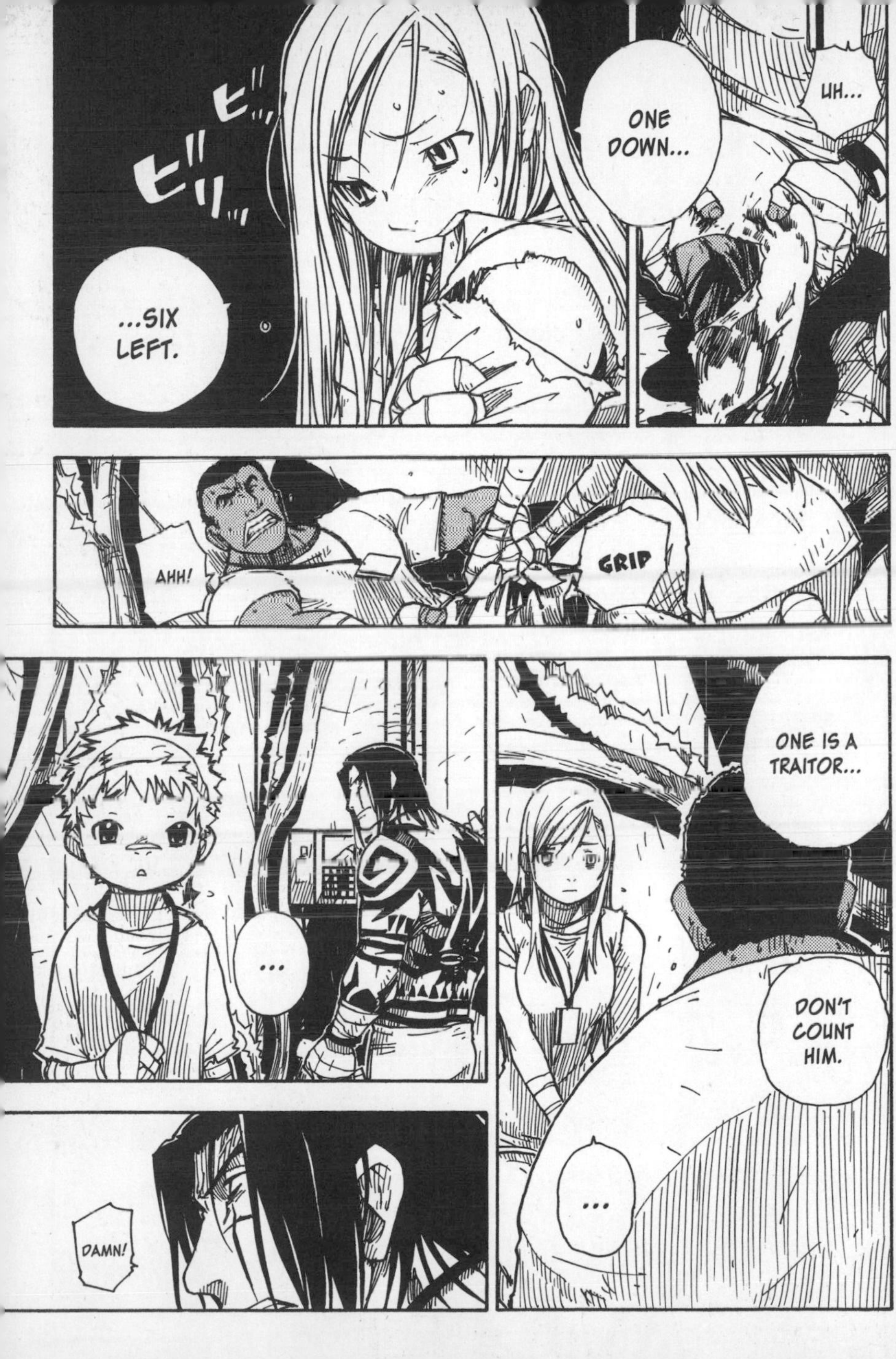
UH...
ONE DOWN...
...SIX LEFT.
GRIP
AHH!
ONE IS A TRAITOR...
DON'T COUNT HIM.
...
...
DAMN!

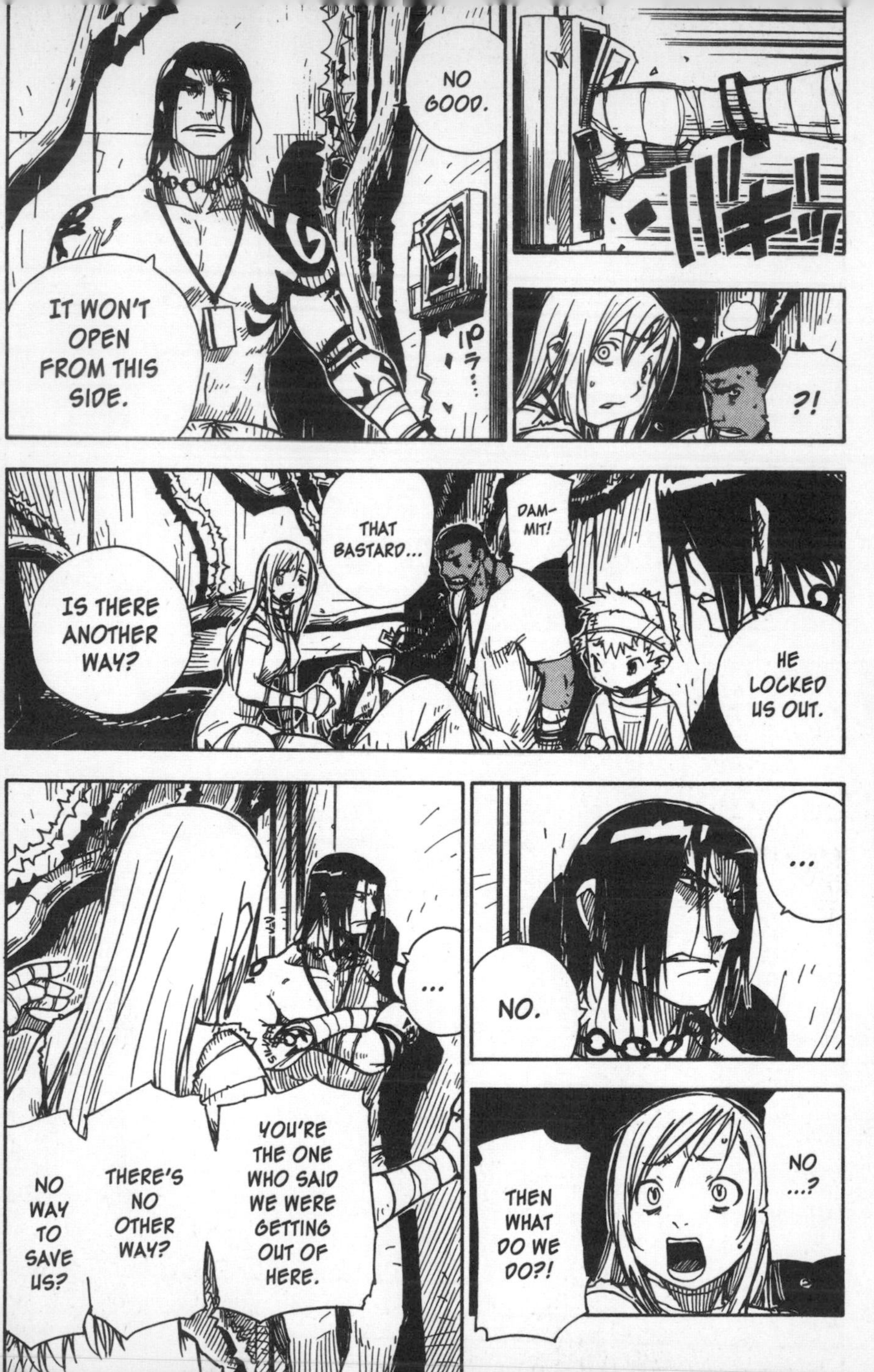
?!
NO GOOD.
IT WON'T OPEN FROM THIS SIDE.
HE LOCKED US OUT.
DAM-MIT!
THAT BASTARD...
IS THERE ANOTHER WAY?
...
NO.
...
NO ...?
THEN WHAT DO WE DO?!
YOU'RE THE ONE WHO SAID WE WERE GETTING OUT OF HERE.
THERE'S NO OTHER WAY?
NO WAY TO SAVE US?

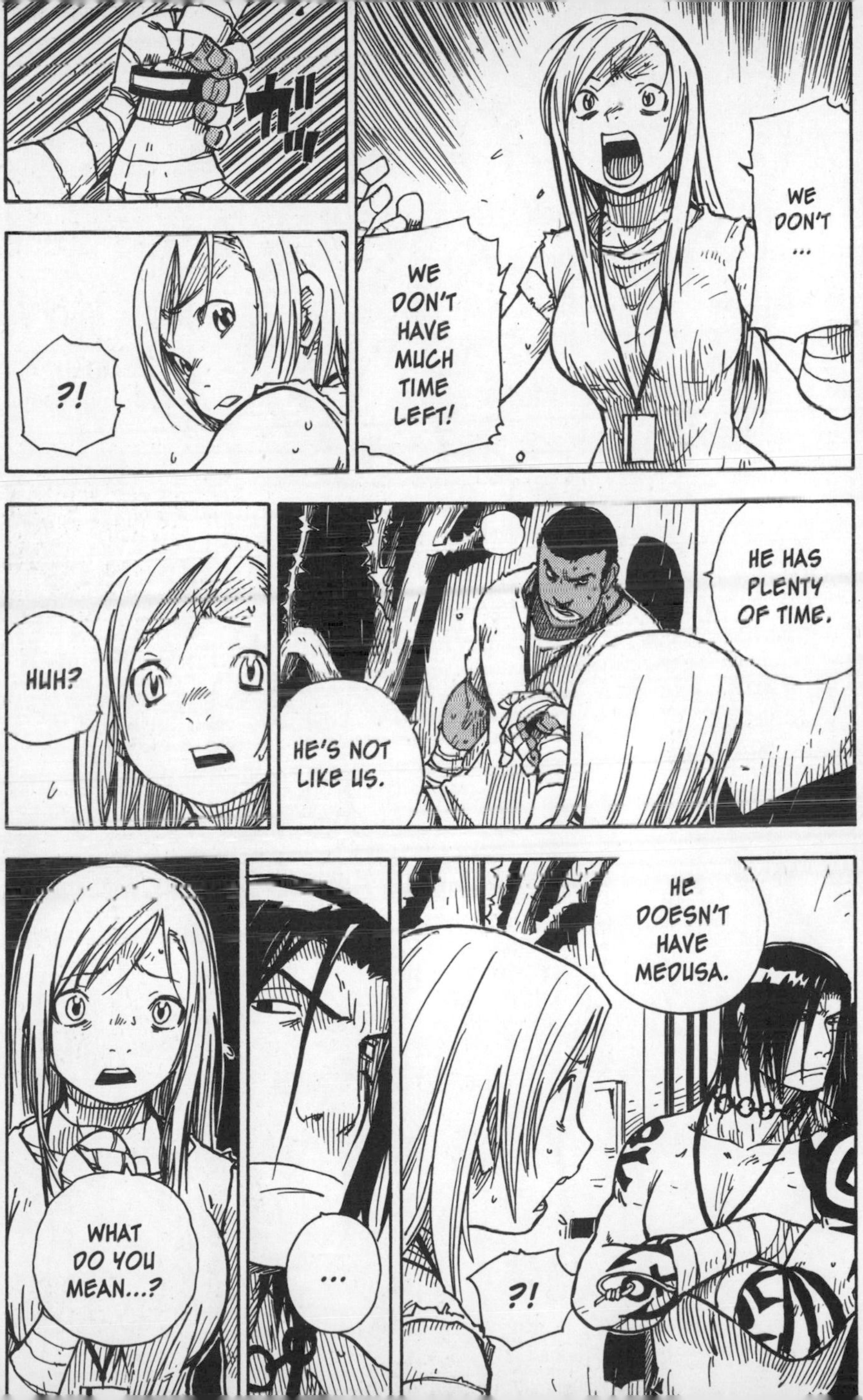
WE DON'T ...
WE DON'T HAVE MUCH TIME LEFT!
?!
HE HAS PLENTY OF TIME.
HE'S NOT LIKE US.
HUH?
HE DOESN'T HAVE MEDUSA.
?!
...
WHAT DO YOU MEAN...?

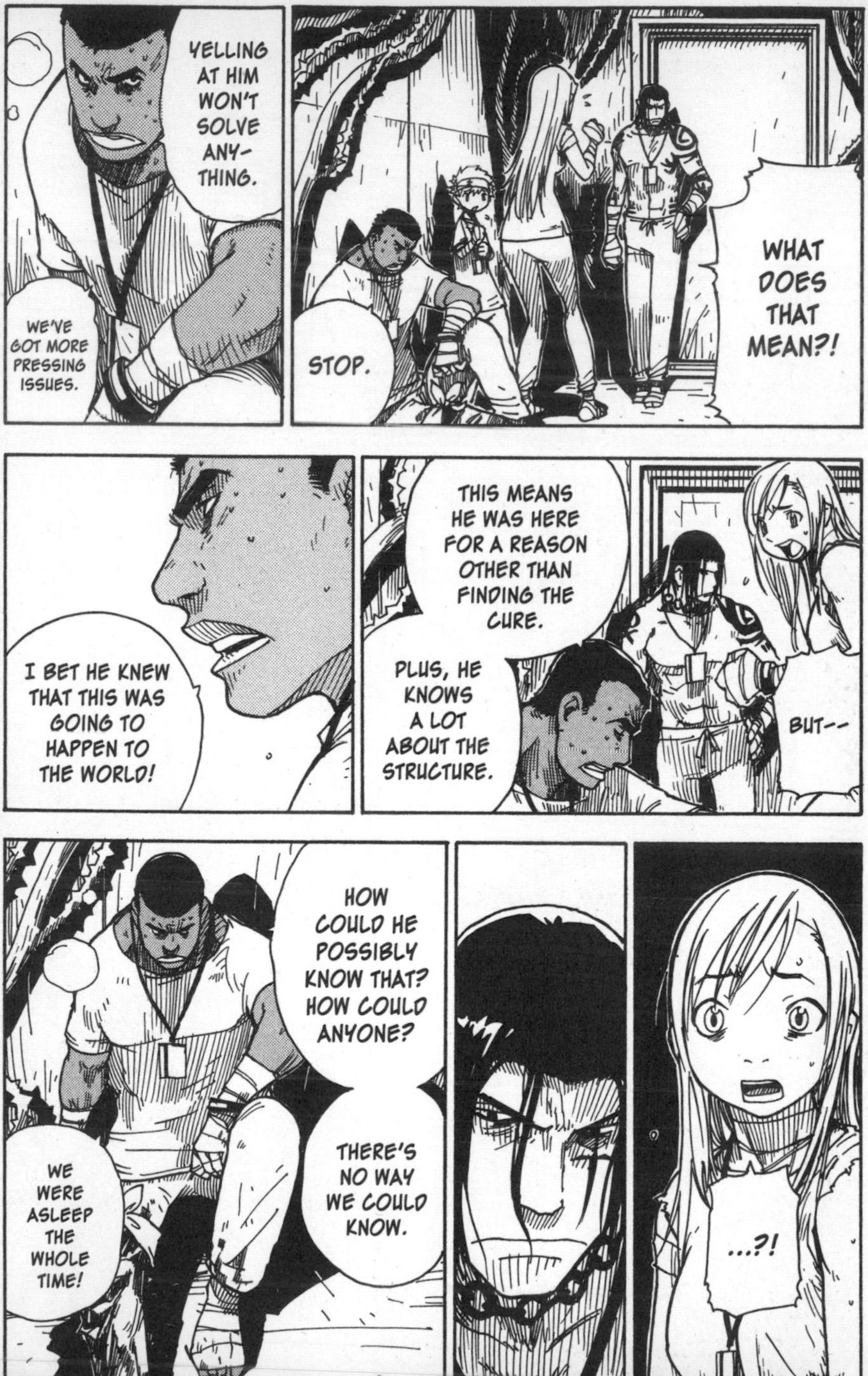

YELLING AT HIM WON'T SOLVE ANYTHING.
WE'VE GOT MORE PRESSING ISSUES.
STOP.
WHAT DOES THAT MEAN?!
I BET HE KNEW THAT THIS WAS GOING TO HAPPEN TO THE WORLD!
THIS MEANS HE WAS HERE FOR A REASON OTHER THAN FINDING THE CURE.
PLUS, HE KNOWS A LOT ABOUT THE STRUCTURE.
BUT--
HOW COULD HE POSSIBLY KNOW THAT? HOW COULD ANYONE?
WE WERE ASLEEP THE WHOLE TIME!
THERE'S NO WAY WE COULD KNOW.
...?!

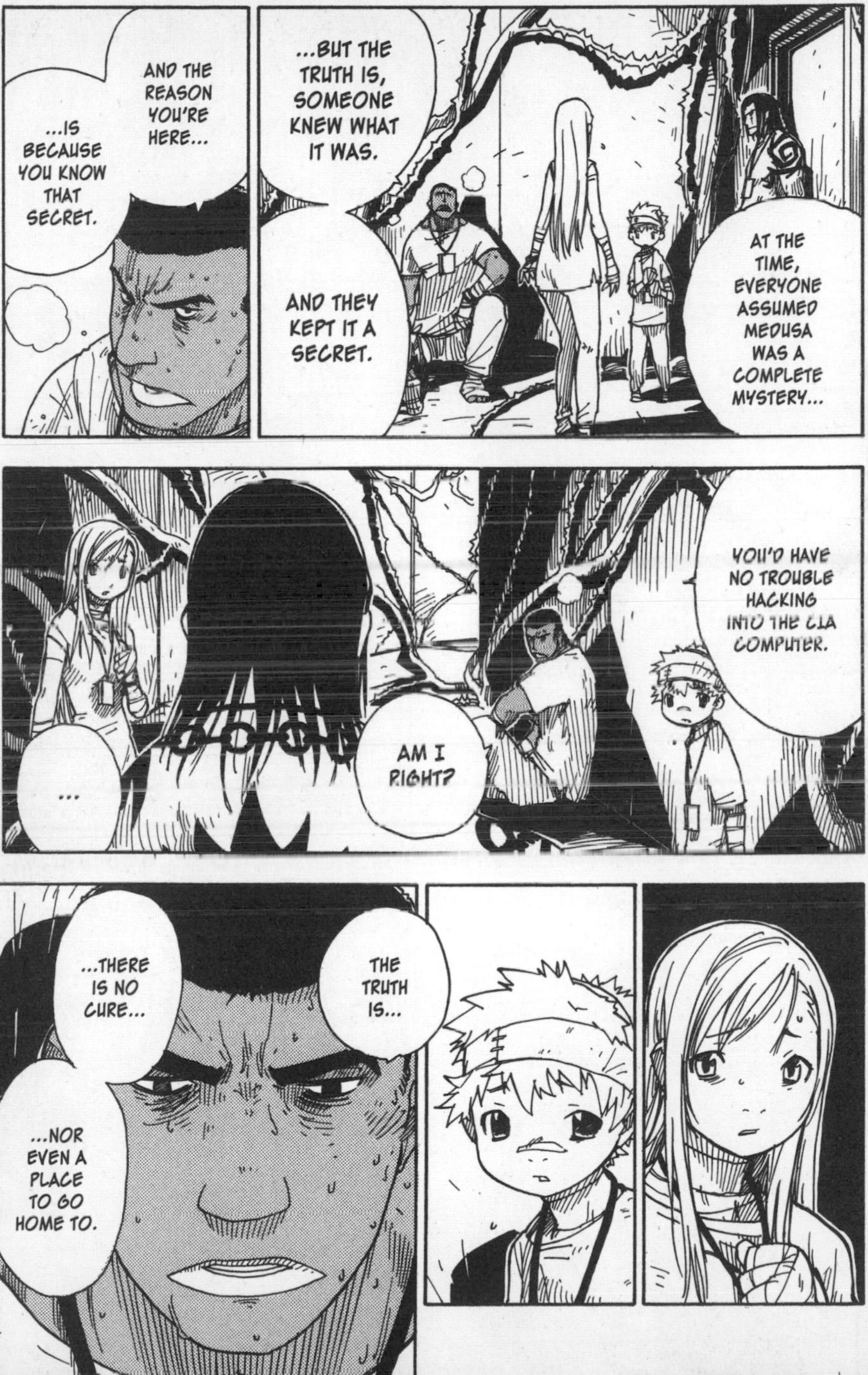
AT THE TIME, EVERYONE ASSUMED MEDUSA WAS A COMPLETE MYSTERY...
...BUT THE TRUTH IS, SOMEONE KNEW WHAT IT WAS.
AND THEY KEPT IT A SECRET.
AND THE REASON YOU'RE HERE...
...IS BECAUSE YOU KNOW THAT SECRET.
YOU'D HAVE NO TROUBLE HACKING INTO THE CIA COMPUTER.
AM I RIGHT?
...
THE TRUTH IS...
...THERE IS NO CURE...
...NOR EVEN A PLACE TO GO HOME TO.

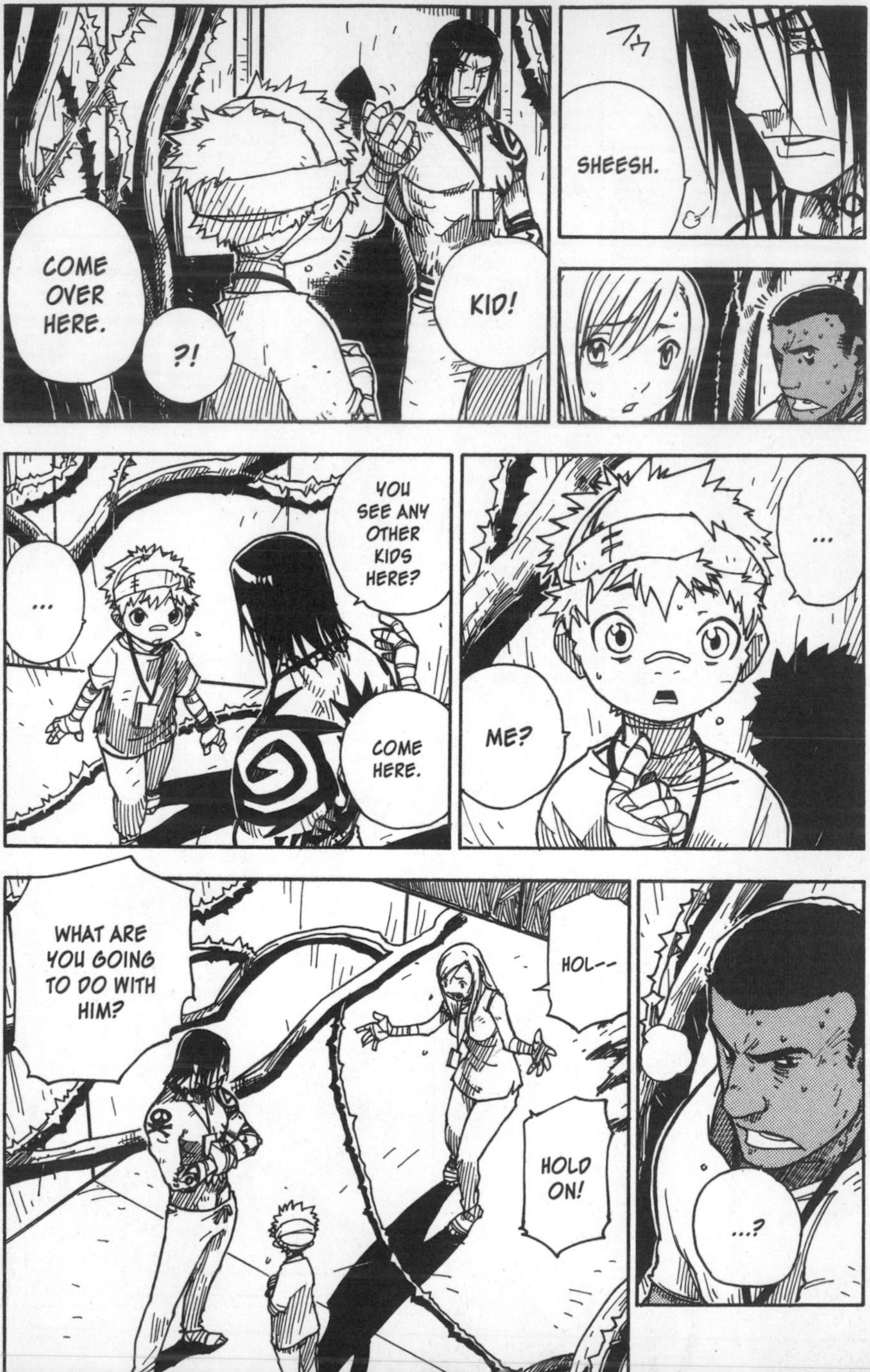
KID!
?!
COME OVER HERE.
SHEESH.
YOU SEE ANY OTHER KIDS HERE?
...
COME HERE.
...
ME?
WHAT ARE YOU GOING TO DO WITH HIM?
HOL--
HOLD ON!
...?

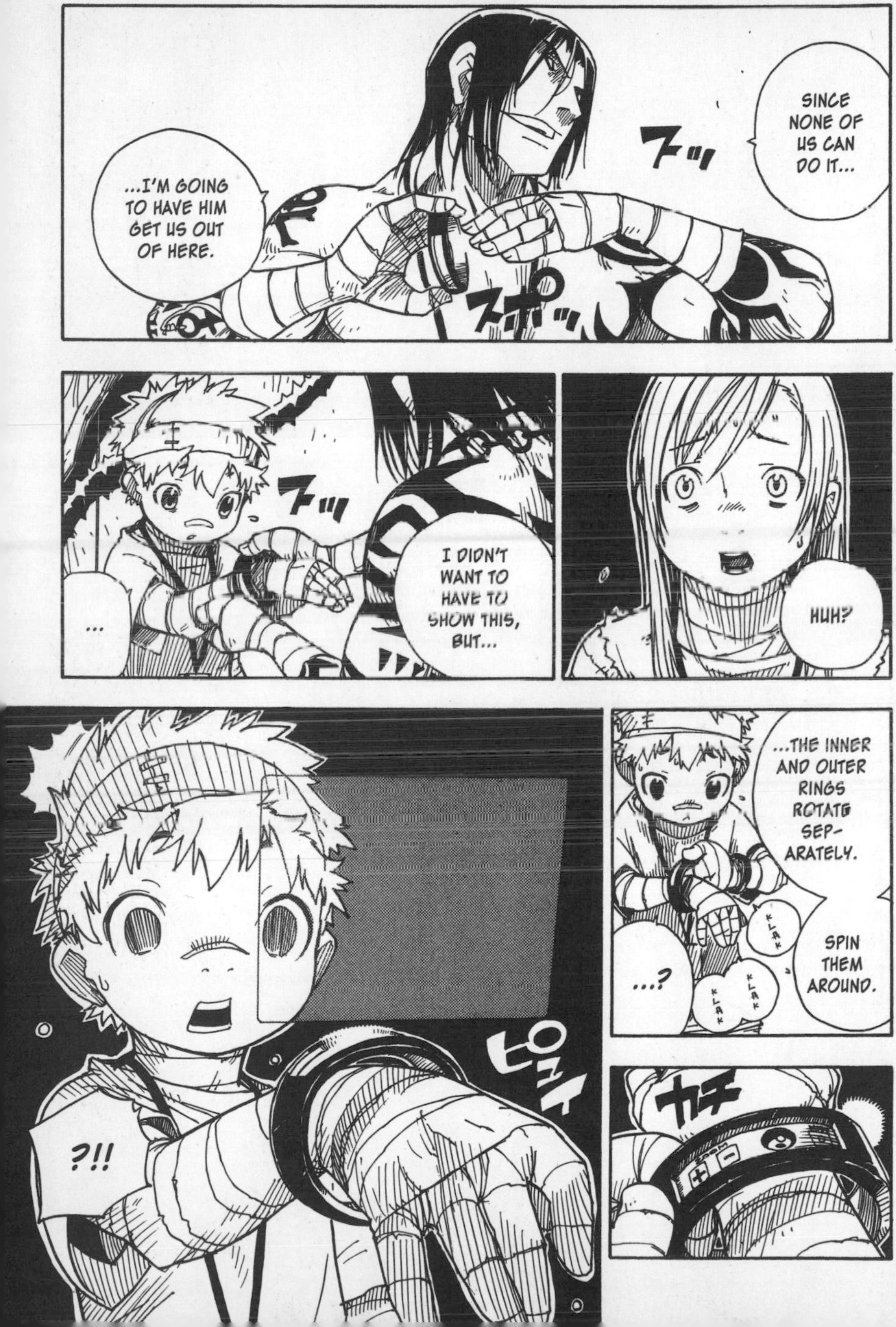
SINCE NONE OF US CAN DO IT...
...I'M GOING TO HAVE HIM GET US OUT OF HERE.
HUH?
I DIDN'T WANT TO HAVE TO SHOW THIS, BUT...
...
...THE INNER AND OUTER RINGS ROTATE SEP-ARATELY.
SPIN THEM AROUND.
KLAK
KLAK
KLAK
...?
?!!

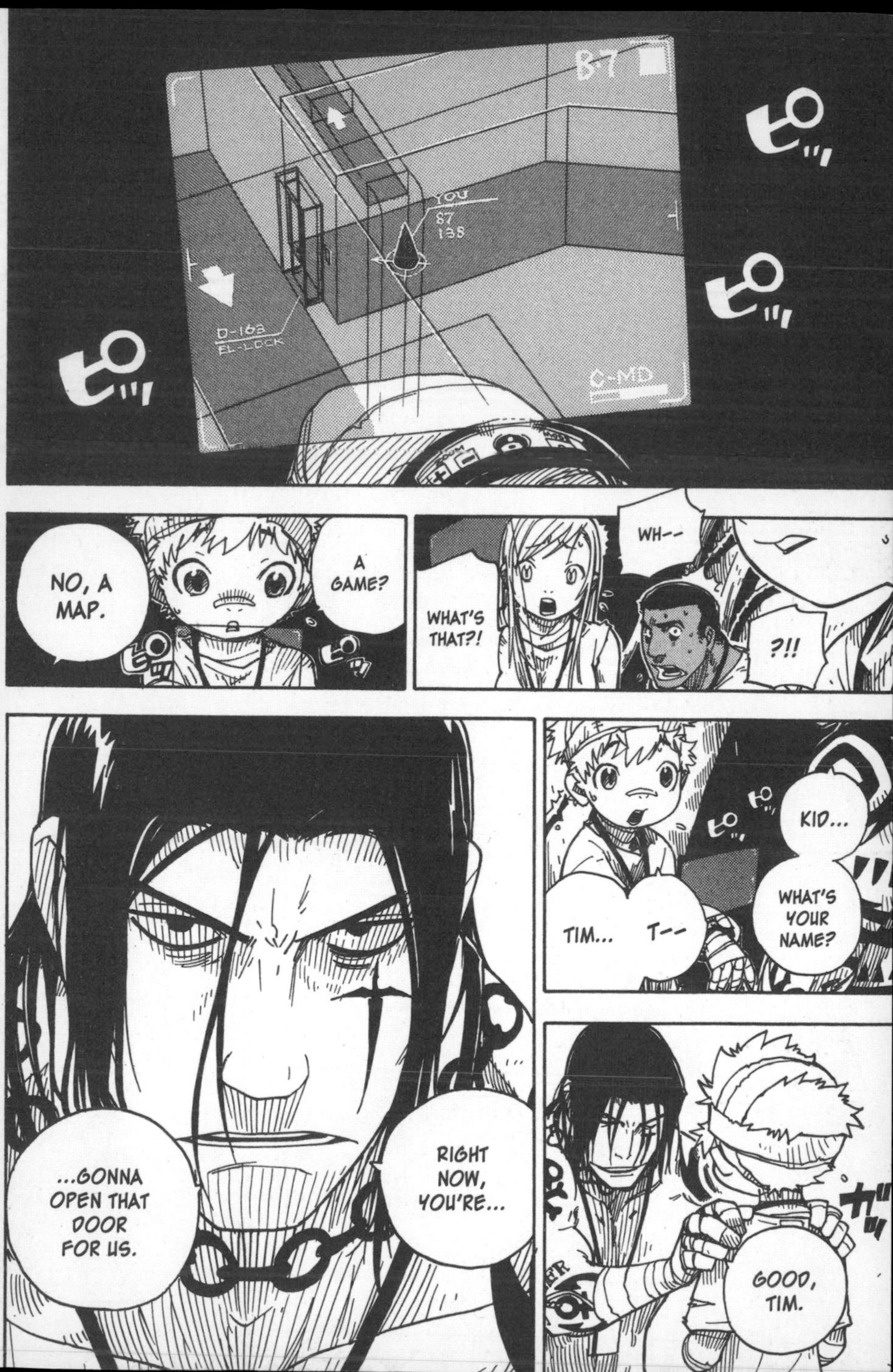
B-7
YOU
87
138
D-163
EL-LOCK
C-MD
WH--
WHAT'S THAT?!
?!!
A GAME?
NO, A MAP.
KID...
WHAT'S YOUR NAME?
TIM... T--
GOOD, TIM.
RIGHT NOW, YOU'RE...
...GONNA OPEN THAT DOOR FOR US.

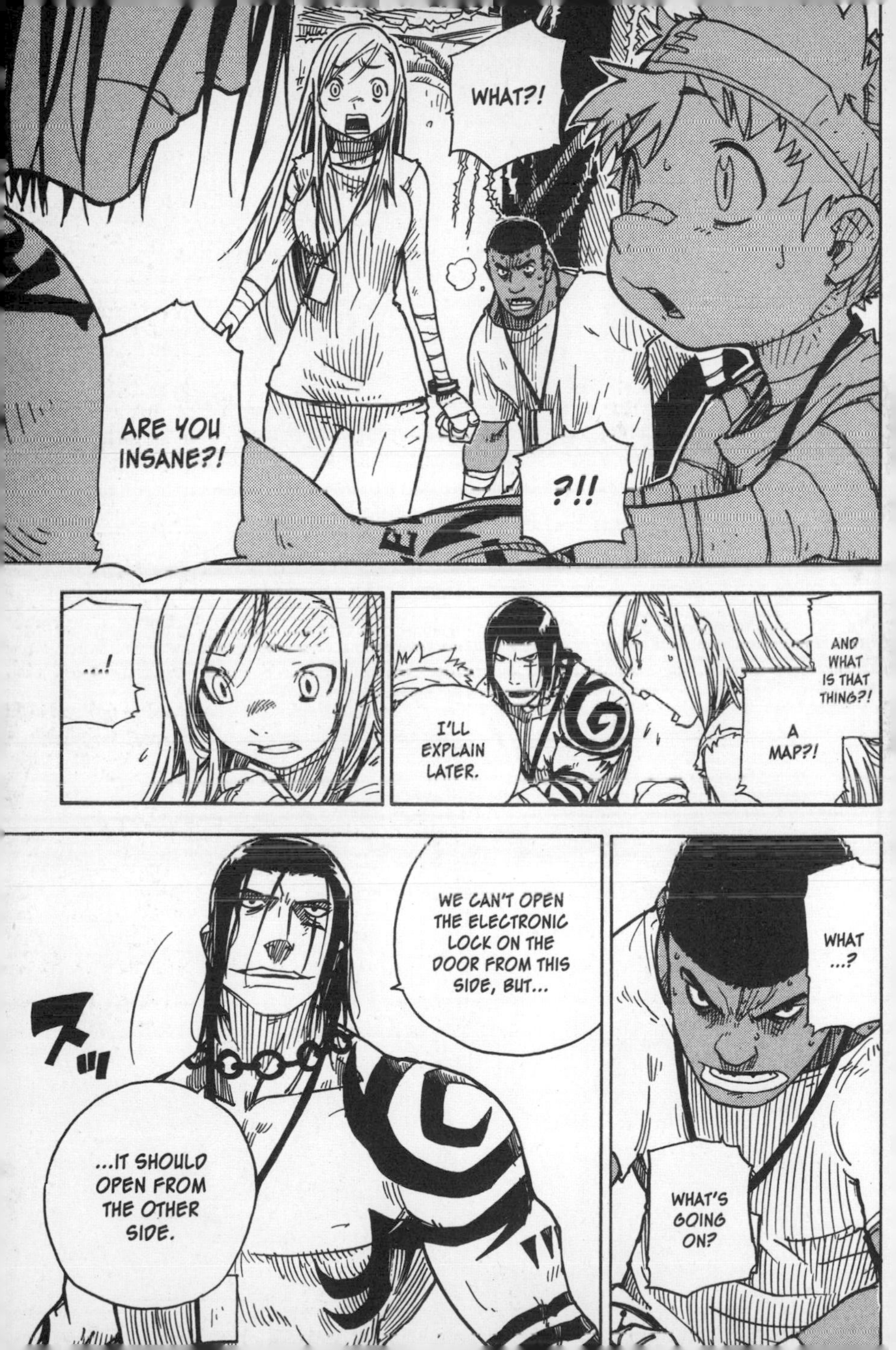
WHAT?!
?!!
ARE YOU INSANE?!
AND WHAT IS THAT THING?!
A MAP?!
I'LL EXPLAIN LATER.
...!
WHAT ...?
WHAT'S GOING ON?
WE CAN'T OPEN THE ELECTRONIC LOCK ON THE DOOR FROM THIS SIDE, BUT...
...IT SHOULD OPEN FROM THE OTHER SIDE.

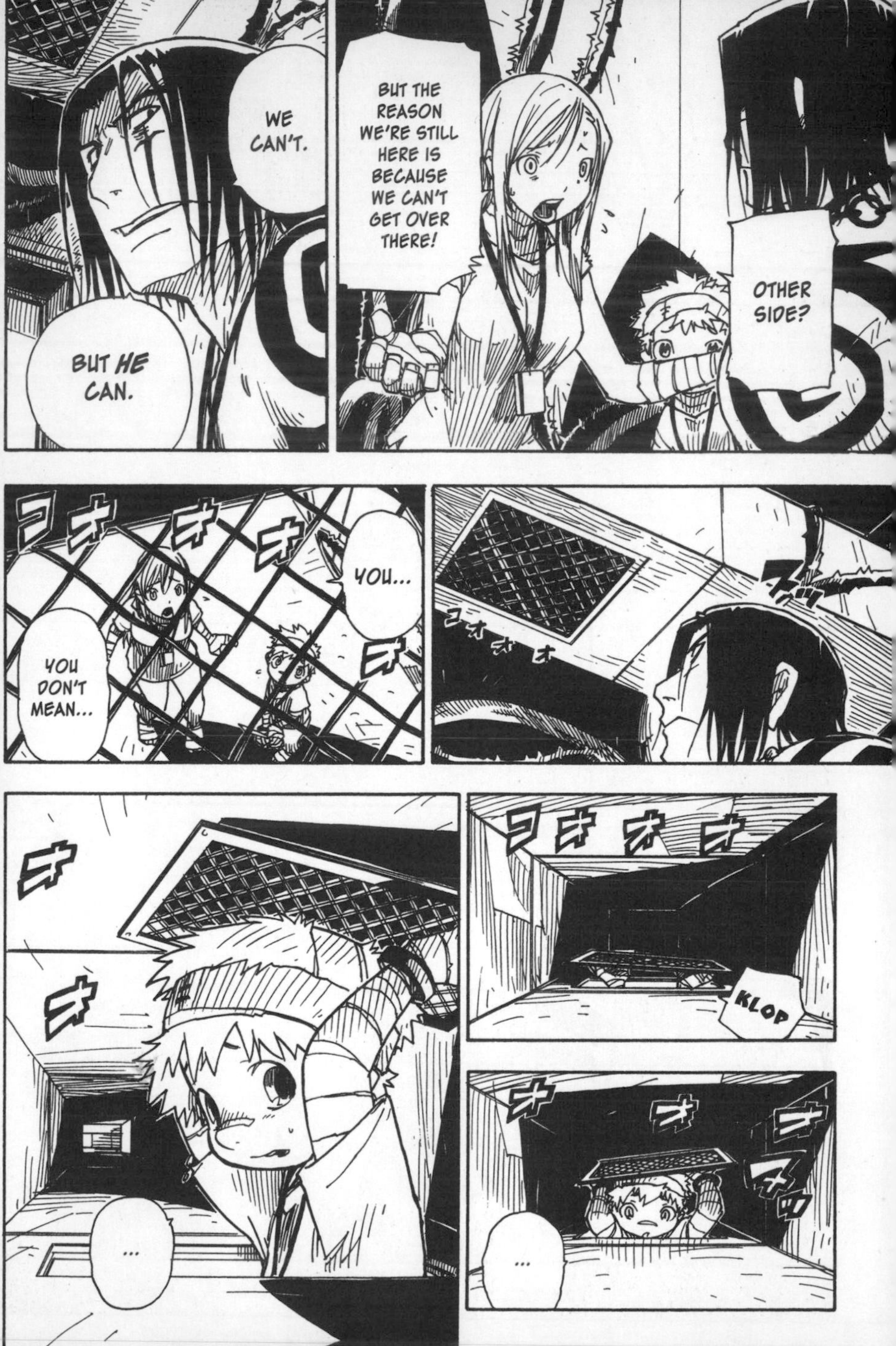
OTHER SIDE?
BUT THE REASON WE'RE STILL HERE IS BECAUSE WE CAN'T GET OVER THERE!
WE CAN'T.
BUT HE CAN.
YOU...
YOU DON'T MEAN...
KLOP
...
...

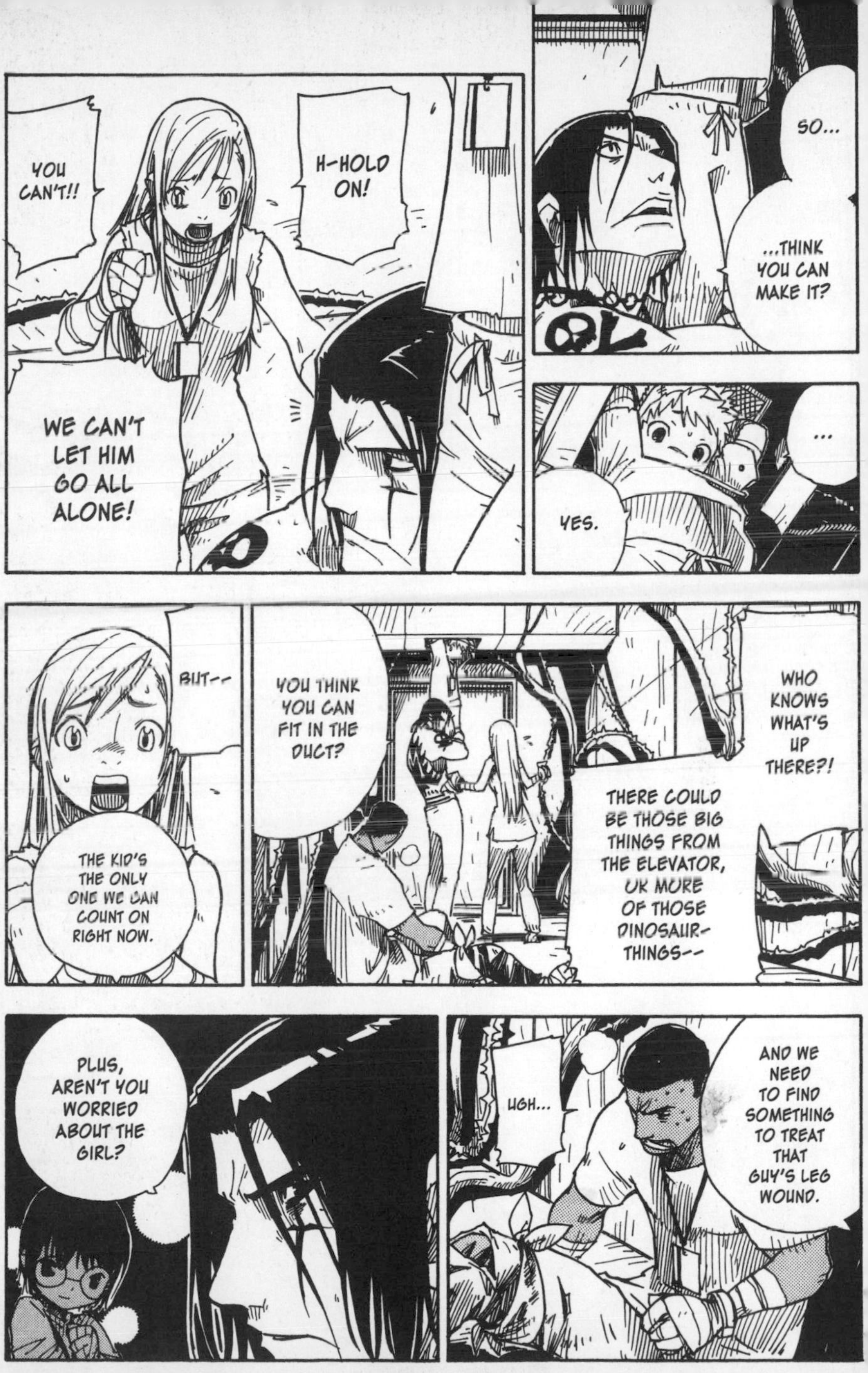
SO...
...THINK YOU CAN MAKE IT?
...
YES.
H-HOLD ON!
YOU CAN'T!!
WE CAN'T LET HIM GO ALL ALONE!
WHO KNOWS WHAT'S UP THERE?!
THERE COULD BE THOSE BIG THINGS FROM THE ELEVATOR, OR MORE OF THOSE DINOSAUR-THINGS--
YOU THINK YOU CAN FIT IN THE DUCT?
BUT--
THE KID'S THE ONLY ONE WE CAN COUNT ON RIGHT NOW.
AND WE NEED TO FIND SOMETHING TO TREAT THAT GUY'S LEG WOUND.
UGH...
PLUS, AREN'T YOU WORRIED ABOUT THE GIRL?

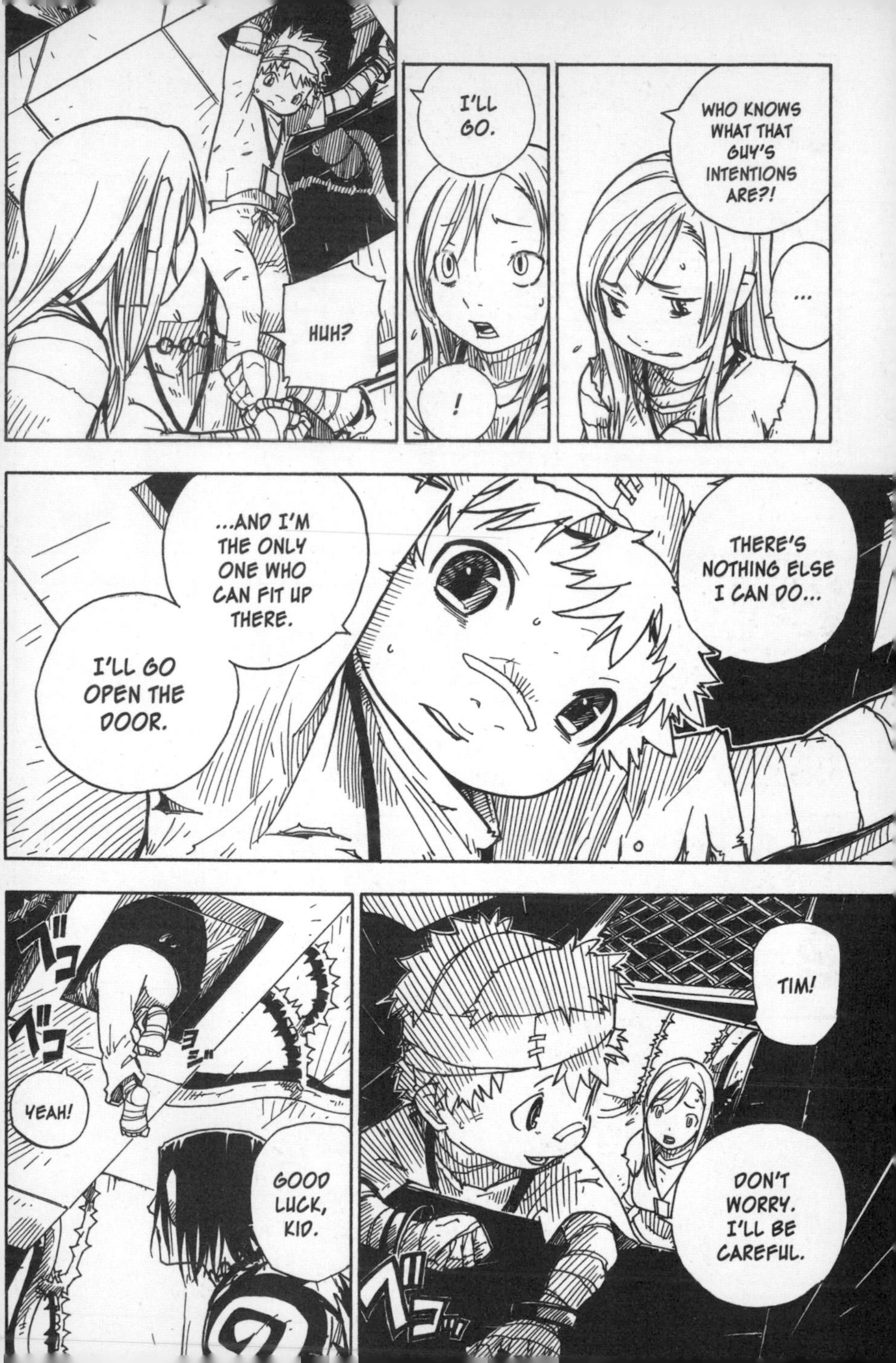
WHO KNOWS WHAT THAT GUY'S INTENTIONS ARE?!
...
I'LL GO.
!
HUH?
THERE'S NOTHING ELSE I CAN DO...
...AND I'M THE ONLY ONE WHO CAN FIT UP THERE.
I'LL GO OPEN THE DOOR.
TIM!
DON'T WORRY. I'LL BE CAREFUL.
GOOD LUCK, KID.
YEAH!

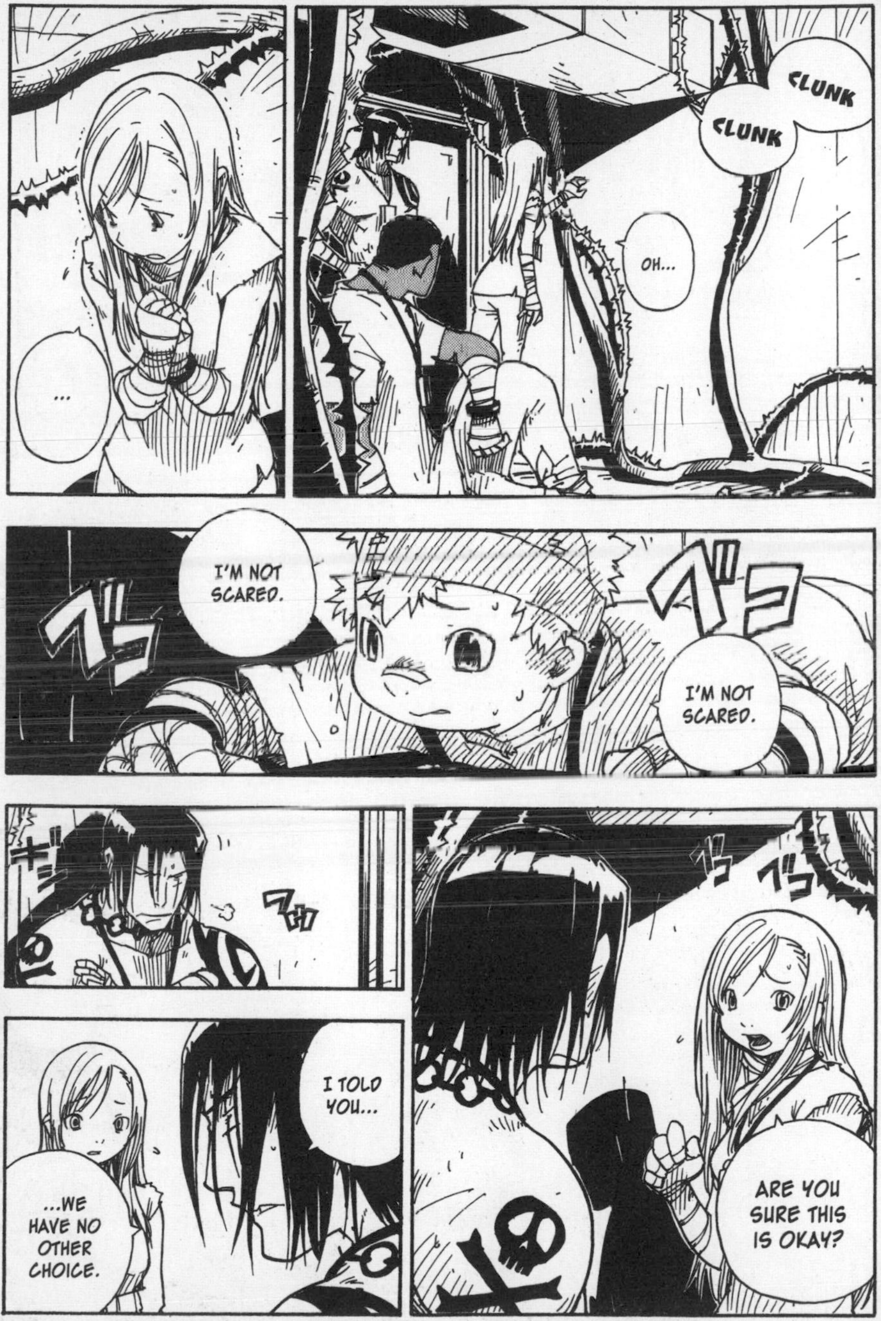
CLUNK
CLUNK
OH...
...
I'M NOT SCARED.
I'M NOT SCARED.
ARE YOU SURE THIS IS OKAY?
I TOLD YOU...
...WE HAVE NO OTHER CHOICE.

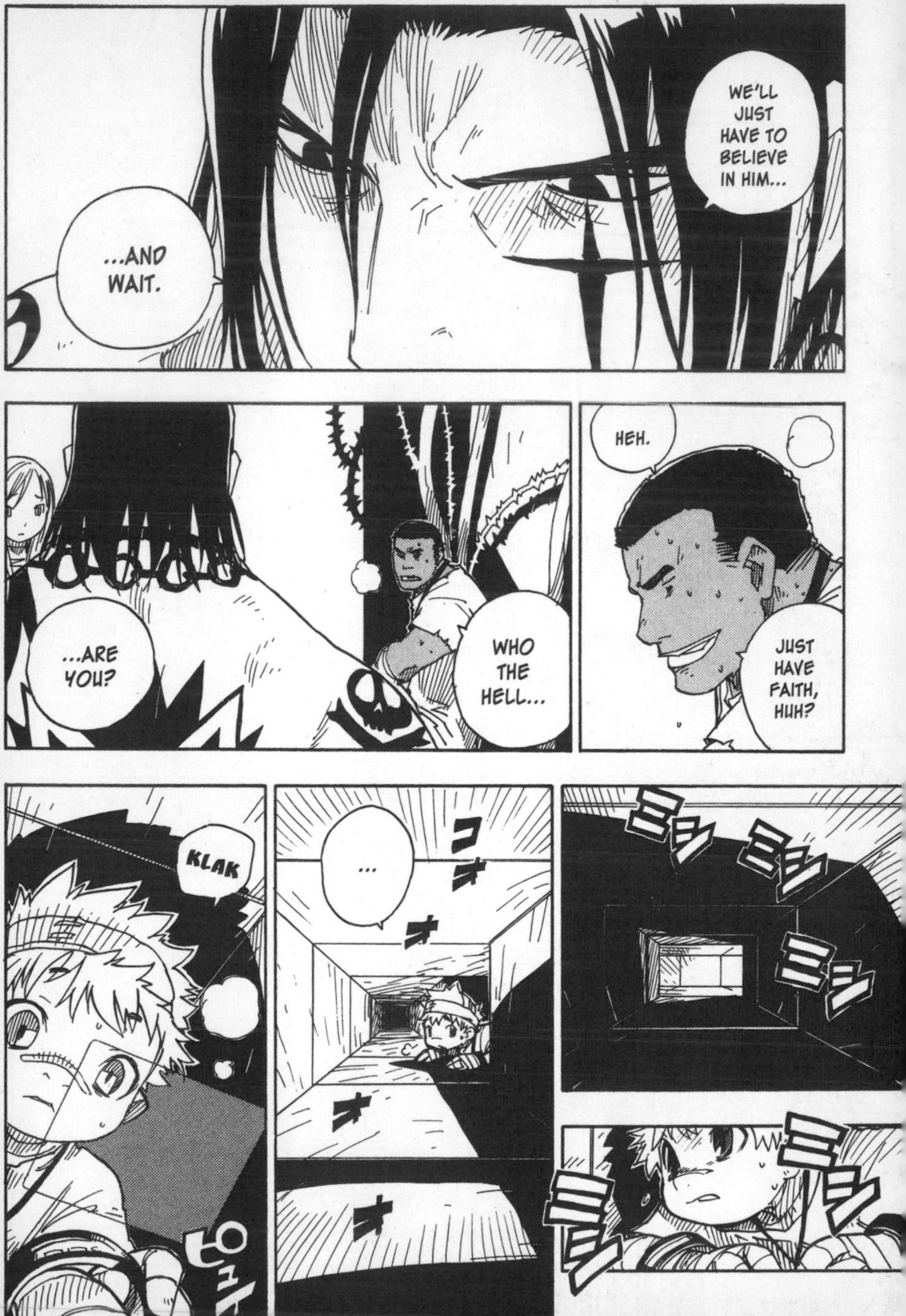
WE'LL JUST HAVE TO BELIEVE IN HIM...
...AND WAIT.
HEH.
JUST HAVE FAITH, HUH?
WHO THE HELL...
...ARE YOU?
ミシ ミシ
ミシ
ミシ ミシ
コォォォォ
...
KLAK

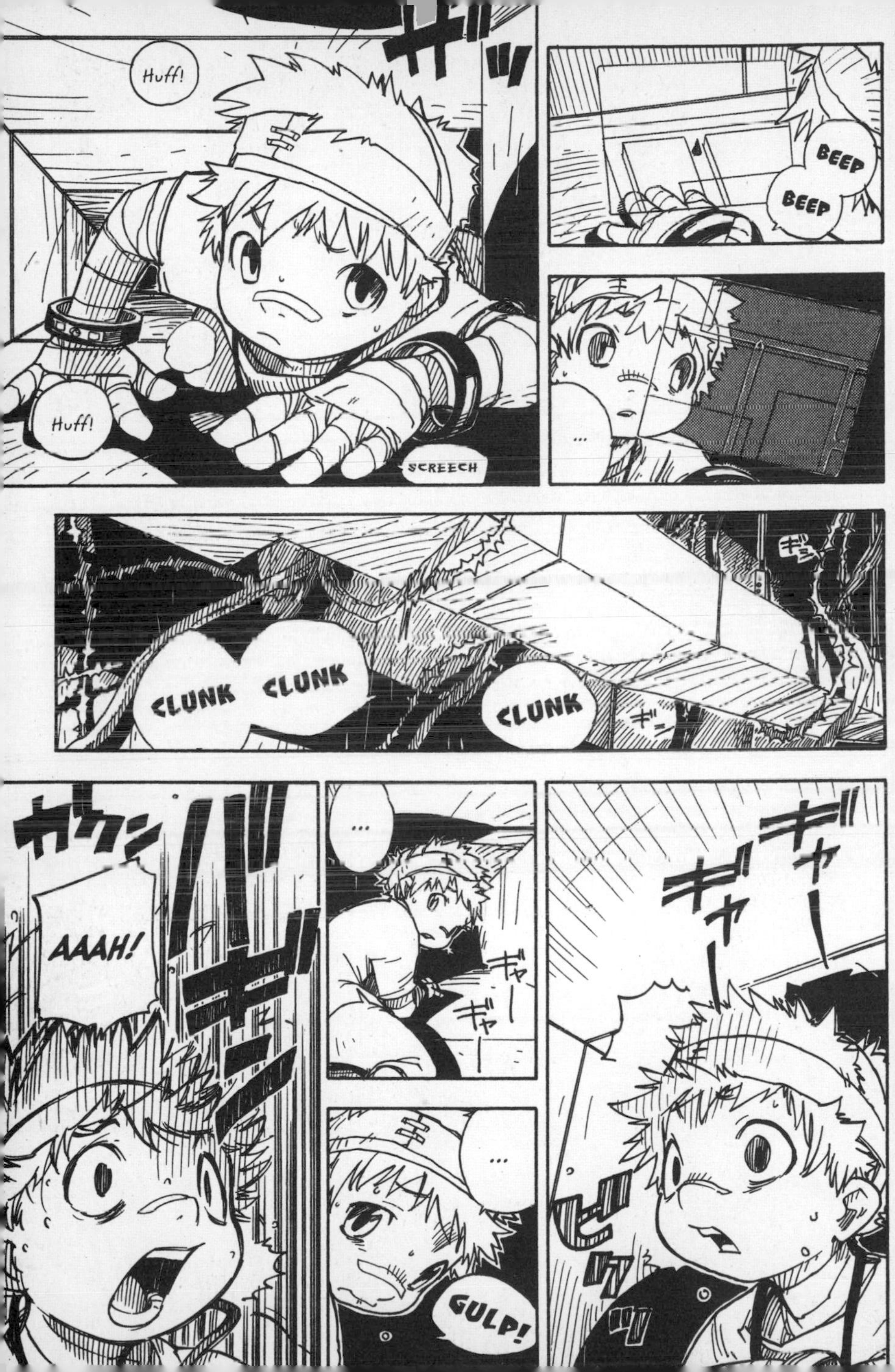
Huff!
Huff!
SCREECH
BEEP
BEEP
...
CLUNK
CLUNK
CLUNK
AAAH!
...
...
GULP!

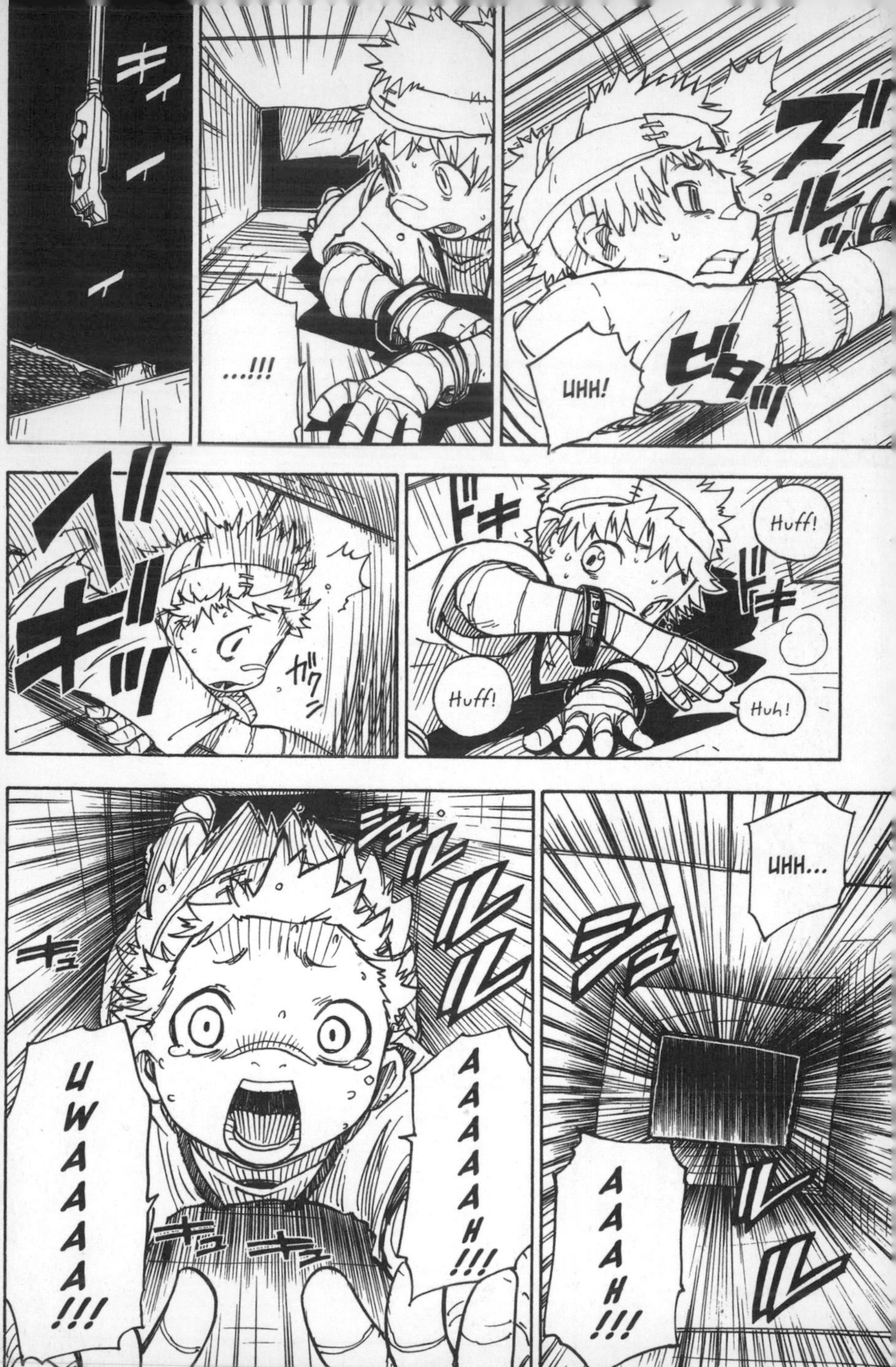
UHH!
...!!!
Huff!
Huh!
Huff!
UHH...
AAAAH!!!
AAAAAAAH!!!
UWAAAAAA!!!

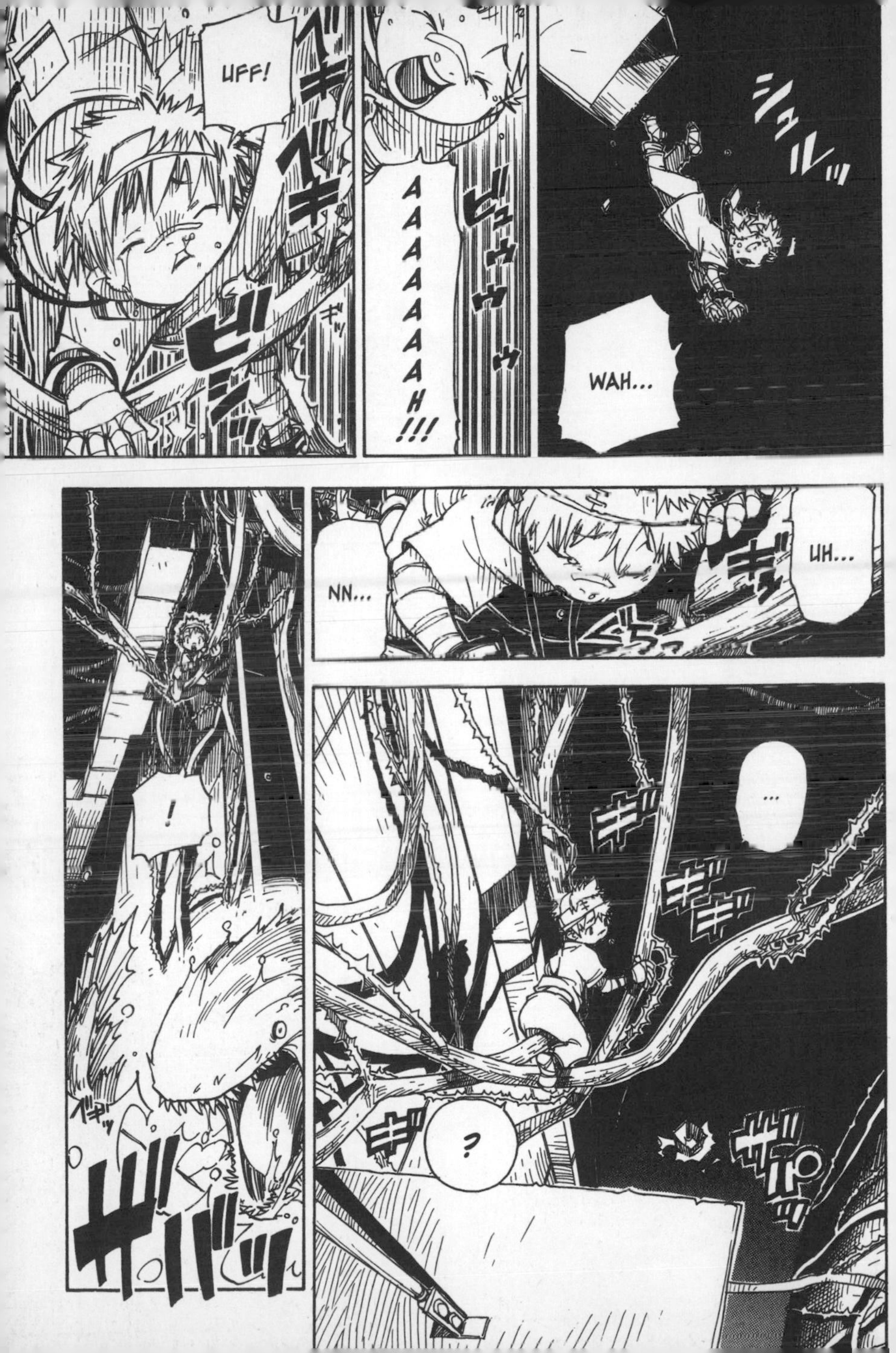

シュルッ
WAH...
AAAAAAAAAH!!!
UFF!
UH...
NN...
...
?
!

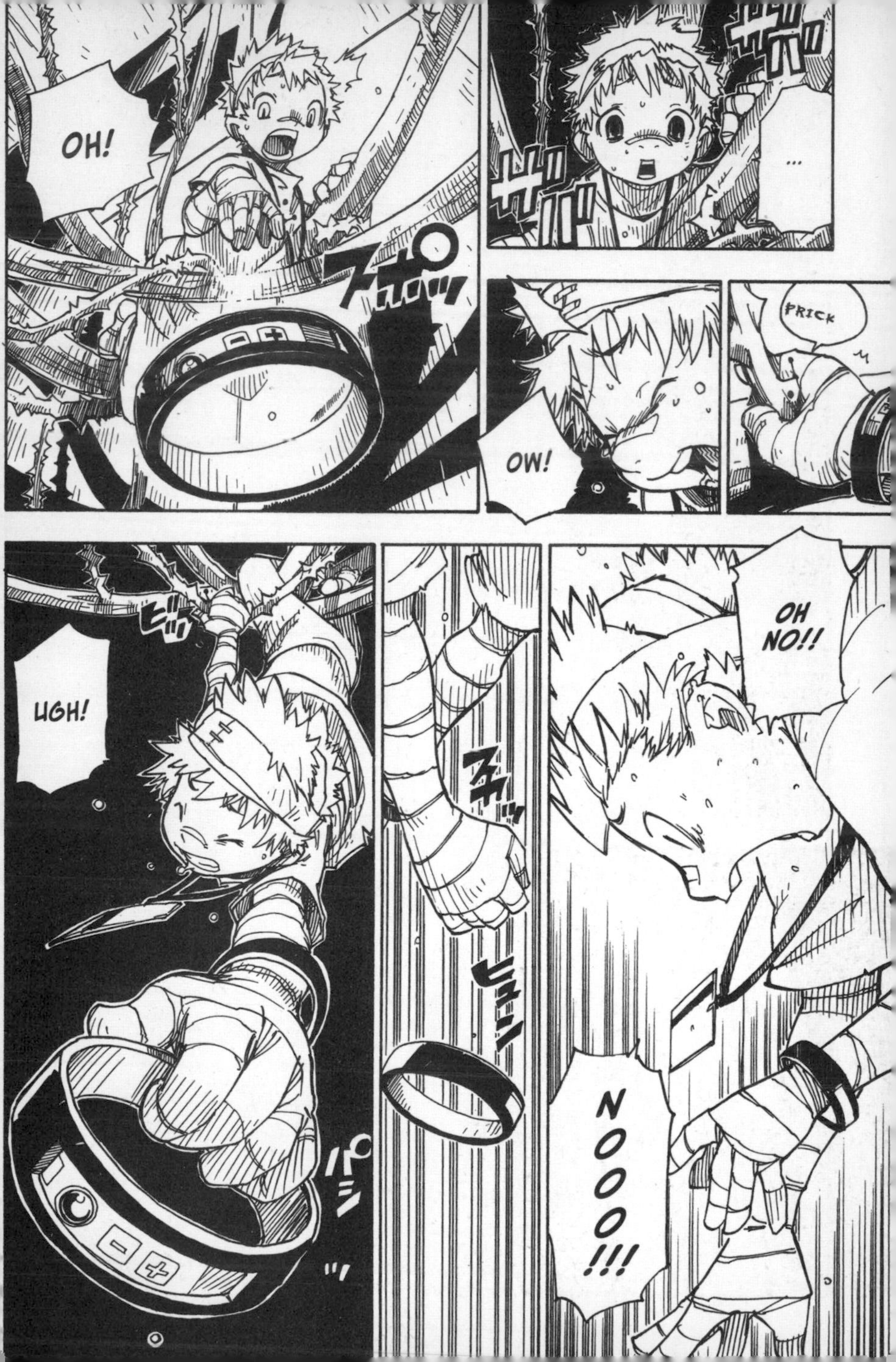
...
OH!
OW!
PRICK
OH NO!!
NOOOO!!!
UGH!

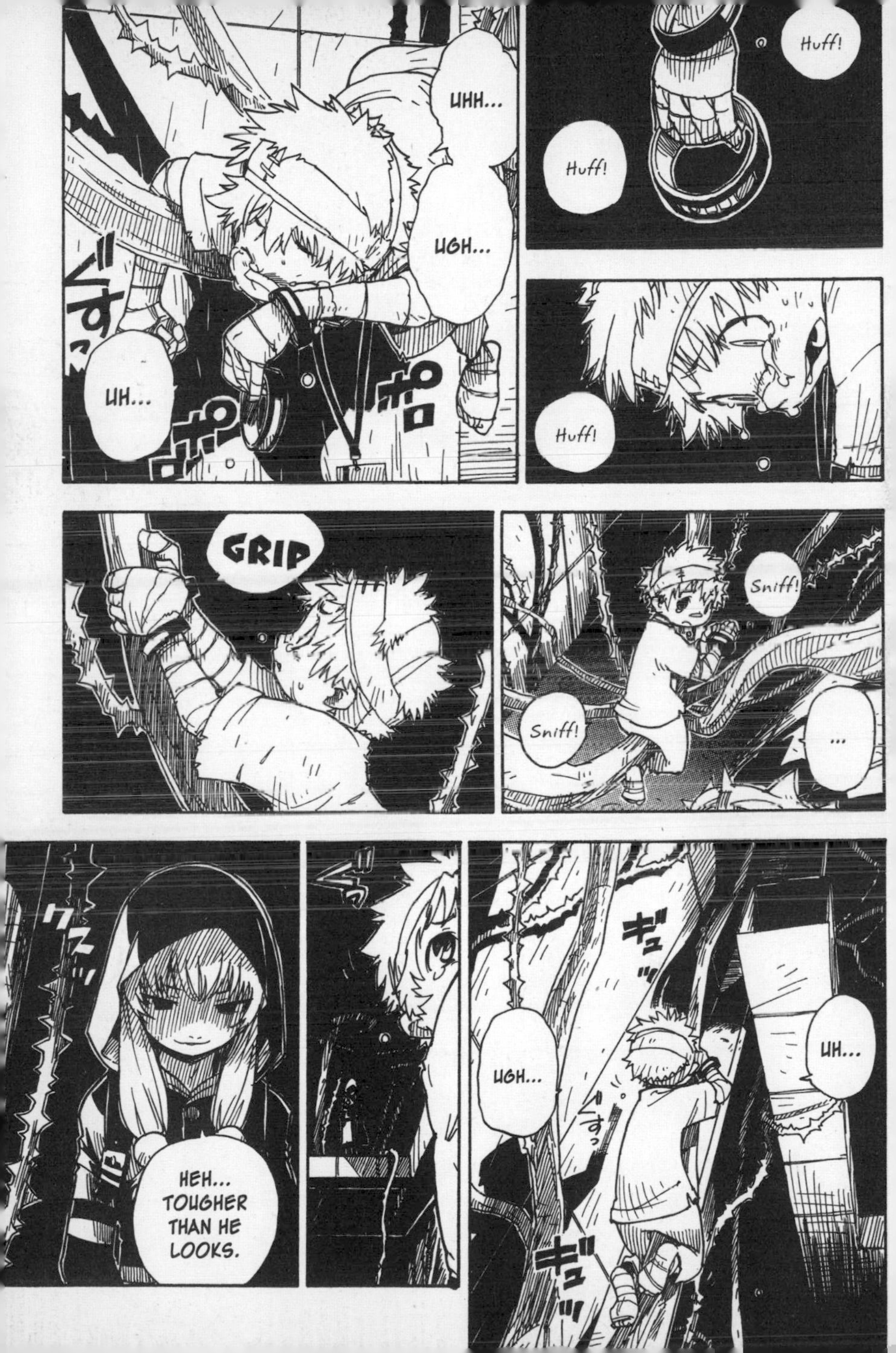
Huff!
Huff!
Huff!
UHH...
UGH...
UH...
ぐすっ
ポロ
ポロ
Sniff!
Sniff!
...
GRIP
UH...
UGH...
ぐすっ
ギュッ
ギュッ
クスッ
HEH... TOUGHER THAN HE LOOKS.

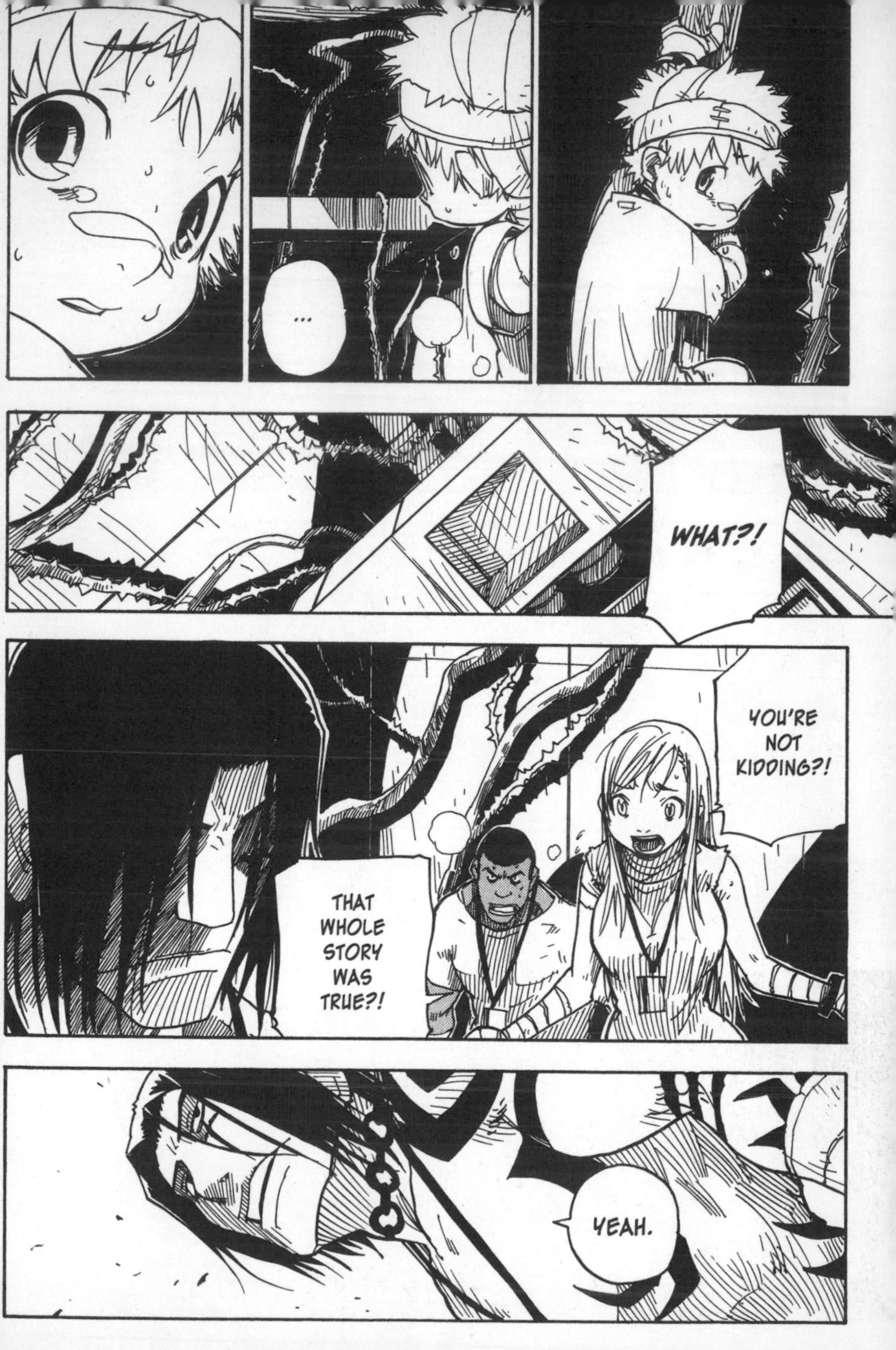
...
WHAT?!
YOU'RE NOT KIDDING?!
THAT WHOLE STORY WAS TRUE?!
YEAH.

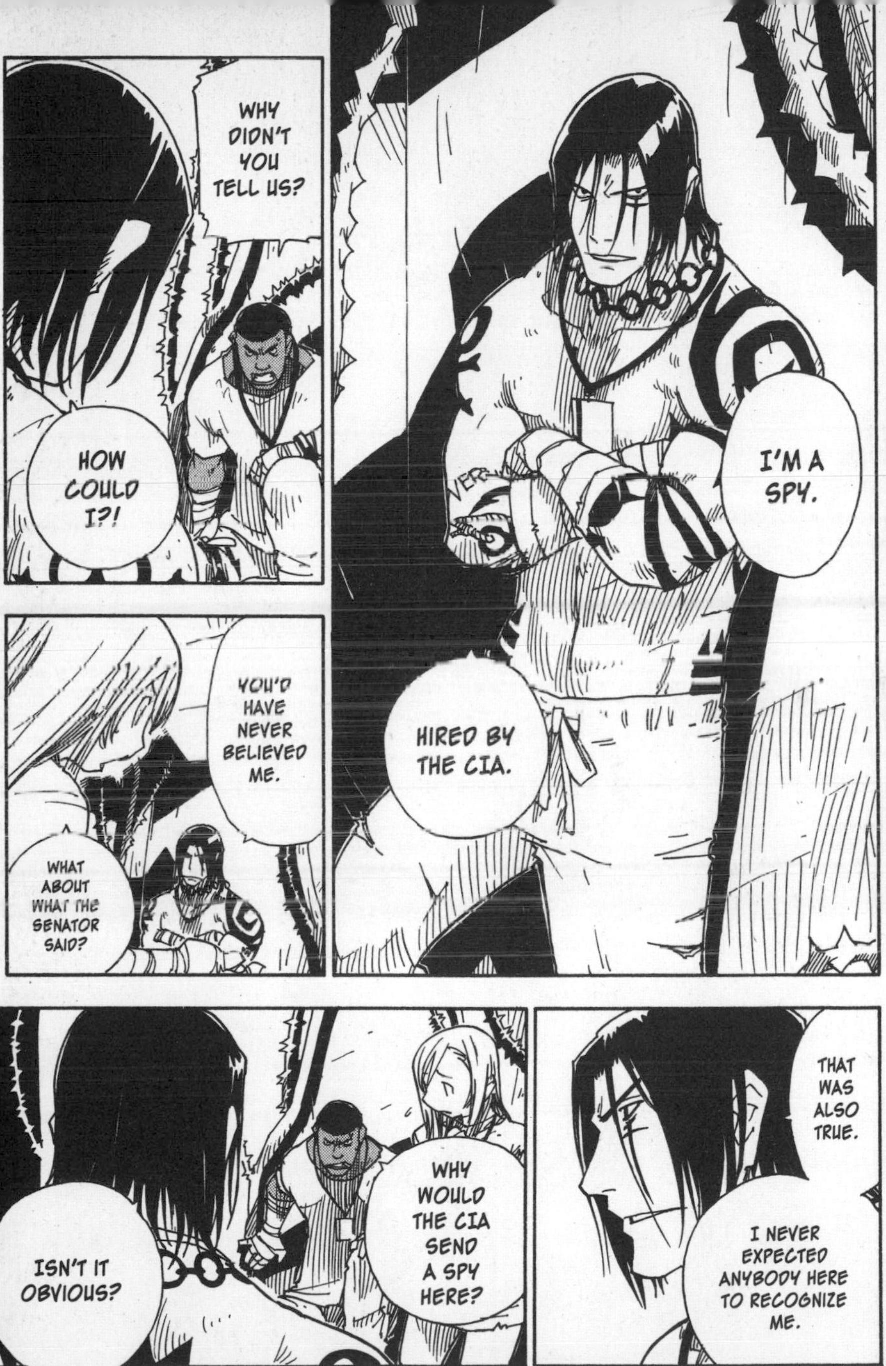
WHY DIDN'T YOU TELL US?
HOW COULD I?!
I'M A SPY.
HIRED BY THE CIA.
YOU'D HAVE NEVER BELIEVED ME.
WHAT ABOUT WHAT THE SENATOR SAID?
THAT WAS ALSO TRUE.
I NEVER EXPECTED ANYBODY HERE TO RECOGNIZE ME.
WHY WOULD THE CIA SEND A SPY HERE?
ISN'T IT OBVIOUS?

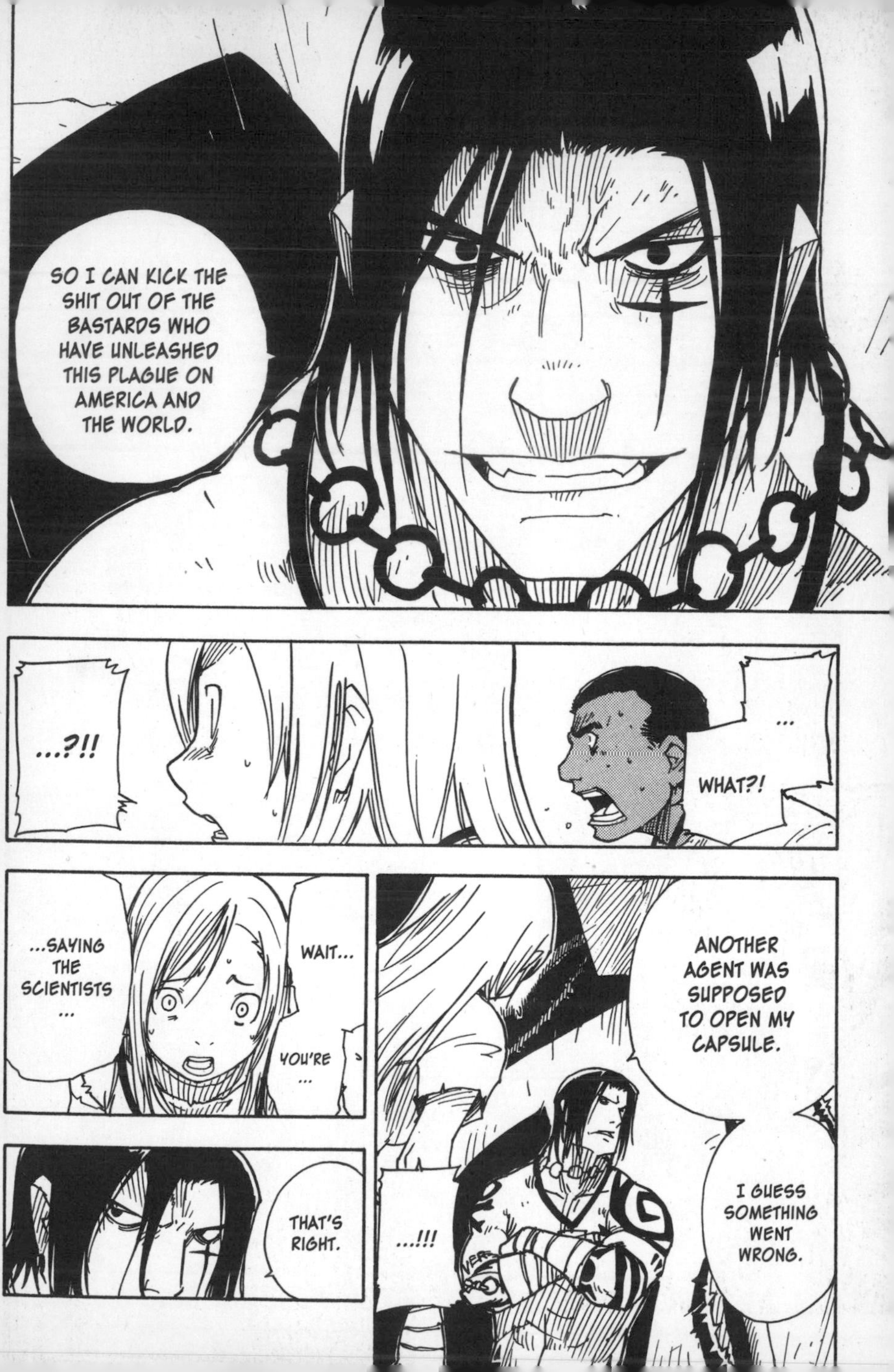
SO I CAN KICK THE SHIT OUT OF THE BASTARDS WHO HAVE UNLEASHED THIS PLAGUE ON AMERICA AND THE WORLD.
...?!!
...
WHAT?!
WAIT...
YOU'RE ...
...SAYING THE SCIENTISTS ...
THAT'S RIGHT.
ANOTHER AGENT WAS SUPPOSED TO OPEN MY CAPSULE.
I GUESS SOMETHING WENT WRONG.
...!!!

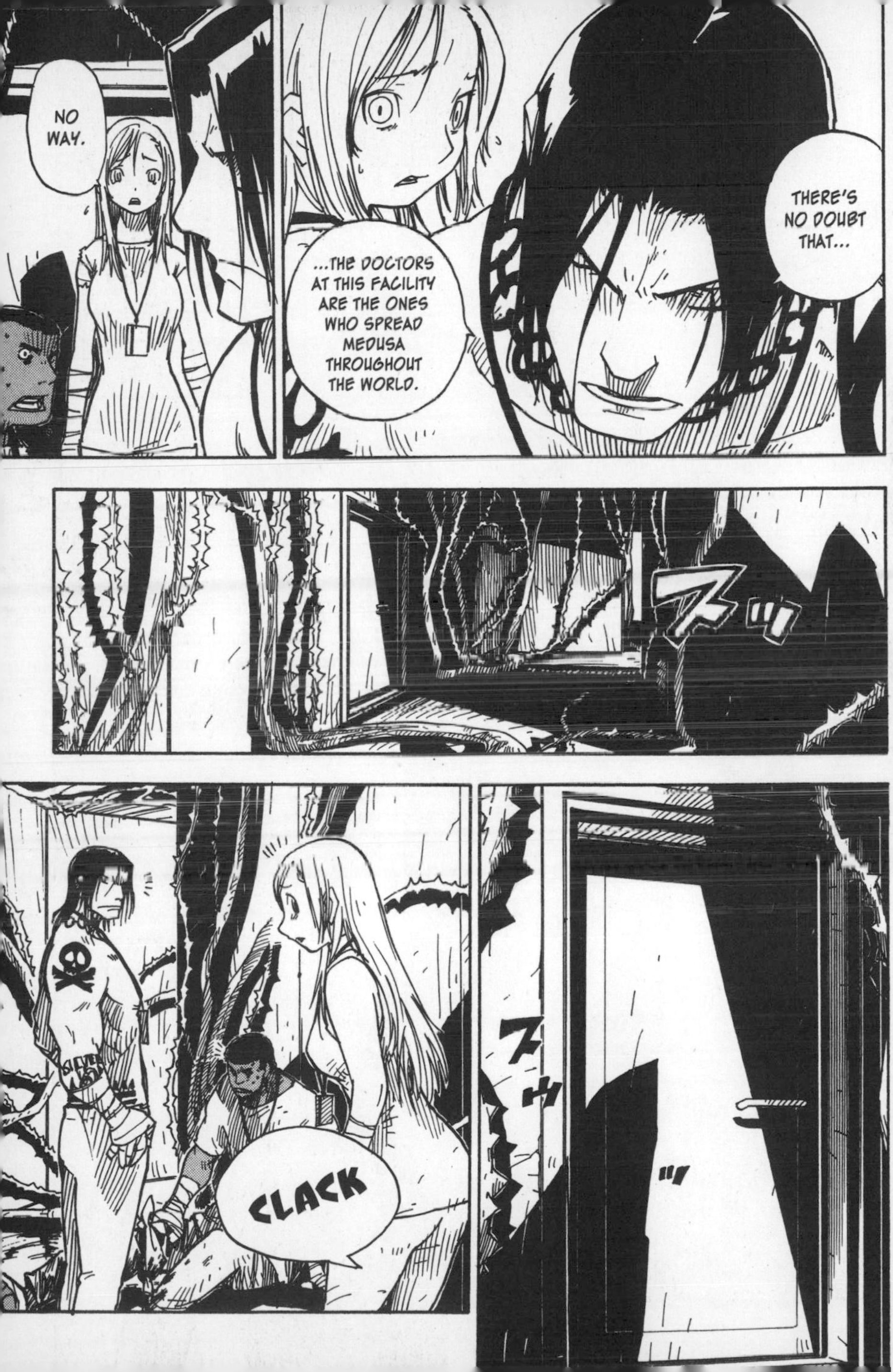
THERE'S NO DOUBT THAT...
...THE DOCTORS AT THIS FACILITY ARE THE ONES WHO SPREAD MEDUSA THROUGHOUT THE WORLD.
NO WAY.
CLACK

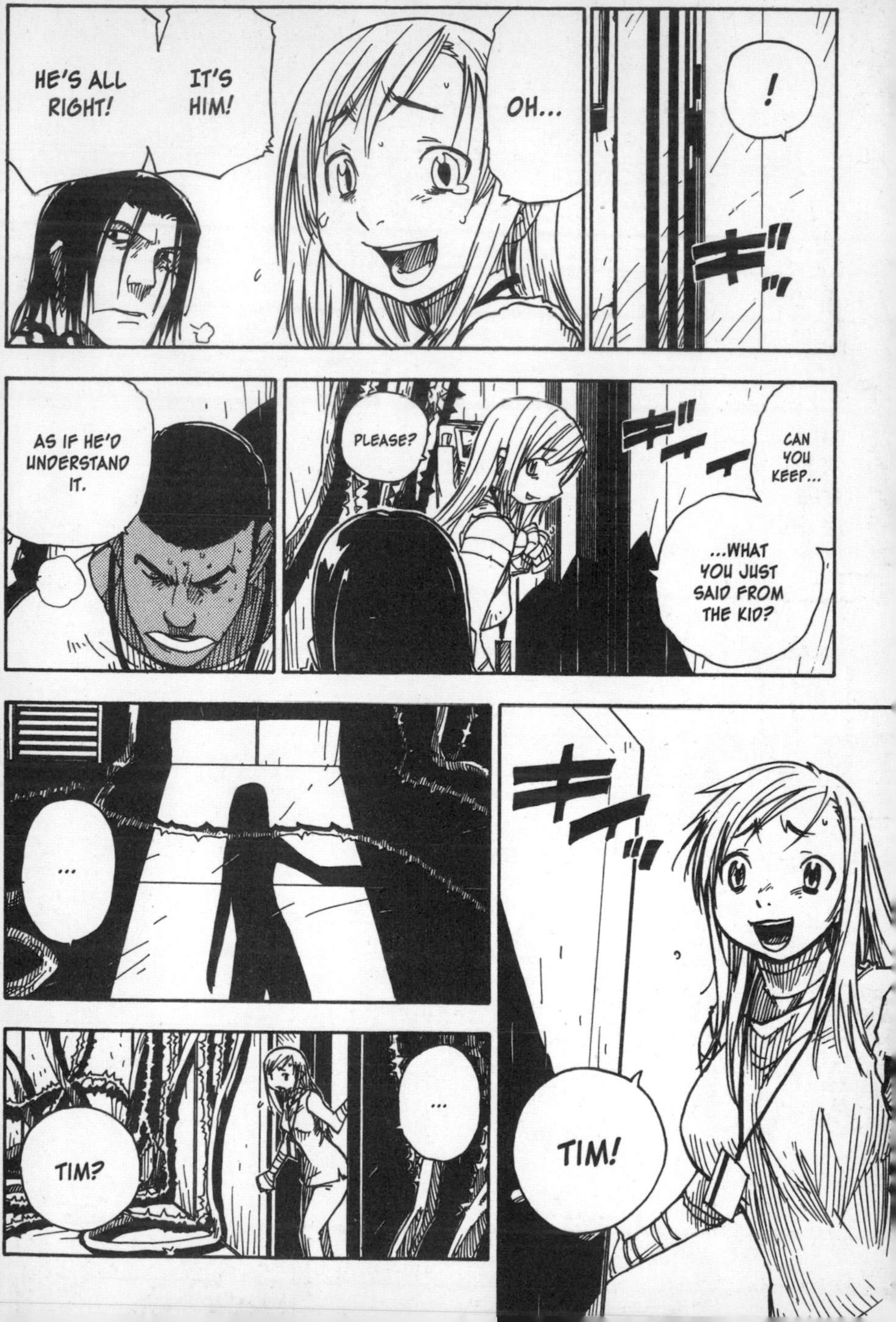
!
OH...
IT'S HIM!
HE'S ALL RIGHT!
CAN YOU KEEP...
...WHAT YOU JUST SAID FROM THE KID?
PLEASE?
AS IF HE'D UNDERSTAND IT.
TIM!
...
...
TIM?

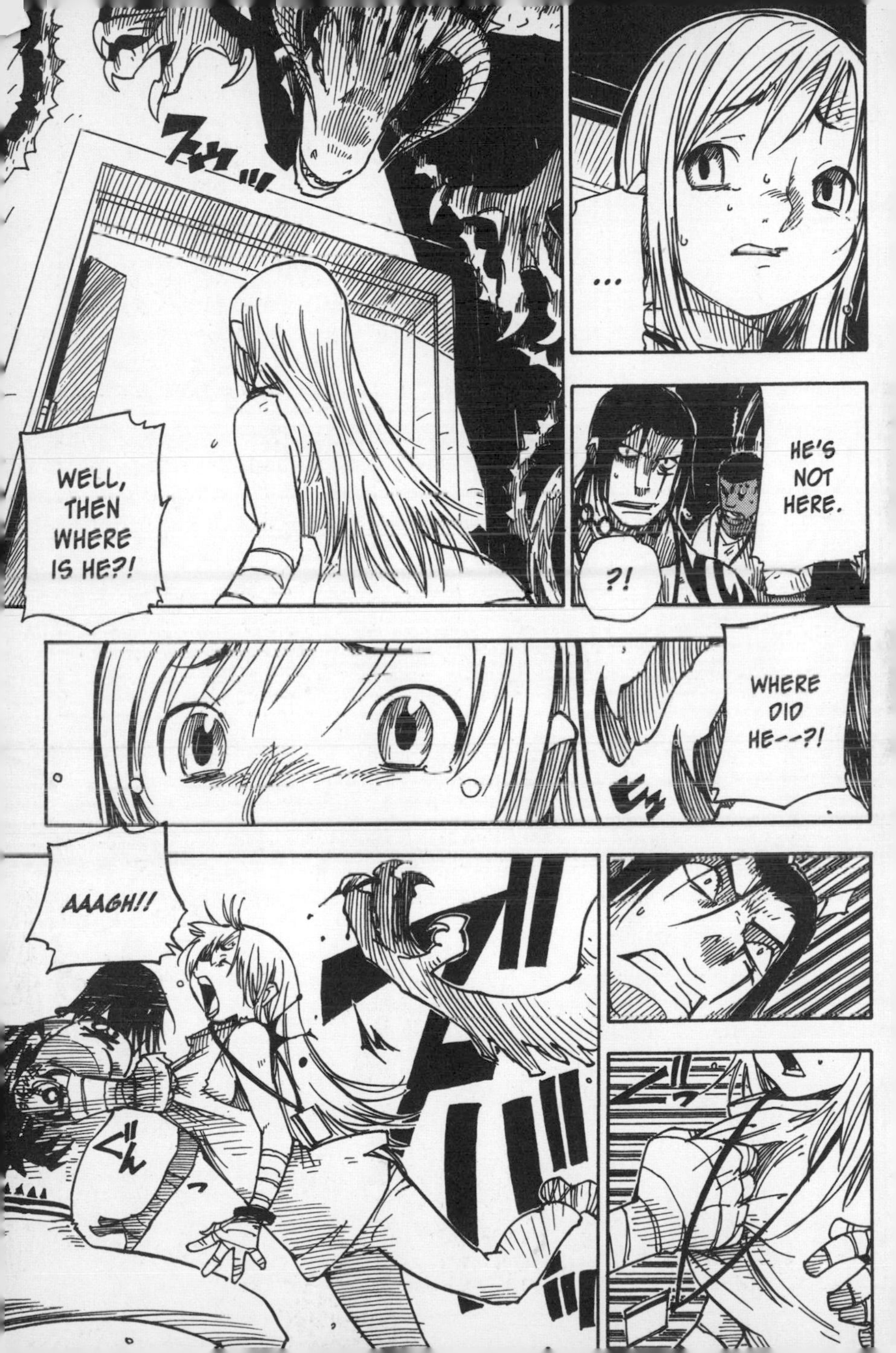
...
HE'S NOT HERE.
?!
WELL, THEN WHERE IS HE?!
WHERE DID HE--?!
AAAGH!!
ぐん

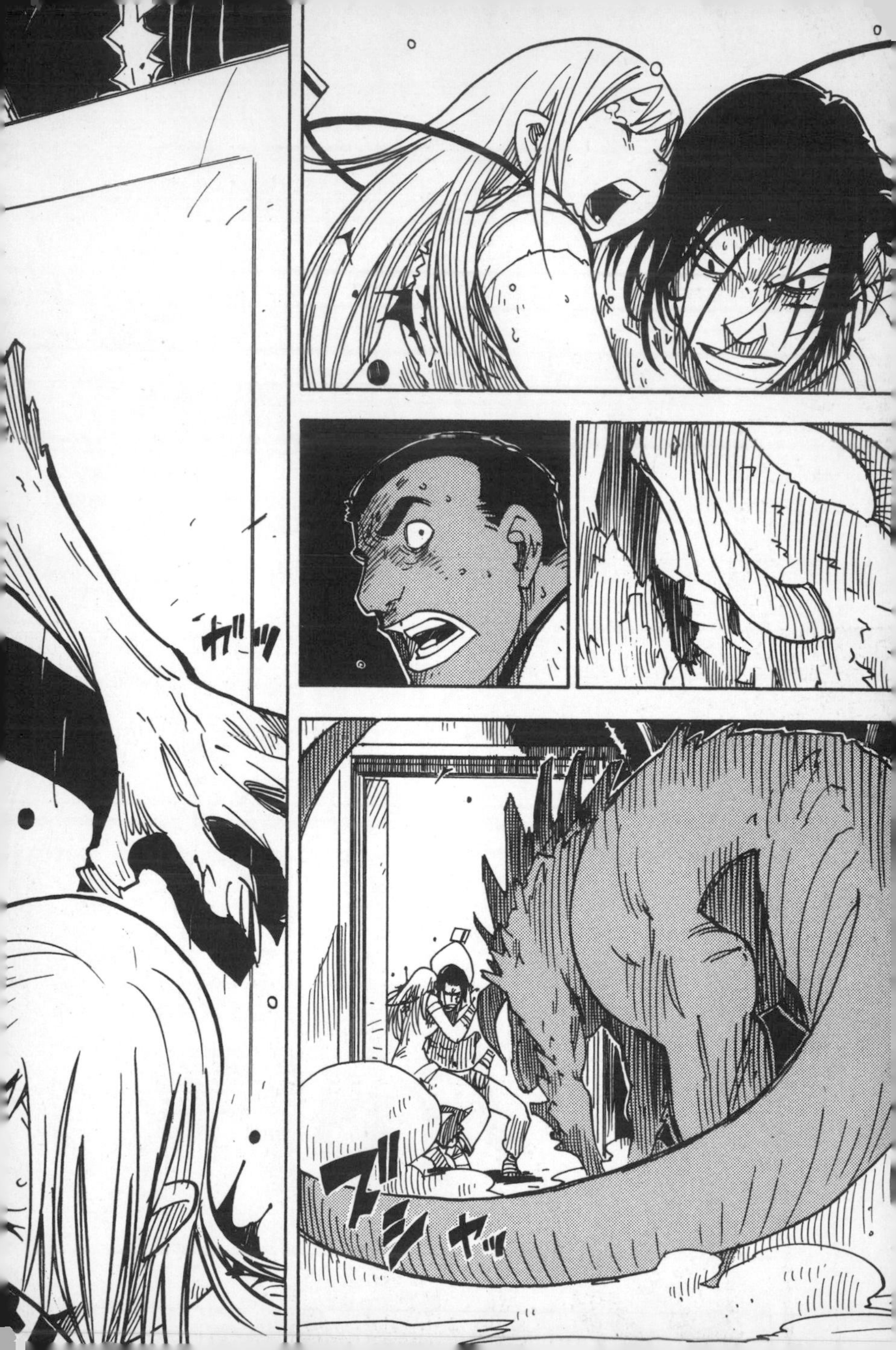
ブシャッ
ガッ

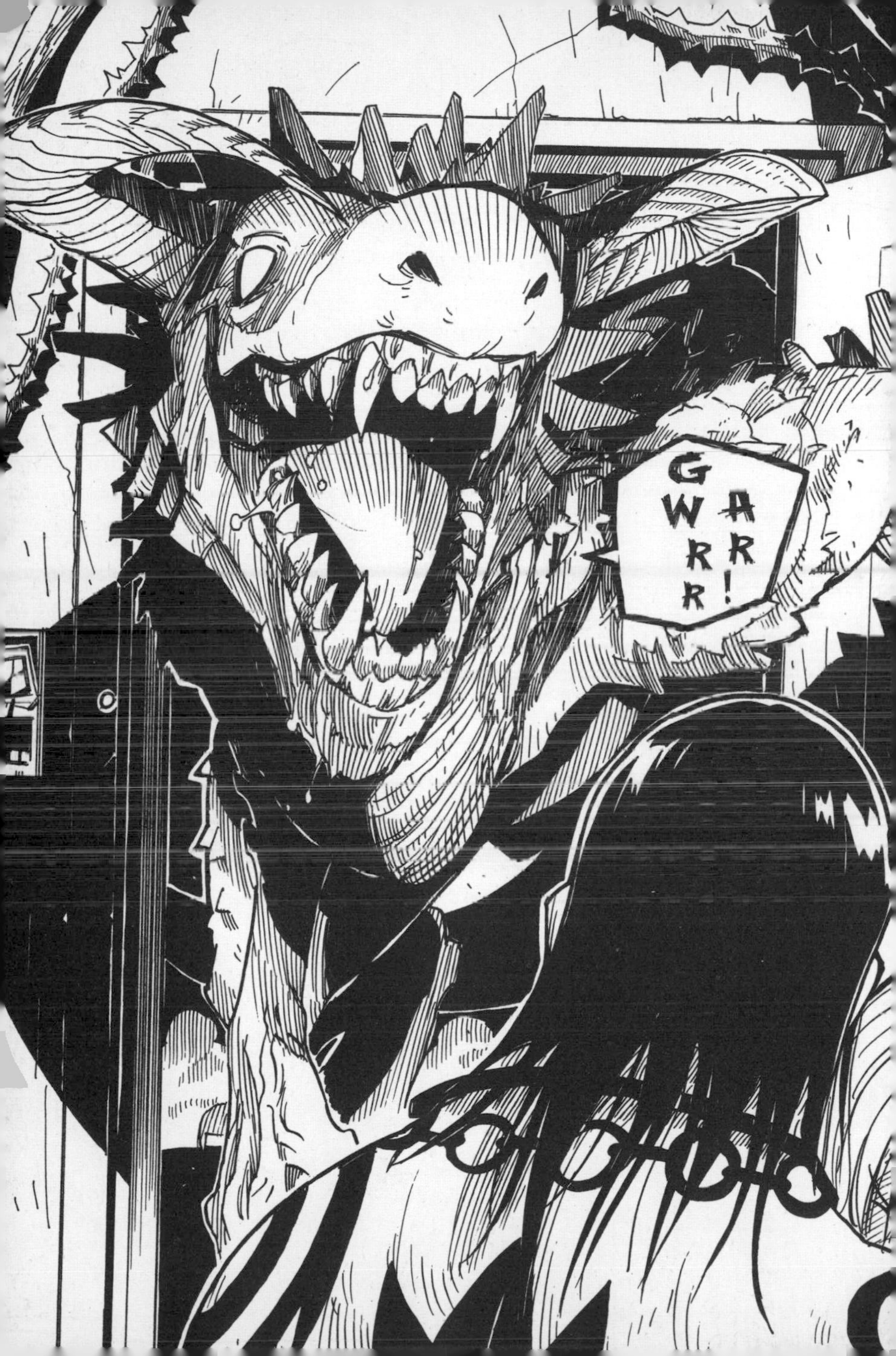
GWRRR ARR!

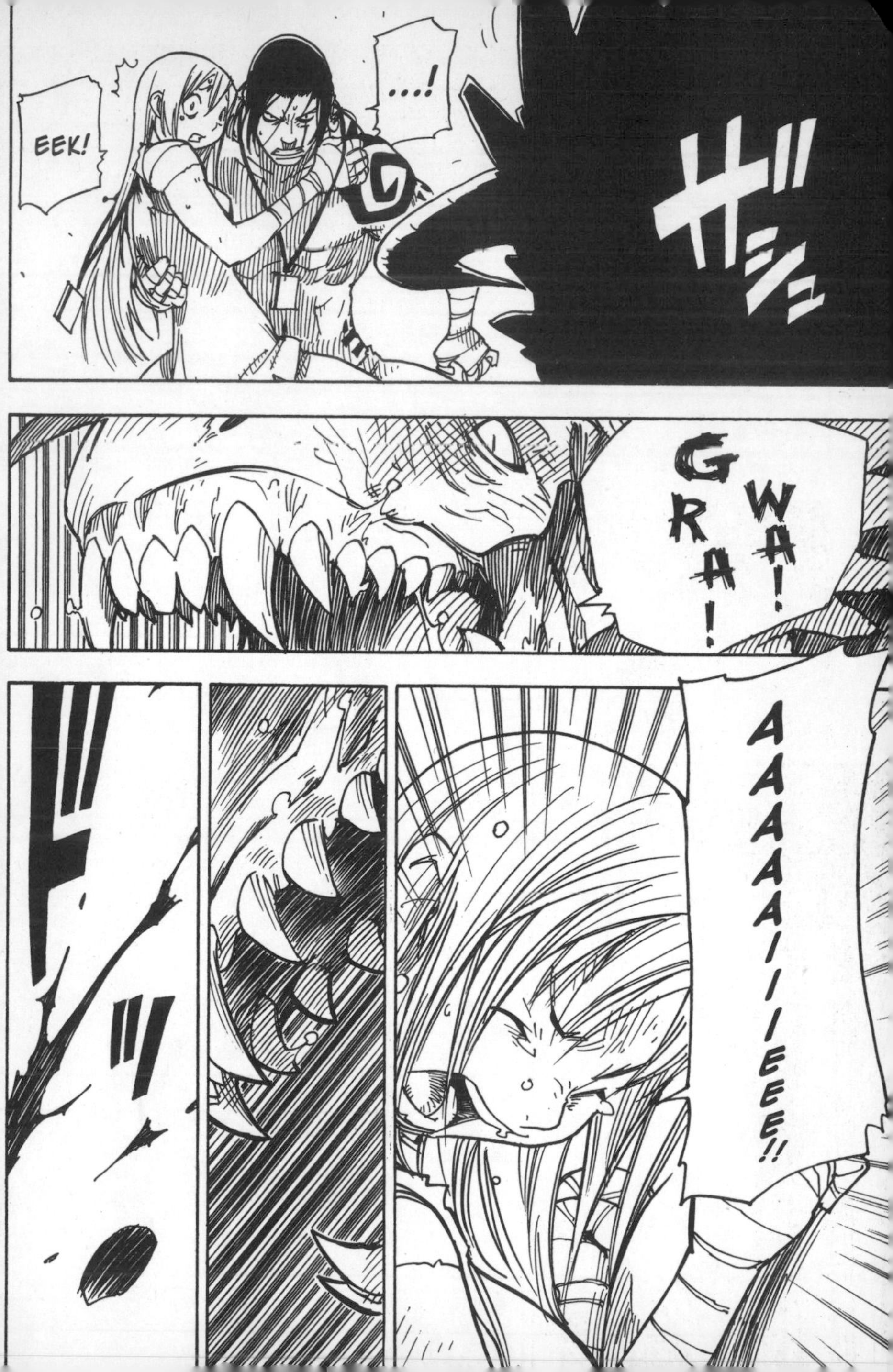

...!
EEK!
ザジュ
GWA! RA!
AAAAAIIIEEEE!!

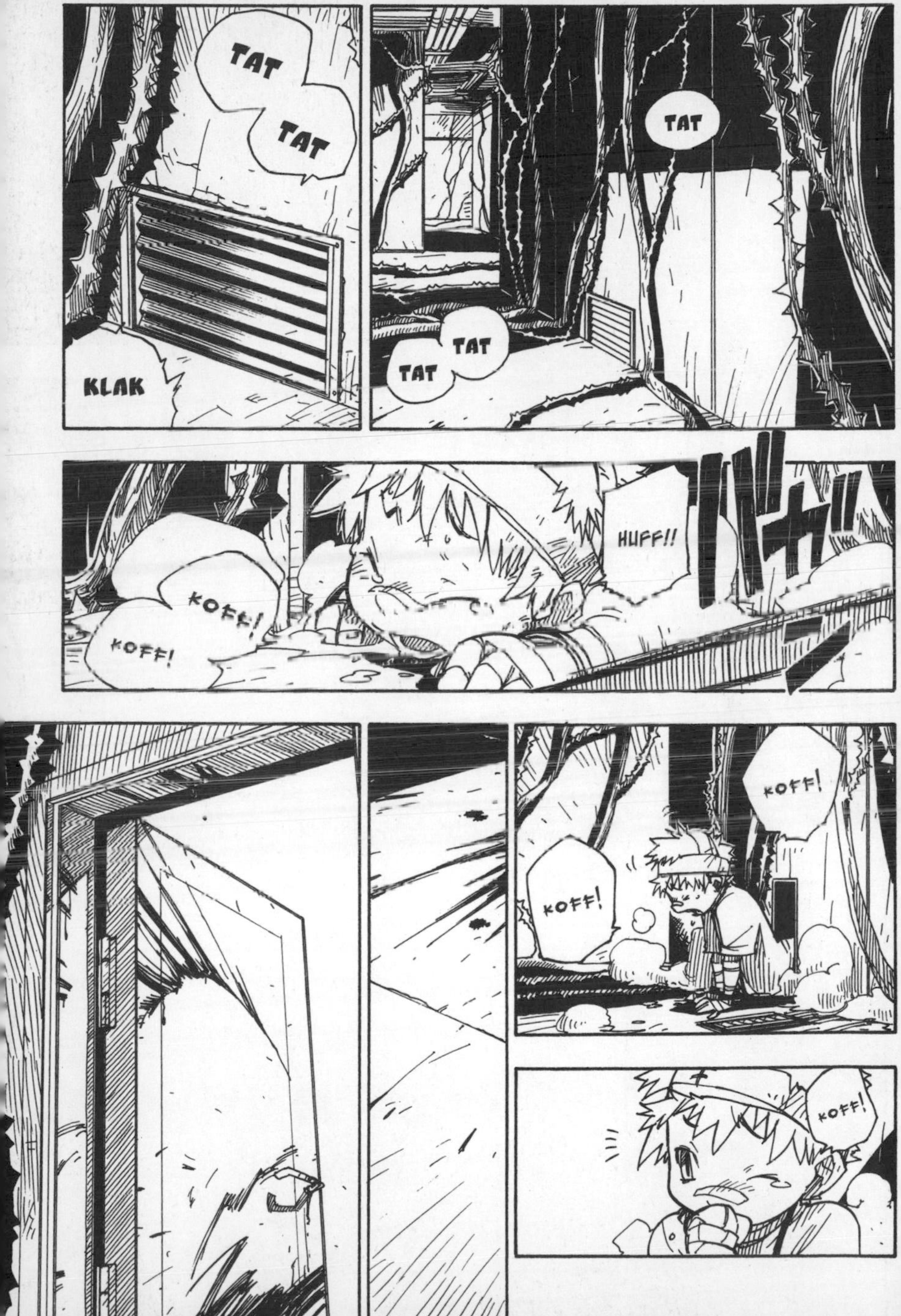
TAT
TAT
TAT
TAT
TAT
KLAK
HUFF!!
KOFF!
KOFF!
KOFF!
KOFF!
KOFF!

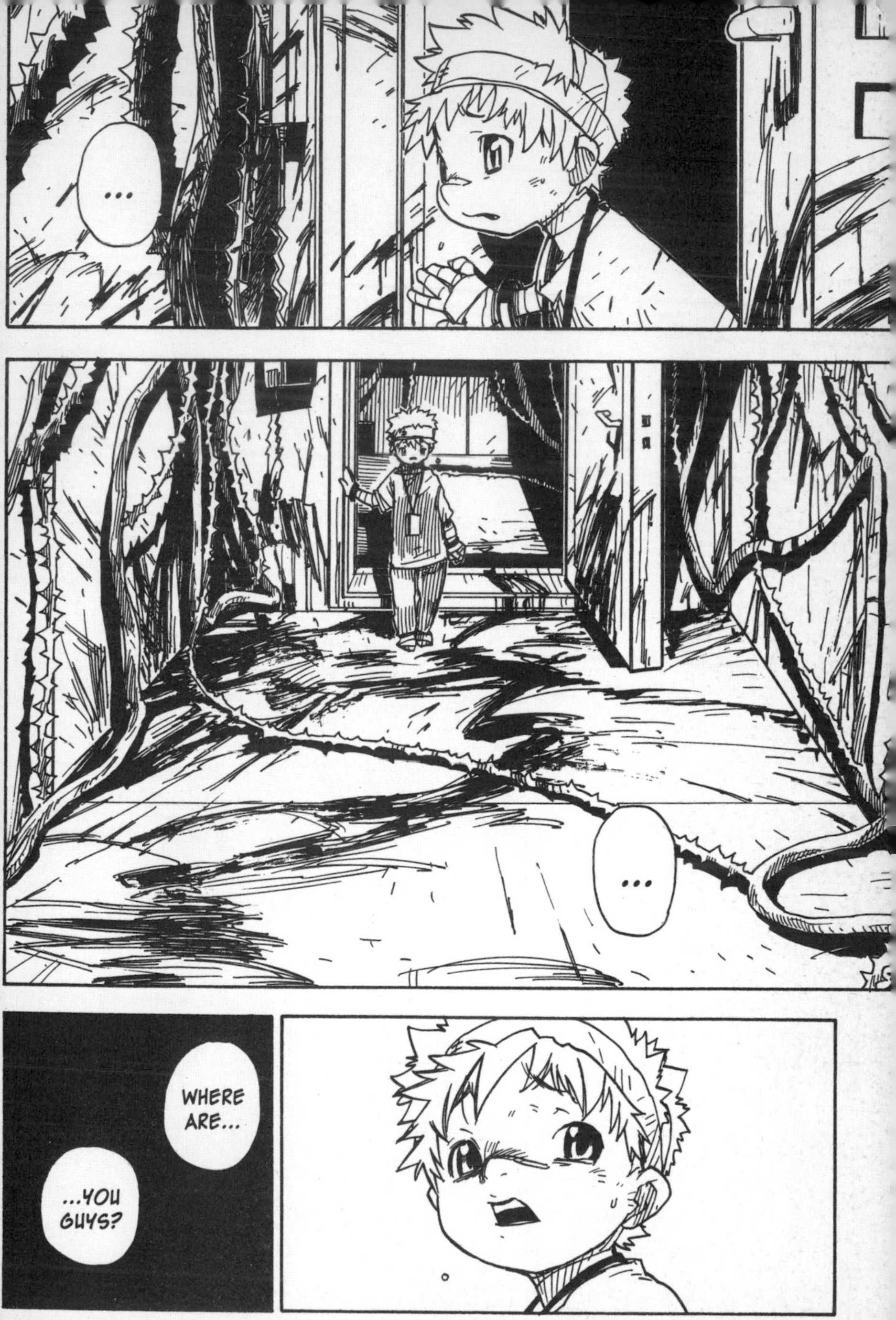
...
...
WHERE ARE...
...YOU GUYS?

CHAPTER 8
A STEP TO THE TRUTH

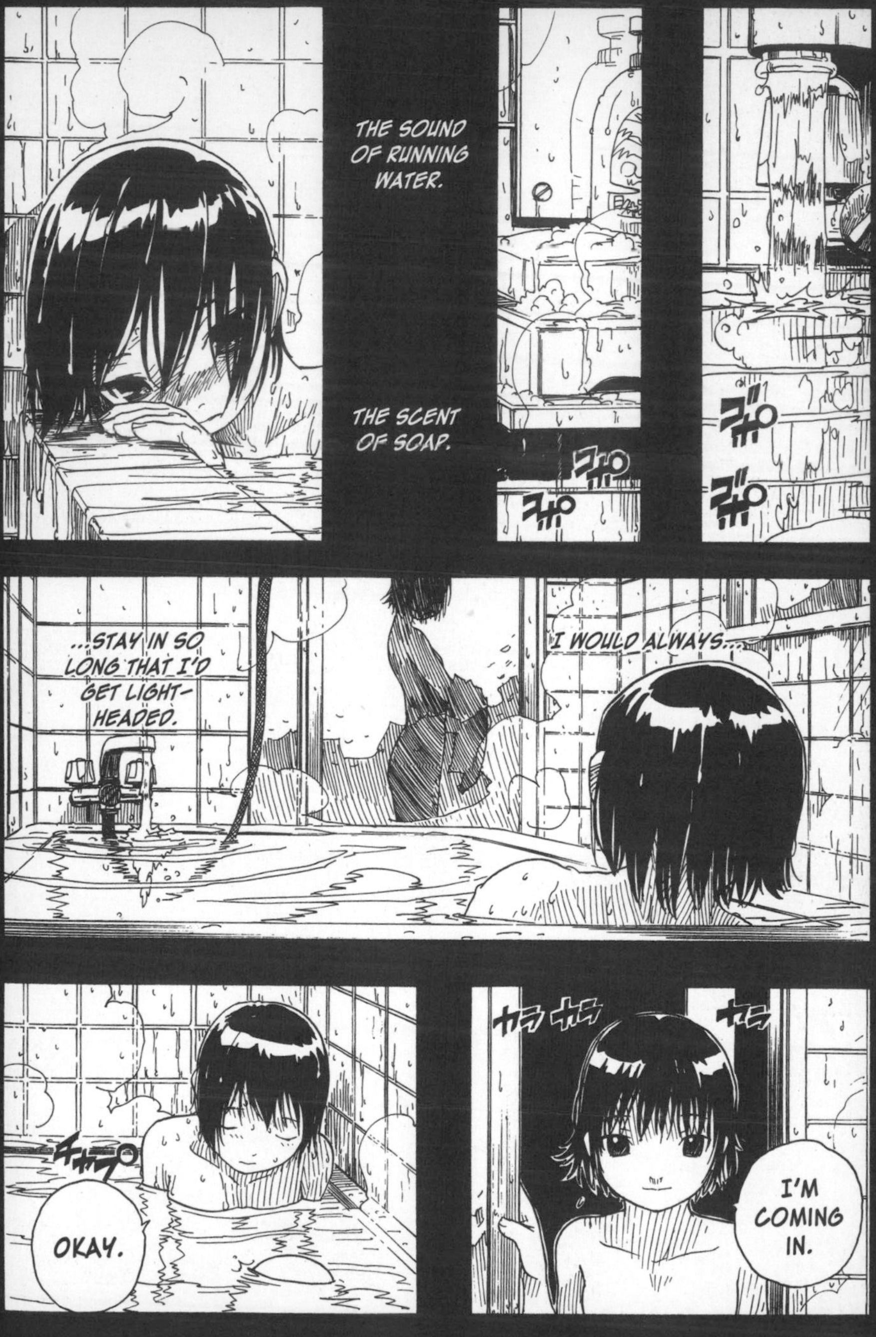
THE SOUND OF RUNNING WATER.
THE SCENT OF SOAP.
I WOULD ALWAYS...
...STAY IN SO LONG THAT I'D GET LIGHT-HEADED.
I'M COMING IN.
OKAY.

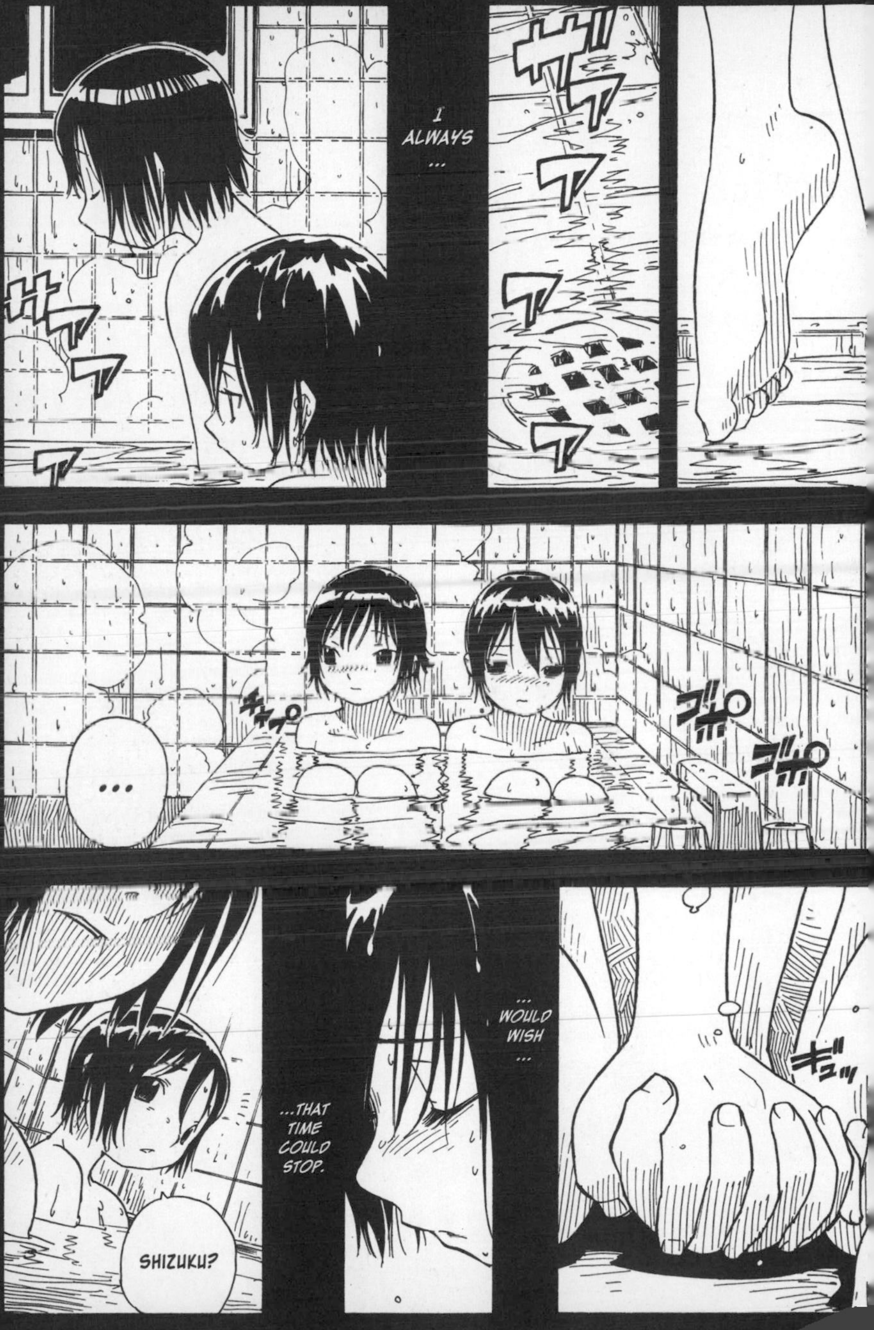
I ALWAYS ...
...
... WOULD WISH ...
...THAT TIME COULD STOP.
SHIZUKU?

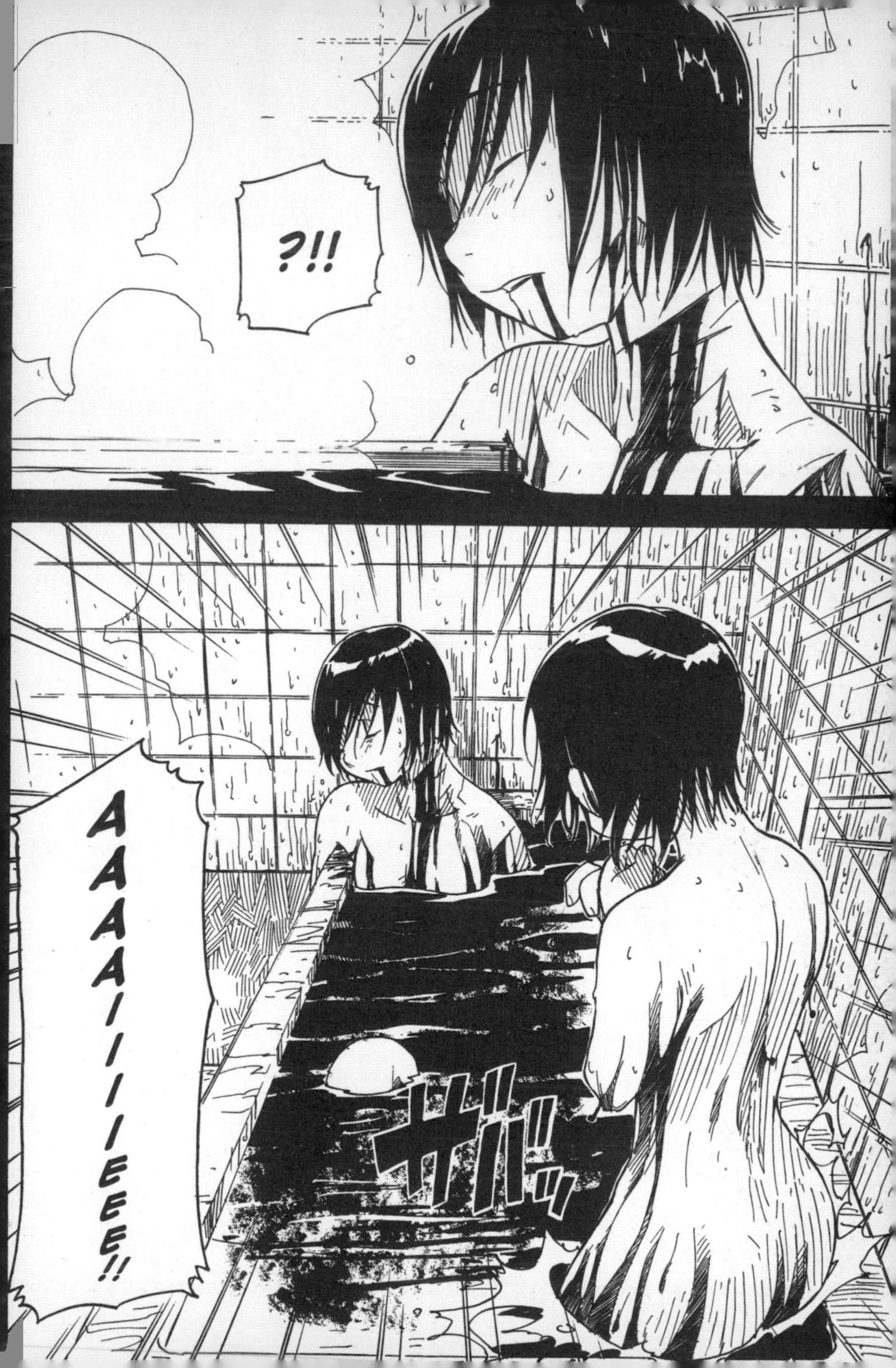

?!!
AAAAIIIIIEEE!!

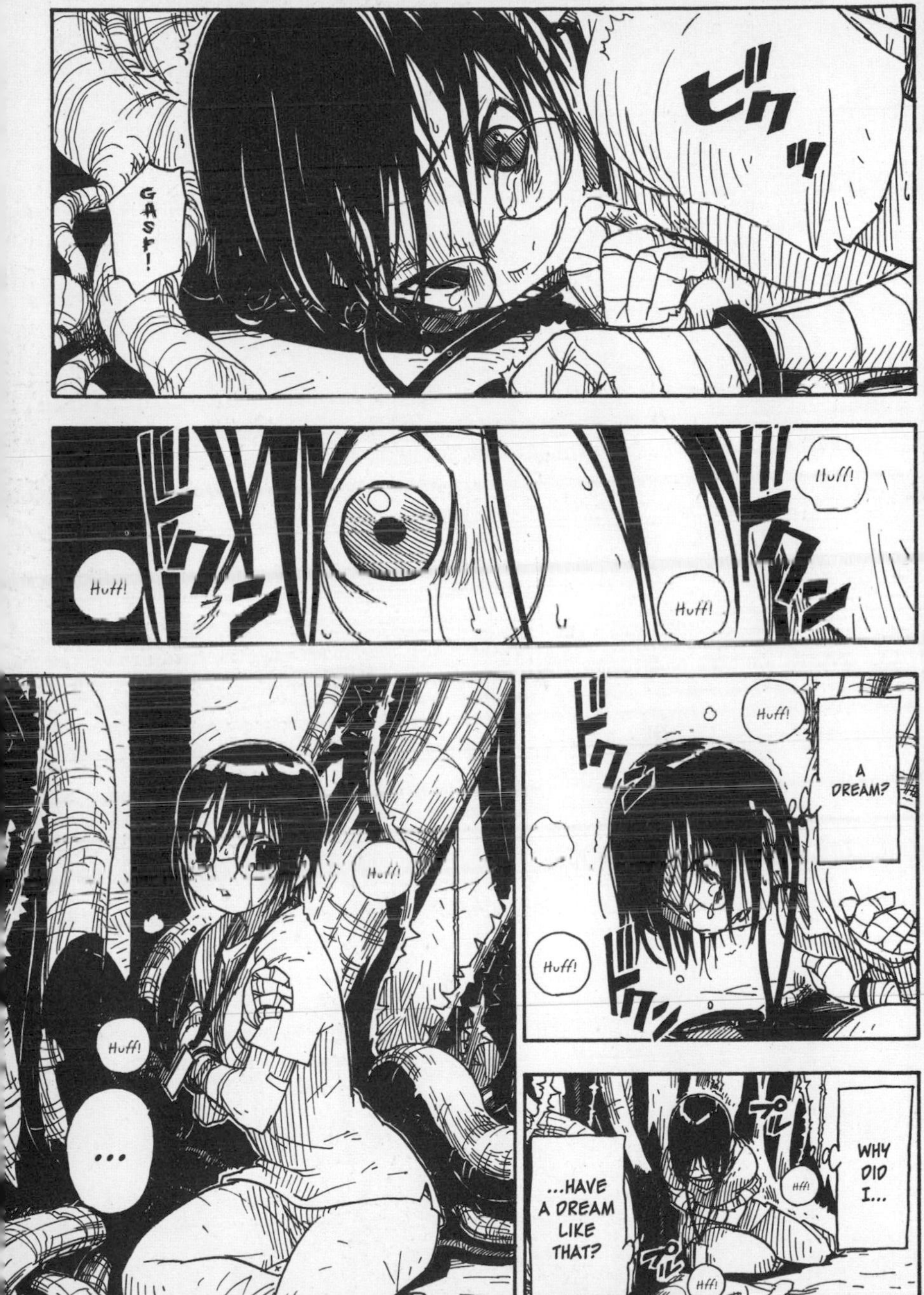
ビクッ
GASP!
Huff!
ドクン
Huff!
ドクン
Huff!
Huff!
A DREAM?
Huff!
WHY DID I...
Hff!
...HAVE A DREAM LIKE THAT?
Hff!
Huff!
Huff!
...

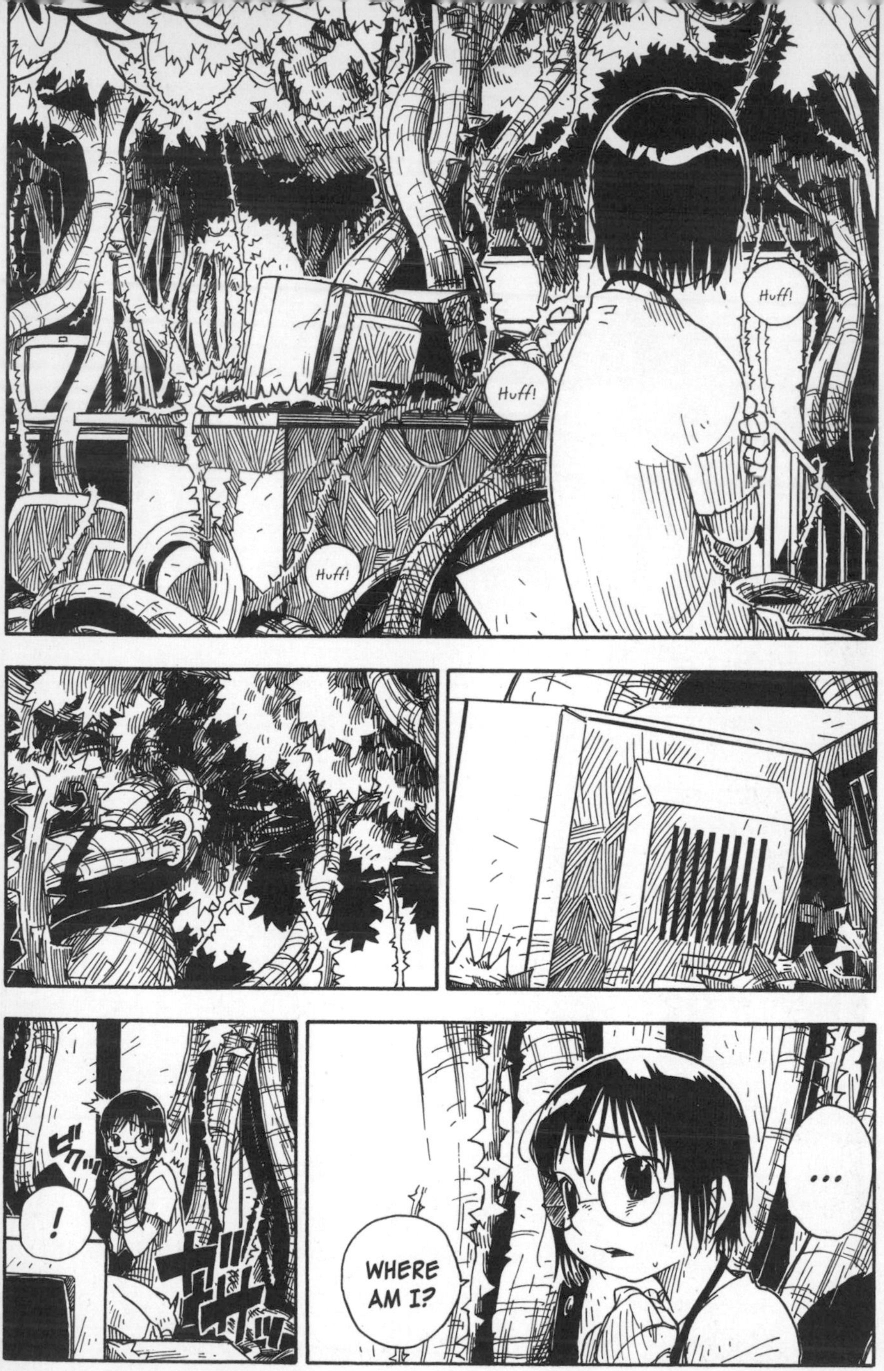

Huff!
Huff!
Huff!
...
WHERE AM I?
ビクッ
!

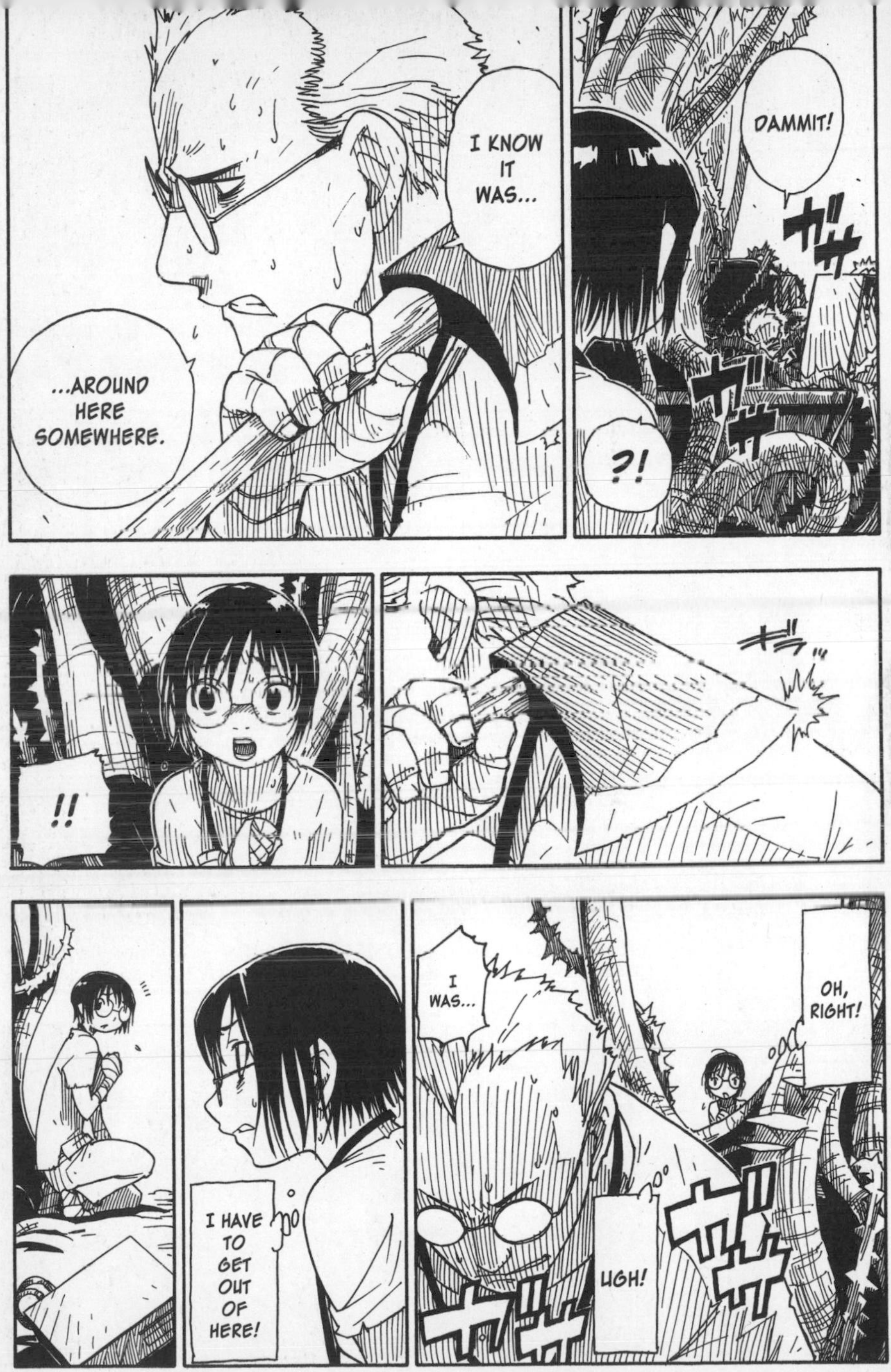
I KNOW IT WAS...
...AROUND HERE SOMEWHERE.
DAMMIT!
?!
!!
OH, RIGHT!
I WAS...
UGH!
I HAVE TO GET OUT OF HERE!

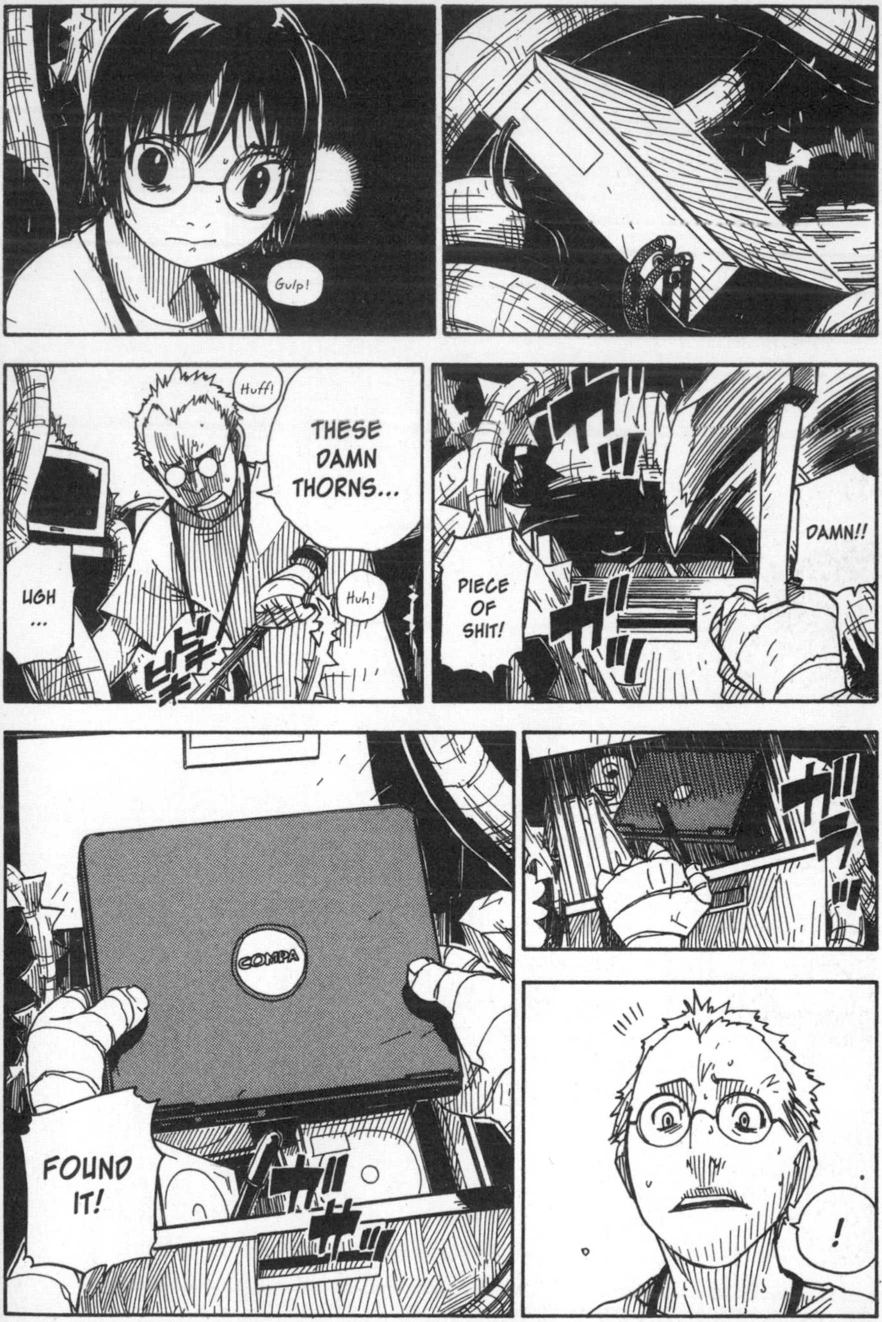
Gulp!
Huff!
THESE DAMN THORNS...
UGH ...
Huh!
DAMN!!
PIECE OF SHIT!
COMPA
FOUND IT!
!

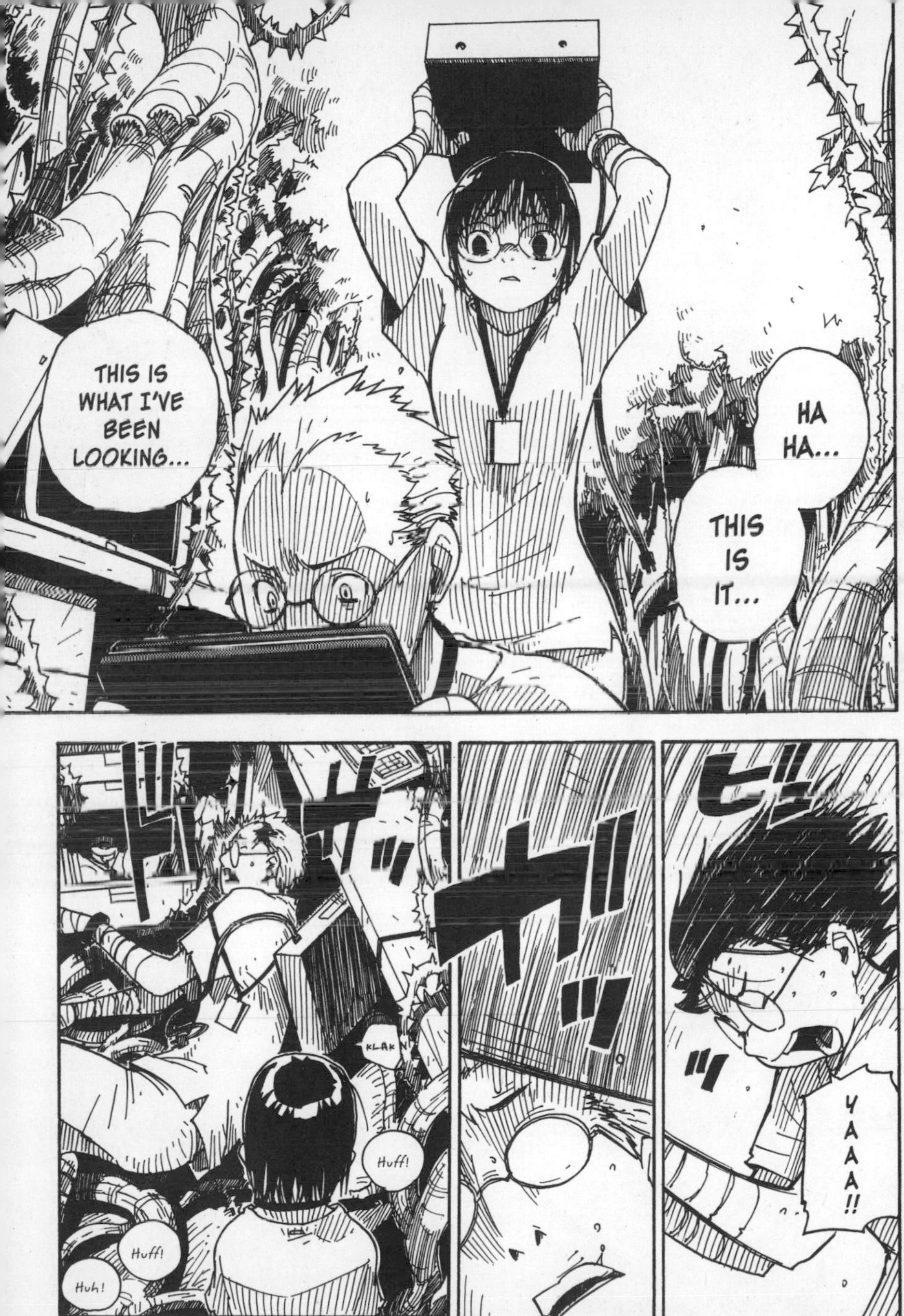
HA HA...
THIS IS IT...
THIS IS WHAT I'VE BEEN LOOKING...
YAAAA!!
KLAK
Huff!
Huff!
Huh!

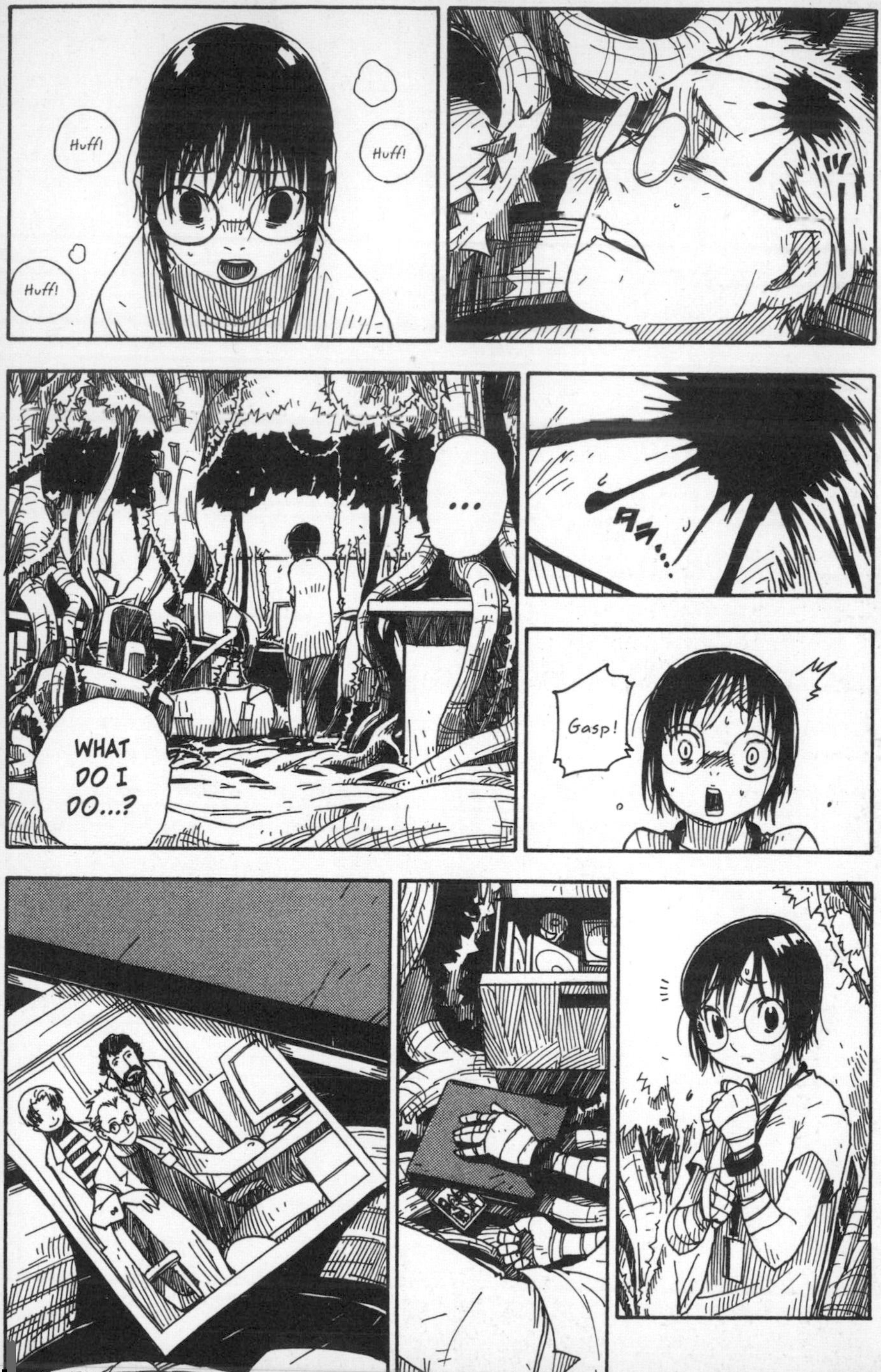

Huff!
Huff!
Huff!
...
WHAT DO I DO...?
Gasp!

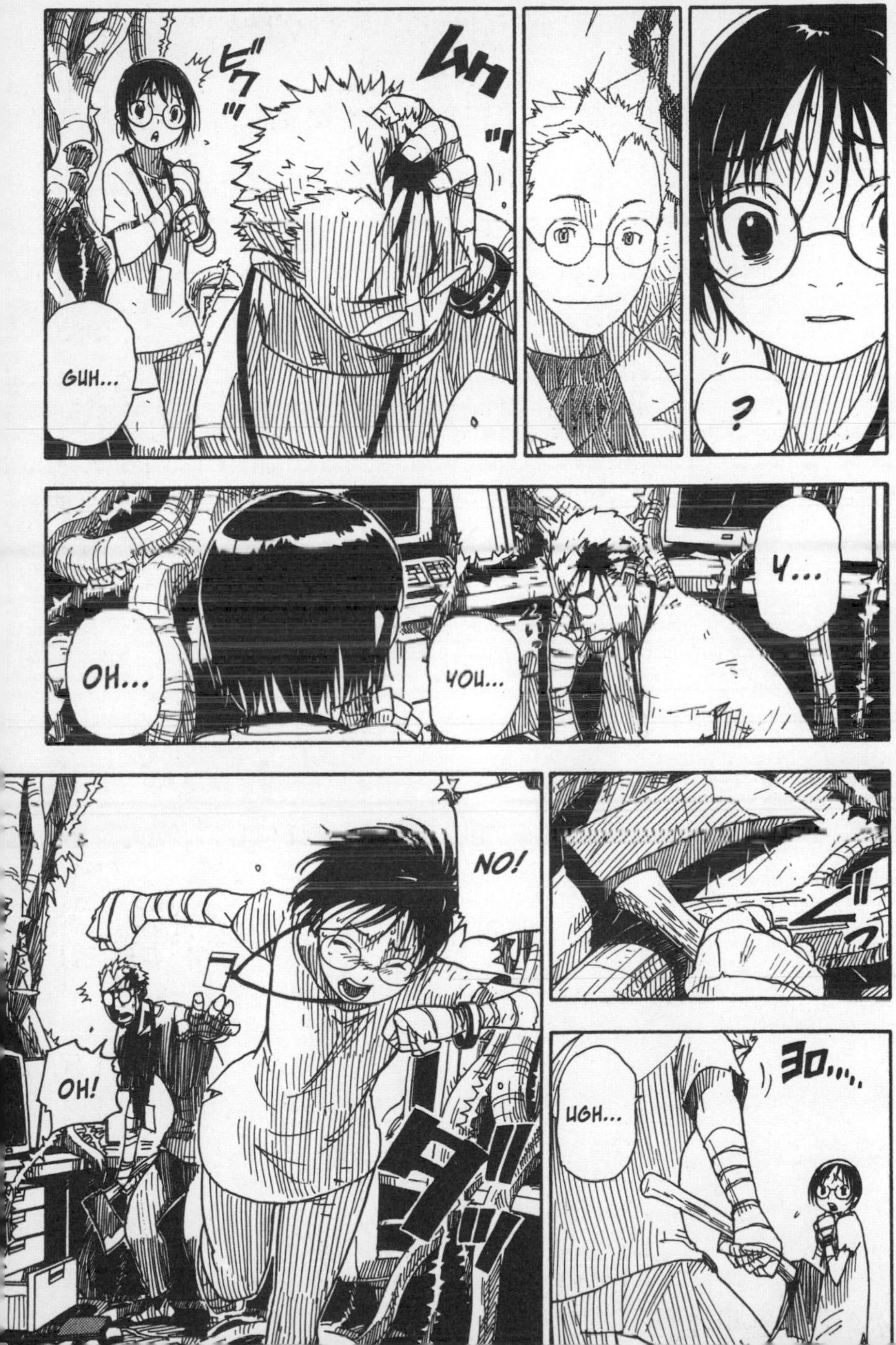
?
GUH...
Y...
YOU...
OH...
NO!
OH!
UGH...

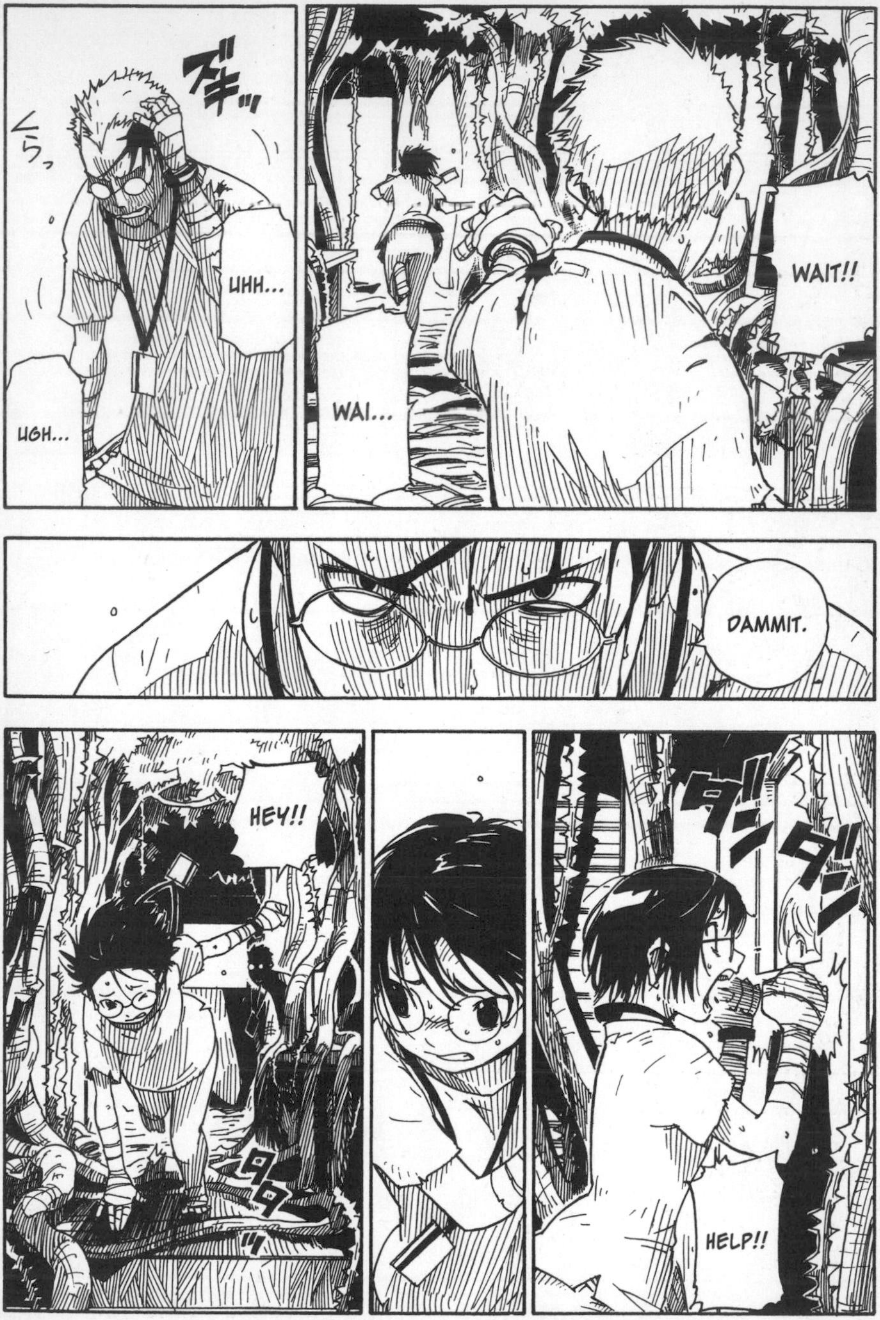
WAIT!!
WAI...
ズキッ
くらっ
UHH...
UGH...
DAMMIT.
ダン ダン
HELP!!
HEY!!

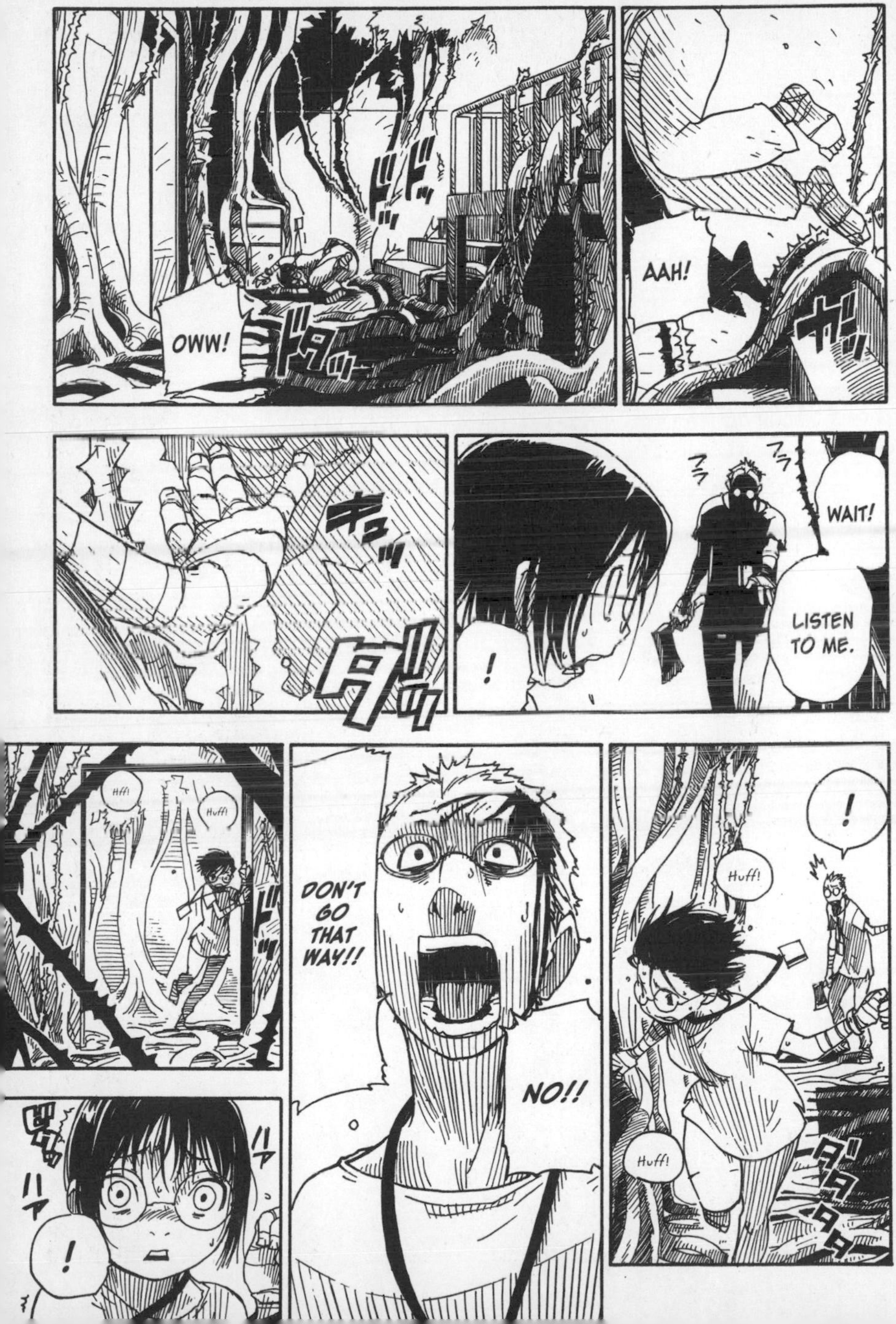
AAH!
OWW!
WAIT!
LISTEN TO ME.
!
!
Huff!
Huff!
DON'T GO THAT WAY!!
NO!!
Huff!
Huff!
!

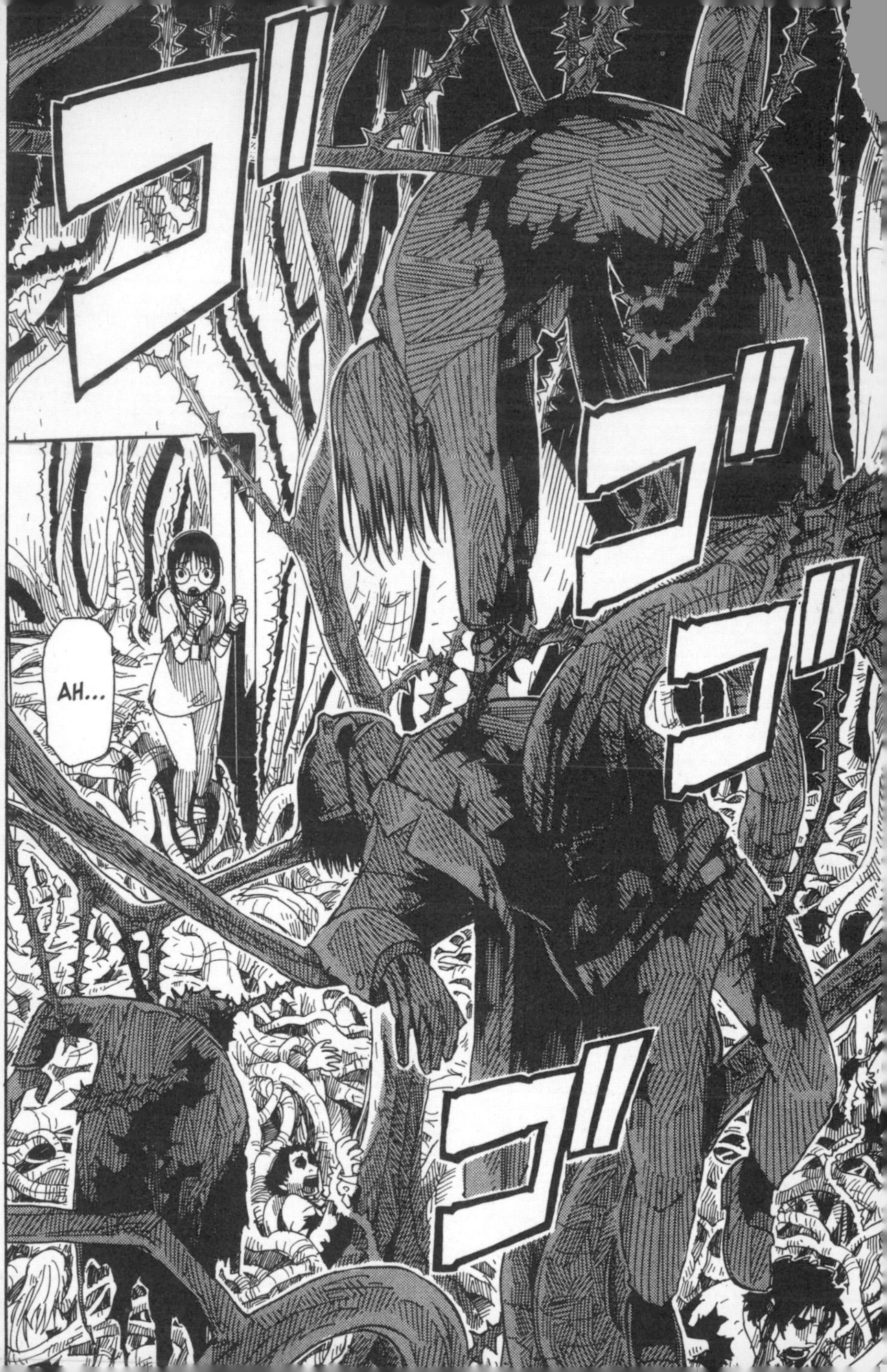
ゴ
ゴ
ゴ
ゴ
AH...

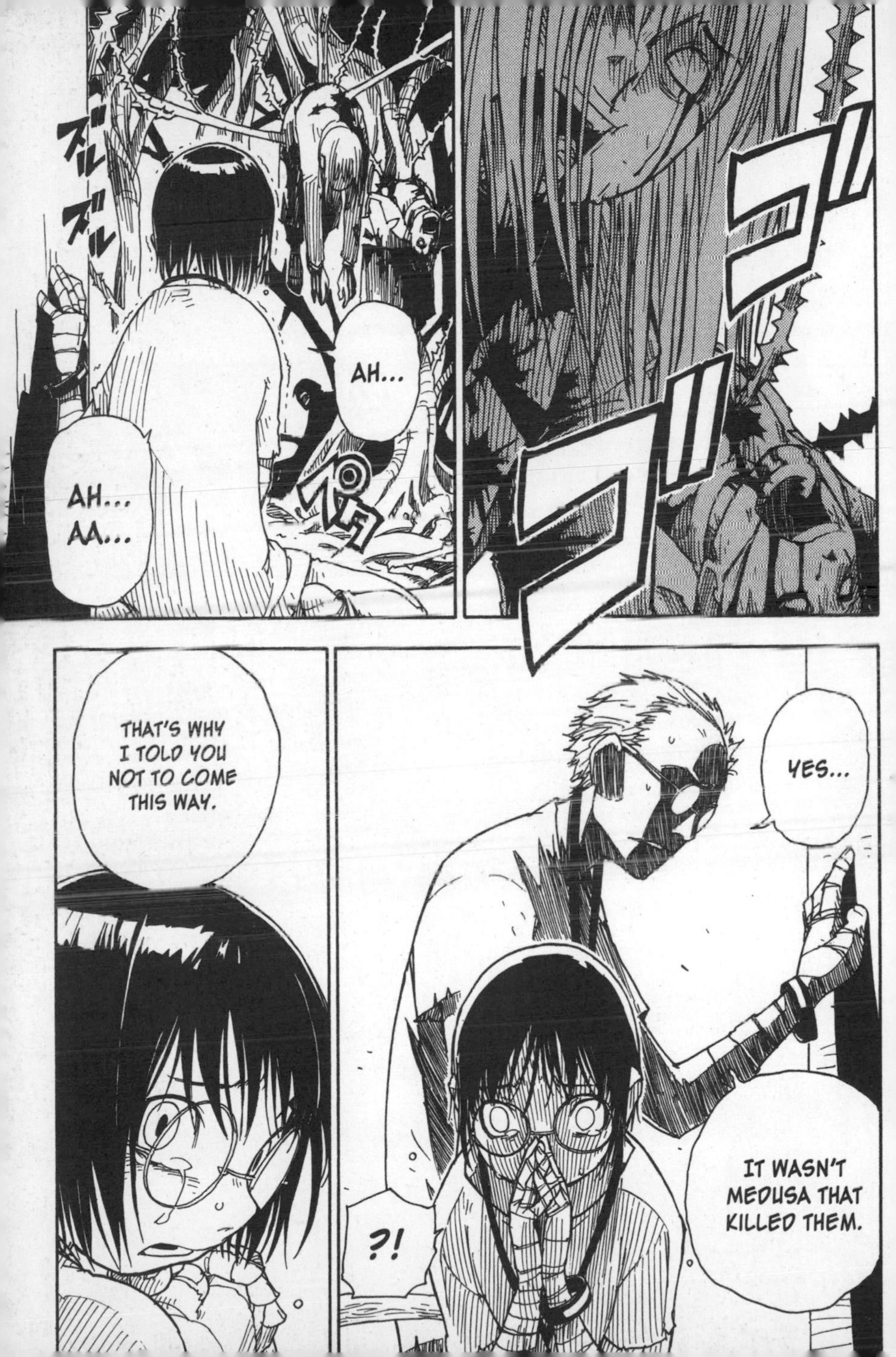
ゴゴ
ズルズル
AH...
AH... AA...
YES...
IT WASN'T MEDUSA THAT KILLED THEM.
?!
THAT'S WHY I TOLD YOU NOT TO COME THIS WAY.

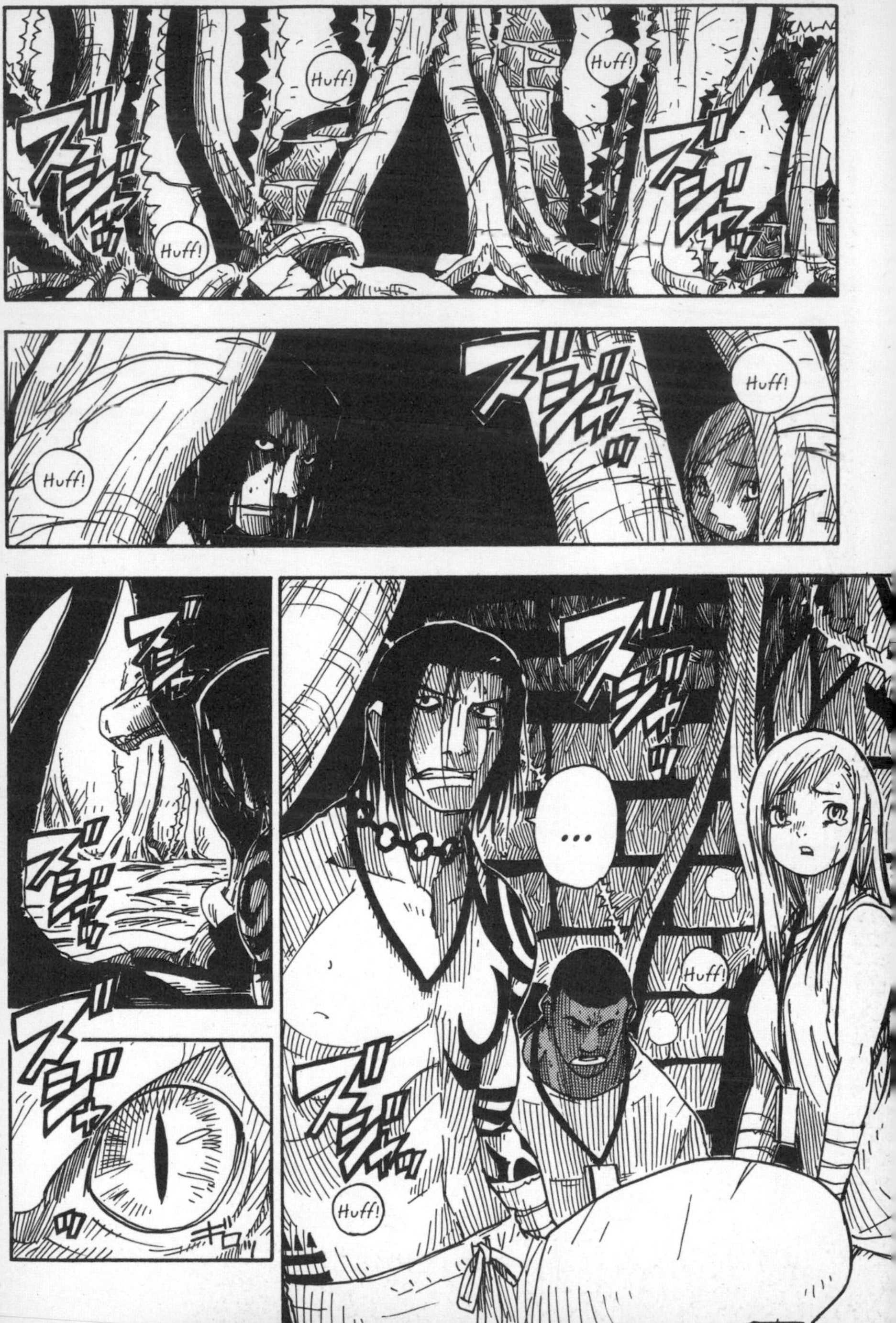
Huff!
Huff!
Huff!
Huff!
Huff!
...
Huff!
Huff!

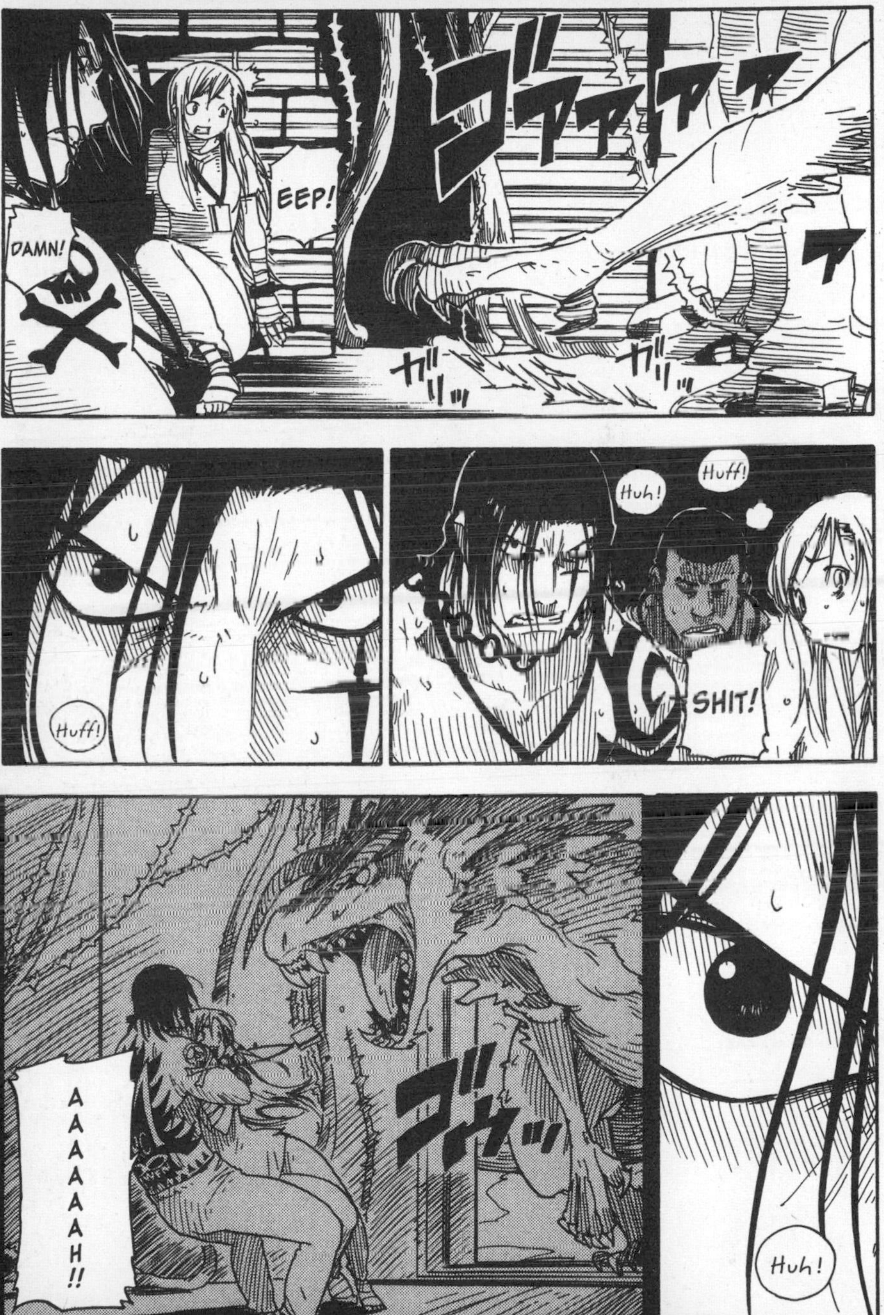
EEP!
DAMN!
Huff!
Huh!
SHIT!
Huff!
Huh!
AAAAAAH!!

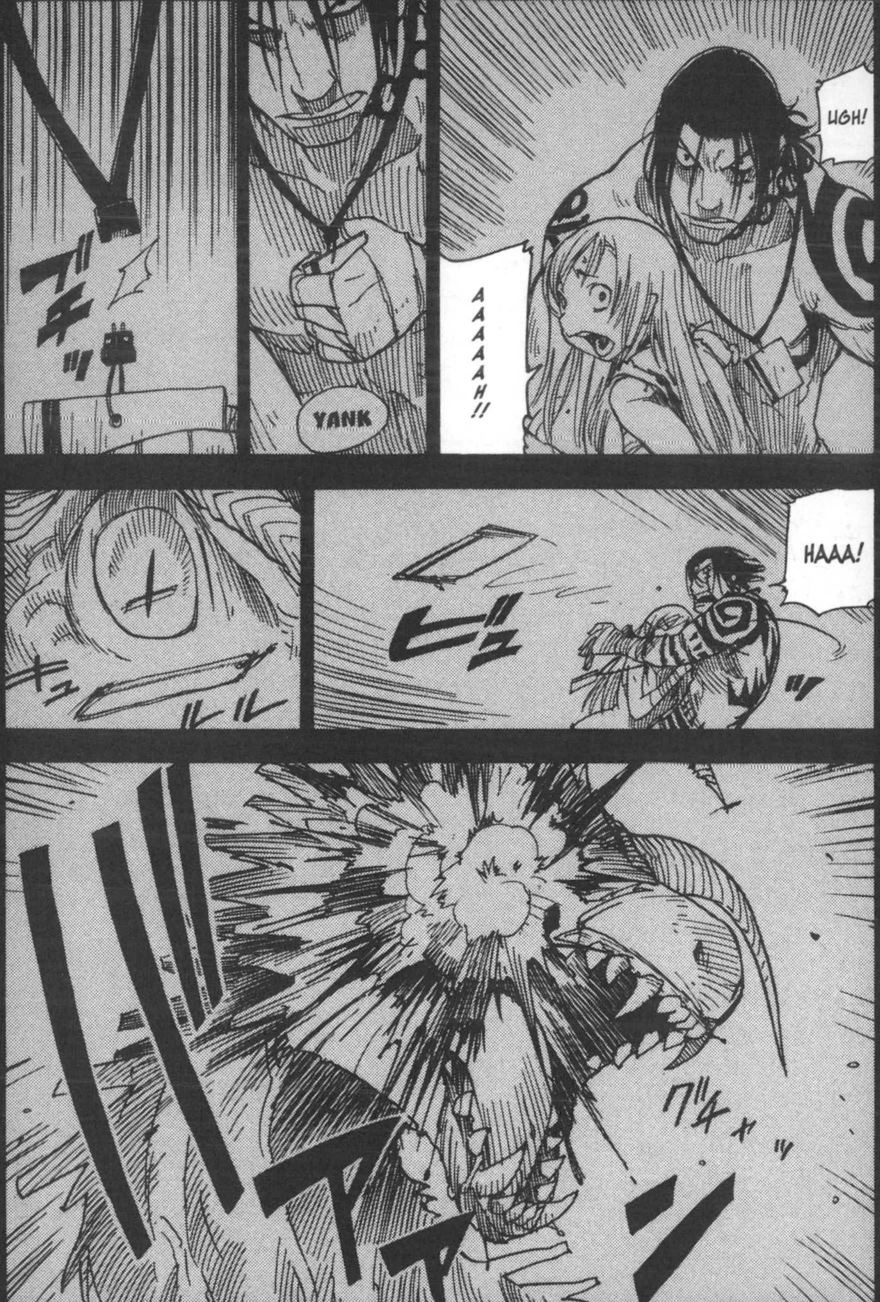
ブチッ
YANK
AAAAAAH!!
UGH!
キュルル
HAAA!
ビュッ
ズバァァン
グシャッ

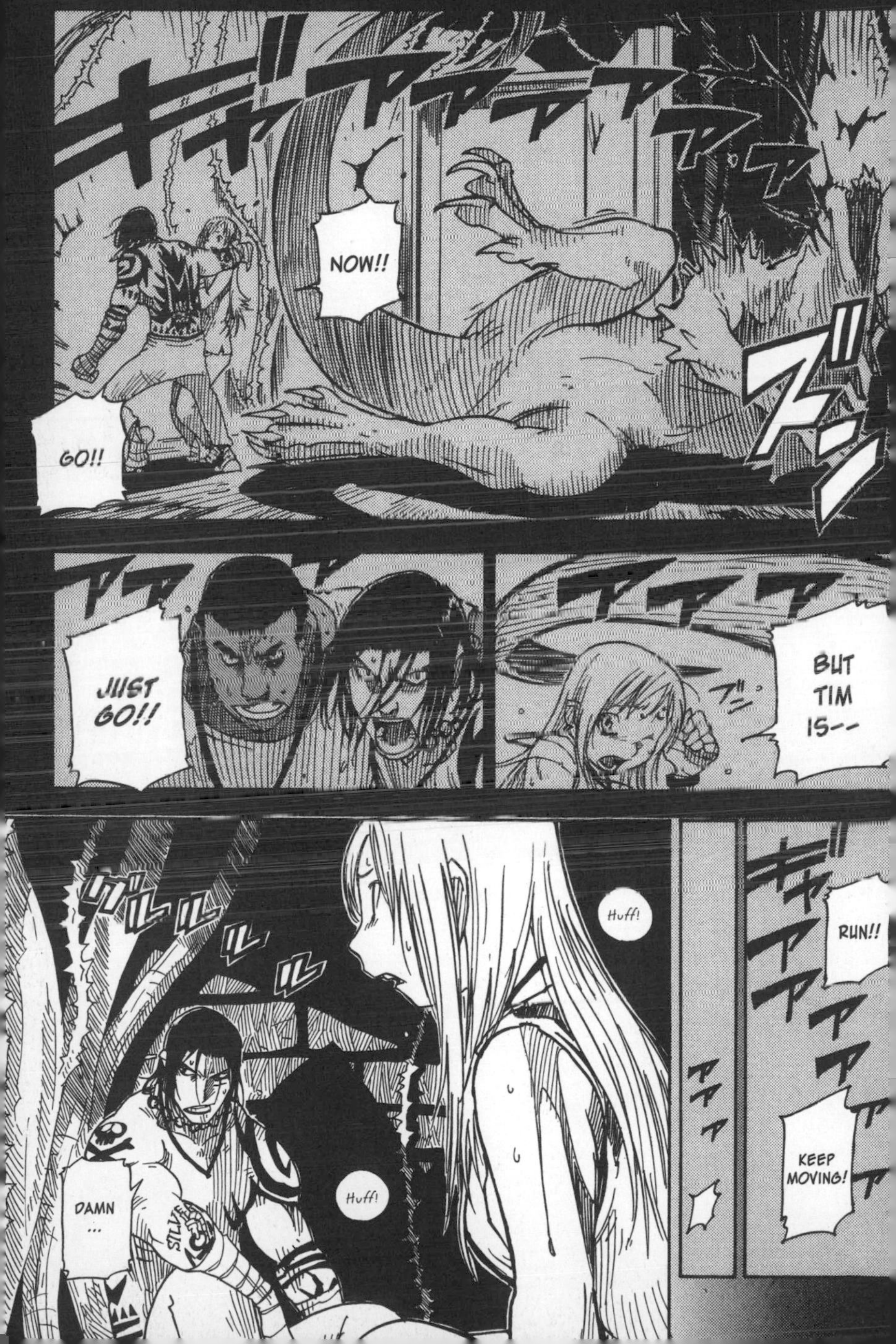
NOW!!
GO!!
BUT TIM IS--
JUST GO!!
RUN!!
KEEP MOVING!
Huff!
Huff!
DAMN ...

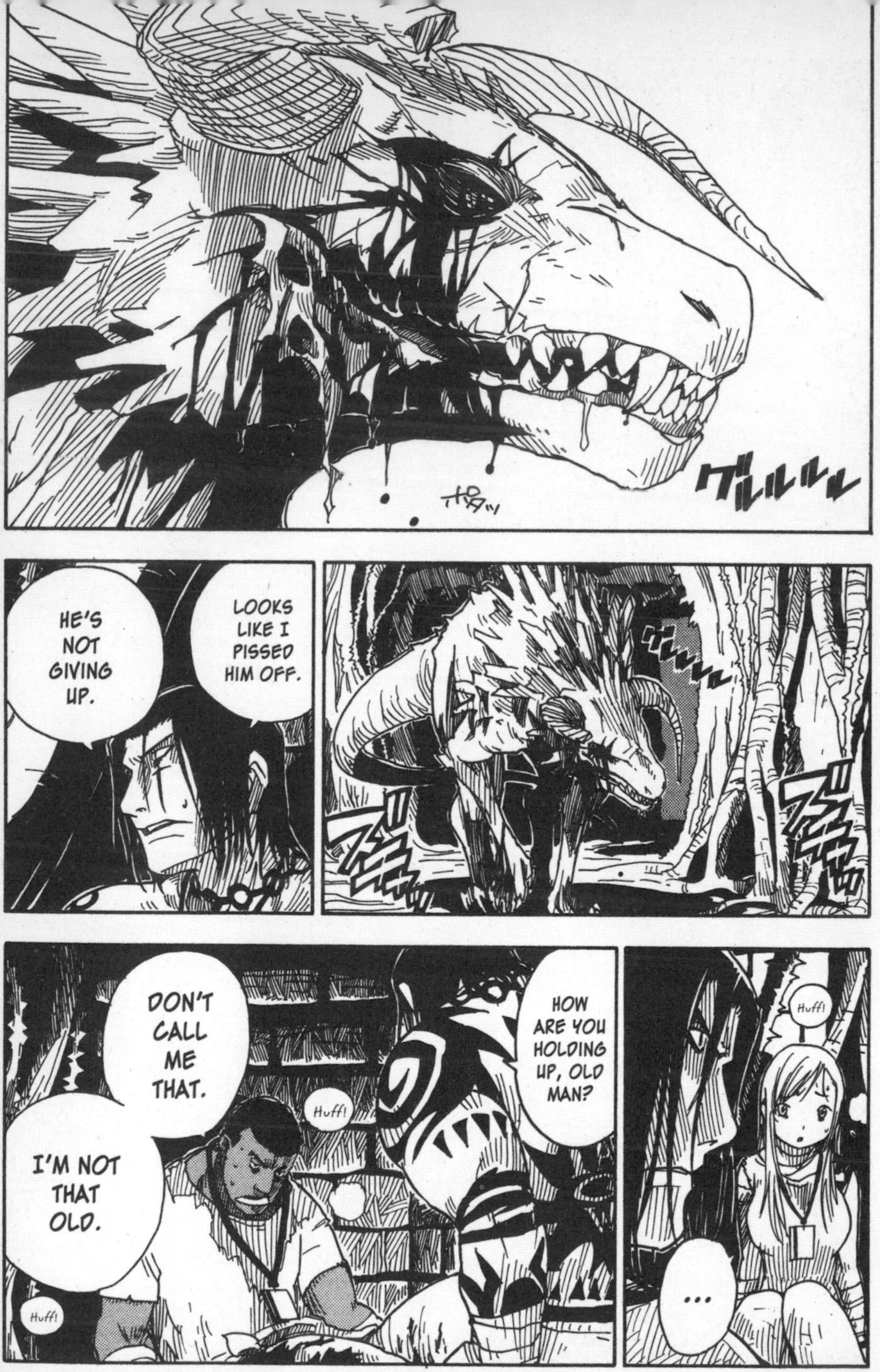
グルルルル
LOOKS LIKE I PISSED HIM OFF.
HE'S NOT GIVING UP.
Huff!
...
HOW ARE YOU HOLDING UP, OLD MAN?
Huff!
DON'T CALL ME THAT.
I'M NOT THAT OLD.
Huff!

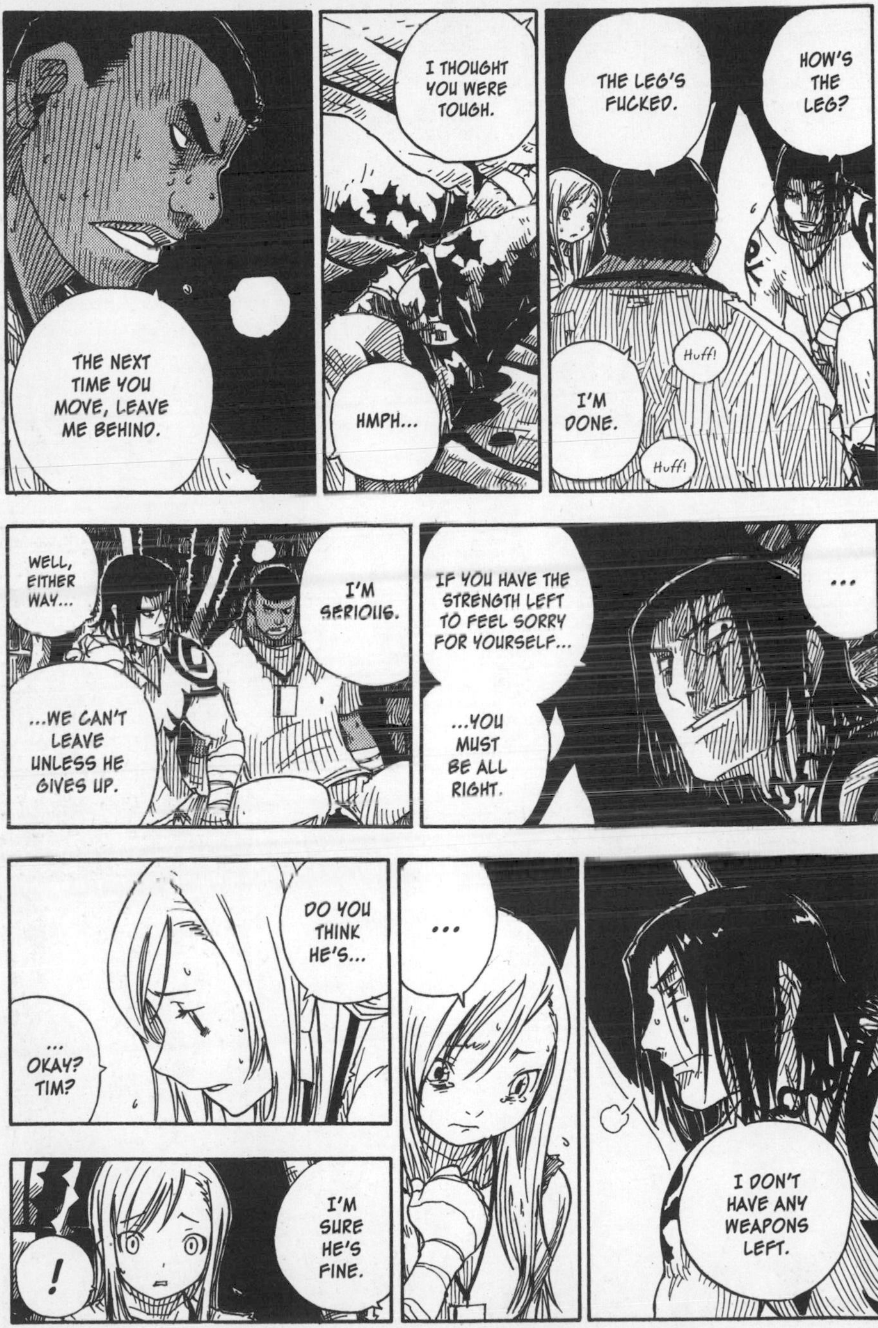
HOW'S THE LEG?
THE LEG'S FUCKED.
Huff!
I'M DONE.
Huff!
I THOUGHT YOU WERE TOUGH.
HMPH...
THE NEXT TIME YOU MOVE, LEAVE ME BEHIND.
...
IF YOU HAVE THE STRENGTH LEFT TO FEEL SORRY FOR YOURSELF...
...YOU MUST BE ALL RIGHT.
I'M SERIOUS.
WELL, EITHER WAY...
...WE CAN'T LEAVE UNLESS HE GIVES UP.
I DON'T HAVE ANY WEAPONS LEFT.
...
DO YOU THINK HE'S...
... OKAY? TIM?
I'M SURE HE'S FINE.
!

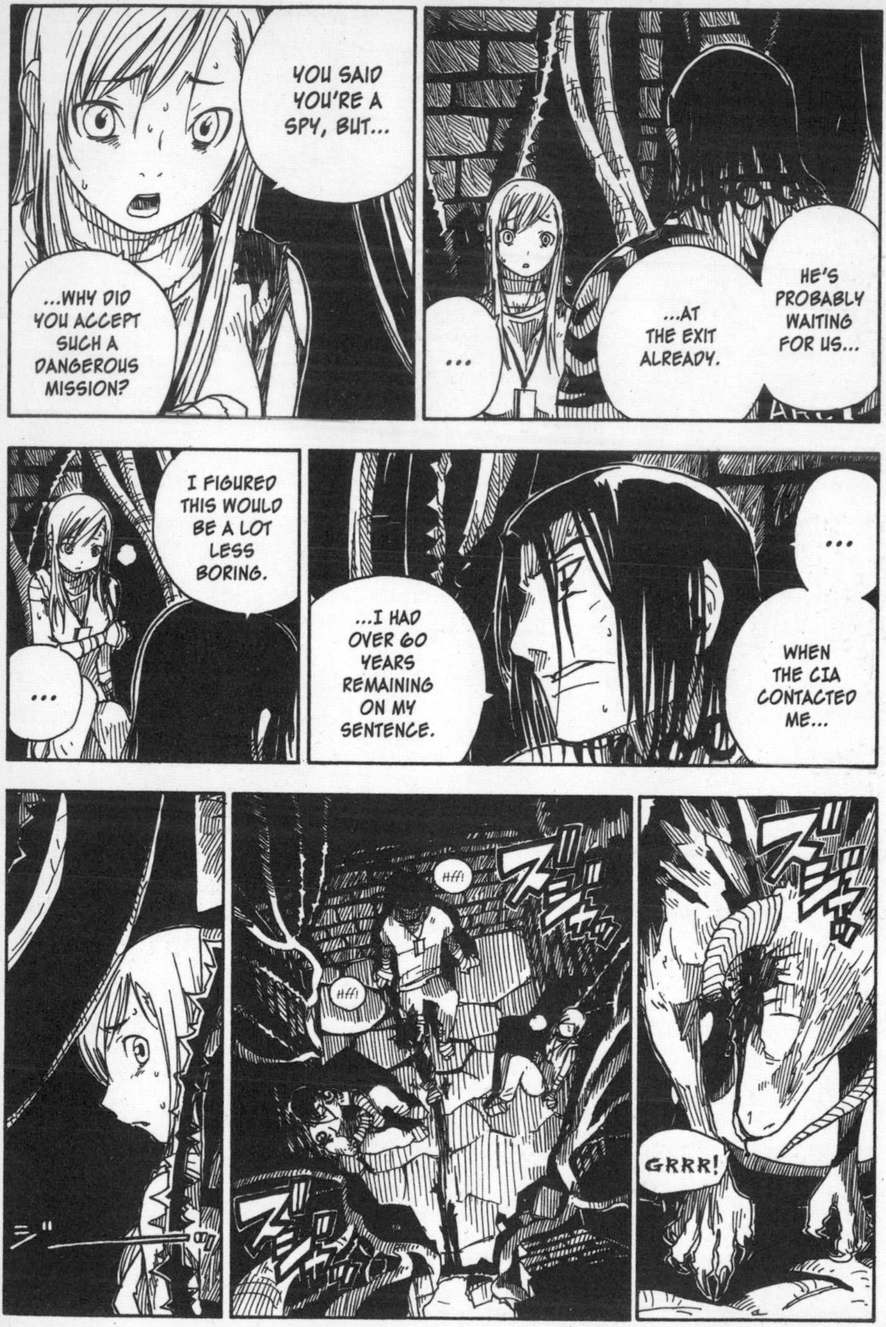

HE'S PROBABLY WAITING FOR US...
...AT THE EXIT ALREADY.
...
YOU SAID YOU'RE A SPY, BUT...
...WHY DID YOU ACCEPT SUCH A DANGEROUS MISSION?
...
WHEN THE CIA CONTACTED ME...
...I HAD OVER 60 YEARS REMAINING ON MY SENTENCE.
I FIGURED THIS WOULD BE A LOT LESS BORING.
...
GRRR!
Hff!
Hff!

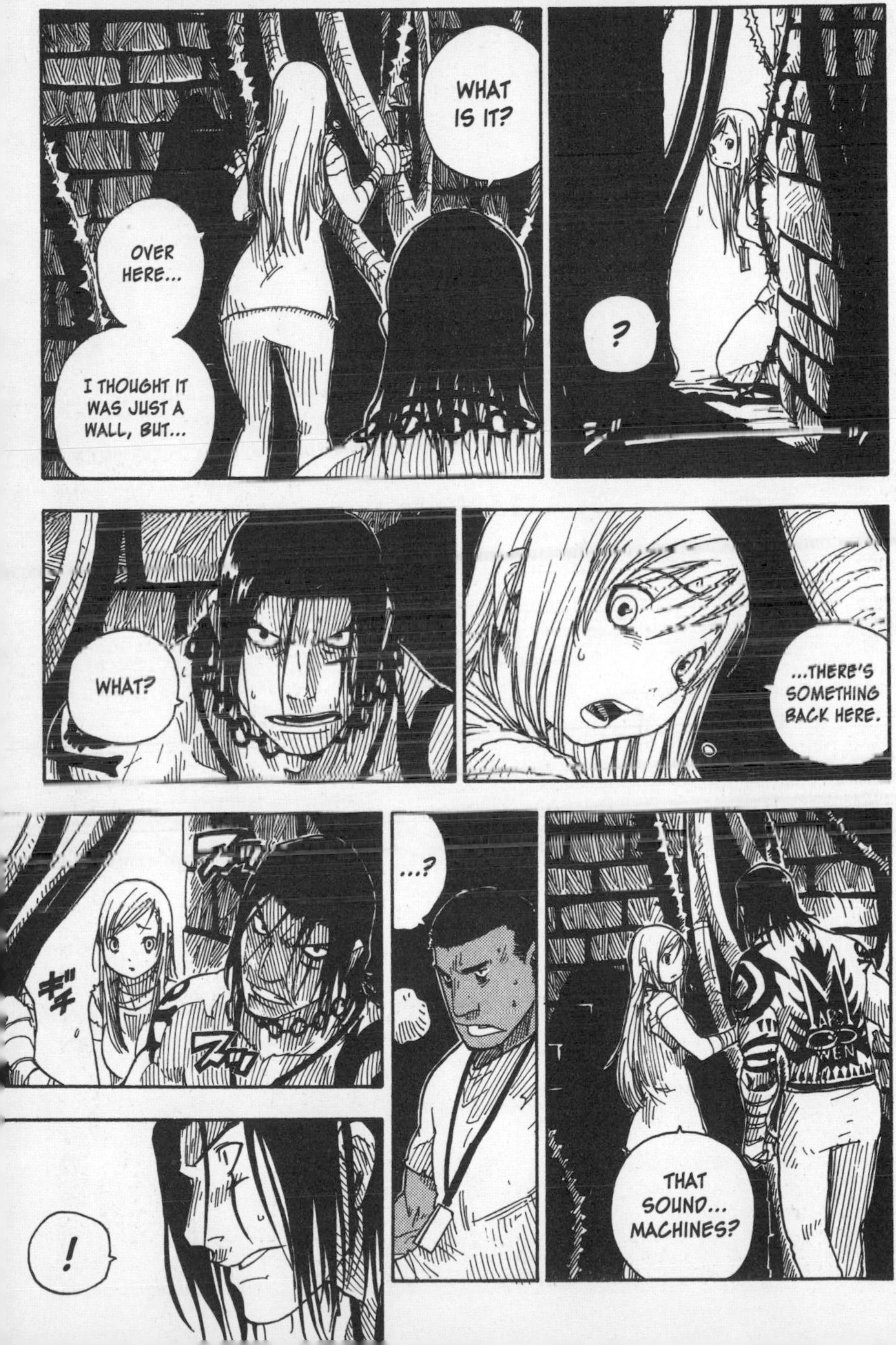
WHAT IS IT?
OVER HERE...
I THOUGHT IT WAS JUST A WALL, BUT...
?
WHAT?
...THERE'S SOMETHING BACK HERE.
...?
THAT SOUND... MACHINES?
!

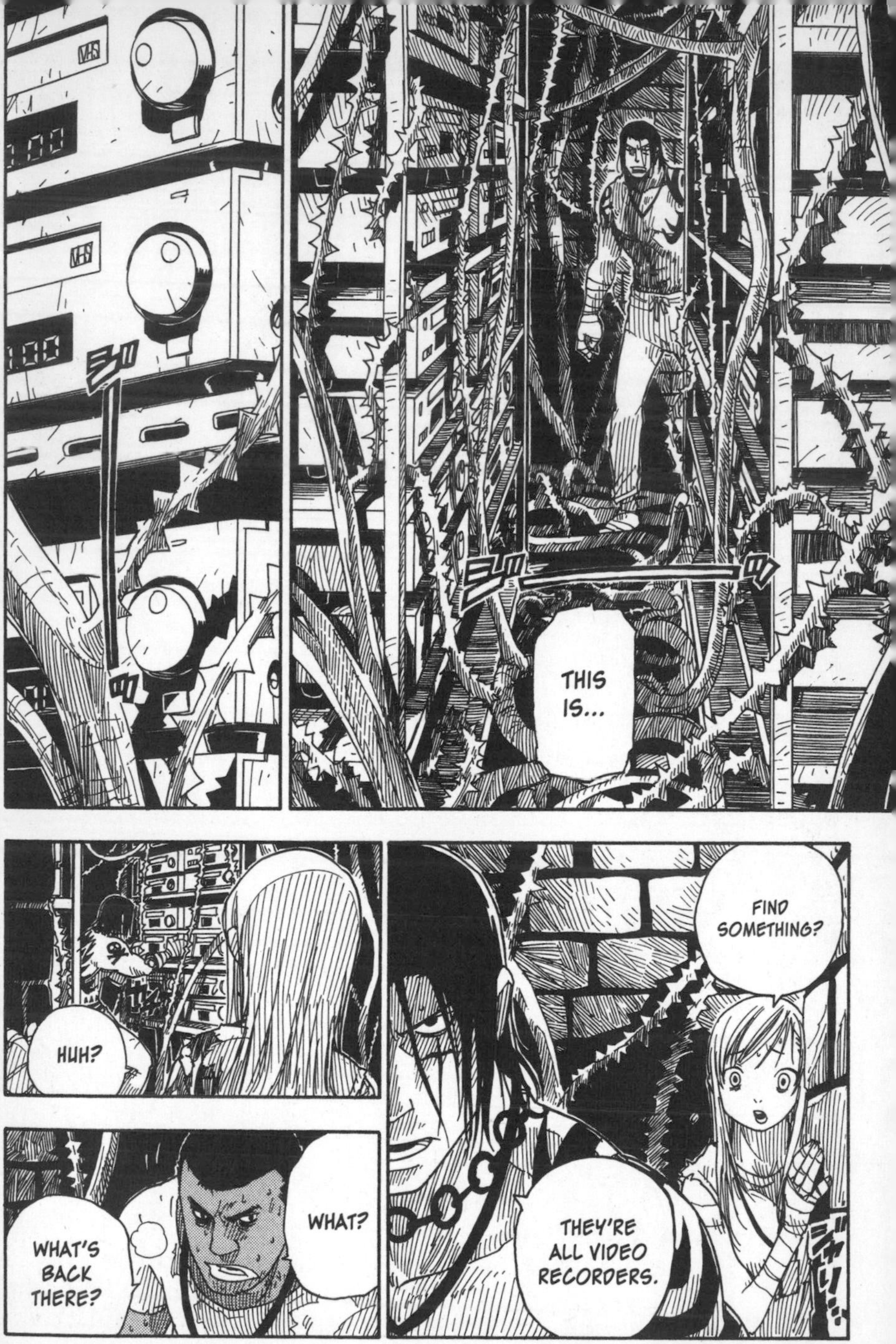
THIS IS...
FIND SOMETHING?
THEY'RE ALL VIDEO RECORDERS.
HUH?
WHAT?
WHAT'S BACK THERE?

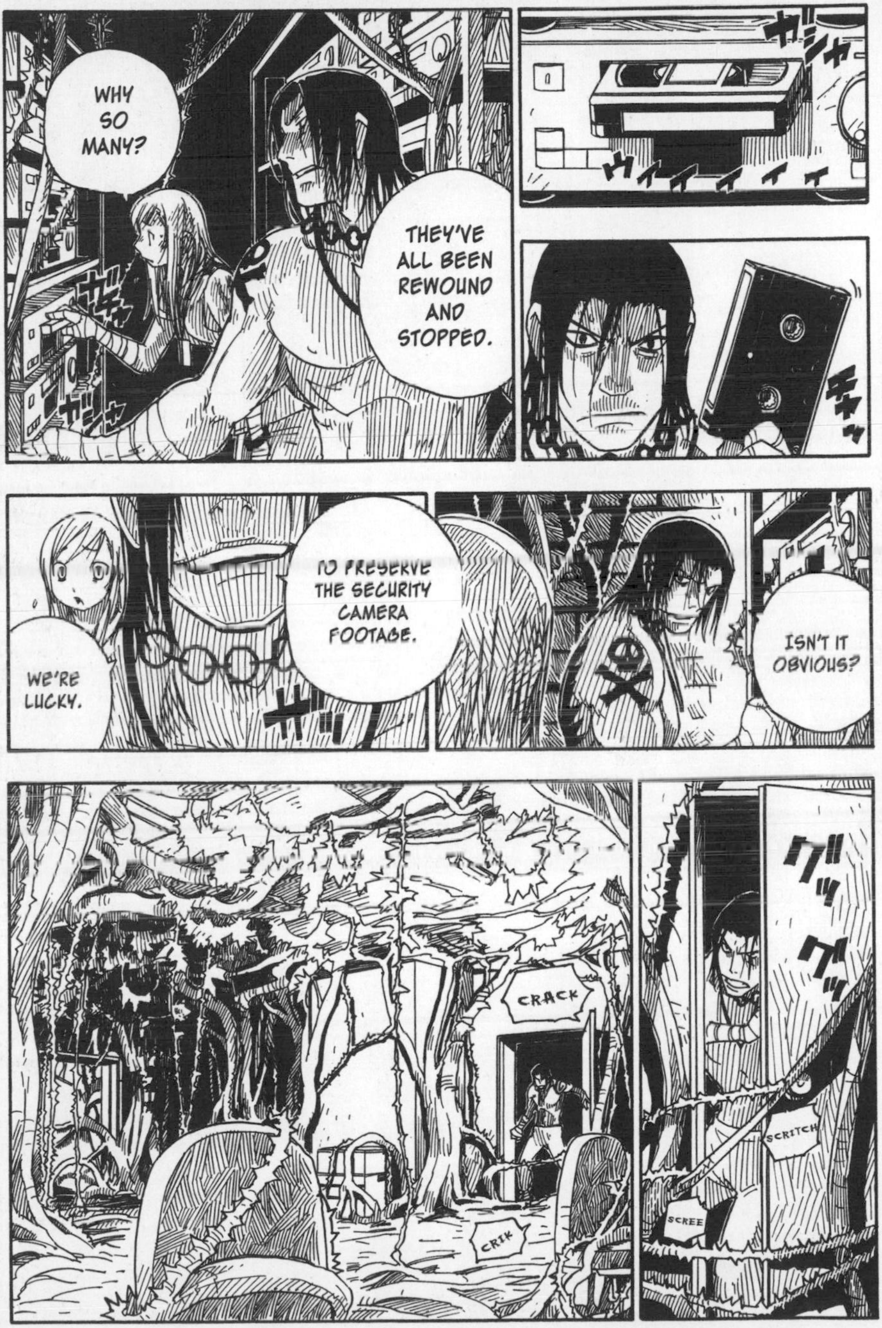
WHY SO MANY?
THEY'VE ALL BEEN REWOUND AND STOPPED.
TO PRESERVE THE SECURITY CAMERA FOOTAGE.
WE'RE LUCKY.
ISN'T IT OBVIOUS?
CRACK
CRIK
SCRITCH
SCREE

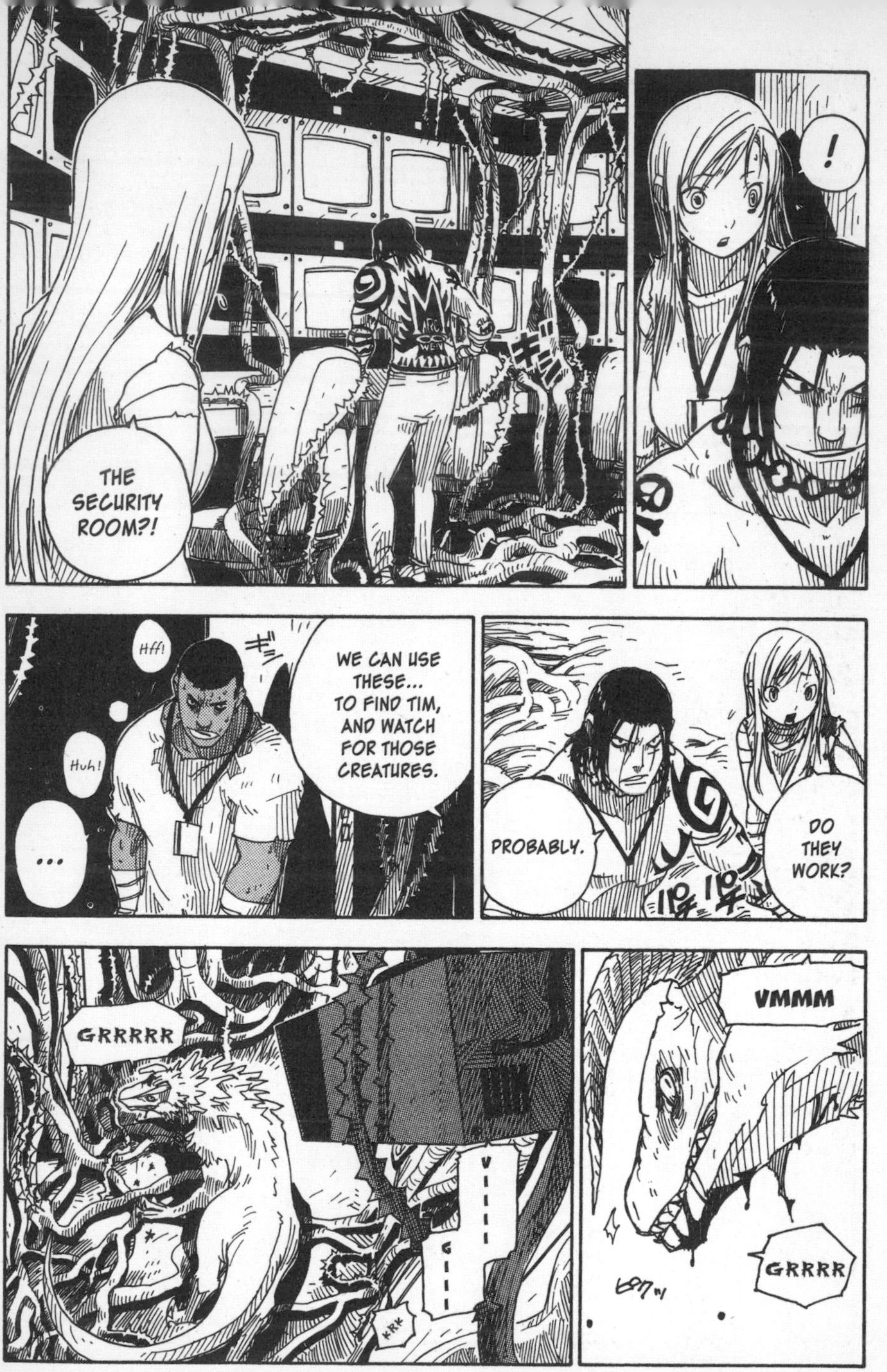
THE SECURITY ROOM?!
!
Hff!
Huh!
...
WE CAN USE THESE... TO FIND TIM, AND WATCH FOR THOSE CREATURES.
DO THEY WORK?
PROBABLY.
GRRRRR
V- - - -
G- - - -
KRK
VMMM
GRRRR

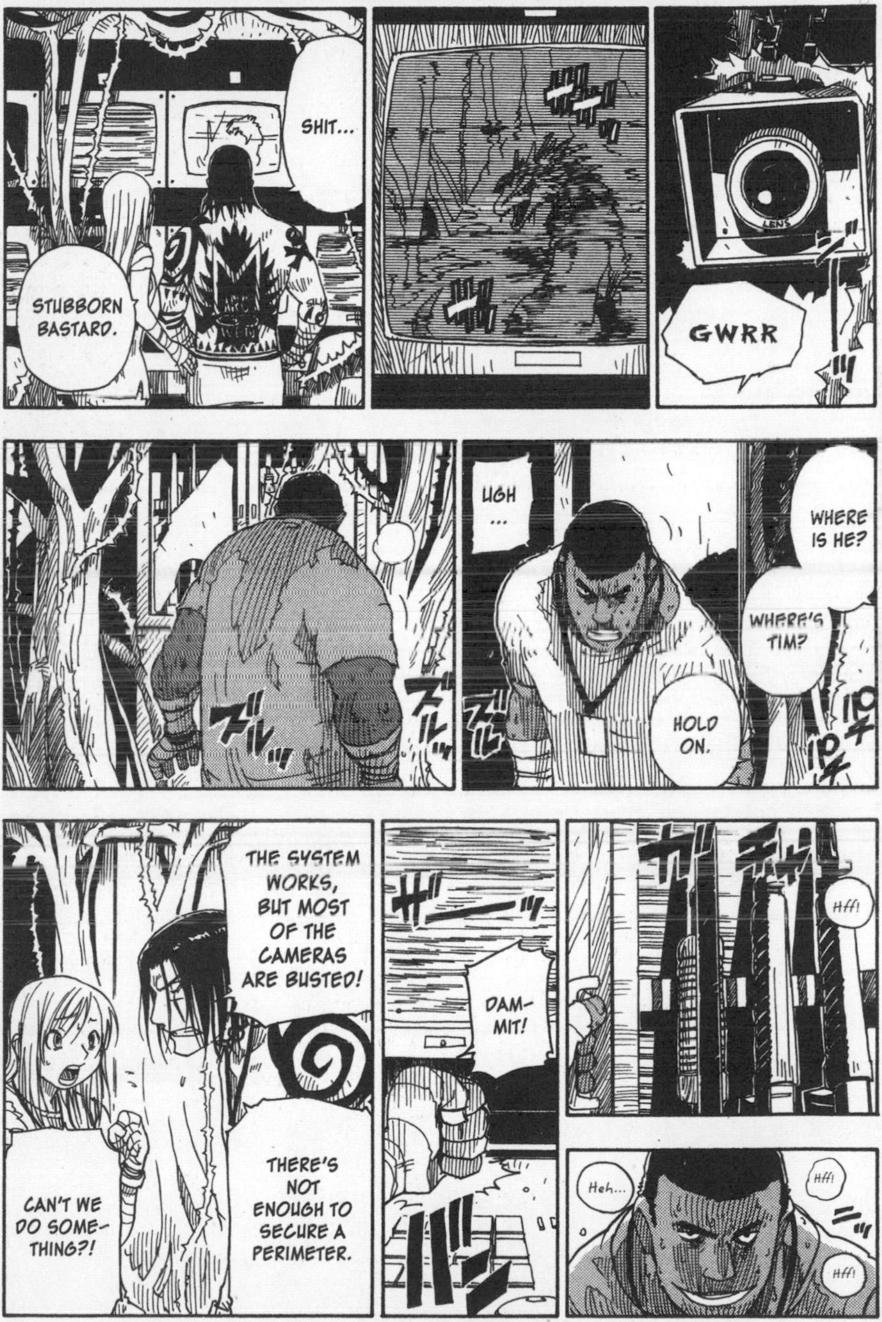
SHIT...
STUBBORN BASTARD.
GWRR
UGH ...
WHERE IS HE?
WHERE'S TIM?
HOLD ON.
THE SYSTEM WORKS, BUT MOST OF THE CAMERAS ARE BUSTED!
CAN'T WE DO SOME-THING?!
THERE'S NOT ENOUGH TO SECURE A PERIMETER.
DAM-MIT!
Hff!
Heh...
Hff!
Hff!

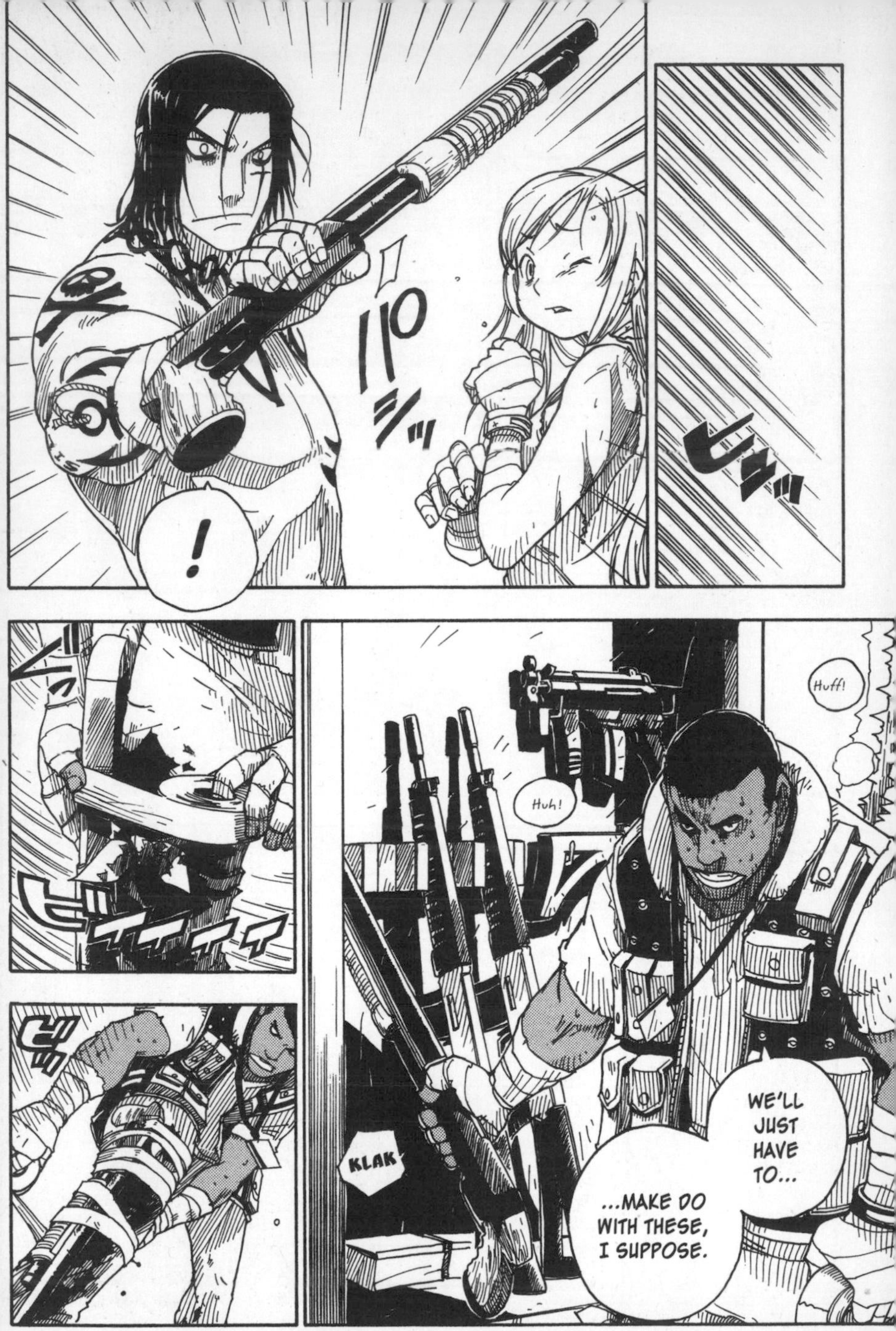
!
Huff!
Huh!
KLAK
WE'LL JUST HAVE TO...
...MAKE DO WITH THESE, I SUPPOSE.

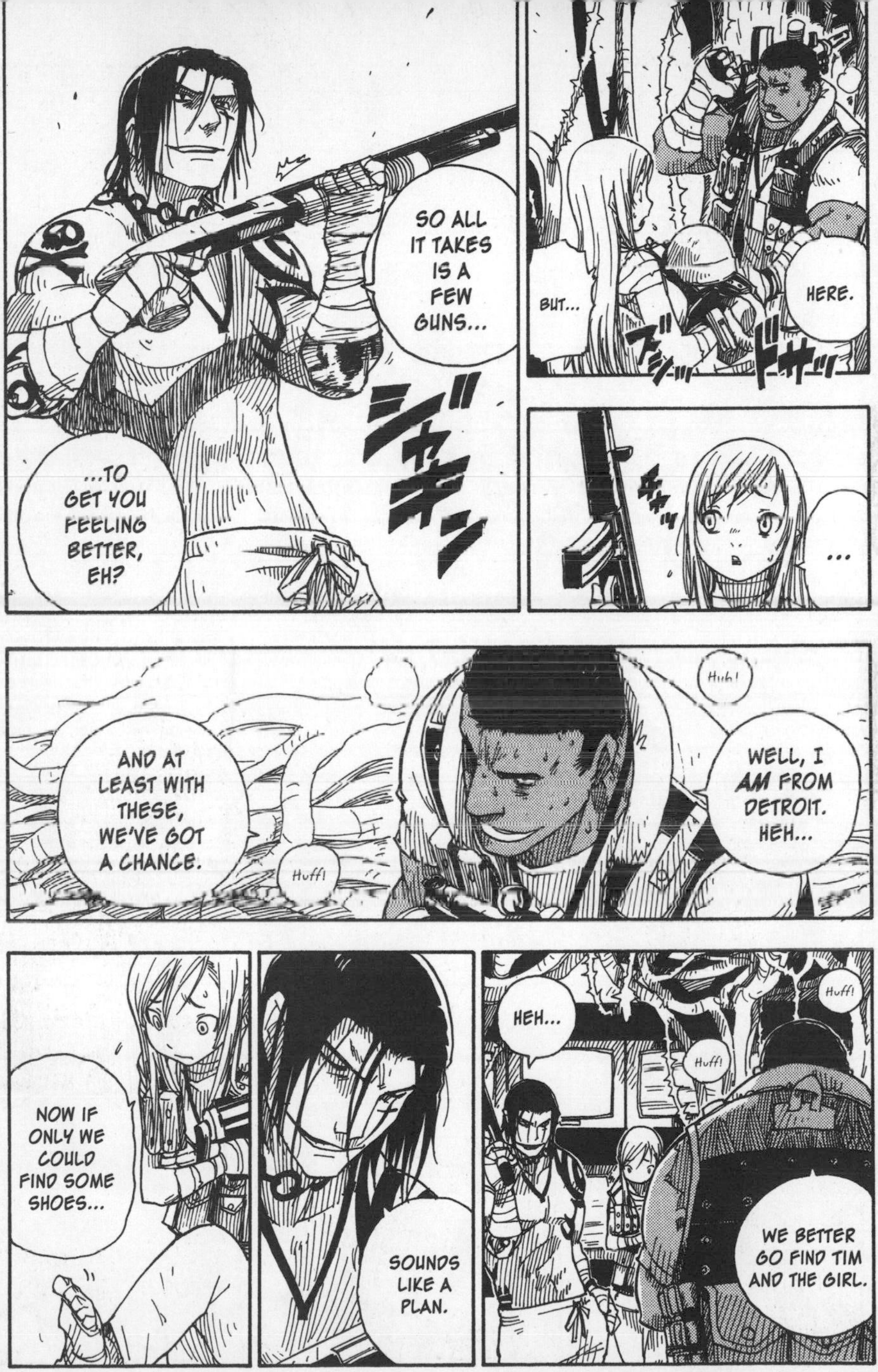
HERE.
BUT...
...
SO ALL IT TAKES IS A FEW GUNS...
...TO GET YOU FEELING BETTER, EH?
Huh!
WELL, I AM FROM DETROIT. HEH...
Huff!
AND AT LEAST WITH THESE, WE'VE GOT A CHANCE.
Huff!
Huff!
HEH...
WE BETTER GO FIND TIM AND THE GIRL.
SOUNDS LIKE A PLAN.
NOW IF ONLY WE COULD FIND SOME SHOES...

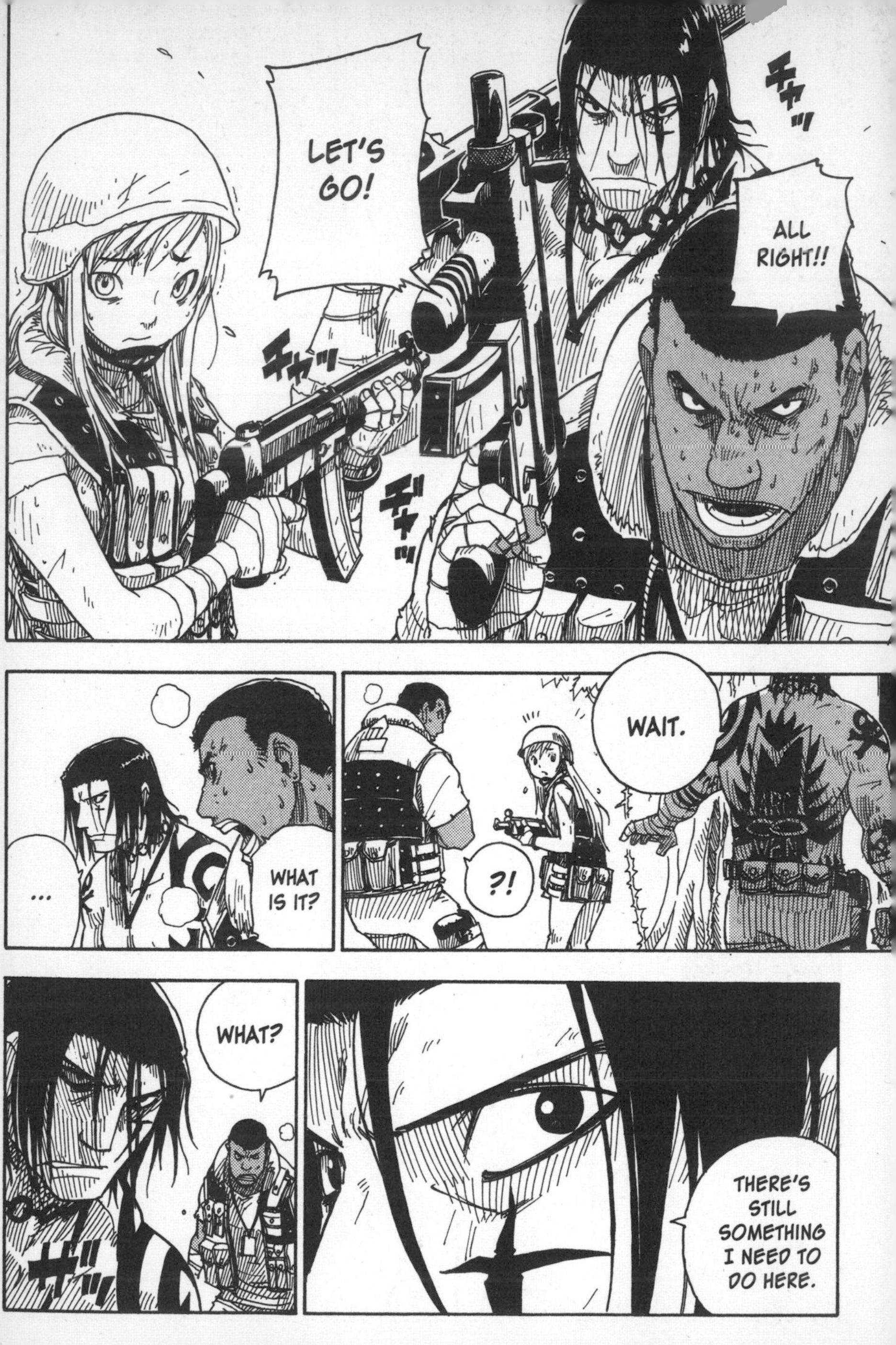
ALL RIGHT!!
LET'S GO!
WAIT.
?!
WHAT IS IT?
...
THERE'S STILL SOMETHING I NEED TO DO HERE.
WHAT?

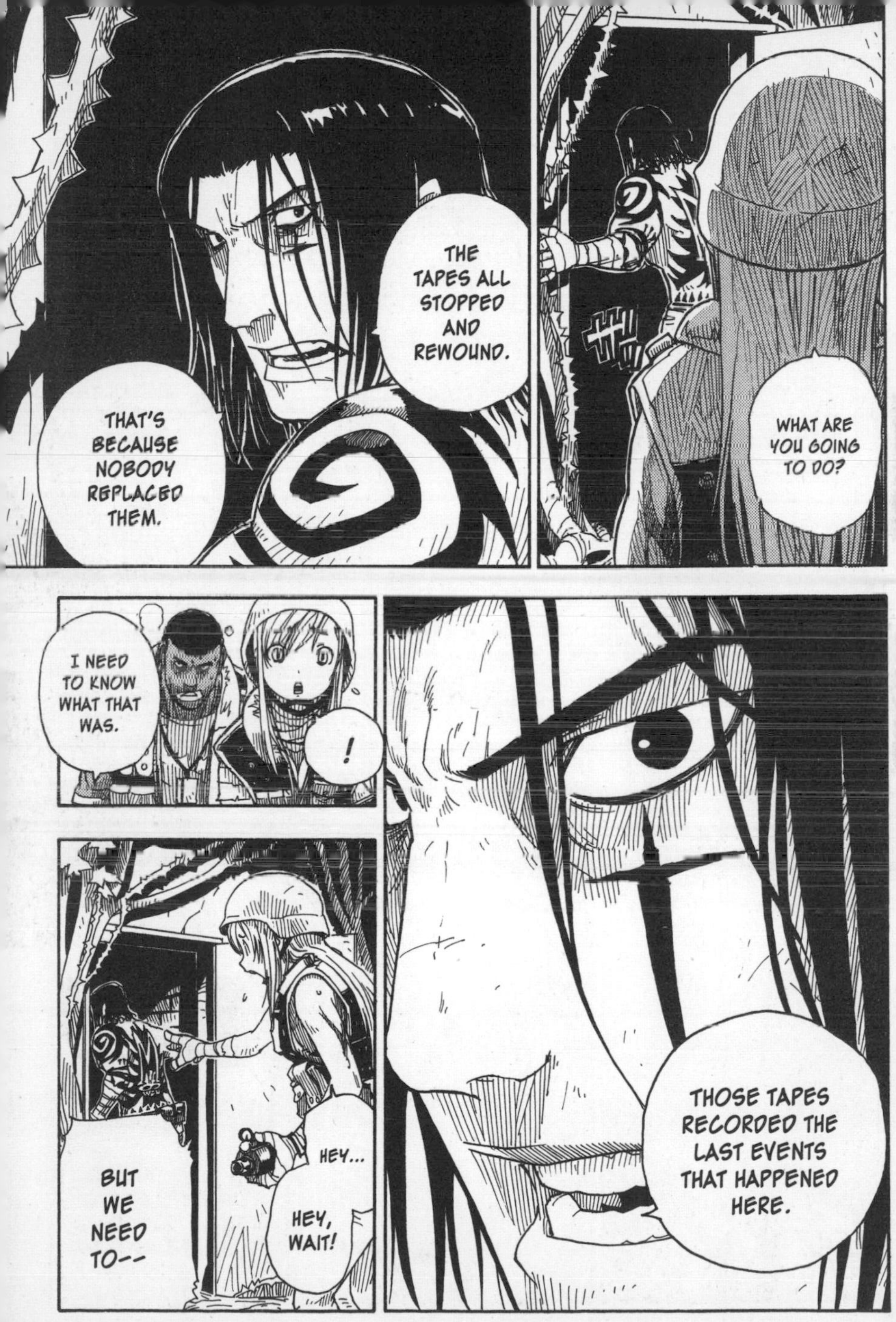
WHAT ARE YOU GOING TO DO?
THE TAPES ALL STOPPED AND REWOUND.
THAT'S BECAUSE NOBODY REPLACED THEM.
THOSE TAPES RECORDED THE LAST EVENTS THAT HAPPENED HERE.
I NEED TO KNOW WHAT THAT WAS.
!
HEY...
HEY, WAIT!
BUT WE NEED TO--

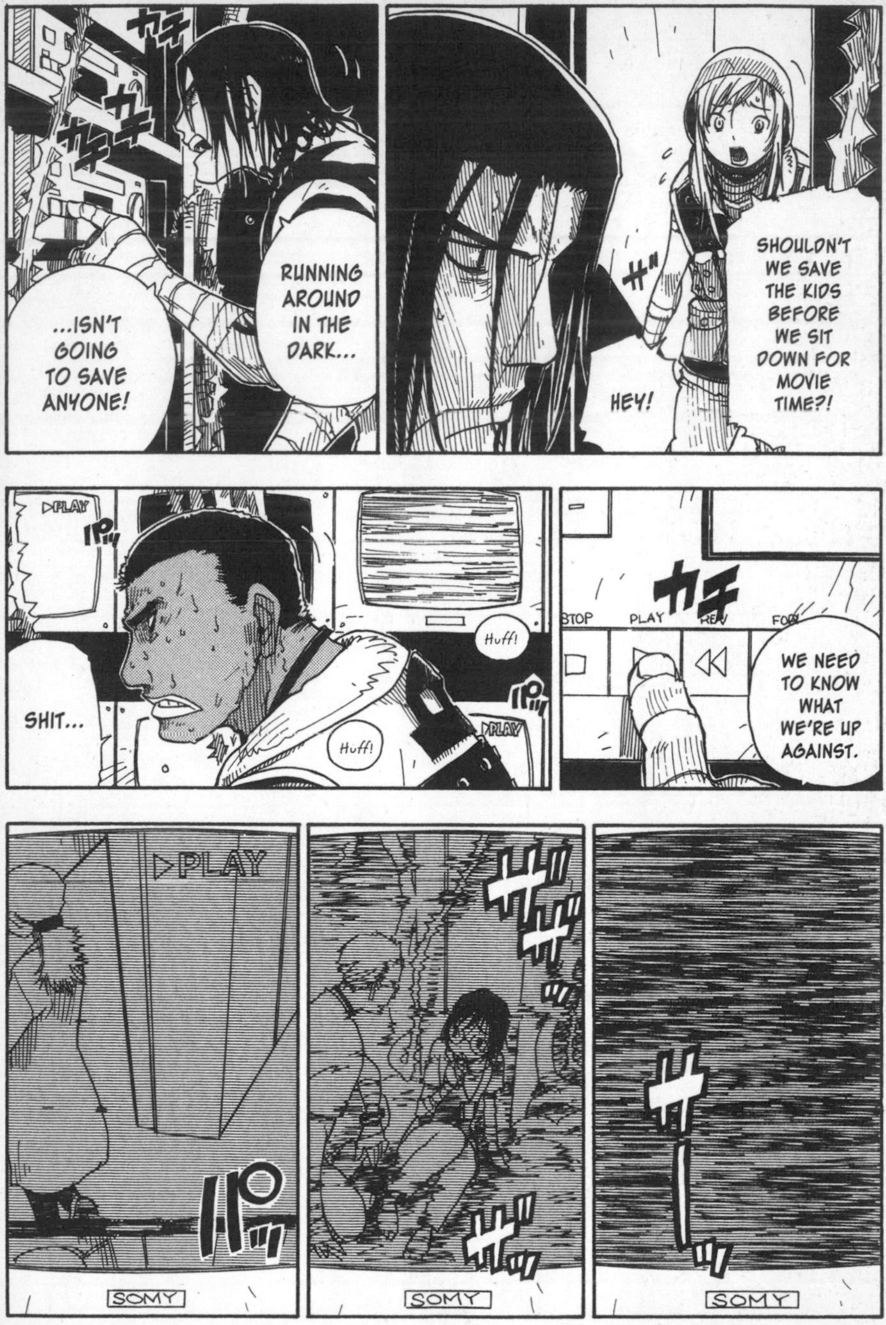
HEY!
SHOULDN'T WE SAVE THE KIDS BEFORE WE SIT DOWN FOR MOVIE TIME?!
RUNNING AROUND IN THE DARK...
...ISN'T GOING TO SAVE ANYONE!
カチ
STOP
PLAY
REW
FOR
WE NEED TO KNOW WHAT WE'RE UP AGAINST.
▷PLAY
Huff!
Huff!
▷PLAY
SHIT...
▷PLAY
SOMY
SOMY
SOMY

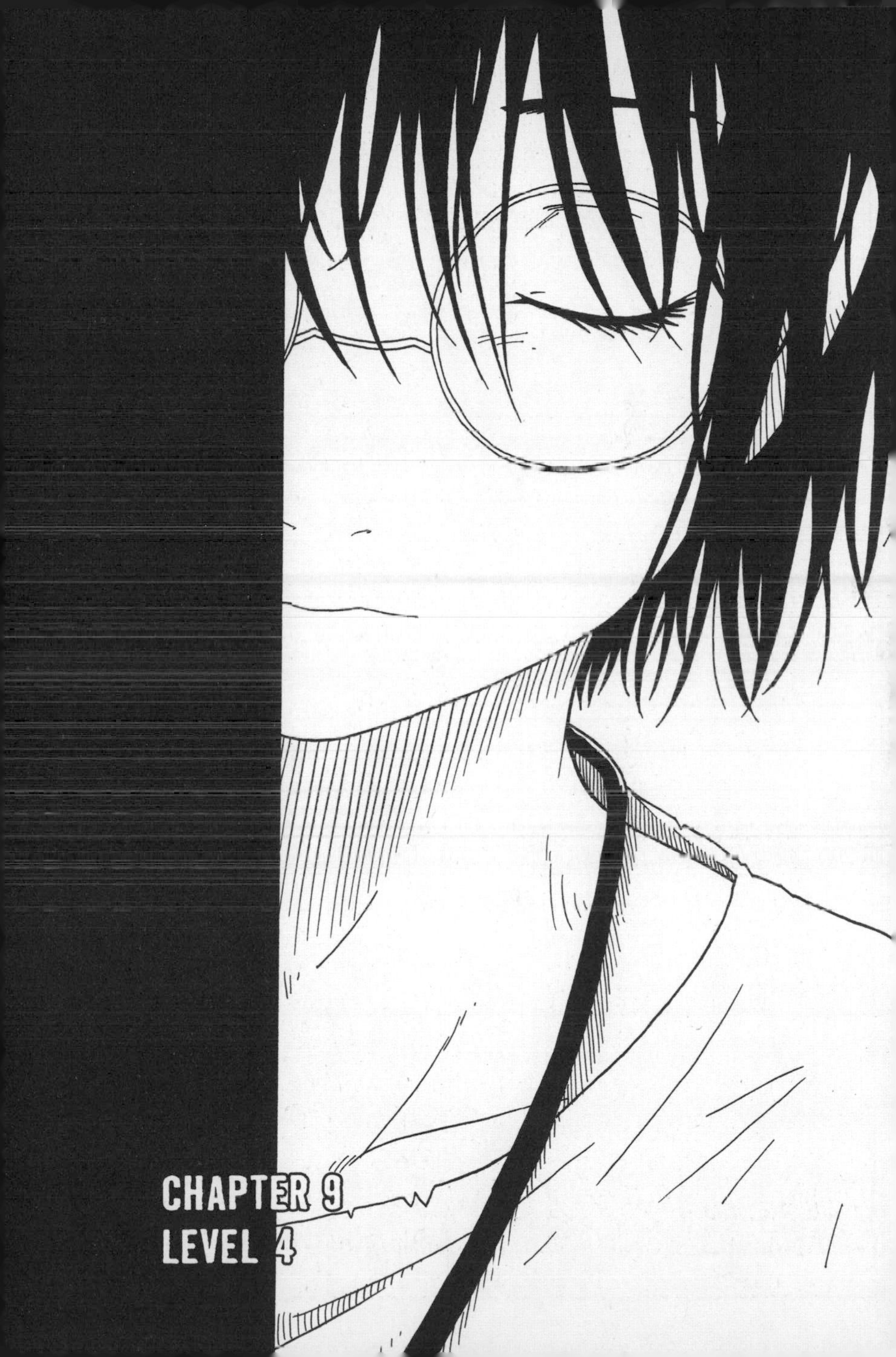

CHAPTER 9
LEVEL 4

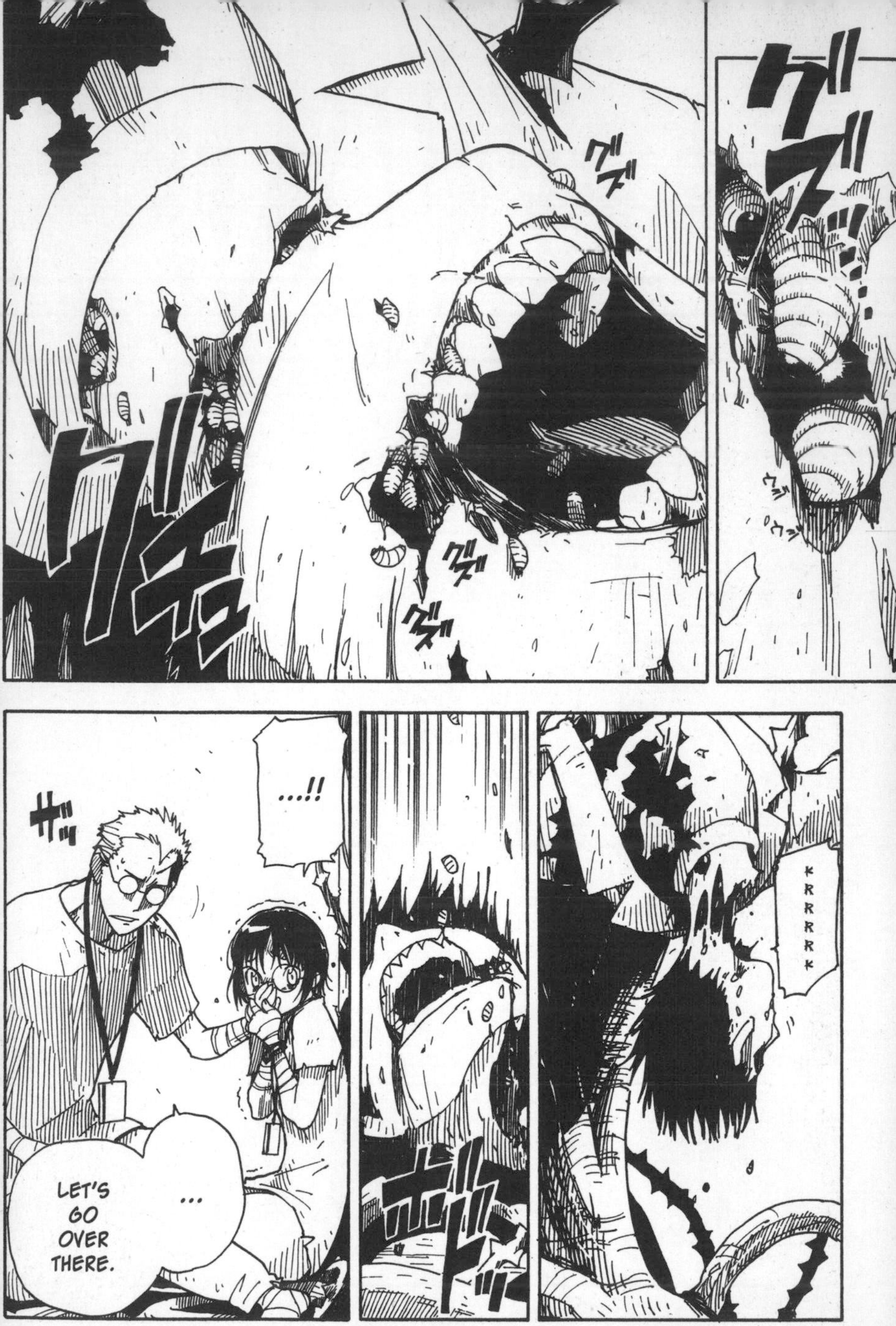
KRRRRK
...!!
...
LET'S GO OVER THERE.

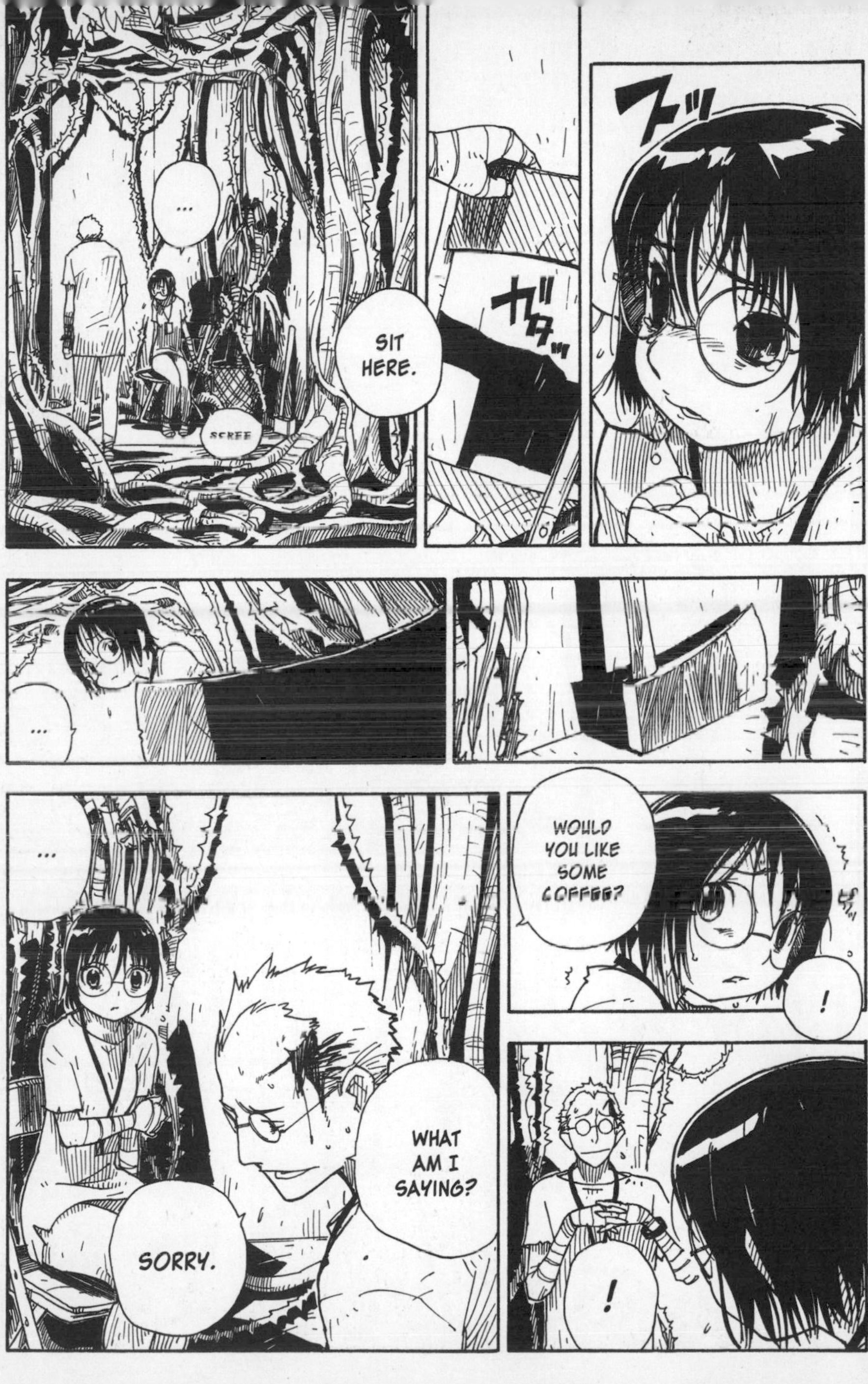

ズッ
ガタ
SIT HERE.
...
SCREE
...
WOULD YOU LIKE SOME COFFEE?
!
...
WHAT AM I SAYING?
SORRY.
!

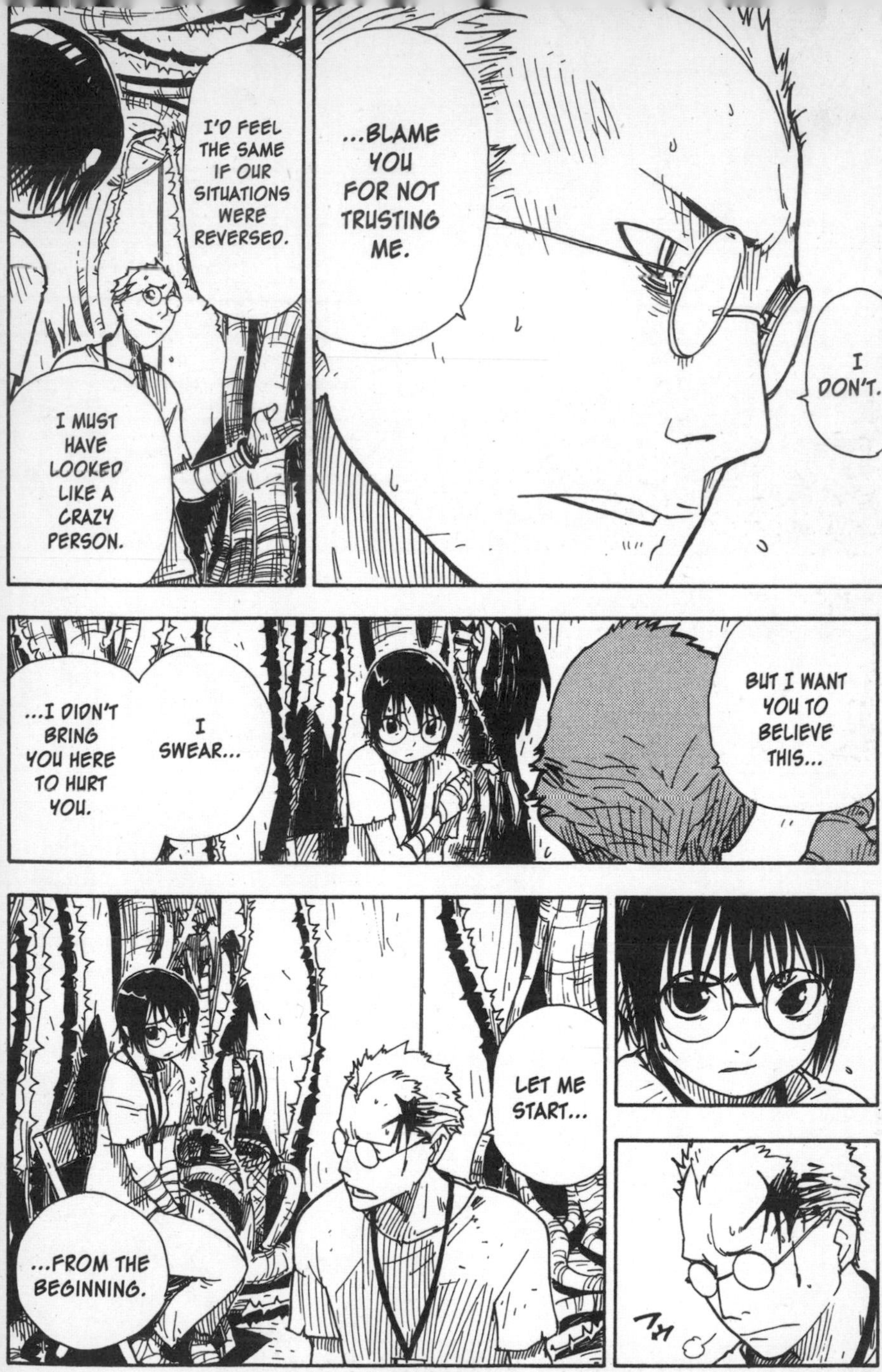
I DON'T...
...BLAME YOU FOR NOT TRUSTING ME.
I'D FEEL THE SAME IF OUR SITUATIONS WERE REVERSED.
I MUST HAVE LOOKED LIKE A CRAZY PERSON.
BUT I WANT YOU TO BELIEVE THIS...
I SWEAR...
...I DIDN'T BRING YOU HERE TO HURT YOU.
LET ME START...
...FROM THE BEGINNING.

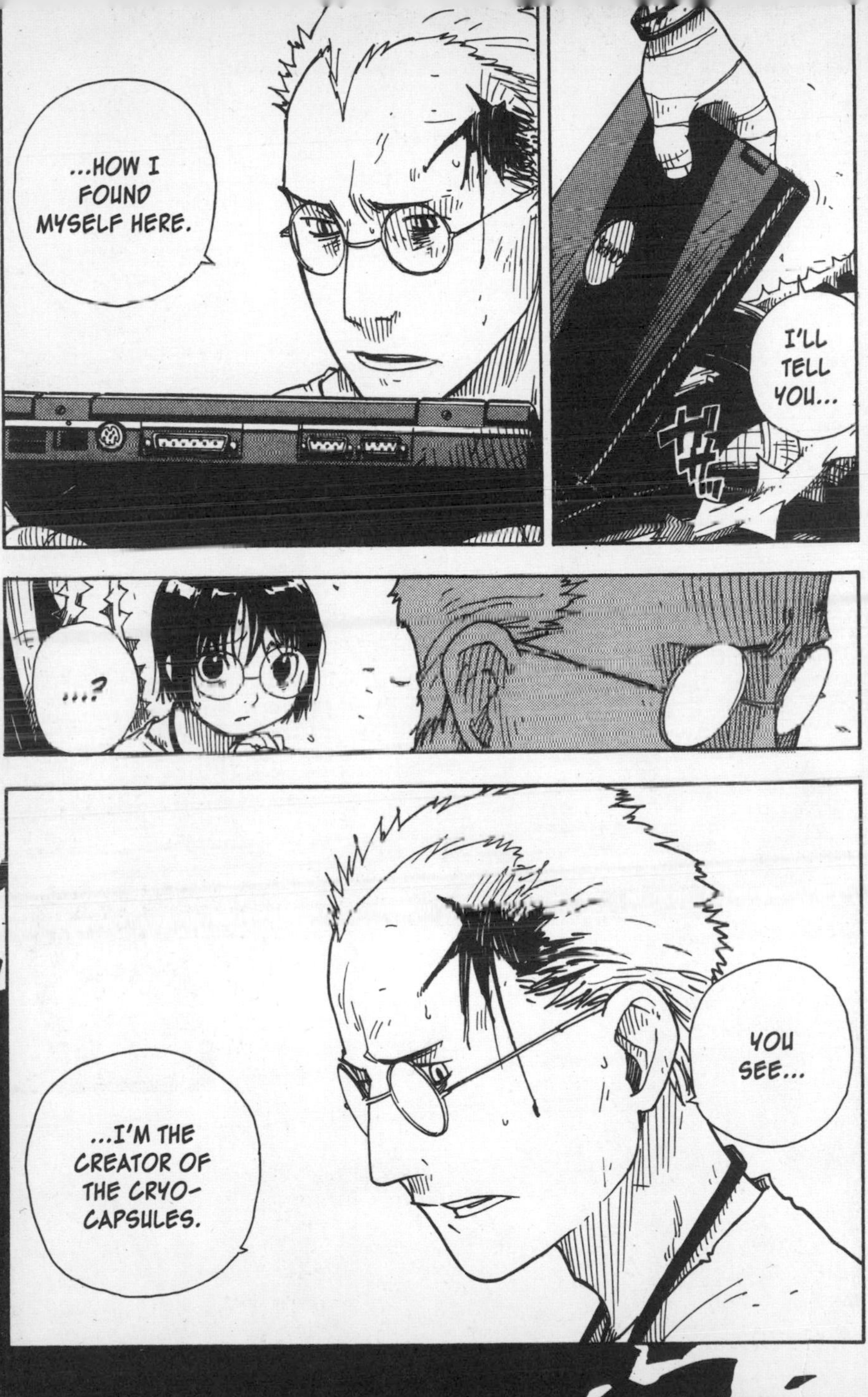
I'LL TELL YOU...
...HOW I FOUND MYSELF HERE.
...?
YOU SEE...
...I'M THE CREATOR OF THE CRYO-CAPSULES.

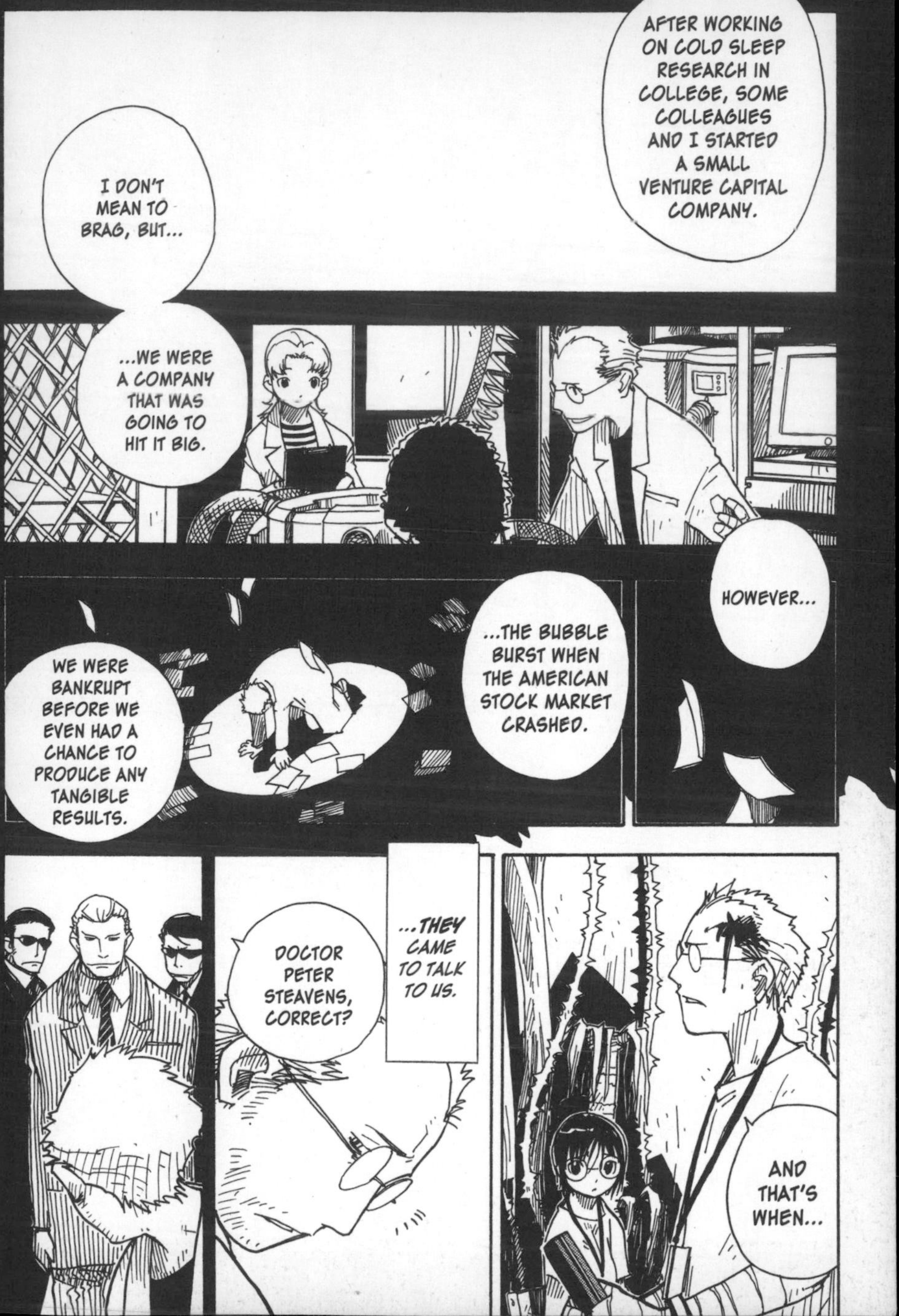
AFTER WORKING ON COLD SLEEP RESEARCH IN COLLEGE, SOME COLLEAGUES AND I STARTED A SMALL VENTURE CAPITAL COMPANY.
I DON'T MEAN TO BRAG, BUT...
...WE WERE A COMPANY THAT WAS GOING TO HIT IT BIG.
HOWEVER...
...THE BUBBLE BURST WHEN THE AMERICAN STOCK MARKET CRASHED.
WE WERE BANKRUPT BEFORE WE EVEN HAD A CHANCE TO PRODUCE ANY TANGIBLE RESULTS.
AND THAT'S WHEN...
...THEY CAME TO TALK TO US.
DOCTOR PETER STEAVENS, CORRECT?

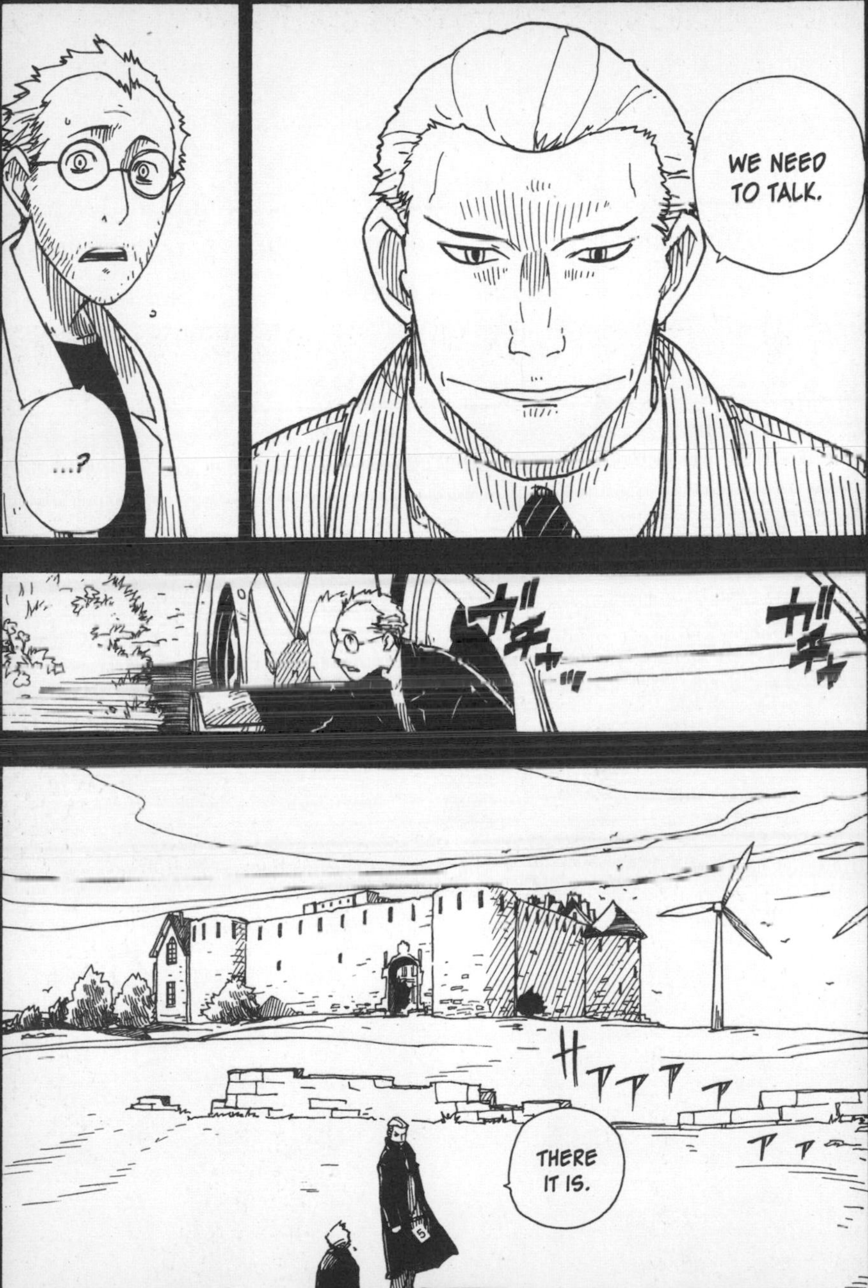
WE NEED TO TALK.
...?
THERE IT IS.

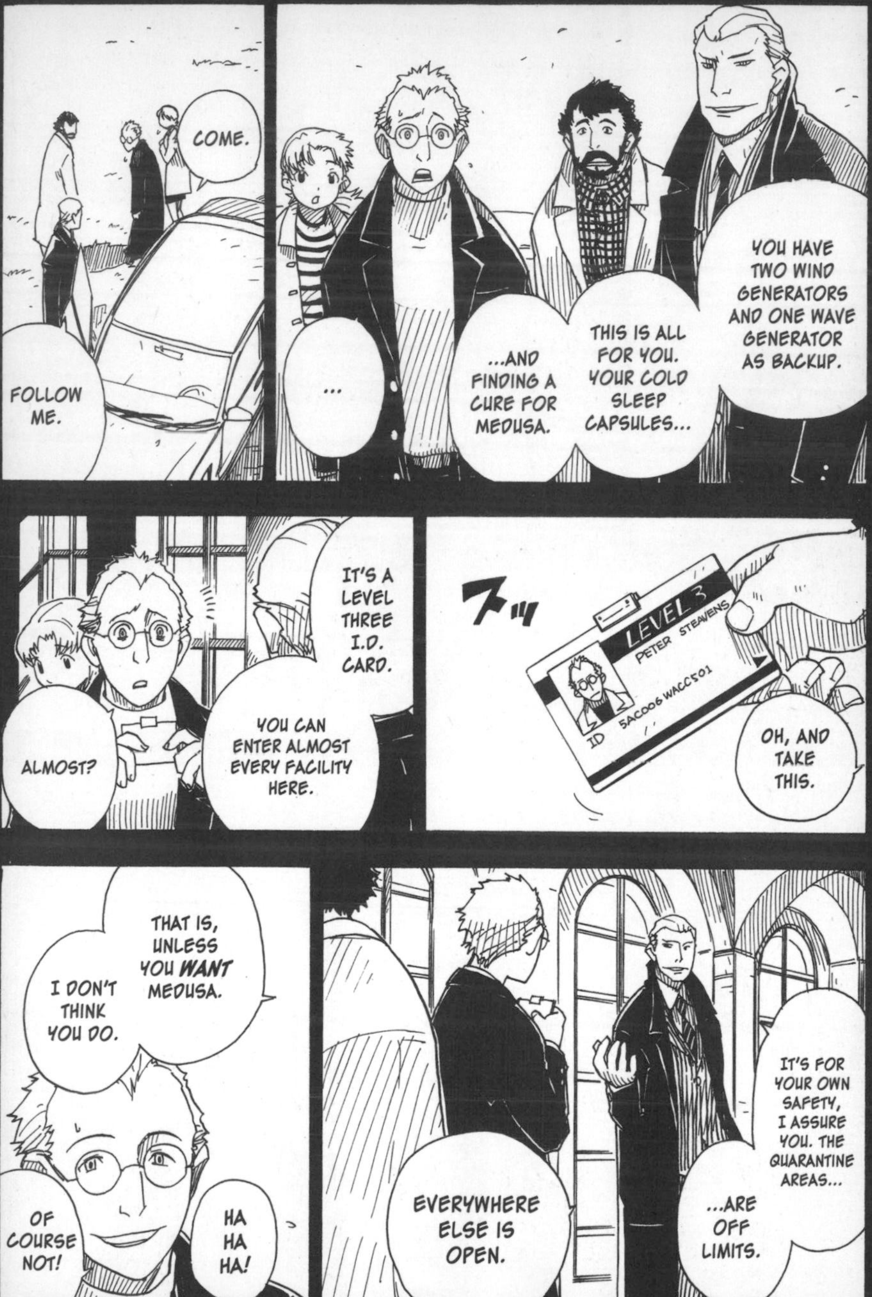

YOU HAVE TWO WIND GENERATORS AND ONE WAVE GENERATOR AS BACKUP.
THIS IS ALL FOR YOU. YOUR COLD SLEEP CAPSULES...
...AND FINDING A CURE FOR MEDUSA.
...
COME.
FOLLOW ME.
OH, AND TAKE THIS.
LEVEL 3
PETER STEAVENS
ID 5AC006 WACC501
フッ
IT'S A LEVEL THREE I.D. CARD.
YOU CAN ENTER ALMOST EVERY FACILITY HERE.
ALMOST?
IT'S FOR YOUR OWN SAFETY, I ASSURE YOU. THE QUARANTINE AREAS...
...ARE OFF LIMITS.
EVERYWHERE ELSE IS OPEN.
THAT IS, UNLESS YOU *WANT* MEDUSA.
I DON'T THINK YOU DO.
OF COURSE NOT!
HA HA HA!

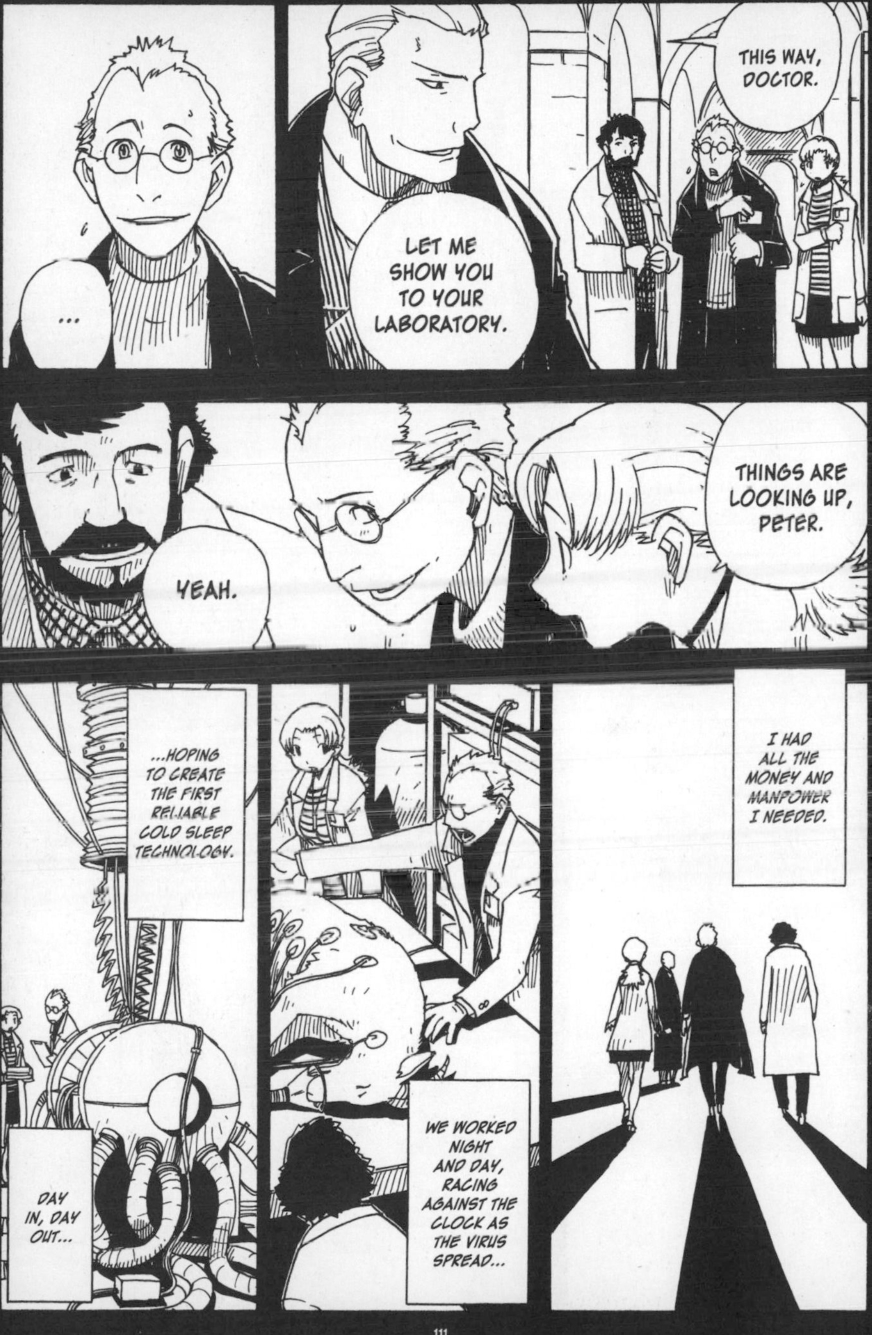
...
LET ME SHOW YOU TO YOUR LABORATORY.
THIS WAY, DOCTOR.
YEAH.
THINGS ARE LOOKING UP, PETER.
...HOPING TO CREATE THE FIRST RELIABLE COLD SLEEP TECHNOLOGY.
DAY IN, DAY OUT...
WE WORKED NIGHT AND DAY, RACING AGAINST THE CLOCK AS THE VIRUS SPREAD...
I HAD ALL THE MONEY AND MANPOWER I NEEDED.

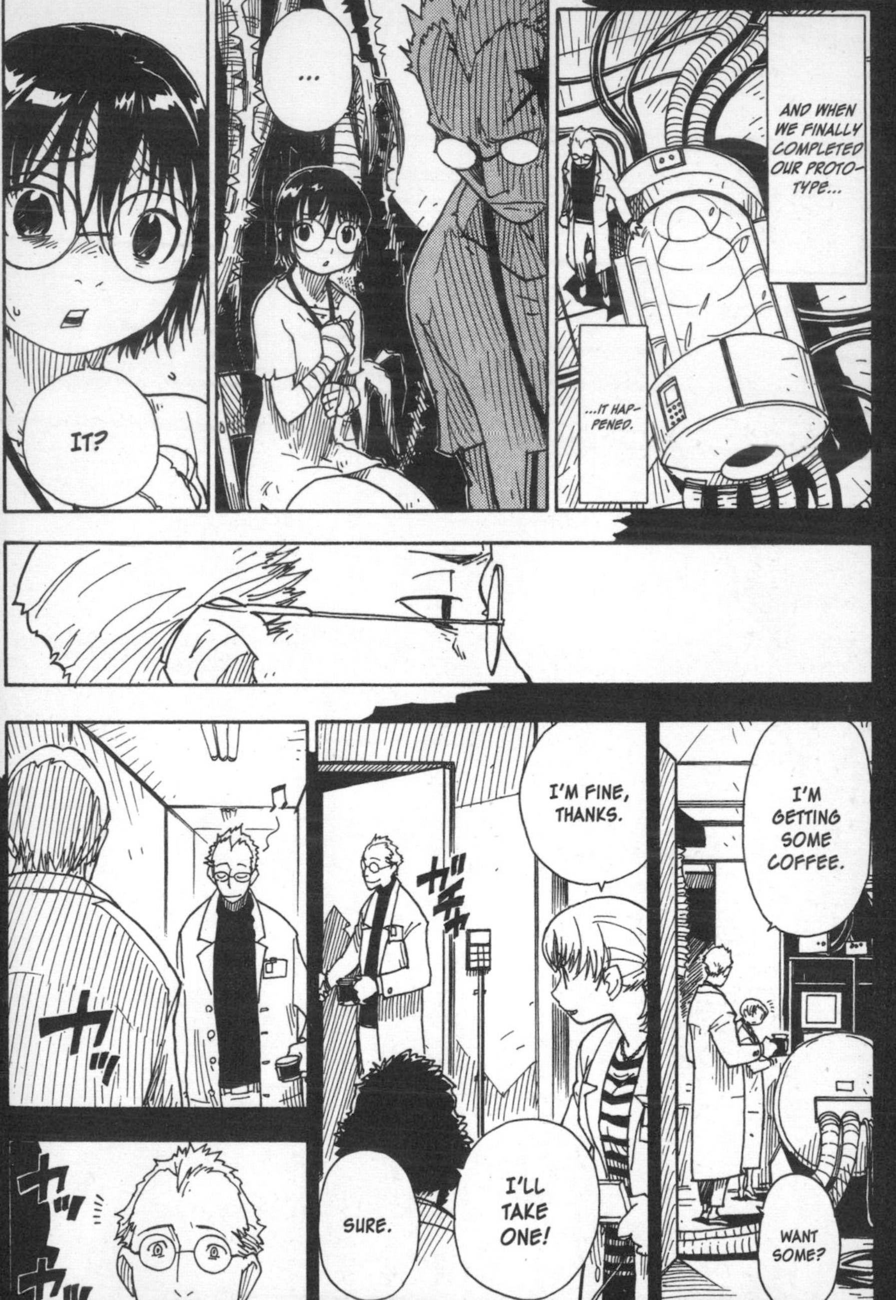
AND WHEN WE FINALLY COMPLETED OUR PROTO-TYPE...
...IT HAP-PENED.
...
IT?
I'M GETTING SOME COFFEE.
WANT SOME?
I'M FINE, THANKS.
I'LL TAKE ONE!
SURE.

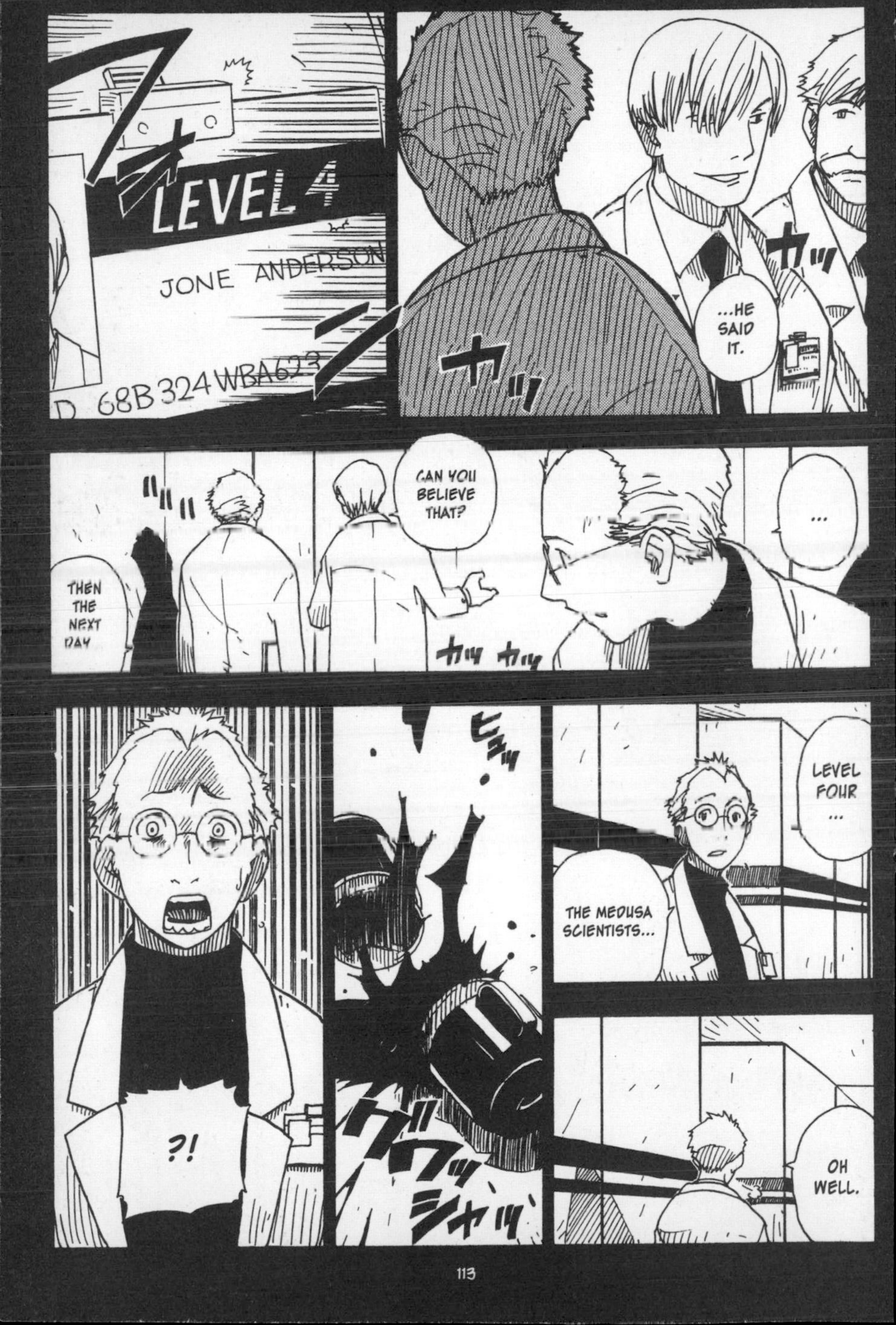
LEVEL 4
JONE ANDERSON
68B 324 WBA623
...HE SAID IT.
THEN THE NEXT DAY
CAN YOU BELIEVE THAT?
...
?!
LEVEL FOUR ...
THE MEDUSA SCIENTISTS...
OH WELL.

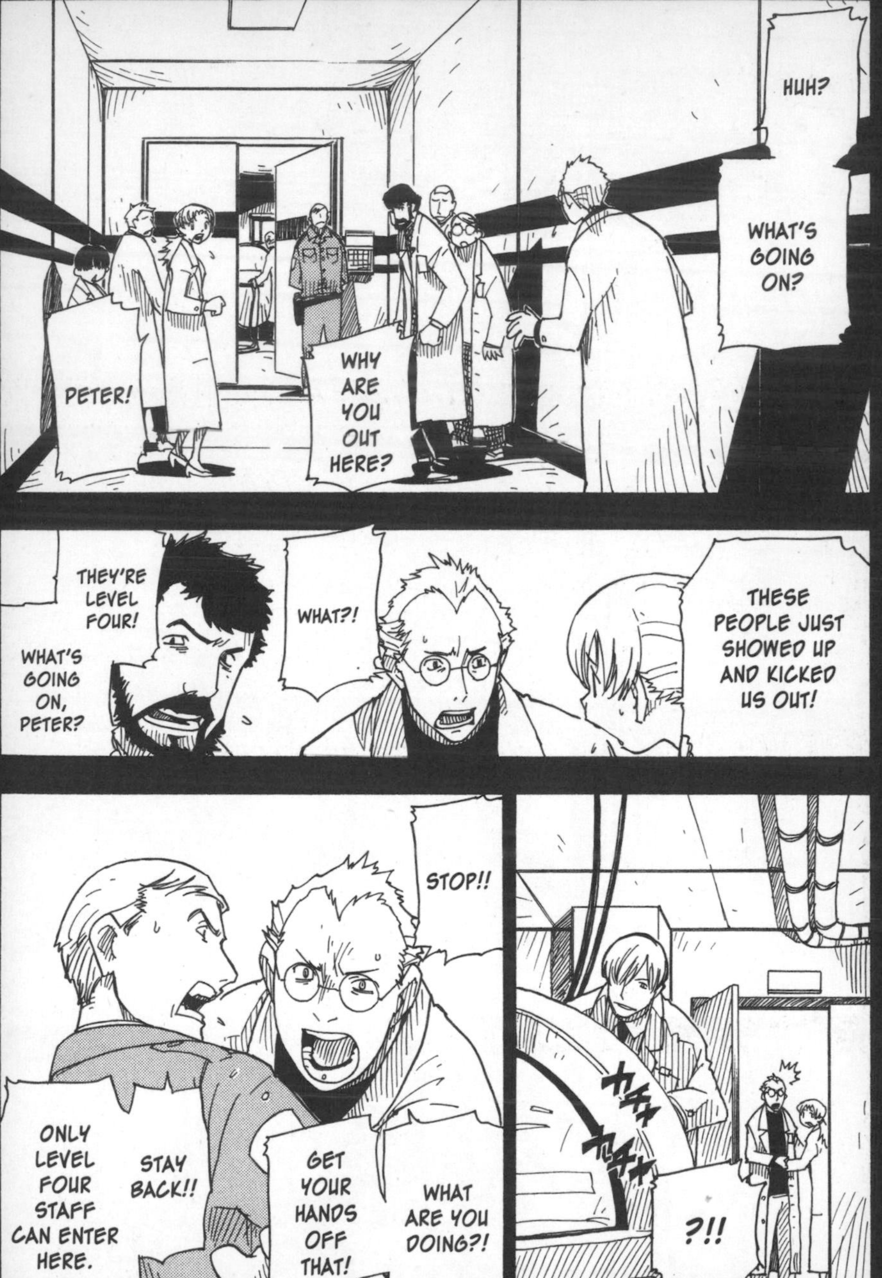
HUH?
WHAT'S GOING ON?
WHY ARE YOU OUT HERE?
PETER!
THESE PEOPLE JUST SHOWED UP AND KICKED US OUT!
WHAT?!
THEY'RE LEVEL FOUR!
WHAT'S GOING ON, PETER?
カチャ
カチャ
?!!
STOP!!
WHAT ARE YOU DOING?!
GET YOUR HANDS OFF THAT!
STAY BACK!!
ONLY LEVEL FOUR STAFF CAN ENTER HERE.

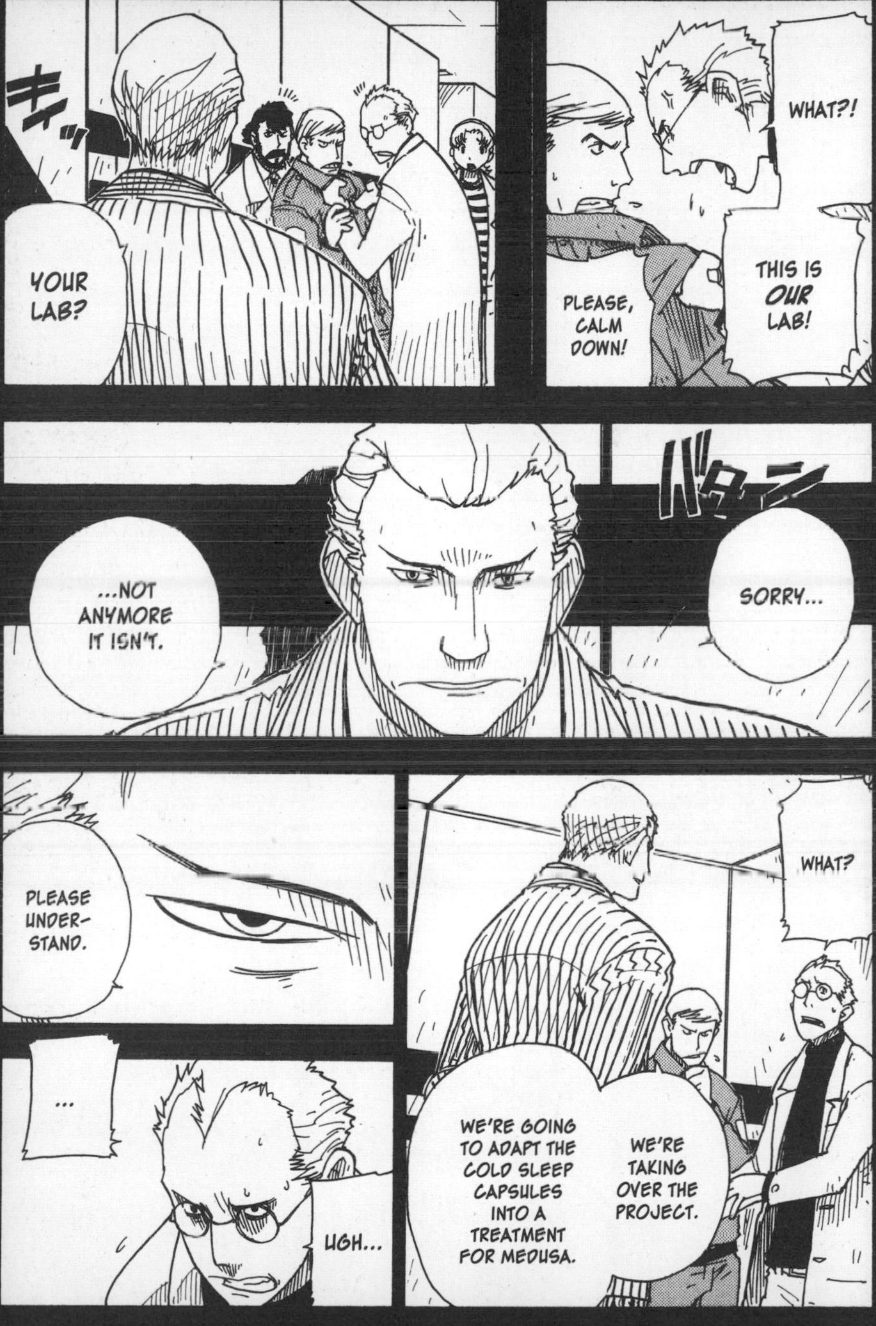
WHAT?!
THIS IS OUR LAB!
PLEASE, CALM DOWN!
キィッ
YOUR LAB?
バタン
SORRY...
...NOT ANYMORE IT ISN'T.
WHAT?
WE'RE TAKING OVER THE PROJECT.
WE'RE GOING TO ADAPT THE COLD SLEEP CAPSULES INTO A TREATMENT FOR MEDUSA.
PLEASE UNDER-STAND.
...
UGH...

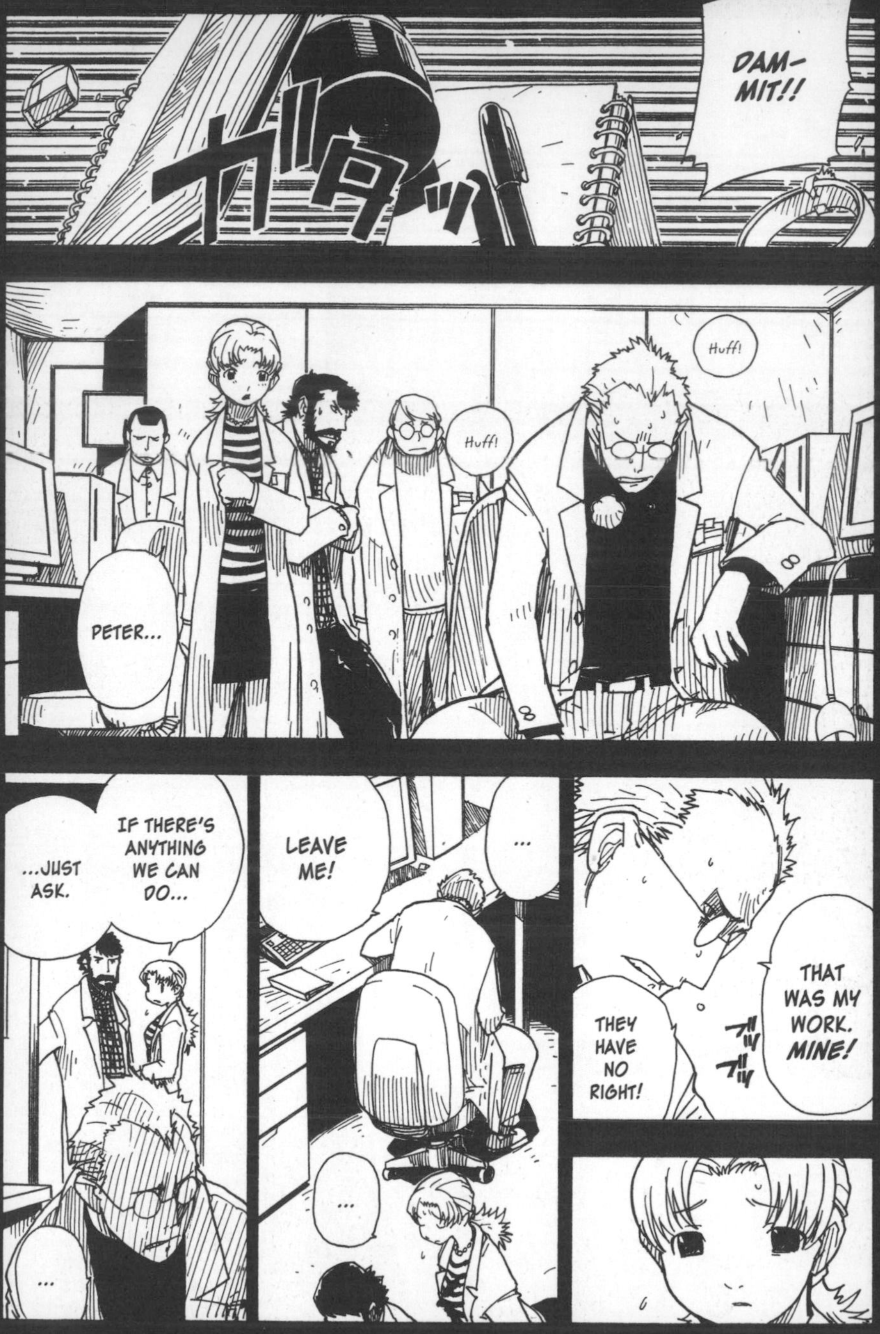

ガタッ
DAM-MIT!!
Huff!
Huff!
PETER...
THAT WAS MY WORK. MINE!
ブツ ブツ
THEY HAVE NO RIGHT!
...
LEAVE ME!
...
IF THERE'S ANYTHING WE CAN DO...
...JUST ASK.
...

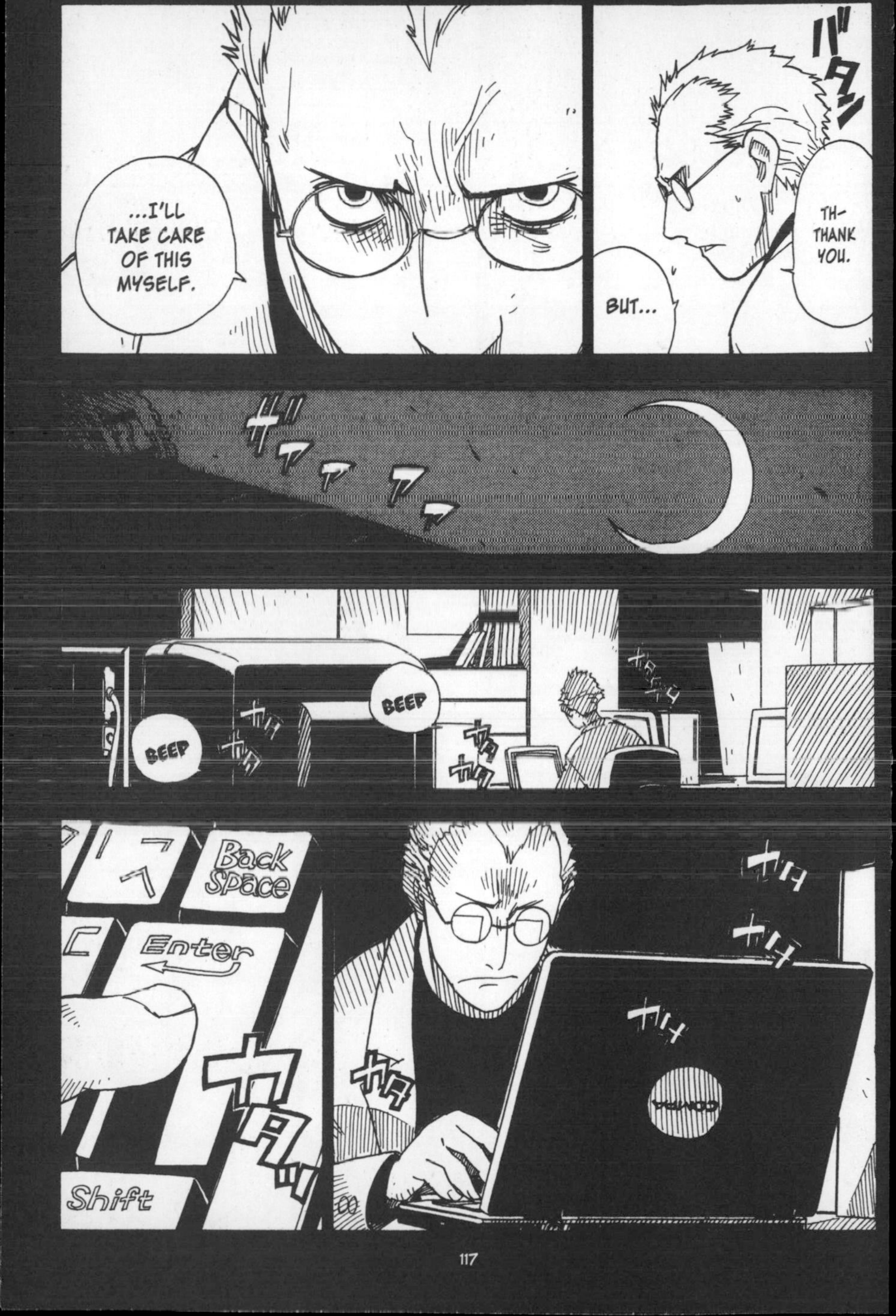
...I'LL TAKE CARE OF THIS MYSELF.
バタン
BUT...
TH-THANK YOU.
BEEP
BEEP
Back Space
Enter
Shift

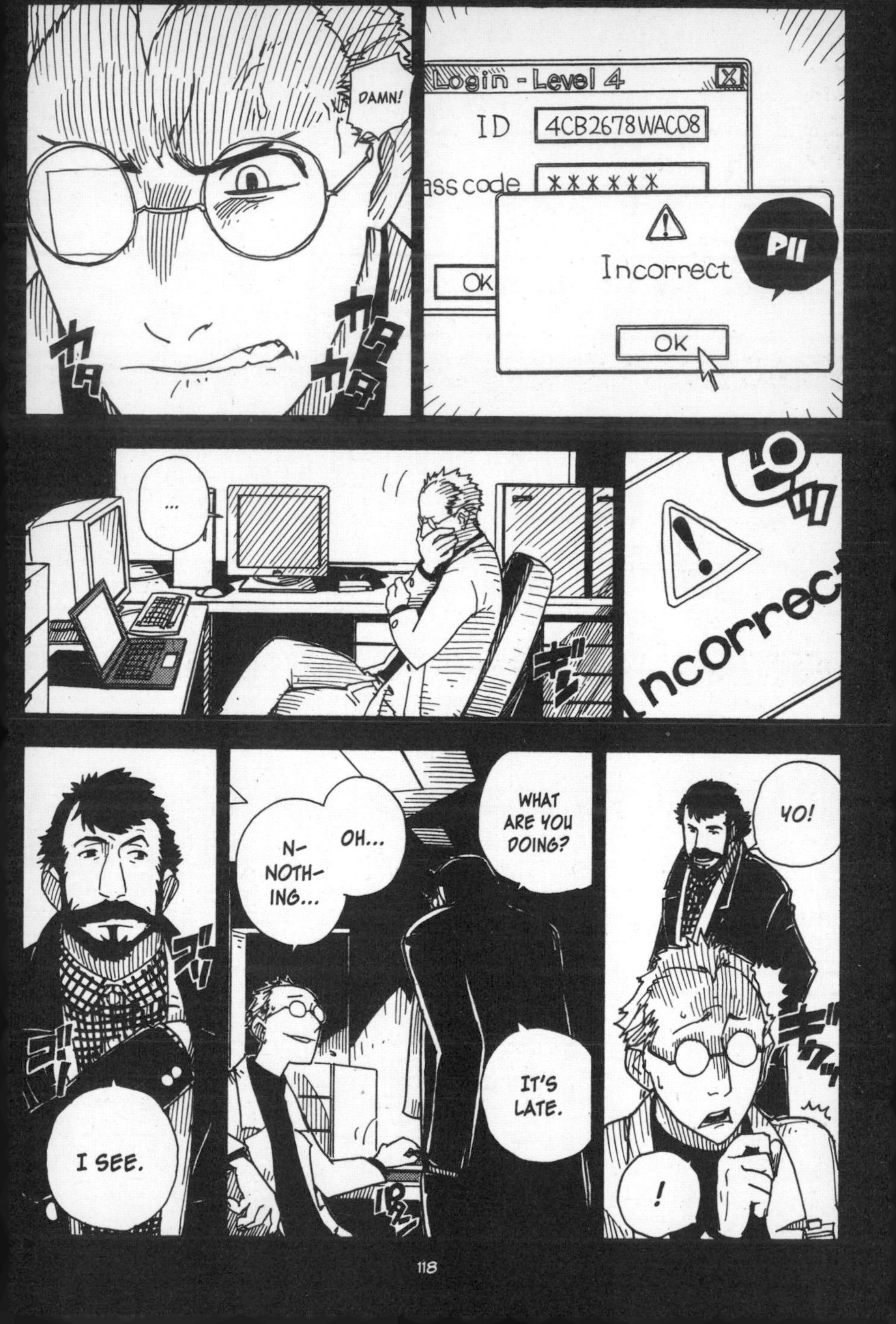
Login - Level 4
ID
4CB2678WAC08
ass code
******
OK
Incorrect
OK
PII
DAMN!
Incorrect
...
YO!
!
WHAT ARE YOU DOING?
OH...
N-NOTHING...
IT'S LATE.
I SEE.

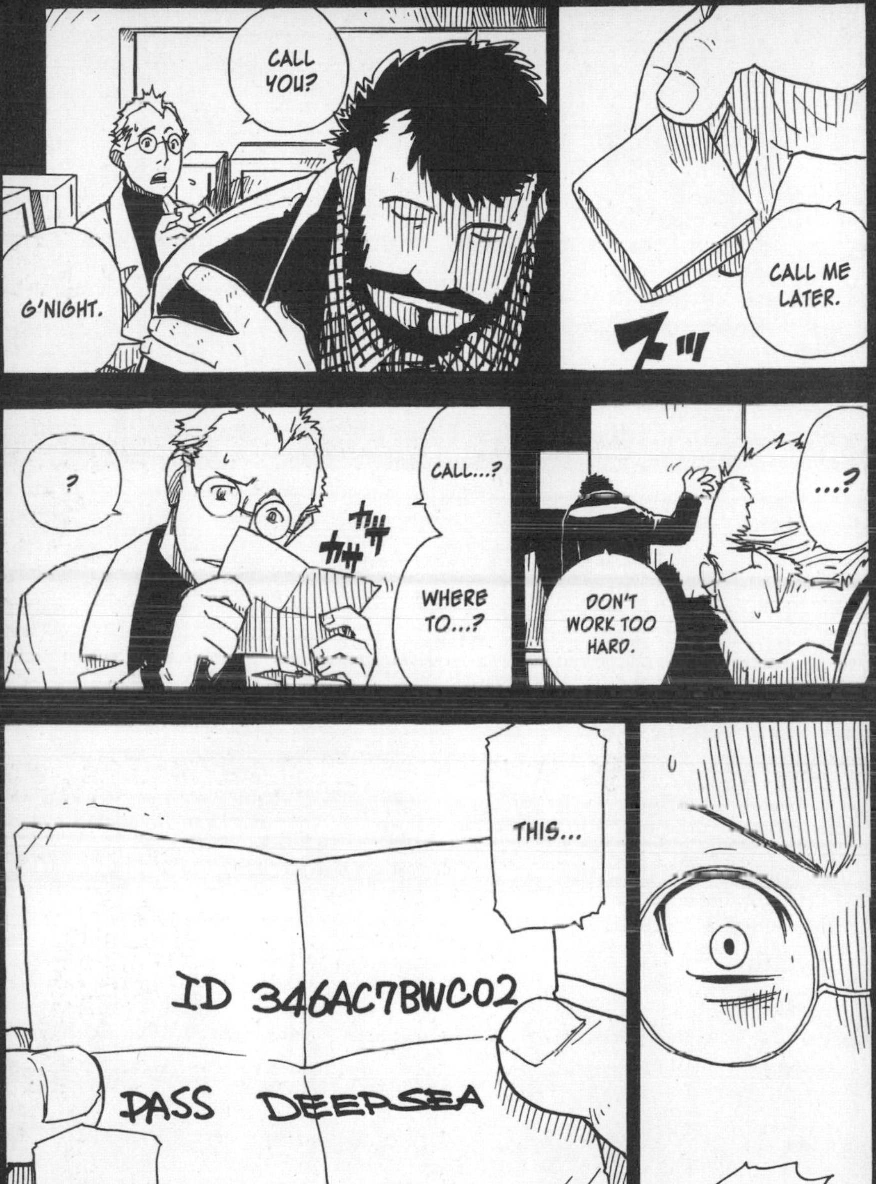
CALL ME LATER.
CALL YOU?
G'NIGHT.
...?
DON'T WORK TOO HARD.
?
CALL...?
WHERE TO...?
!
THIS...
ID 346AC7BWC02
PASS DEEPSEA
THIS IS...

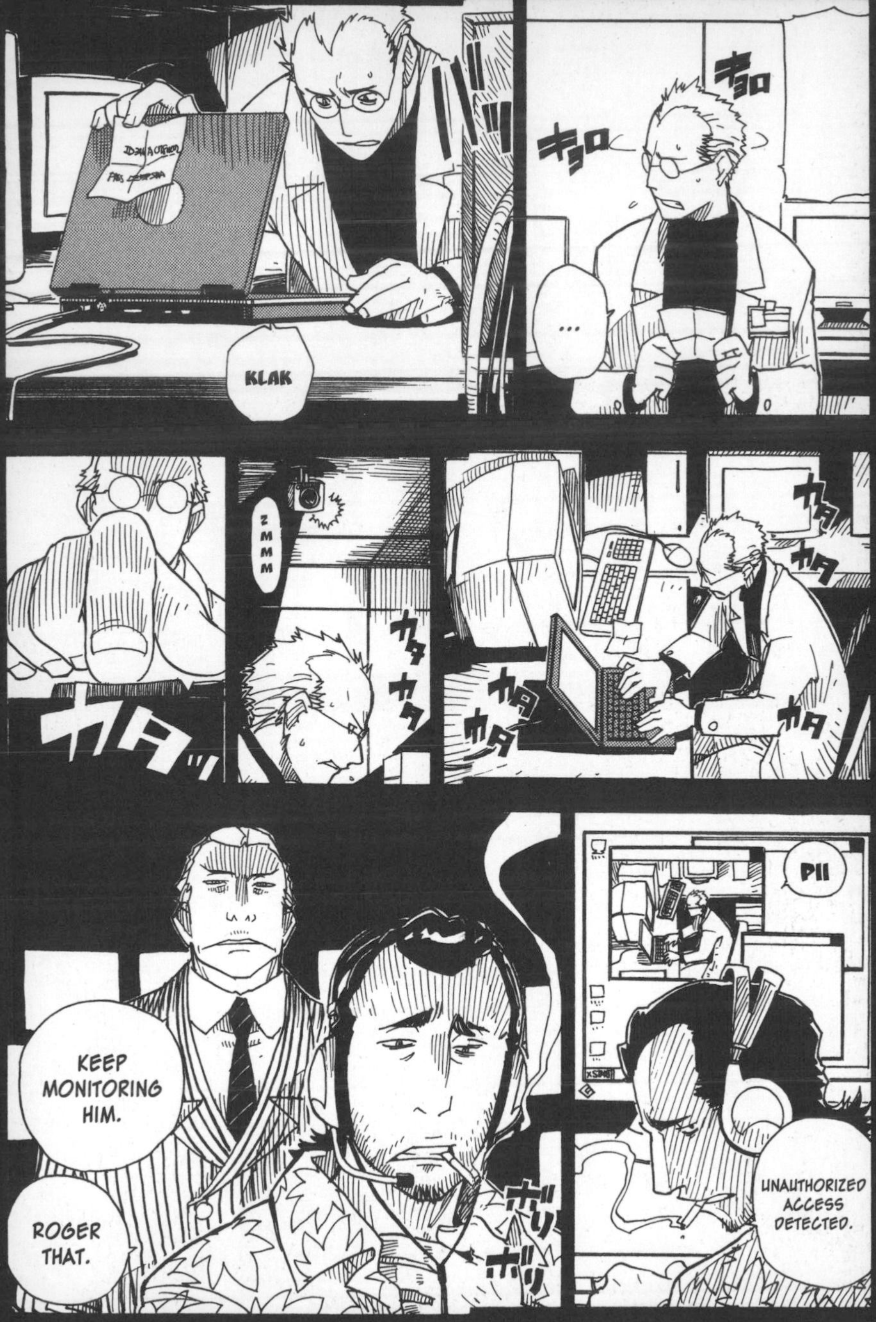
KLAK
キョロ
キョロ
...
ZMMM
カタッ
カタ
カタ
カタ
カタ
カタ
カタ
カタ
カタ
PII
UNAUTHORIZED ACCESS DETECTED.
KEEP MONITORING HIM.
ROGER THAT.
ボリ
ボリ

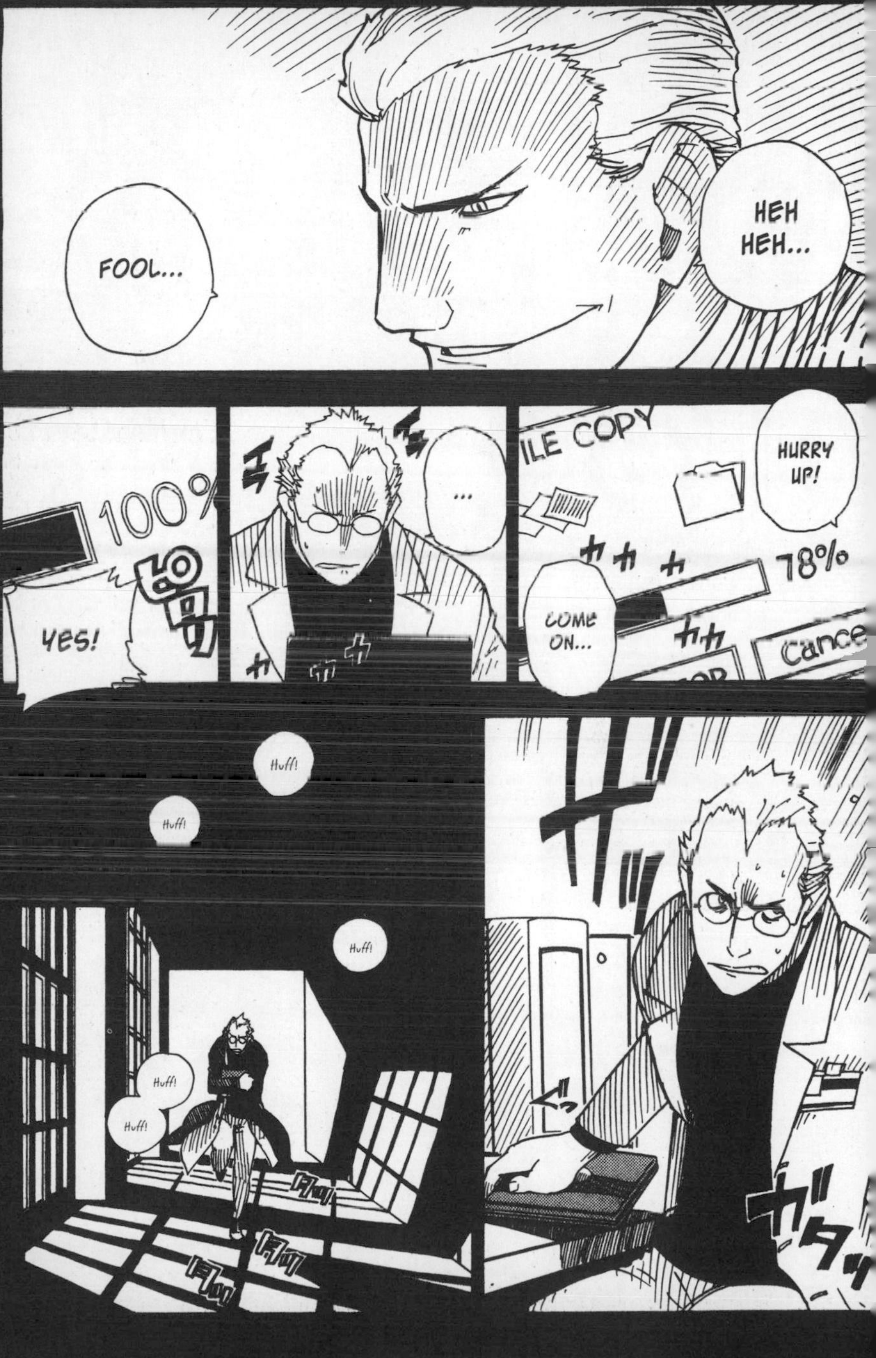
HEH HEH...
FOOL...
HURRY UP!
ILE COPY
78%
COME ON...
...
100%
YES!
Huff!
Huff!
Huff!
Huff!
Huff!

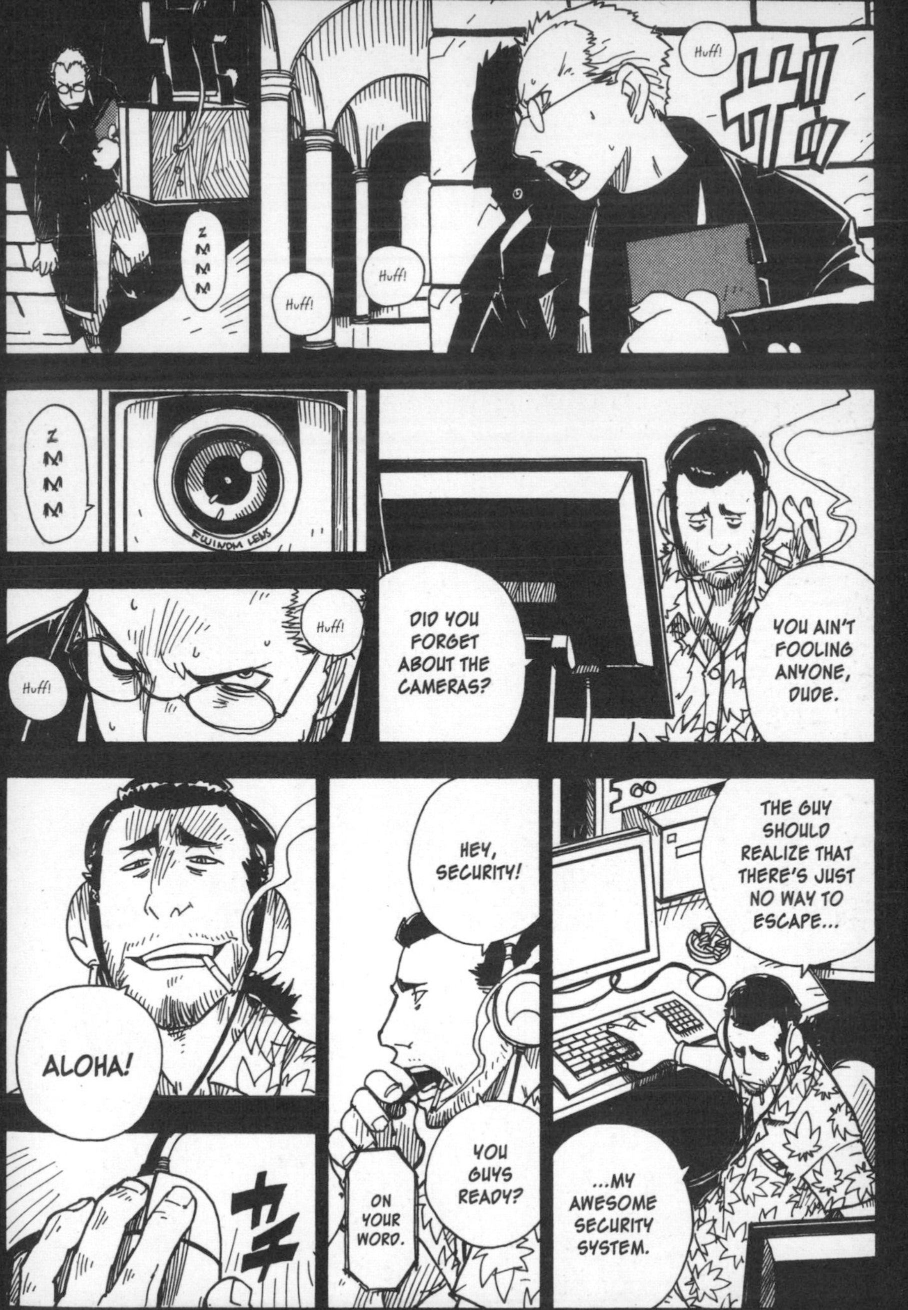
Huff!
Huff!
Huff!
ZMMM
YOU AIN'T FOOLING ANYONE, DUDE.
ZMMM
DID YOU FORGET ABOUT THE CAMERAS?
Huff!
Huff!
THE GUY SHOULD REALIZE THAT THERE'S JUST NO WAY TO ESCAPE...
...MY AWESOME SECURITY SYSTEM.
HEY, SECURITY!
YOU GUYS READY?
ON YOUR WORD.
ALOHA!
カチ

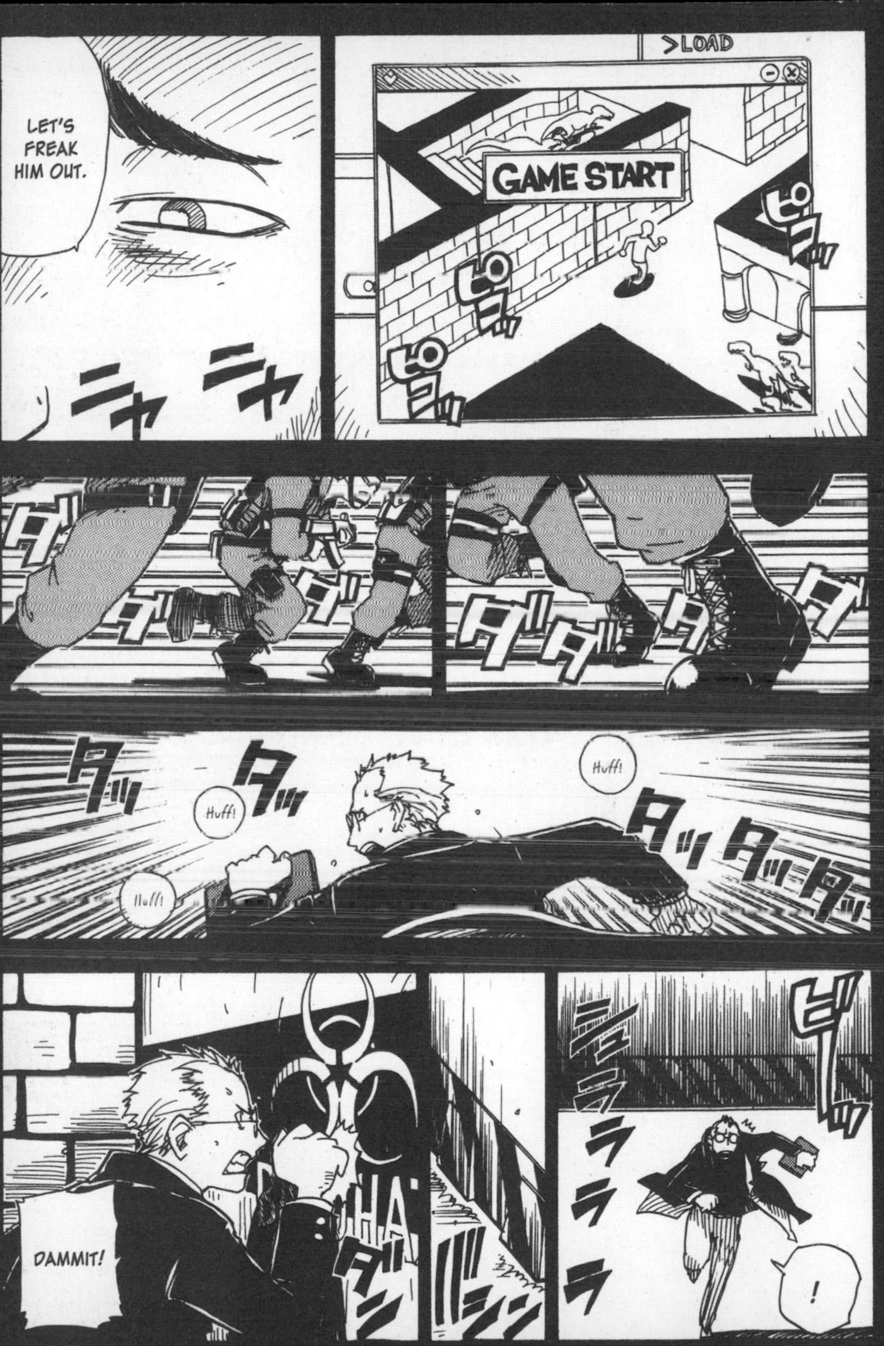
LET'S FREAK HIM OUT.
ニヤ ニヤ
>LOAD
GAME START
Huff!
Huff!
Huff!
DAMMIT!
!

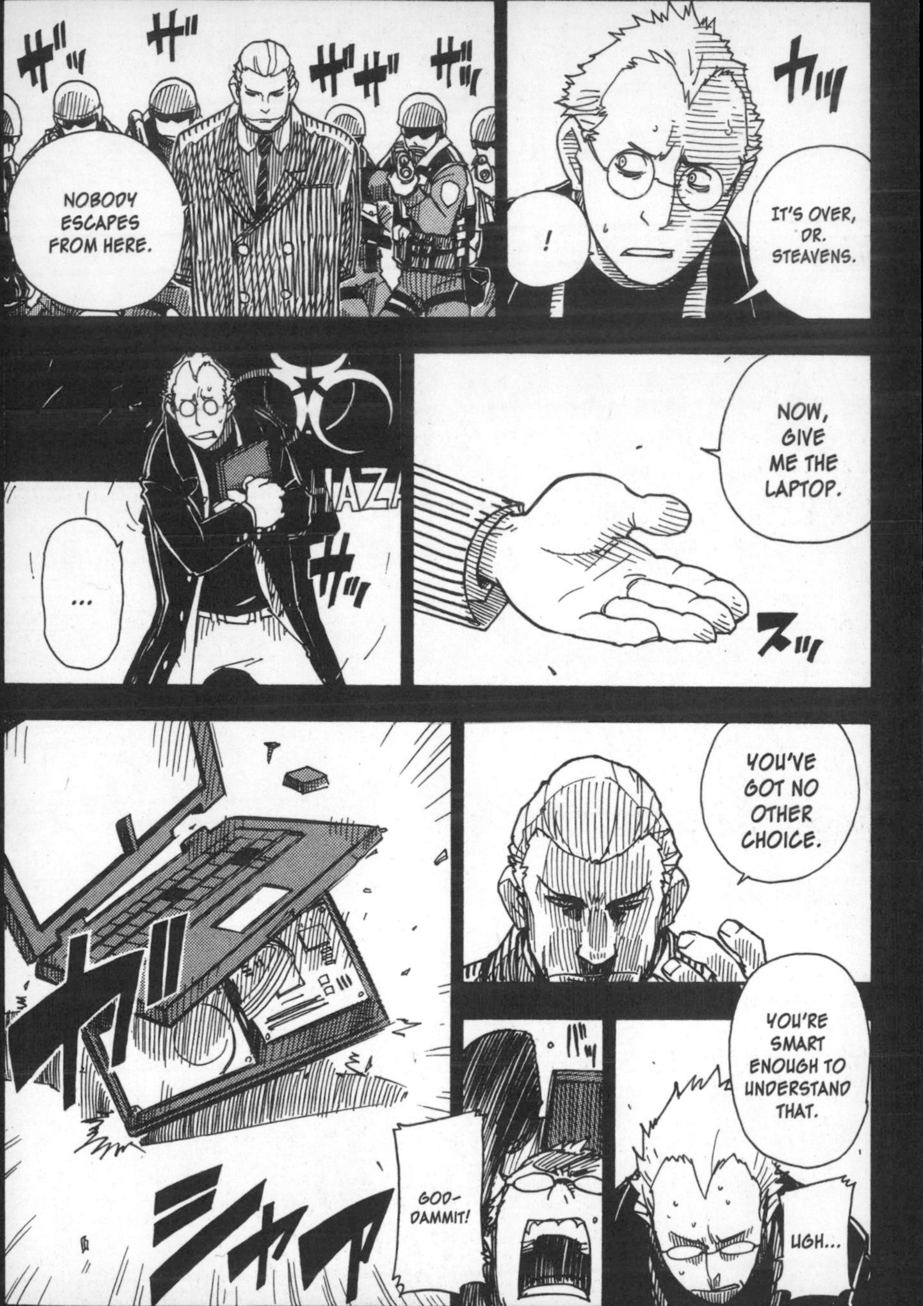
!
IT'S OVER, DR. STEAVENS.
NOBODY ESCAPES FROM HERE.
NOW, GIVE ME THE LAPTOP.
!
...
YOU'VE GOT NO OTHER CHOICE.
YOU'RE SMART ENOUGH TO UNDERSTAND THAT.
UGH...
GOD-DAMMIT!

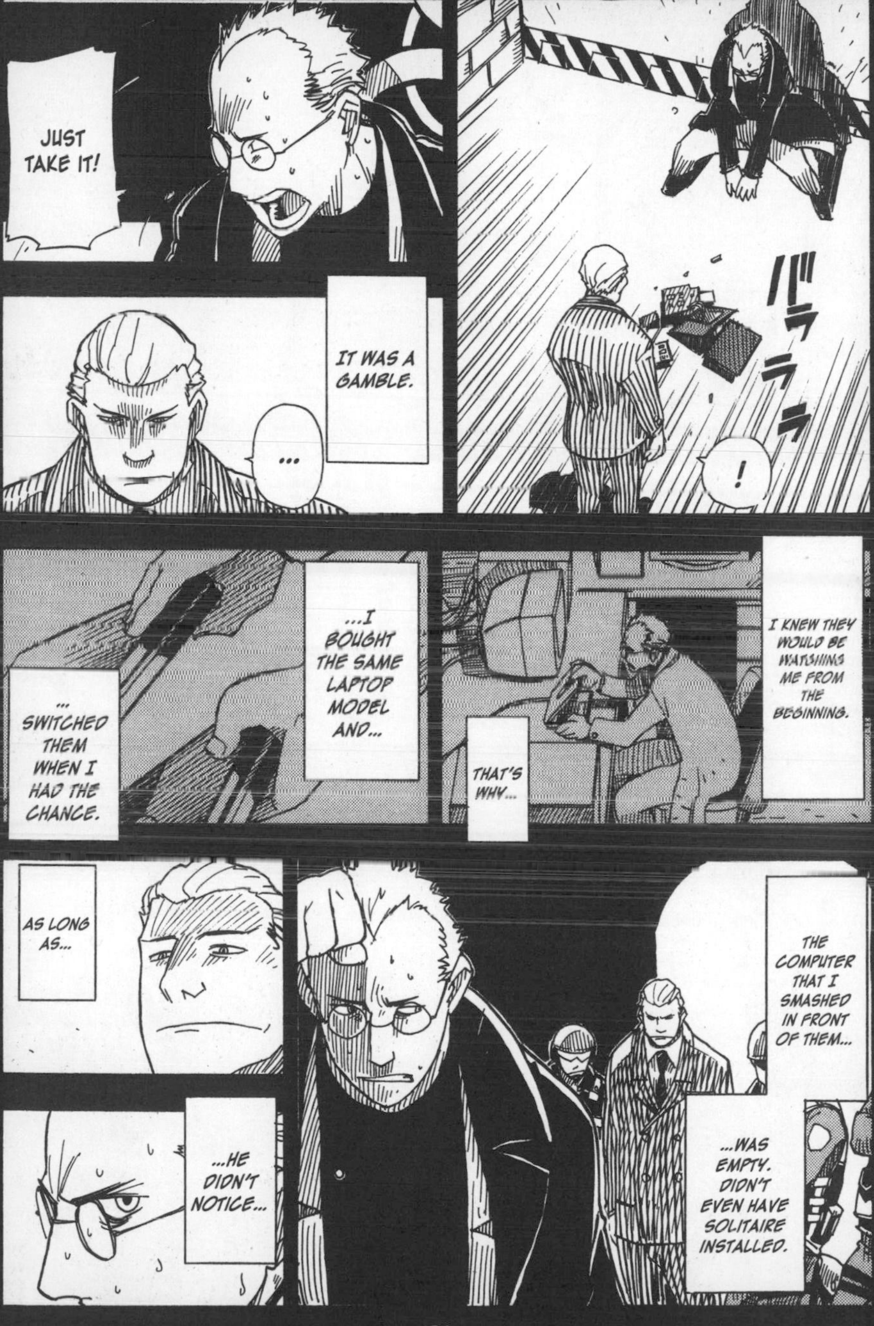
JUST TAKE IT!
IT WAS A GAMBLE.
...
!
I KNEW THEY WOULD BE WATCHING ME FROM THE BEGINNING.
THAT'S WHY...
...I BOUGHT THE SAME LAPTOP MODEL AND...
... SWITCHED THEM WHEN I HAD THE CHANCE.
THE COMPUTER THAT I SMASHED IN FRONT OF THEM...
...WAS EMPTY. DIDN'T EVEN HAVE SOLITAIRE INSTALLED.
AS LONG AS...
...HE DIDN'T NOTICE...

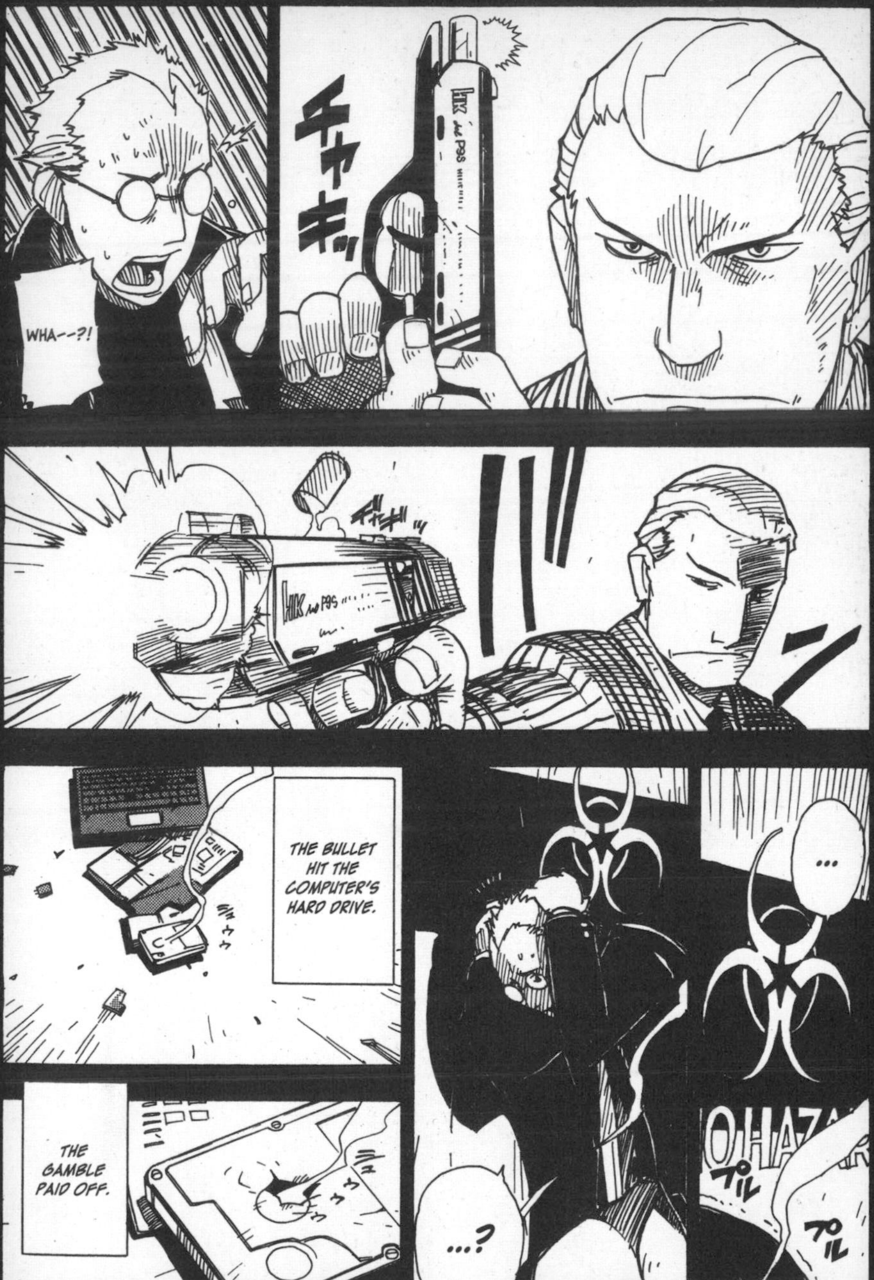
チャキッ
WHA--?!
...
...?
THE BULLET HIT THE COMPUTER'S HARD DRIVE.
THE GAMBLE PAID OFF.

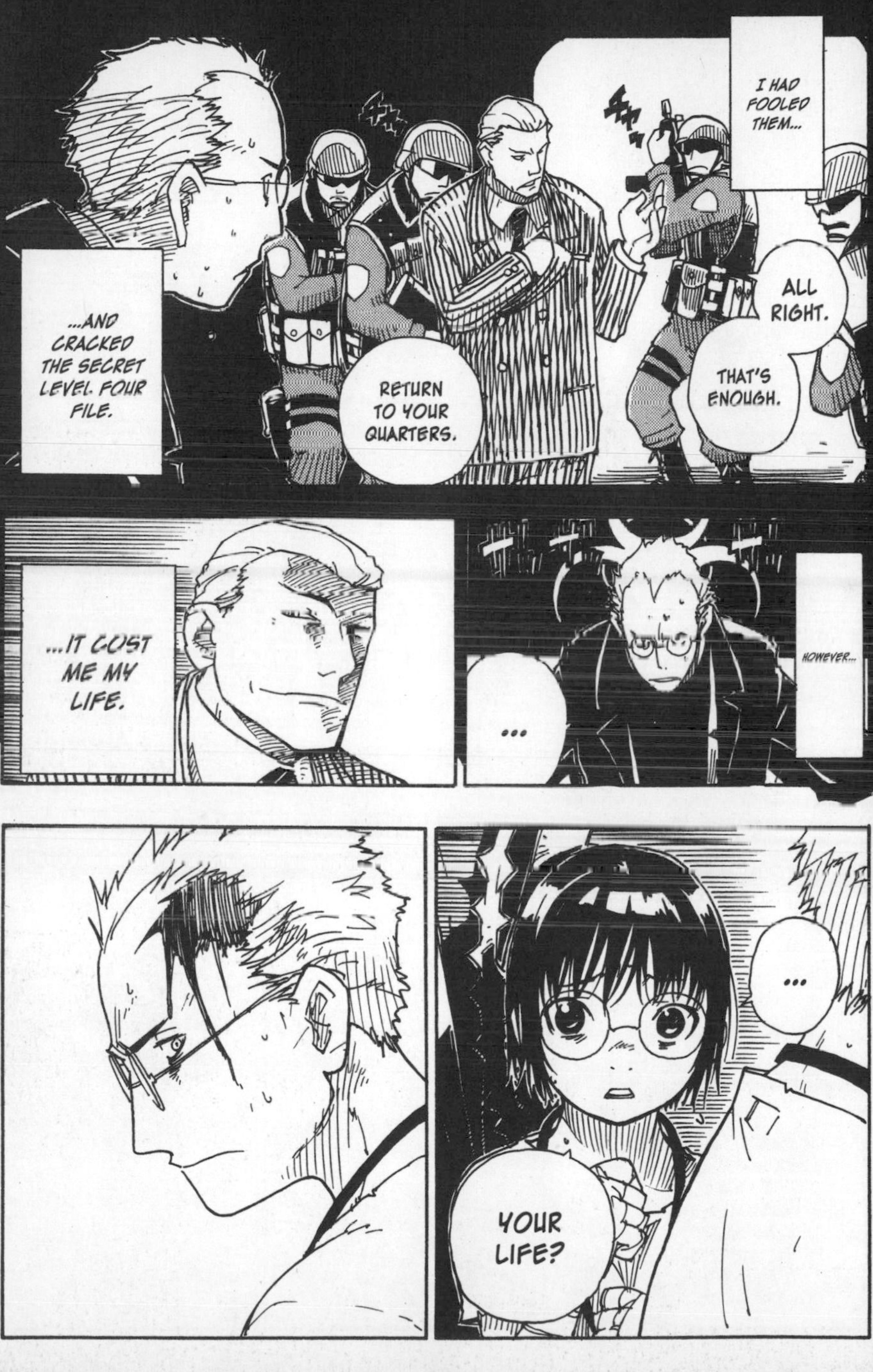
I HAD FOOLED THEM...
...AND CRACKED THE SECRET LEVEL FOUR FILE.
ALL RIGHT.
THAT'S ENOUGH.
RETURN TO YOUR QUARTERS.
HOWEVER...
...
...IT COST ME MY LIFE.
...
YOUR LIFE?

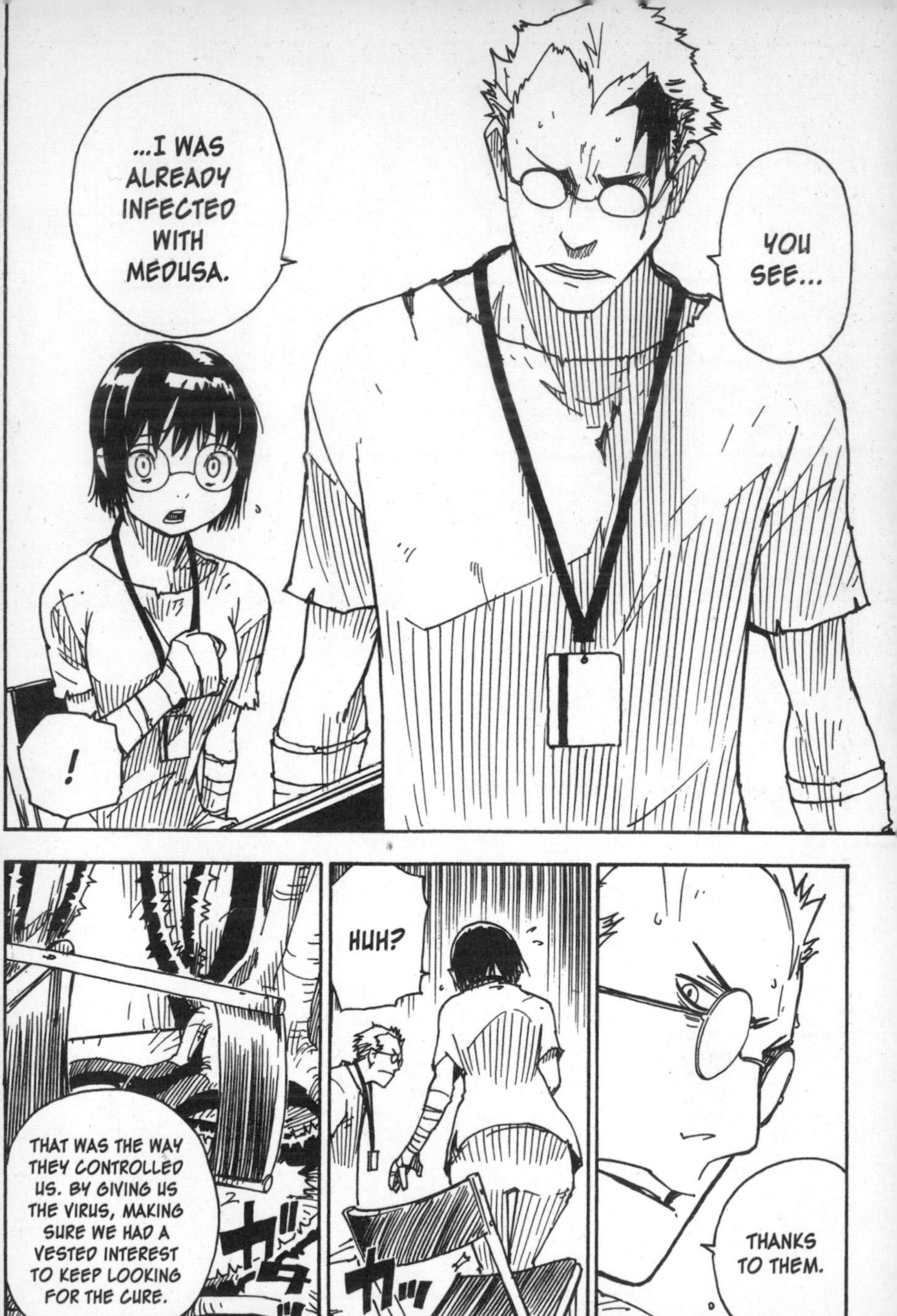
YOU SEE...
...I WAS ALREADY INFECTED WITH MEDUSA.
!
THANKS TO THEM.
HUH?
THAT WAS THE WAY THEY CONTROLLED US. BY GIVING US THE VIRUS, MAKING SURE WE HAD A VESTED INTEREST TO KEEP LOOKING FOR THE CURE.

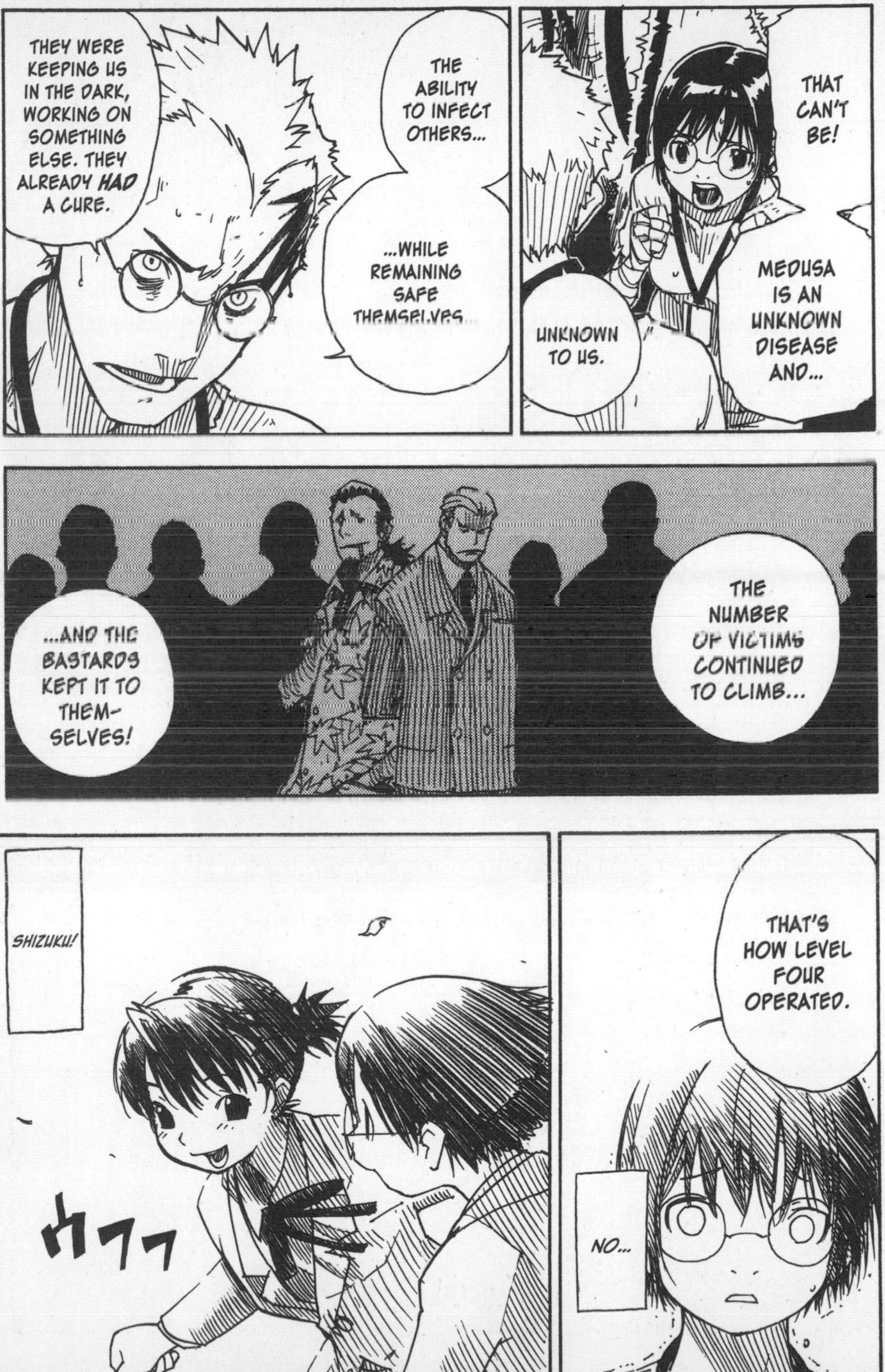
THEY WERE KEEPING US IN THE DARK, WORKING ON SOMETHING ELSE. THEY ALREADY *HAD* A CURE.
THE ABILITY TO INFECT OTHERS...
...WHILE REMAINING SAFE THEMSELVES...
THAT CAN'T BE!
MEDUSA IS AN UNKNOWN DISEASE AND...
UNKNOWN TO US.
...AND THE BASTARDS KEPT IT TO THEM-SELVES!
THE NUMBER OF VICTIMS CONTINUED TO CLIMB...
SHIZUKU!
ウフフ
THAT'S HOW LEVEL FOUR OPERATED.
NO...

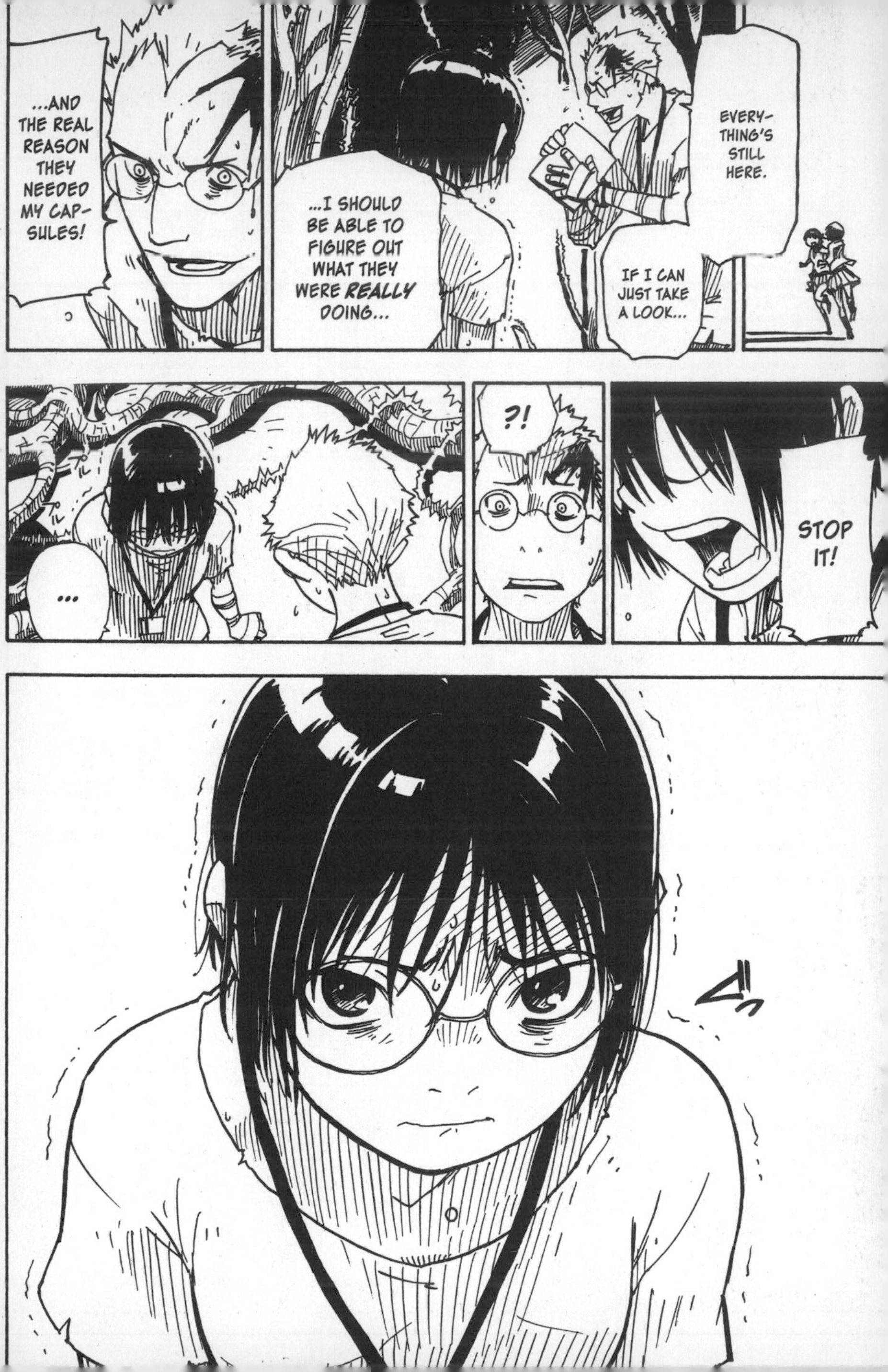
EVERY-THING'S STILL HERE.
IF I CAN JUST TAKE A LOOK...
...I SHOULD BE ABLE TO FIGURE OUT WHAT THEY WERE REALLY DOING...
...AND THE REAL REASON THEY NEEDED MY CAP-SULES!
STOP IT!
?!
...

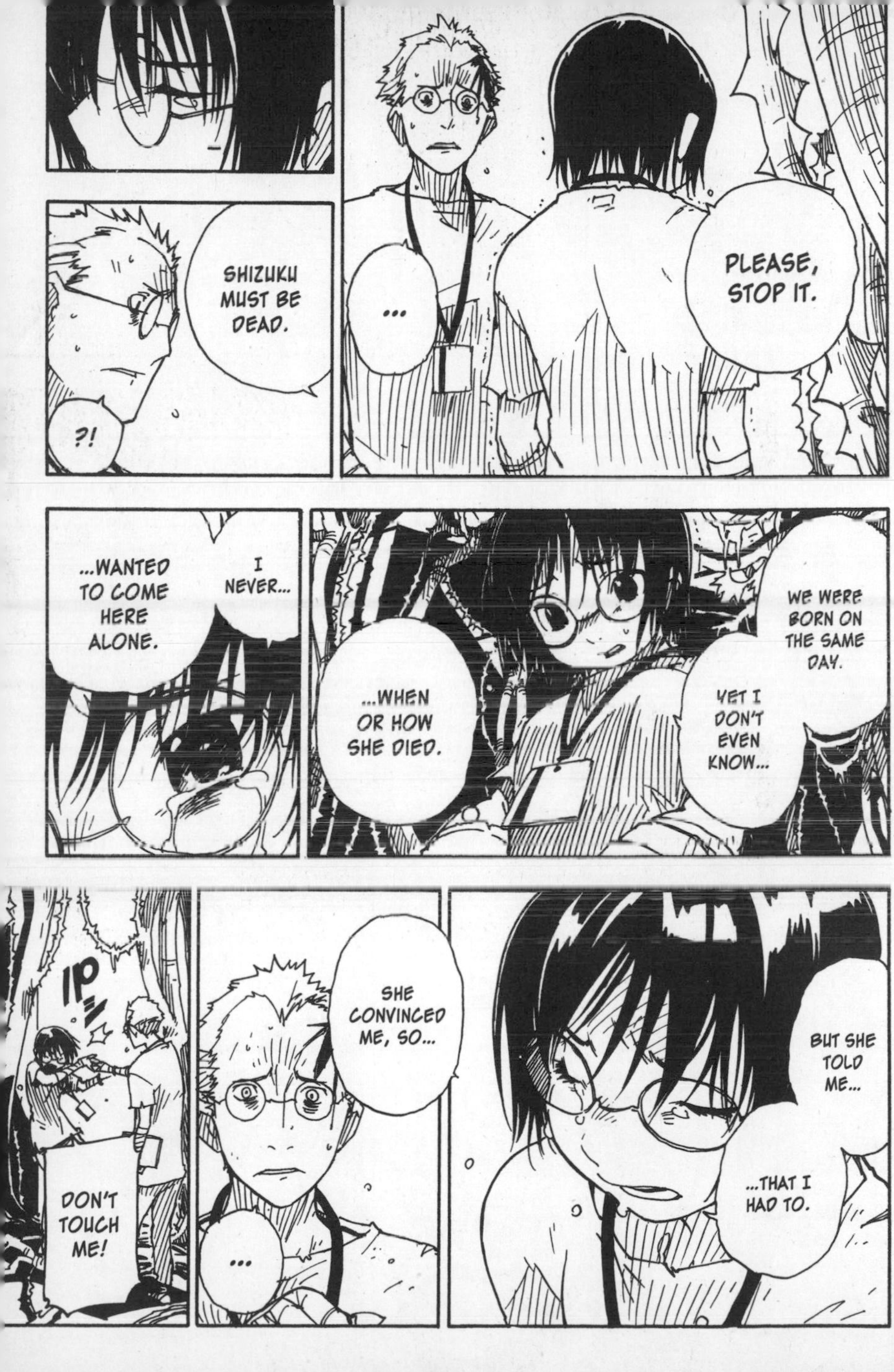
PLEASE, STOP IT.
...
SHIZUKU MUST BE DEAD.
?!
WE WERE BORN ON THE SAME DAY.
YET I DON'T EVEN KNOW...
...WHEN OR HOW SHE DIED.
I NEVER...
...WANTED TO COME HERE ALONE.
BUT SHE TOLD ME...
...THAT I HAD TO.
SHE CONVINCED ME, SO...
...
DON'T TOUCH ME!

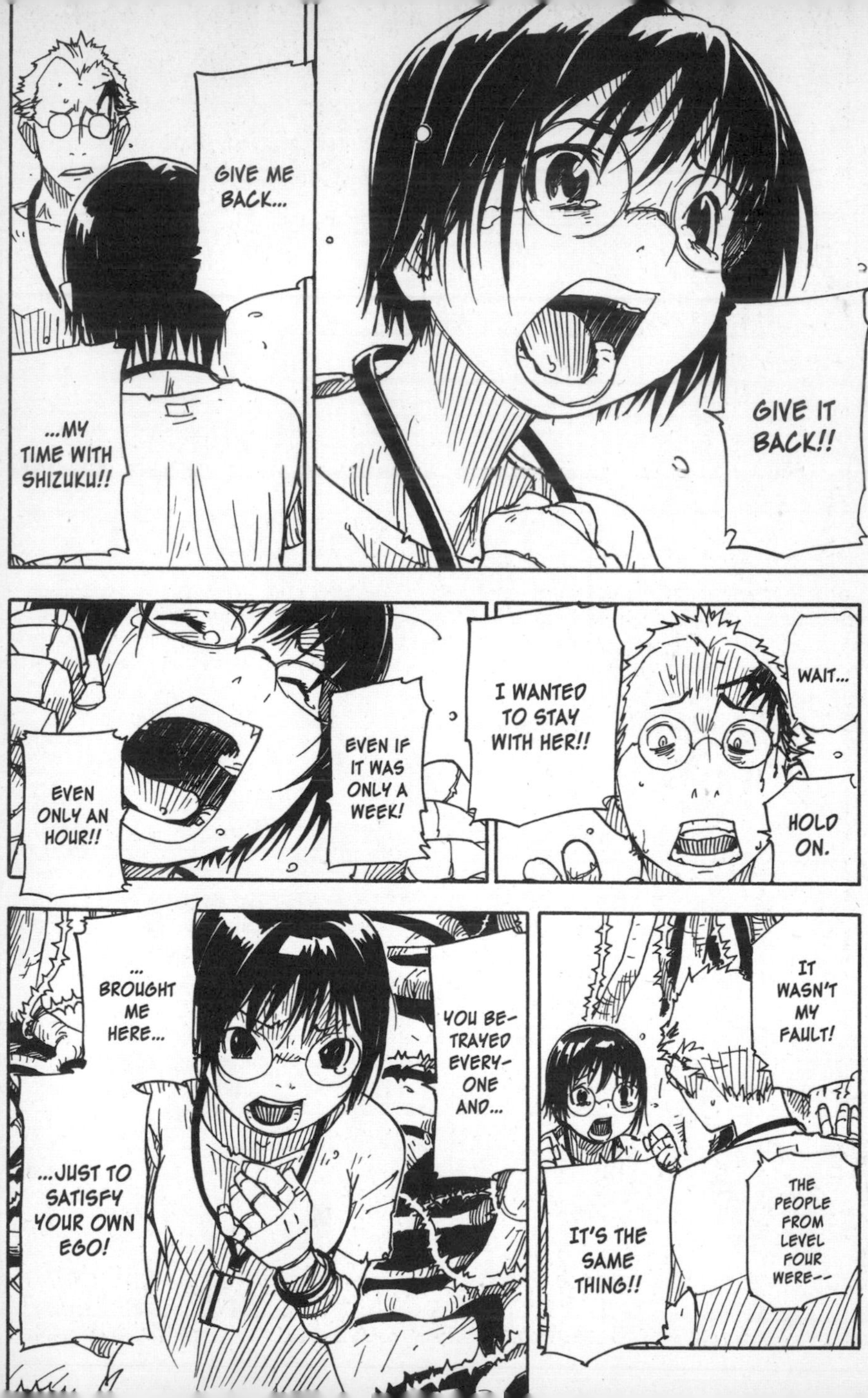
GIVE IT BACK!!
GIVE ME BACK...
...MY TIME WITH SHIZUKU!!
WAIT...
HOLD ON.
I WANTED TO STAY WITH HER!!
EVEN IF IT WAS ONLY A WEEK!
EVEN ONLY AN HOUR!!
IT WASN'T MY FAULT!
THE PEOPLE FROM LEVEL FOUR WERE--
IT'S THE SAME THING!!
YOU BE-TRAYED EVERY-ONE AND...
...BROUGHT ME HERE...
...JUST TO SATISFY YOUR OWN EGO!

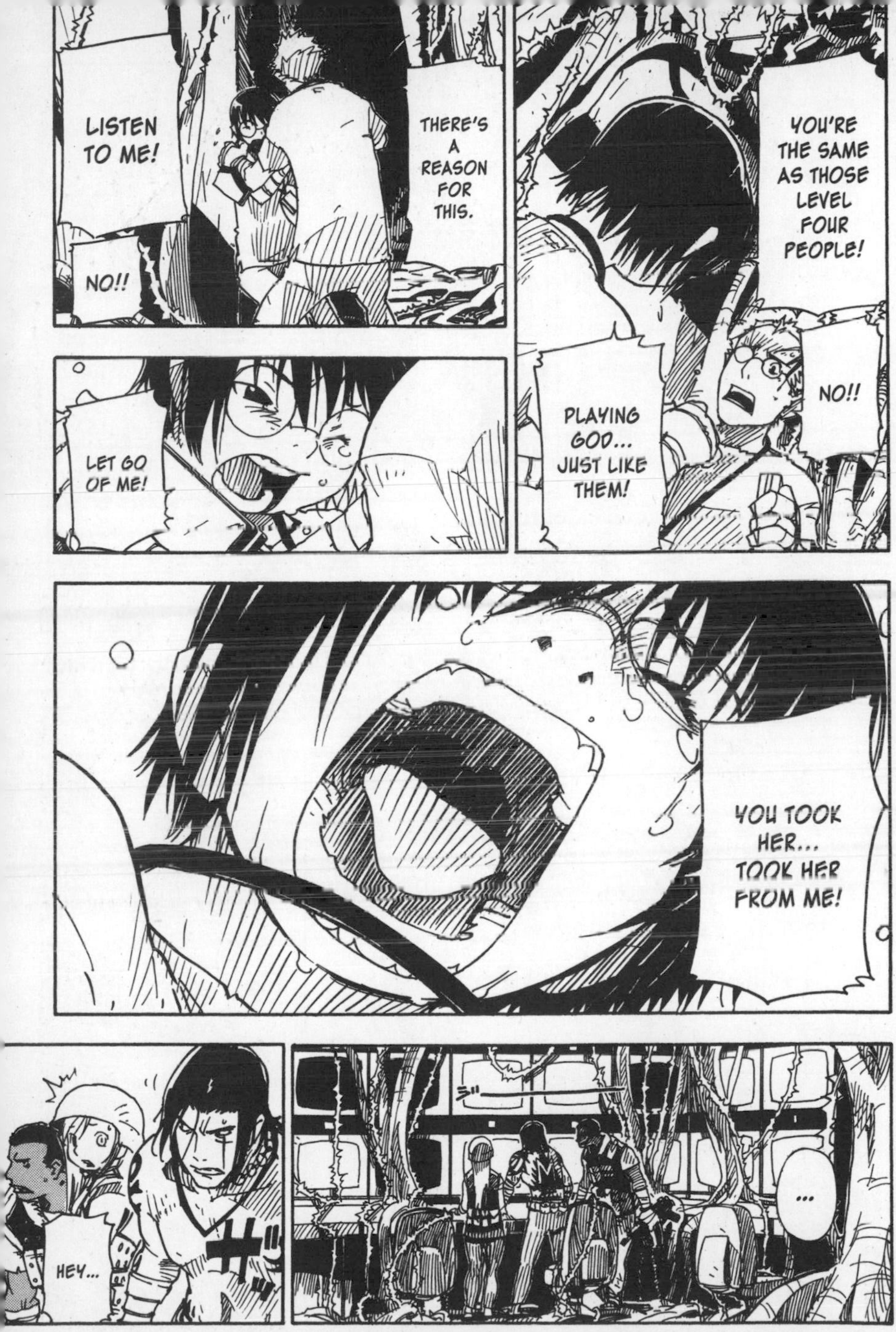
YOU'RE THE SAME AS THOSE LEVEL FOUR PEOPLE!
PLAYING GOD... JUST LIKE THEM!
NO!!
THERE'S A REASON FOR THIS.
LISTEN TO ME!
NO!!
LET GO OF ME!
YOU TOOK HER... TOOK HER FROM ME!
...
HEY...

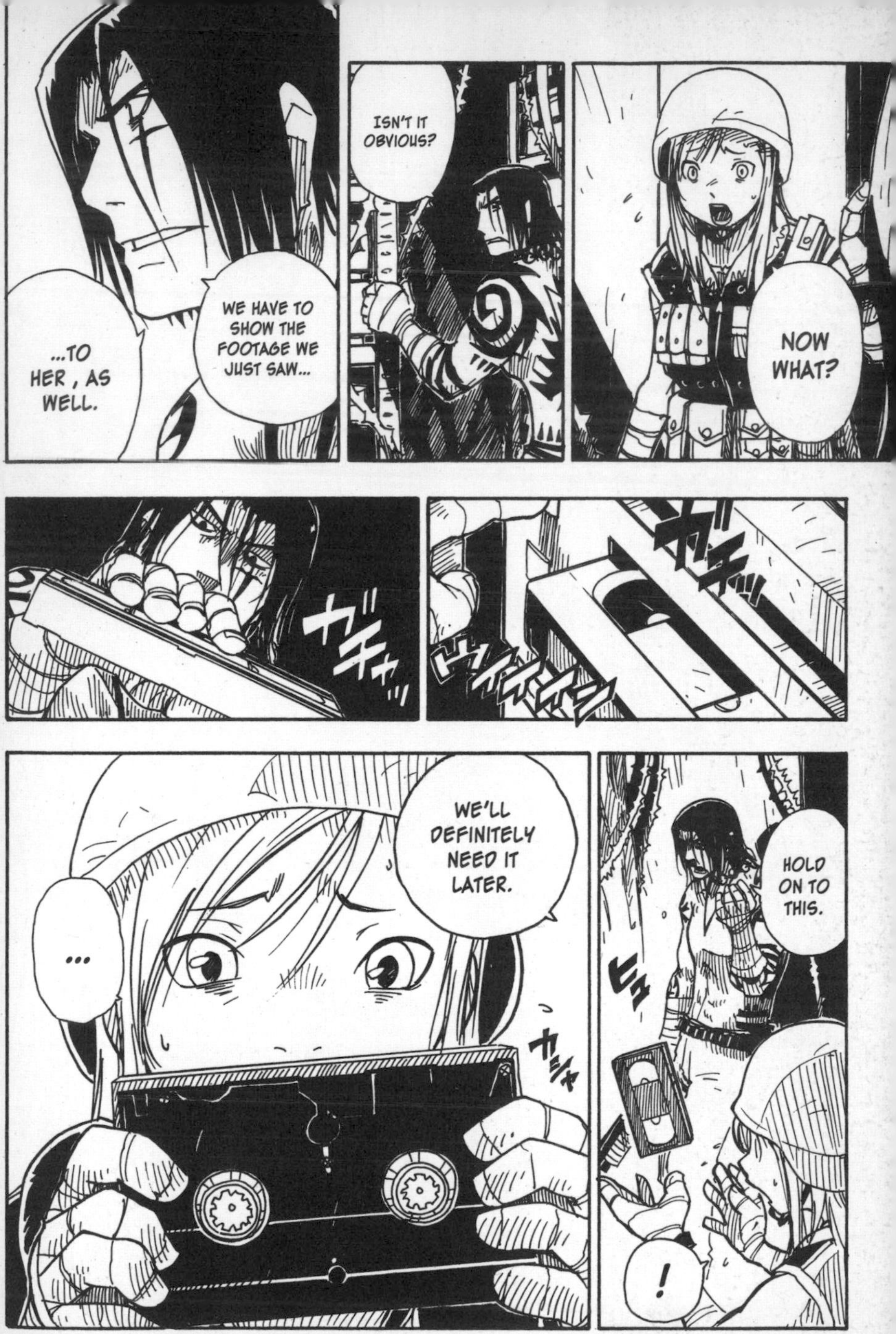
NOW WHAT?
ISN'T IT OBVIOUS?
WE HAVE TO SHOW THE FOOTAGE WE JUST SAW...
...TO HER , AS WELL.
HOLD ON TO THIS.
!
WE'LL DEFINITELY NEED IT LATER.
...

CHAPTER 10
THE BEAT OF BATTLE

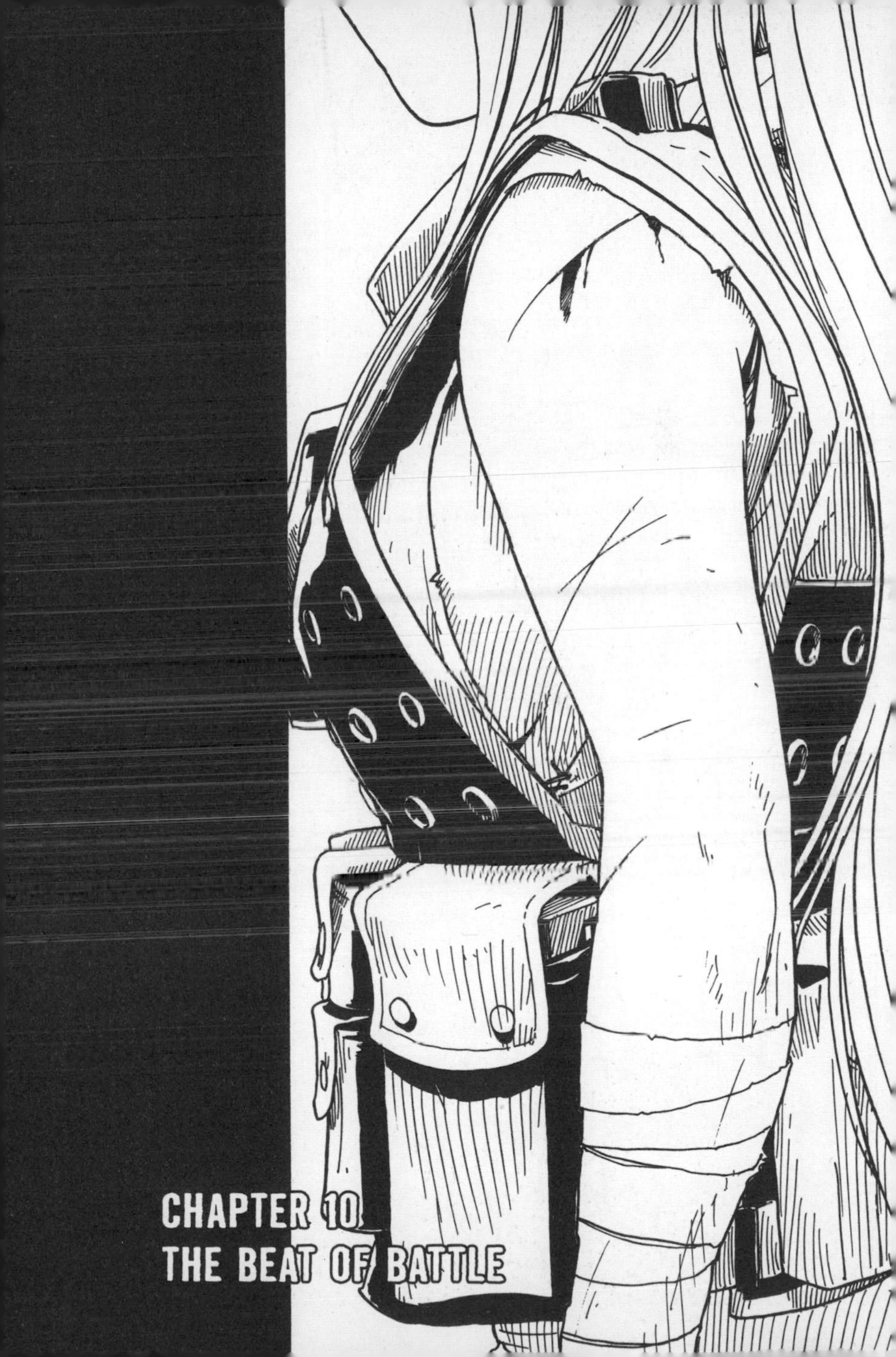

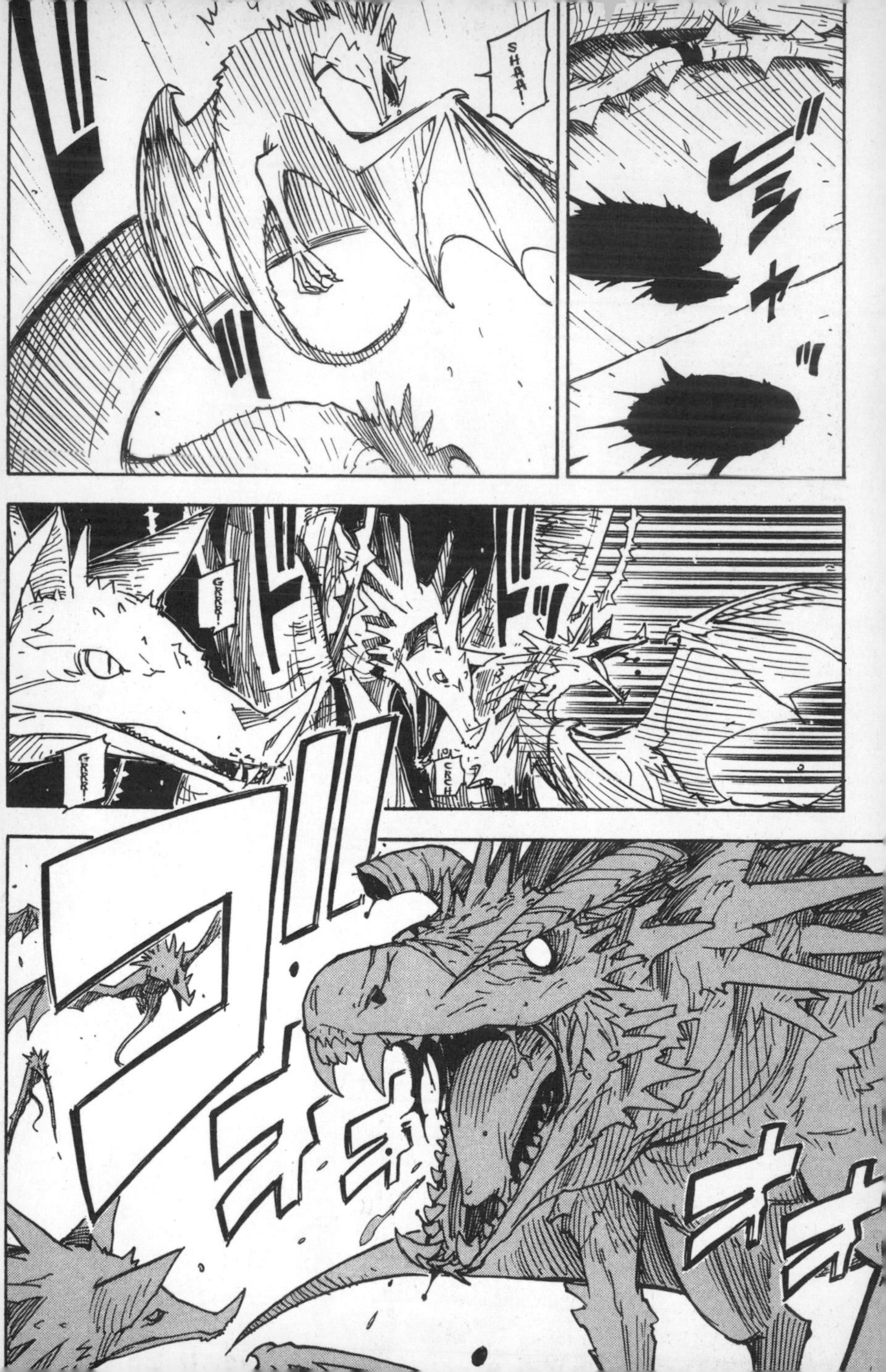
SHAAA!
GRRR!
GRRR!
CRCH

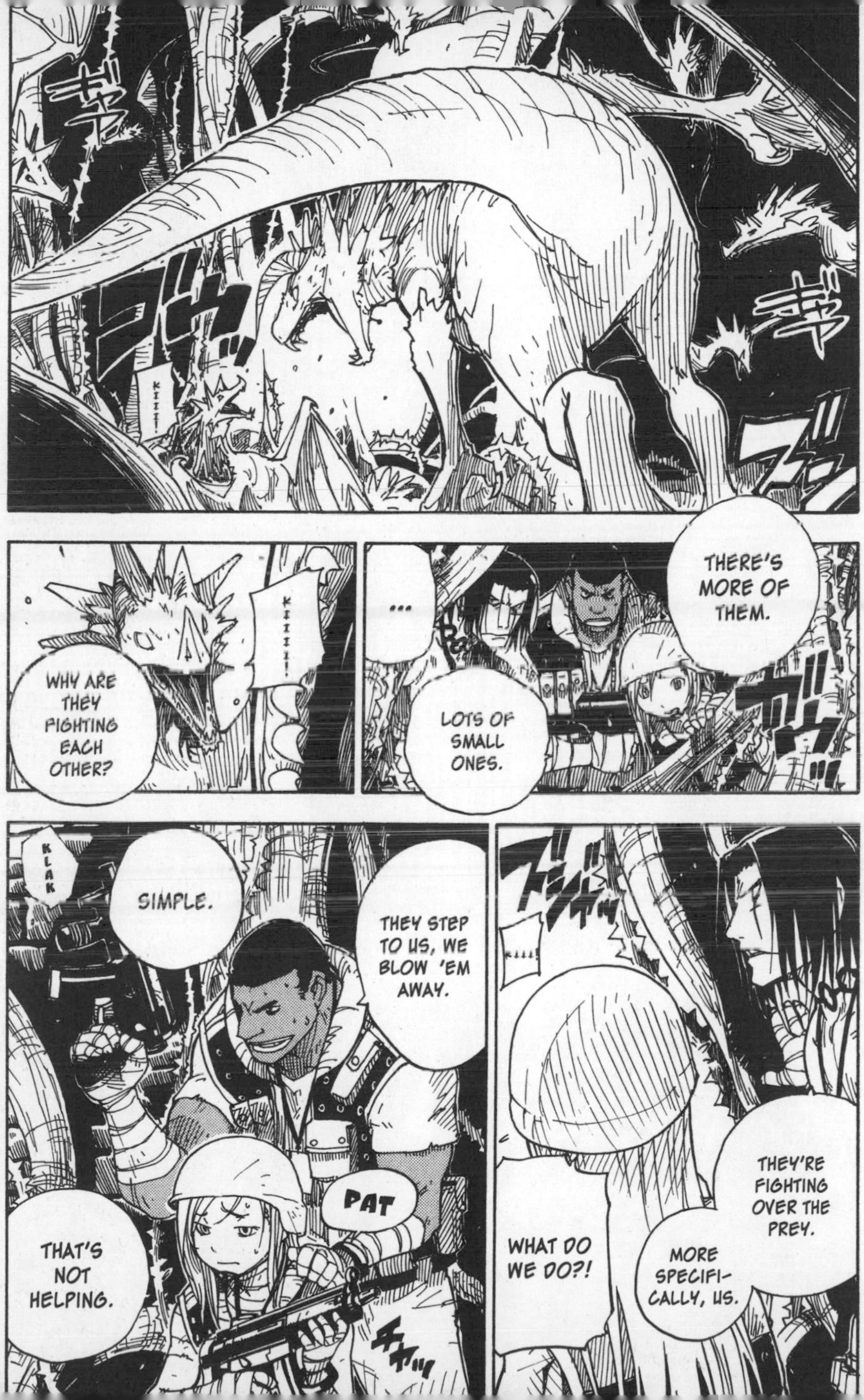
KIII!
THERE'S MORE OF THEM.
...
LOTS OF SMALL ONES.
KIIII!
WHY ARE THEY FIGHTING EACH OTHER?
KIII!
THEY'RE FIGHTING OVER THE PREY.
MORE SPECIFI-CALLY, US.
WHAT DO WE DO?!
KLAK
SIMPLE.
THEY STEP TO US, WE BLOW 'EM AWAY.
PAT
THAT'S NOT HELPING.

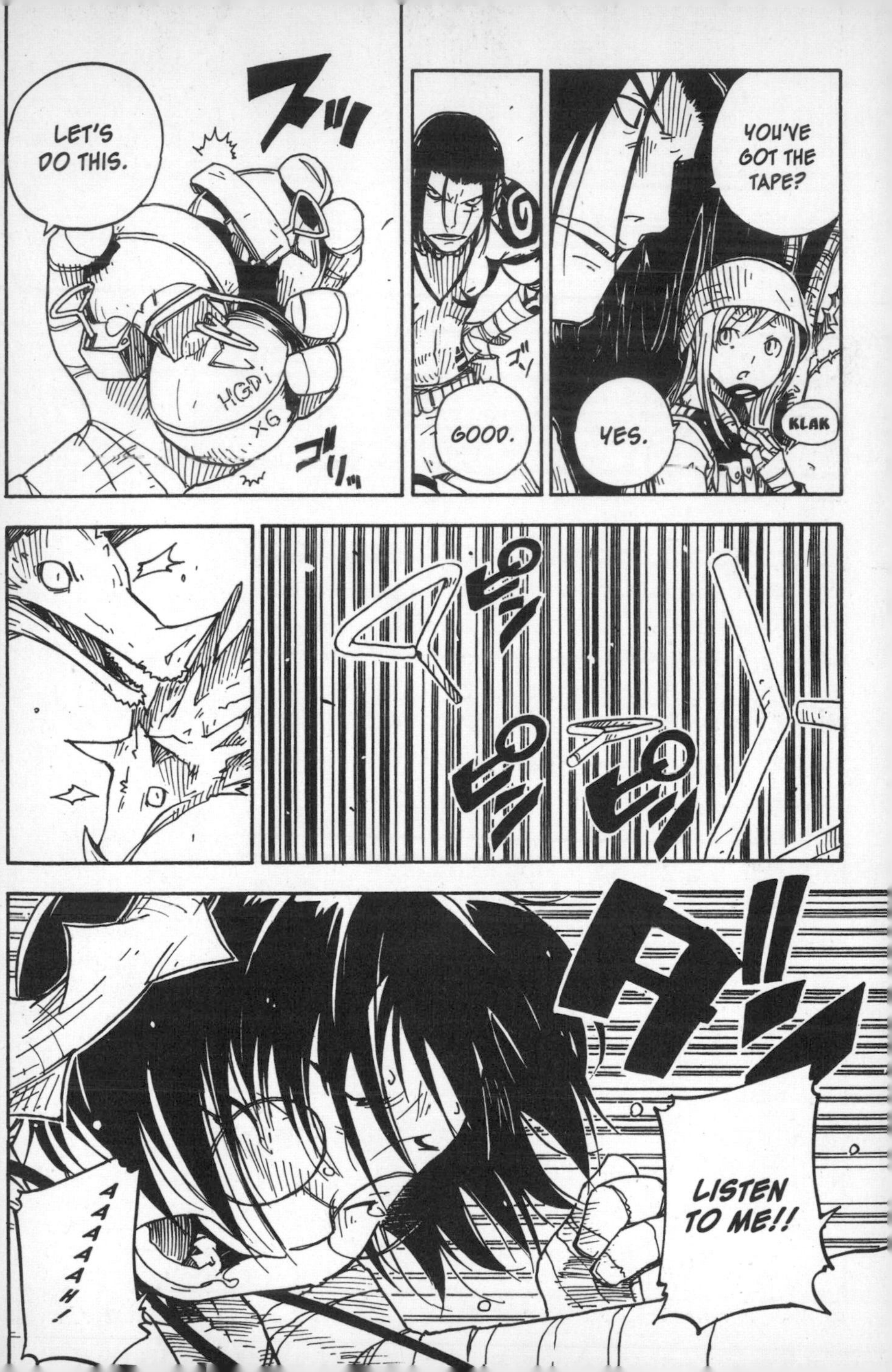
YOU'VE GOT THE TAPE?
YES.
KLAK
GOOD.
LET'S DO THIS.
HGDi
x6
LISTEN TO ME!!
AAAAAAH!

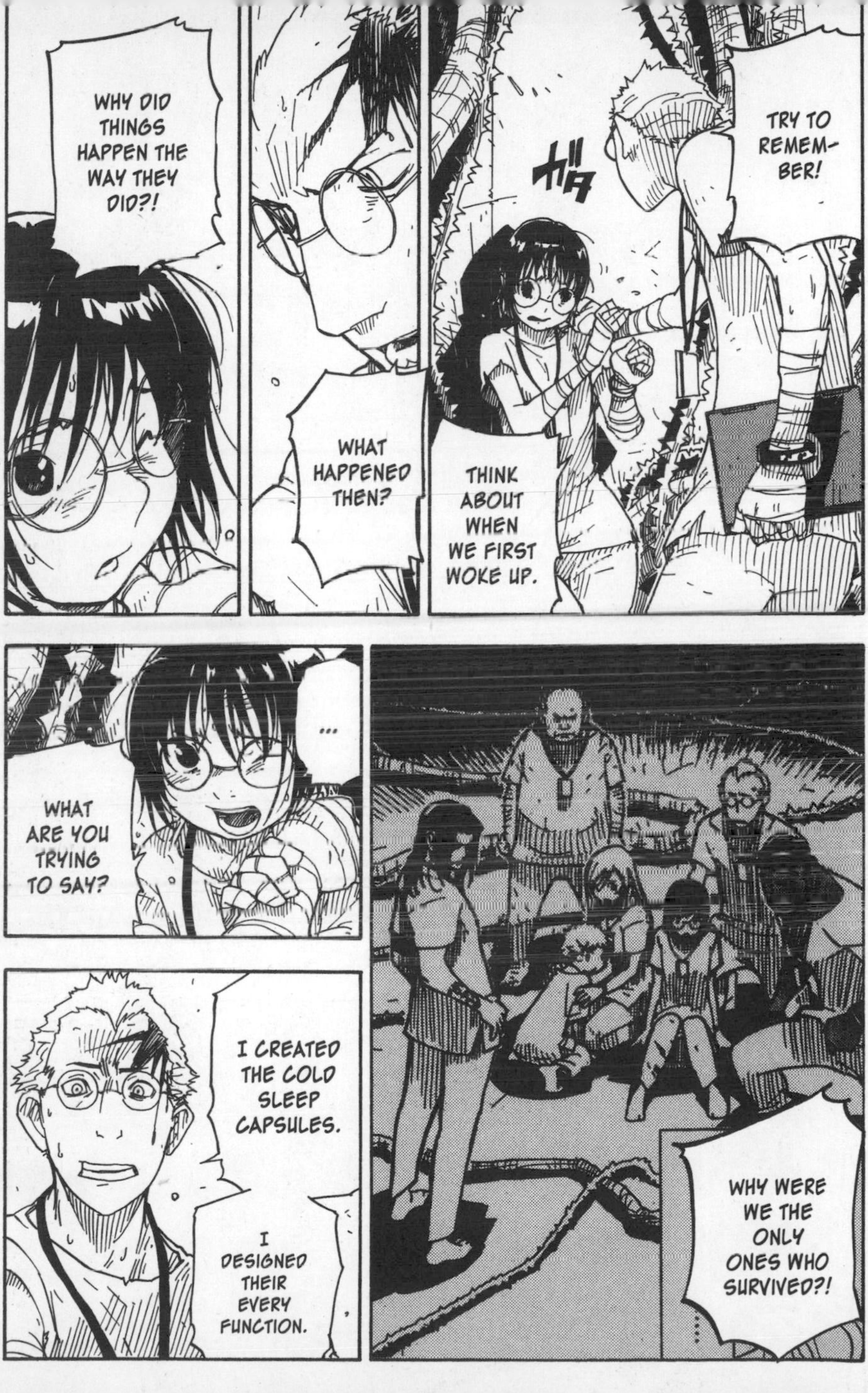
TRY TO REMEMBER!
ガタ
THINK ABOUT WHEN WE FIRST WOKE UP.
WHAT HAPPENED THEN?
WHY DID THINGS HAPPEN THE WAY THEY DID?!
WHY WERE WE THE ONLY ONES WHO SURVIVED?!
...
WHAT ARE YOU TRYING TO SAY?
I CREATED THE COLD SLEEP CAPSULES.
I DESIGNED THEIR EVERY FUNCTION.

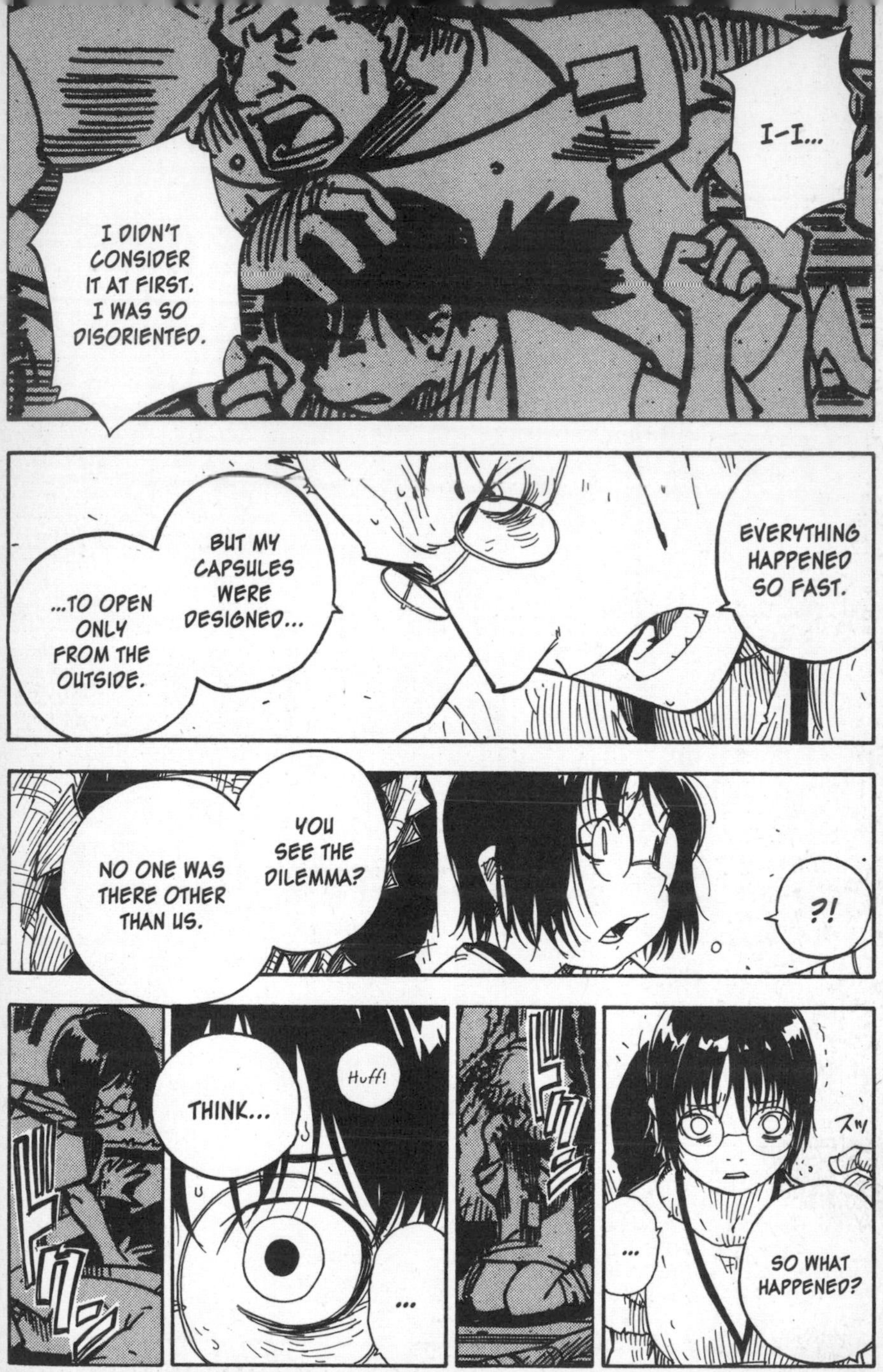
I-I...
I DIDN'T CONSIDER IT AT FIRST. I WAS SO DISORIENTED.
EVERYTHING HAPPENED SO FAST.
BUT MY CAPSULES WERE DESIGNED...
...TO OPEN ONLY FROM THE OUTSIDE.
?!
YOU SEE THE DILEMMA?
NO ONE WAS THERE OTHER THAN US.
ズッ
SO WHAT HAPPENED?
...
...
Huff!
THINK...

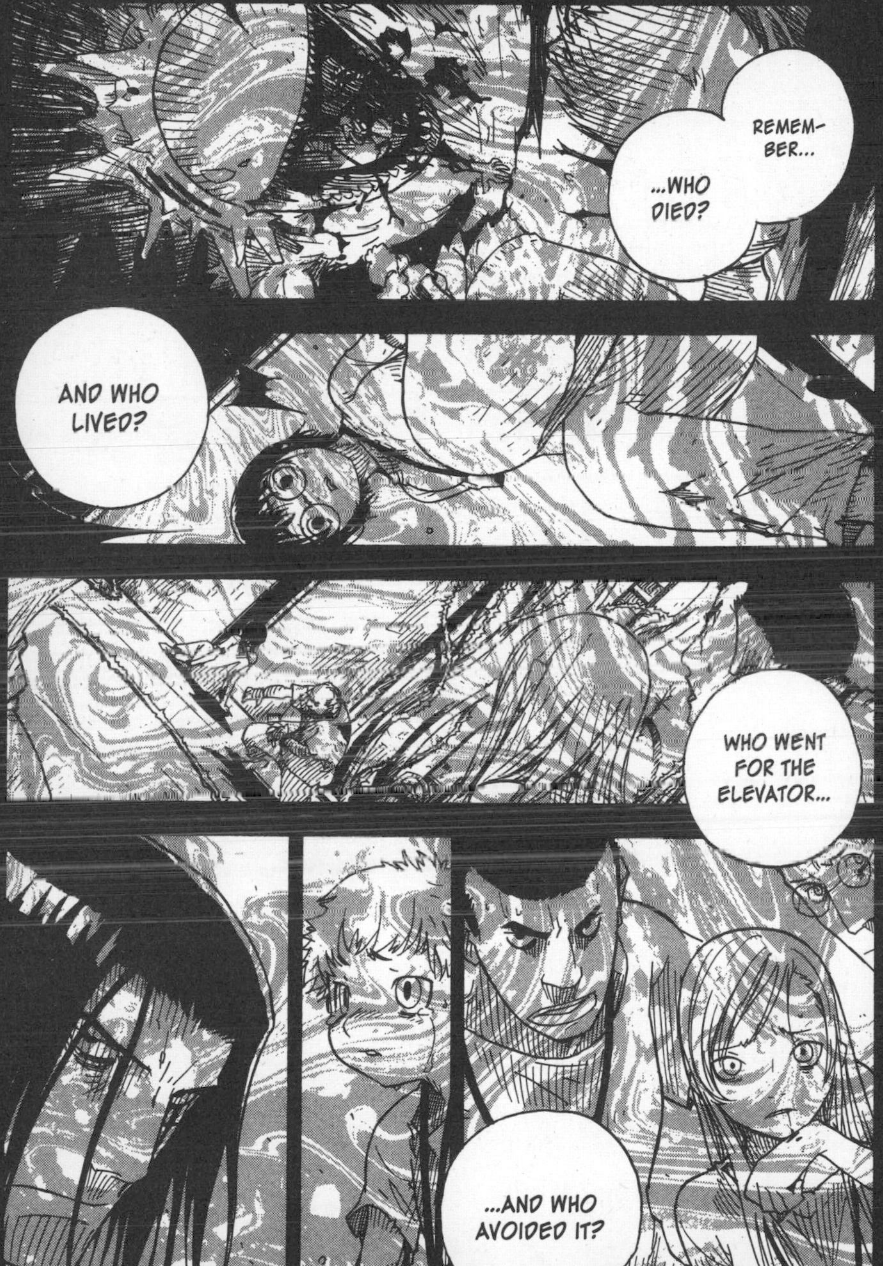
REMEMBER...
...WHO DIED?
AND WHO LIVED?
WHO WENT FOR THE ELEVATOR...
...AND WHO AVOIDED IT?

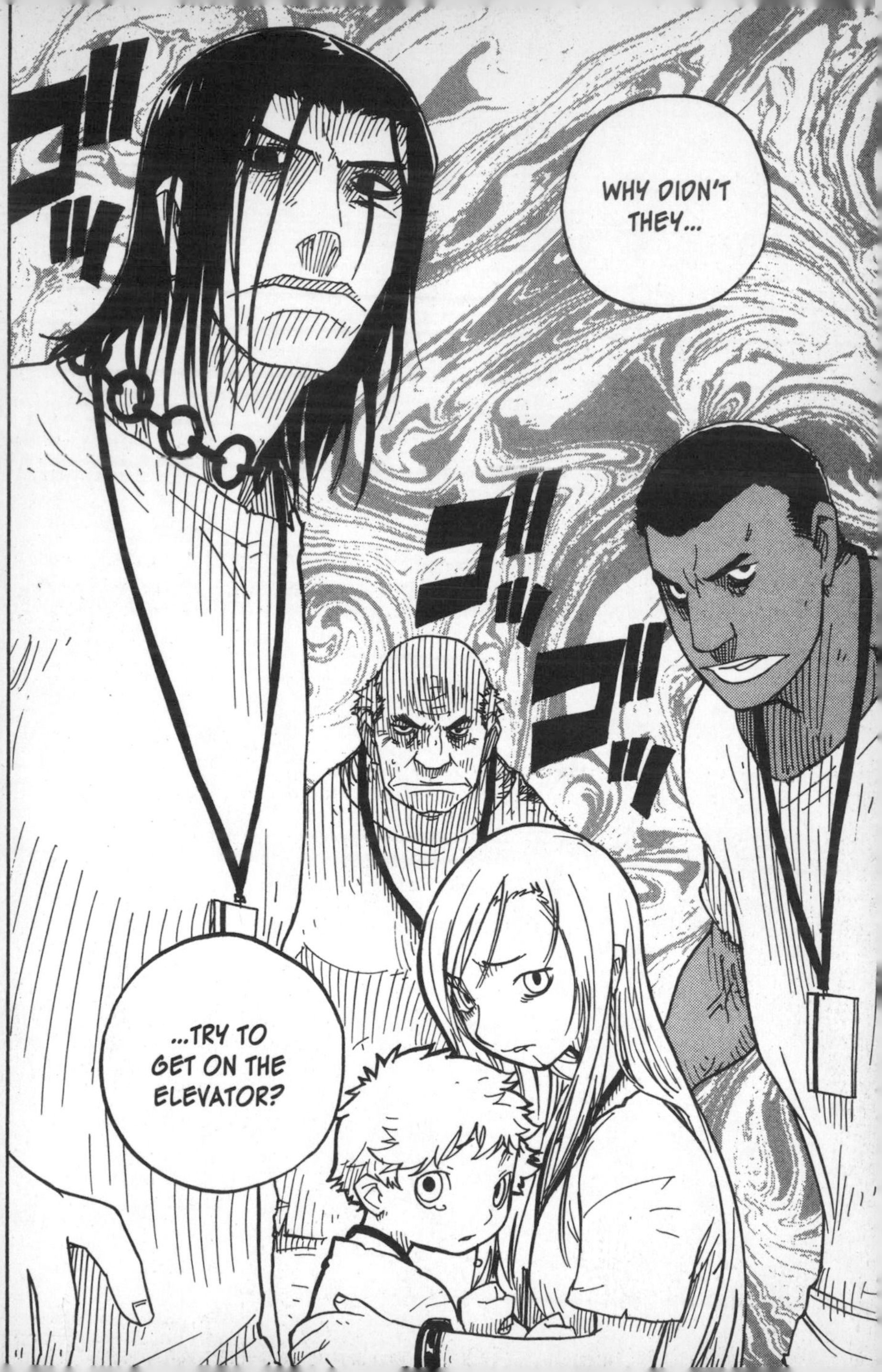
WHY DIDN'T THEY...
...TRY TO GET ON THE ELEVATOR?

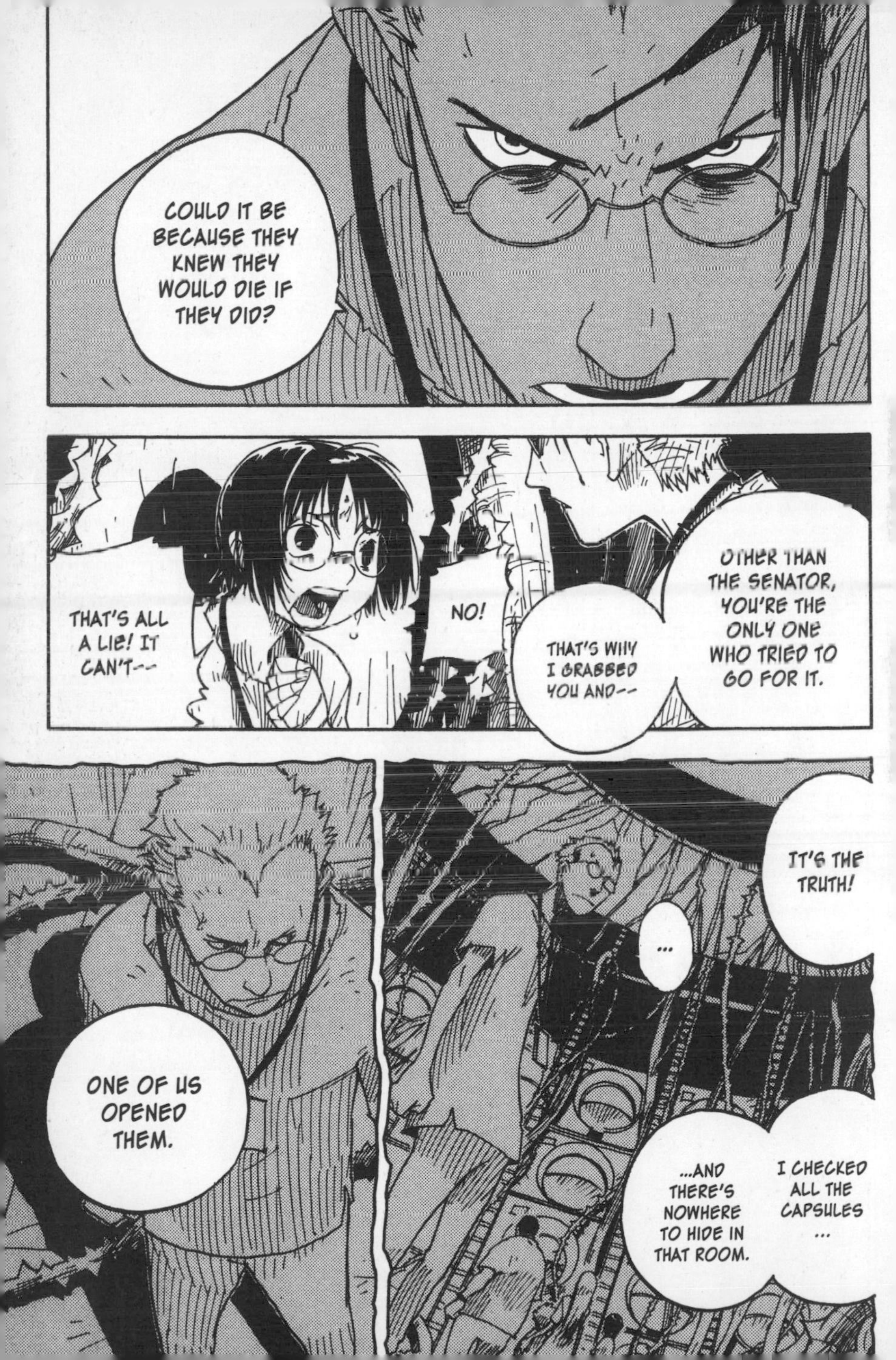
COULD IT BE BECAUSE THEY KNEW THEY WOULD DIE IF THEY DID?
OTHER THAN THE SENATOR, YOU'RE THE ONLY ONE WHO TRIED TO GO FOR IT.
THAT'S WHY I GRABBED YOU AND--
NO!
THAT'S ALL A LIE! IT CAN'T--
IT'S THE TRUTH!
...
I CHECKED ALL THE CAPSULES ...
...AND THERE'S NOWHERE TO HIDE IN THAT ROOM.
ONE OF US OPENED THEM.

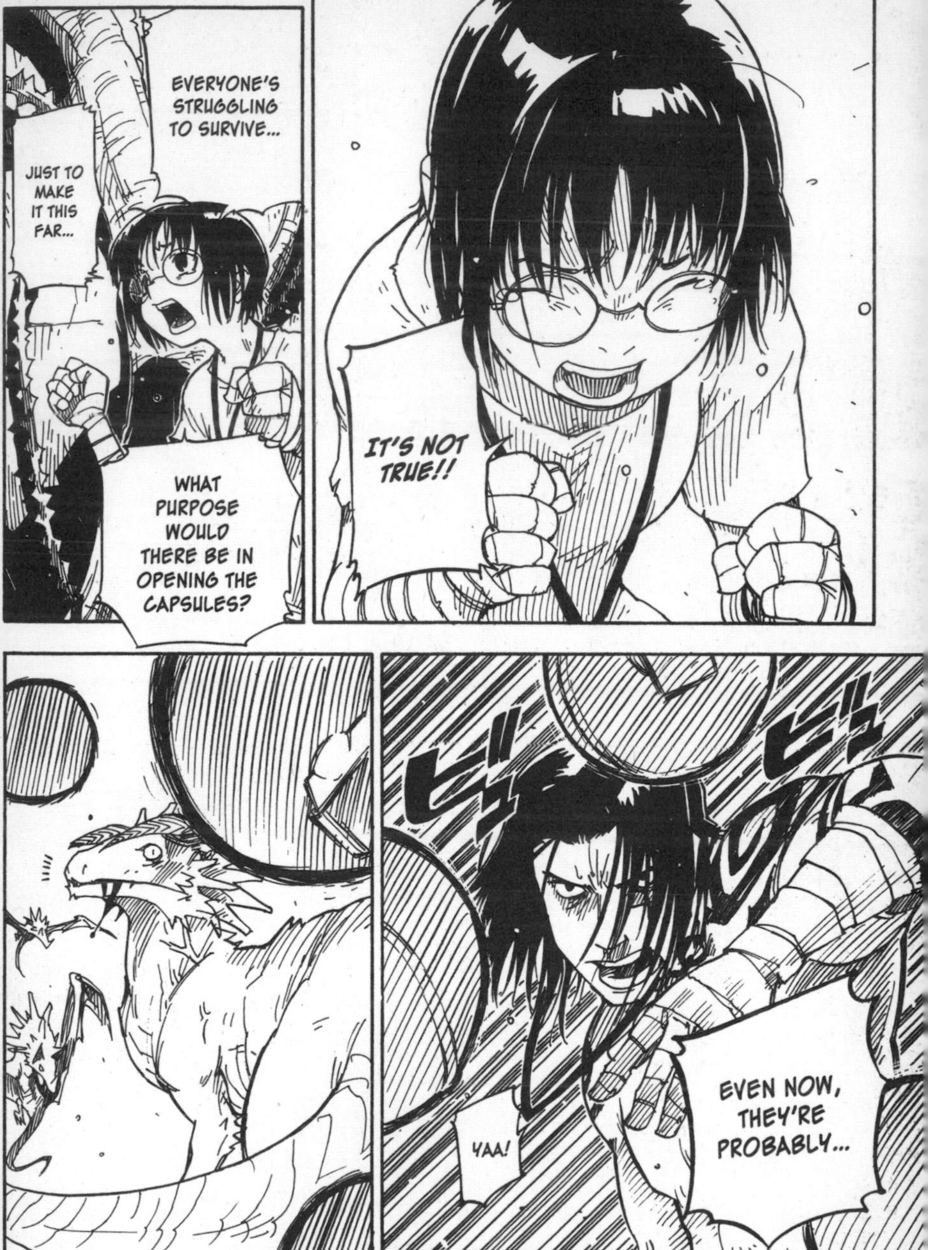
IT'S NOT TRUE!!
EVERYONE'S STRUGGLING TO SURVIVE...
JUST TO MAKE IT THIS FAR...
WHAT PURPOSE WOULD THERE BE IN OPENING THE CAPSULES?
EVEN NOW, THEY'RE PROBABLY...
YAA!

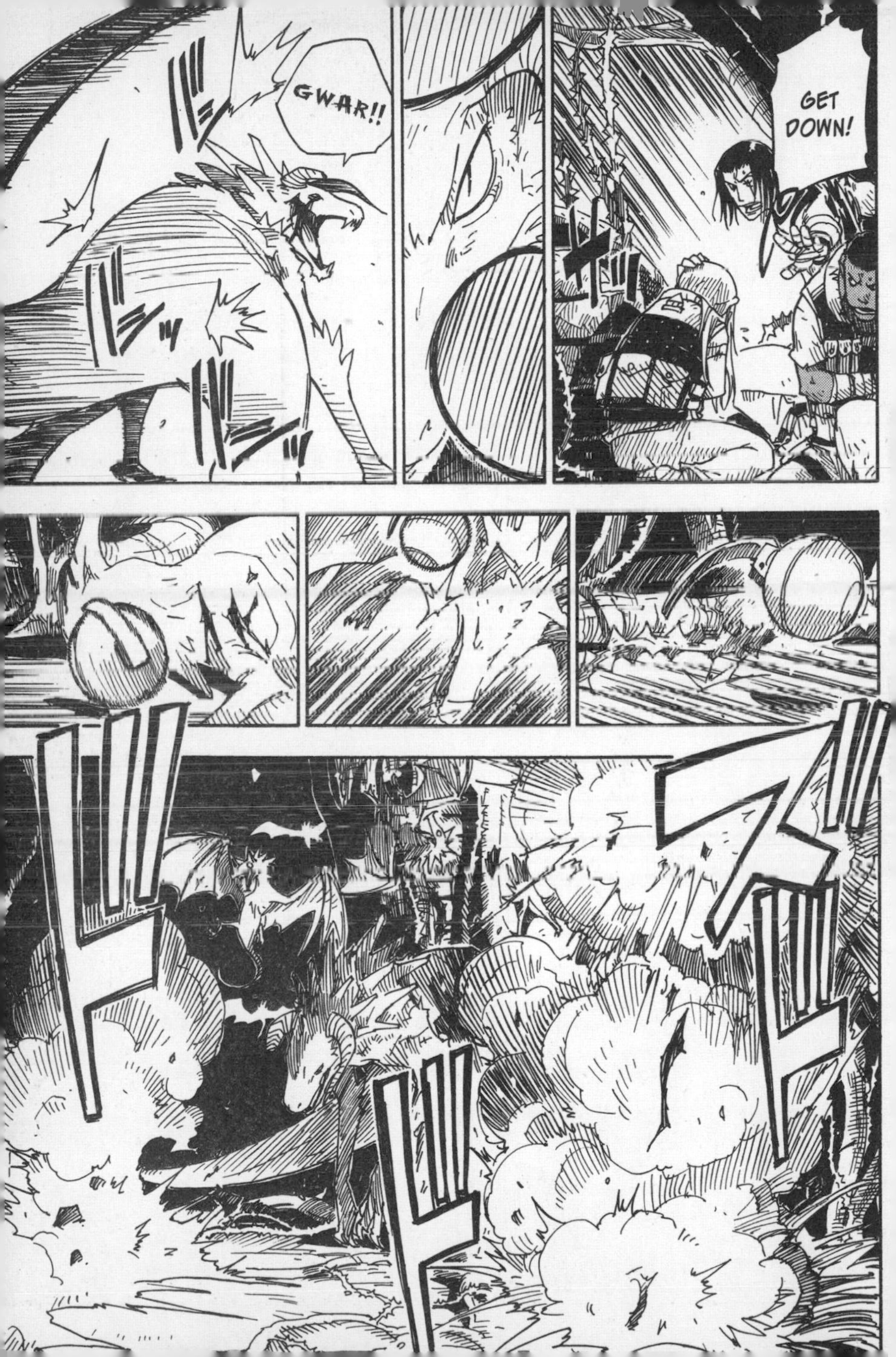
GWAR!!
GET DOWN!

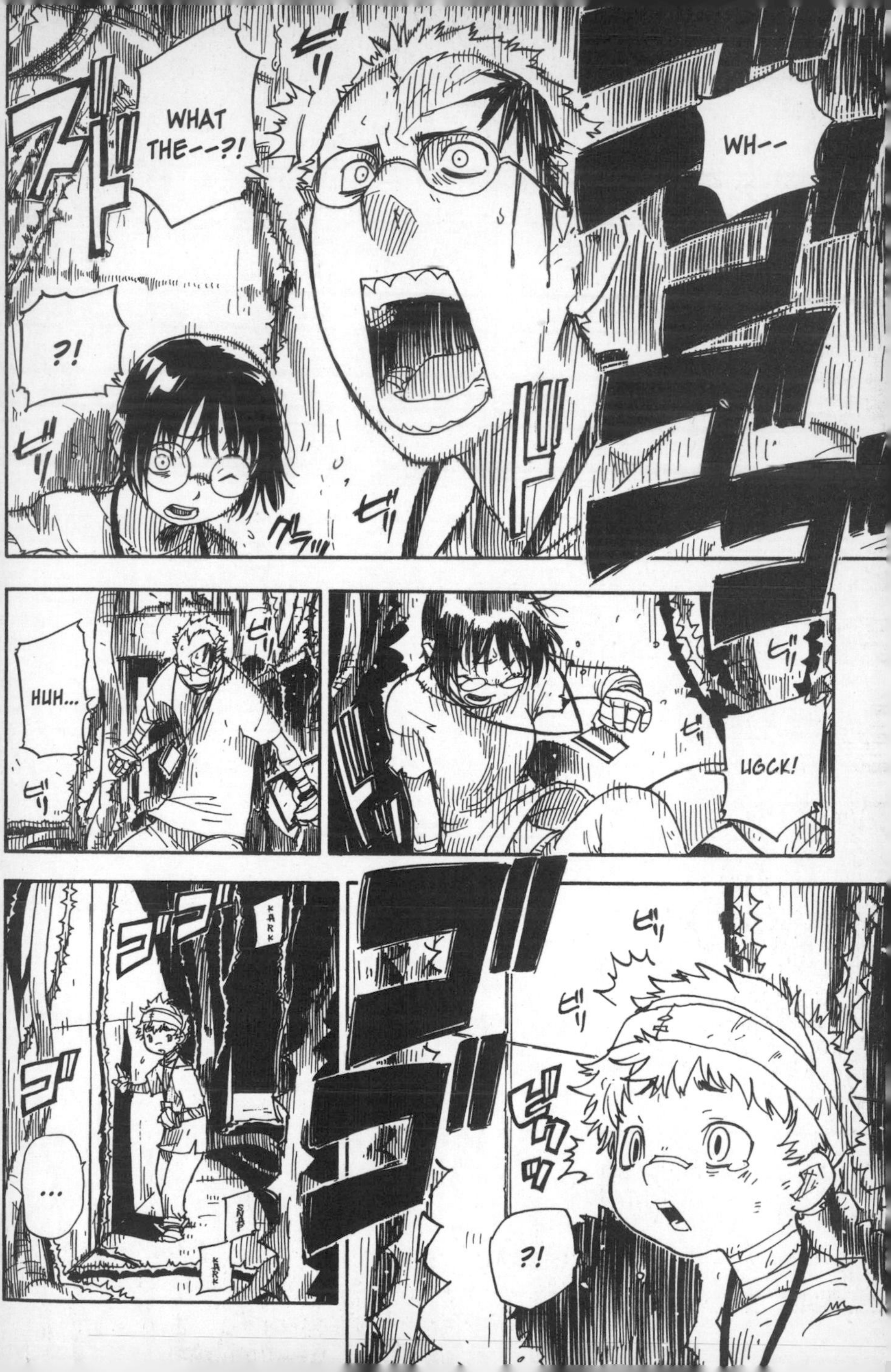
WH--
WHAT THE--?!
?!
UGCK!
HUH...
?!
KARK
...
SNAP
KARK

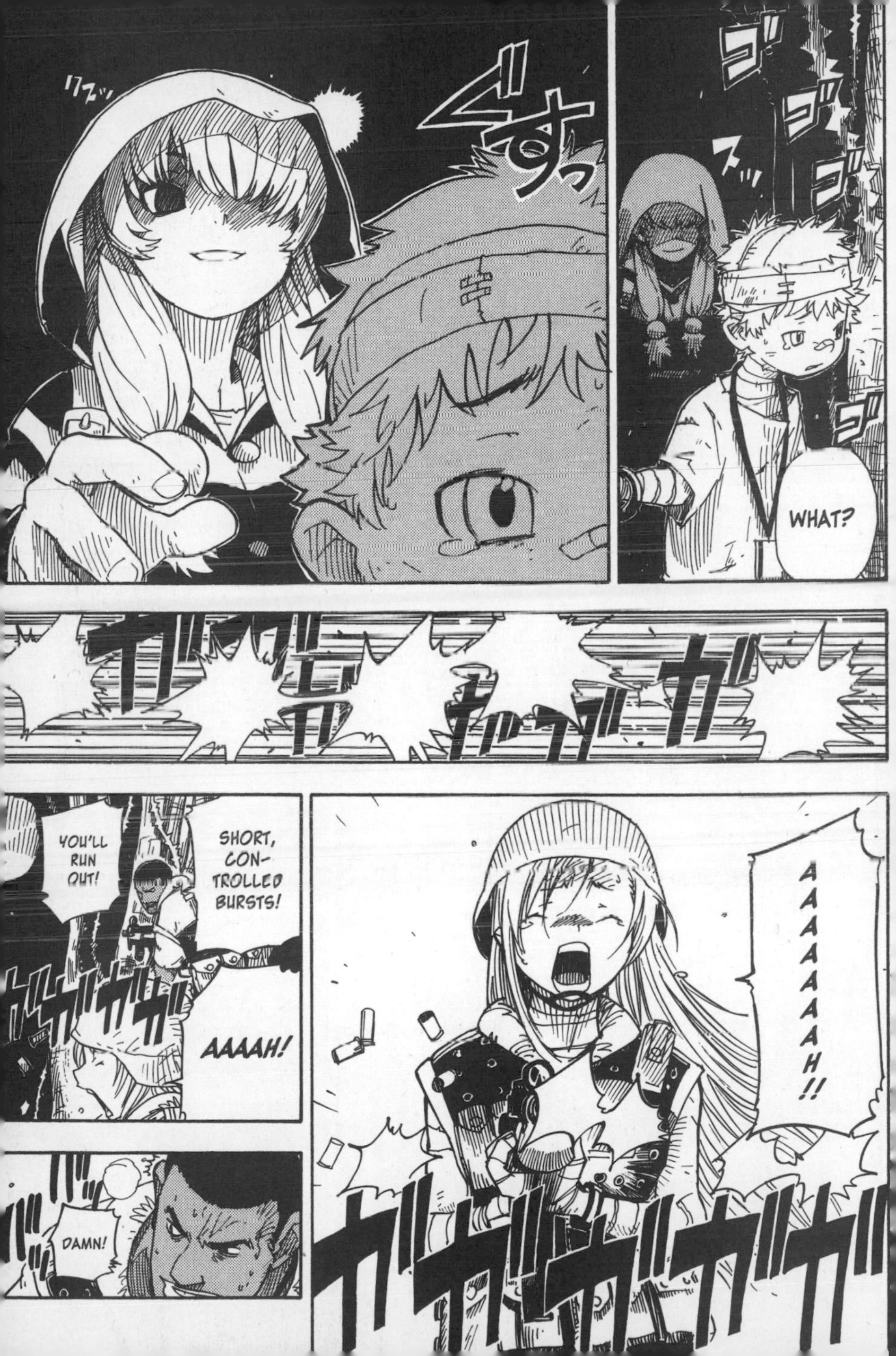
WHAT?
AAAAAAAAAH!!
SHORT, CONTROLLED BURSTS!
YOU'LL RUN OUT!
AAAAH!
DAMN!

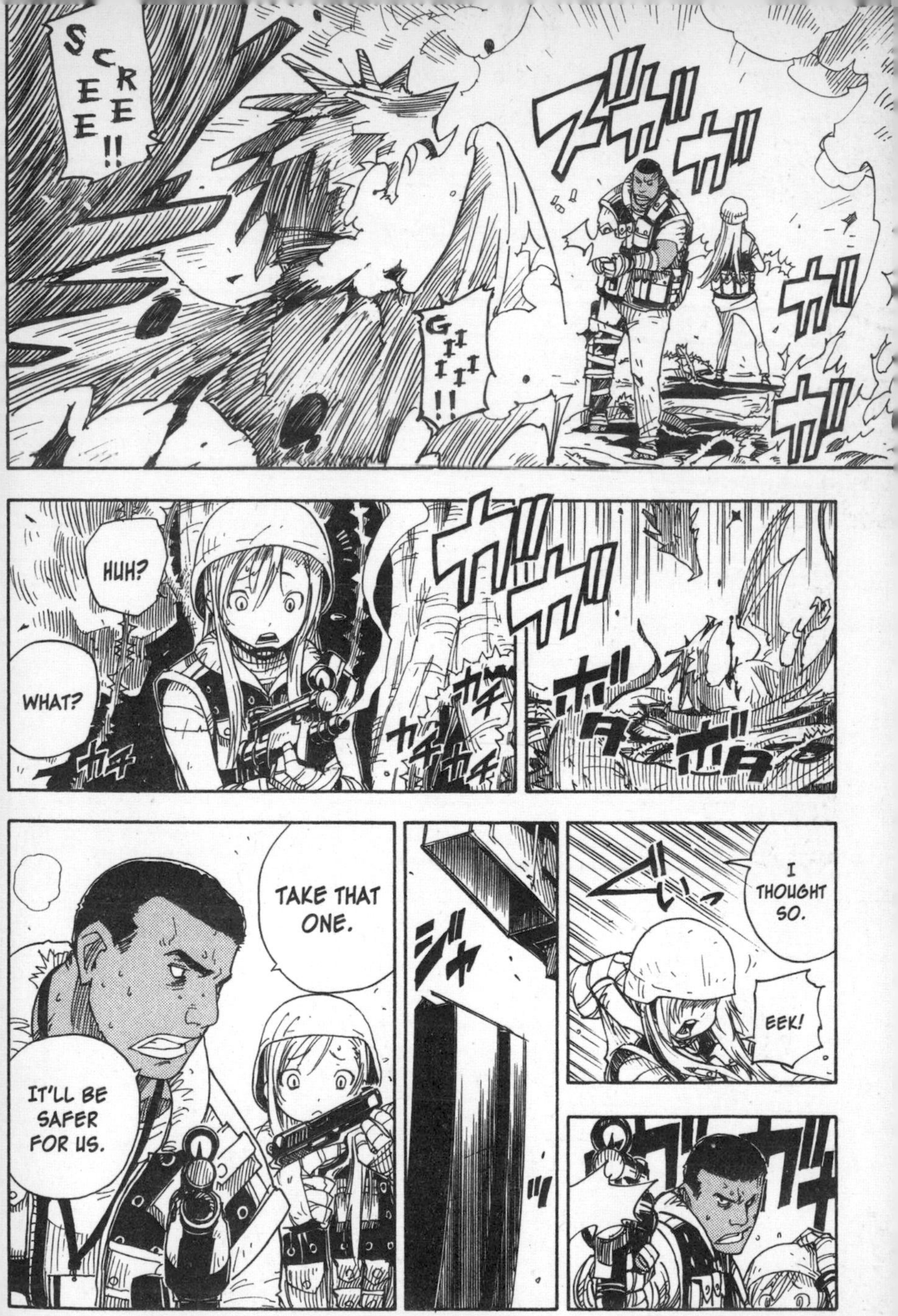
SCREE!!
GIIII!!
HUH?
WHAT?
カチ
I THOUGHT SO.
EEK!
TAKE THAT ONE.
IT'LL BE SAFER FOR US.

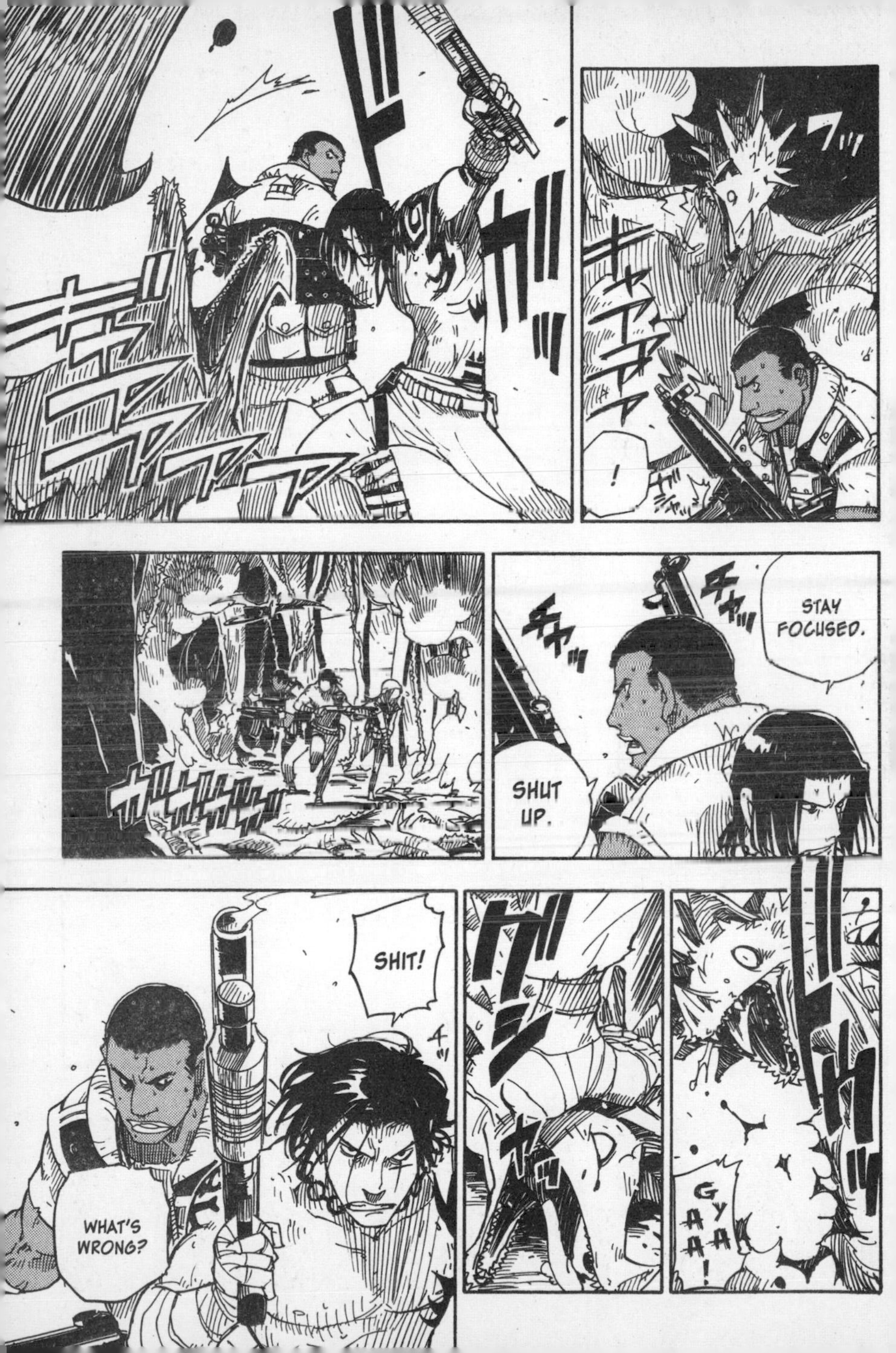
!
STAY FOCUSED.
SHUT UP.
SHIT!
WHAT'S WRONG?
GYAAAA!

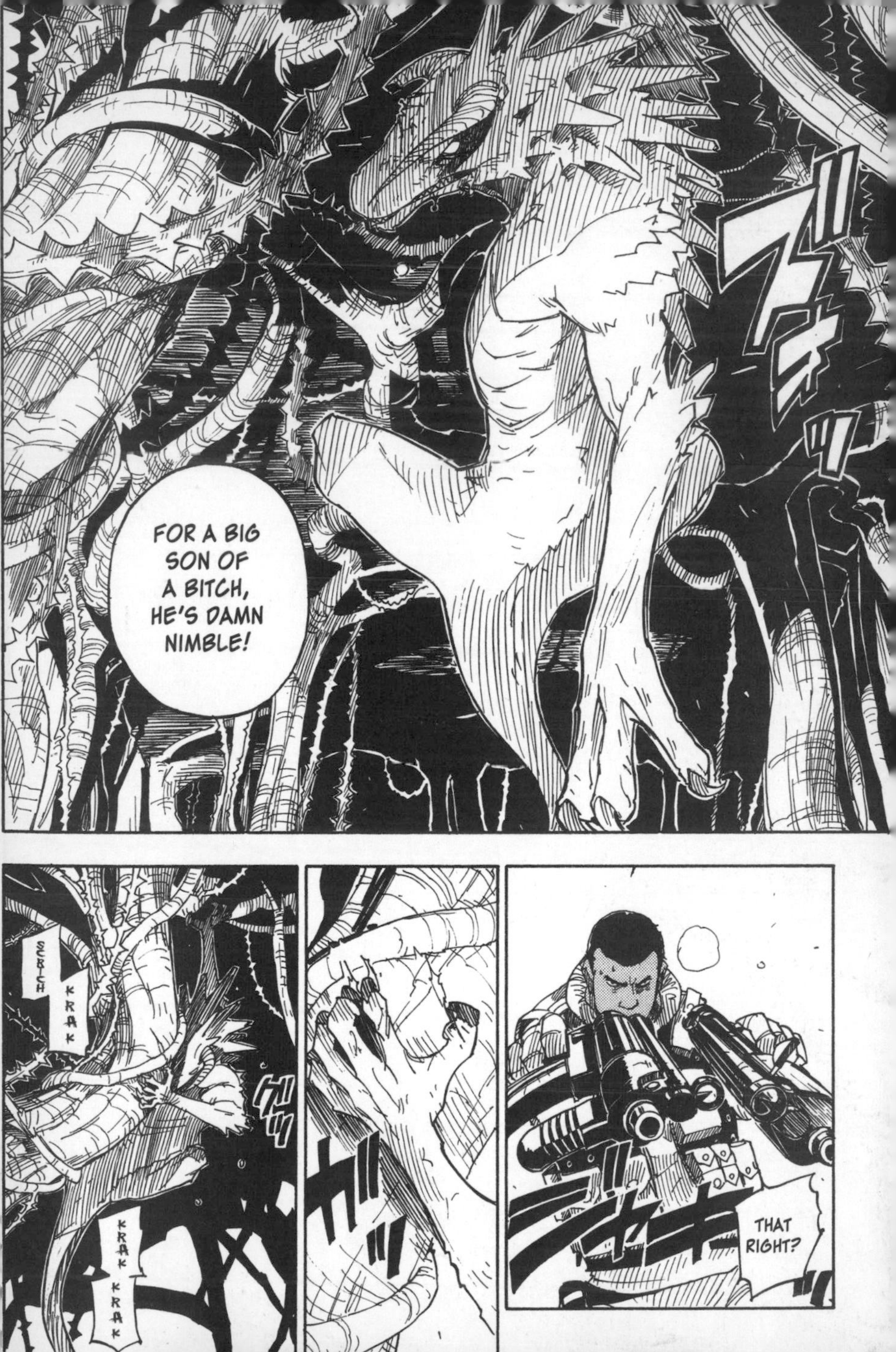
FOR A BIG SON OF A BITCH, HE'S DAMN NIMBLE!
THAT RIGHT?
SCBICH
KRAK
KRAK
KRAK

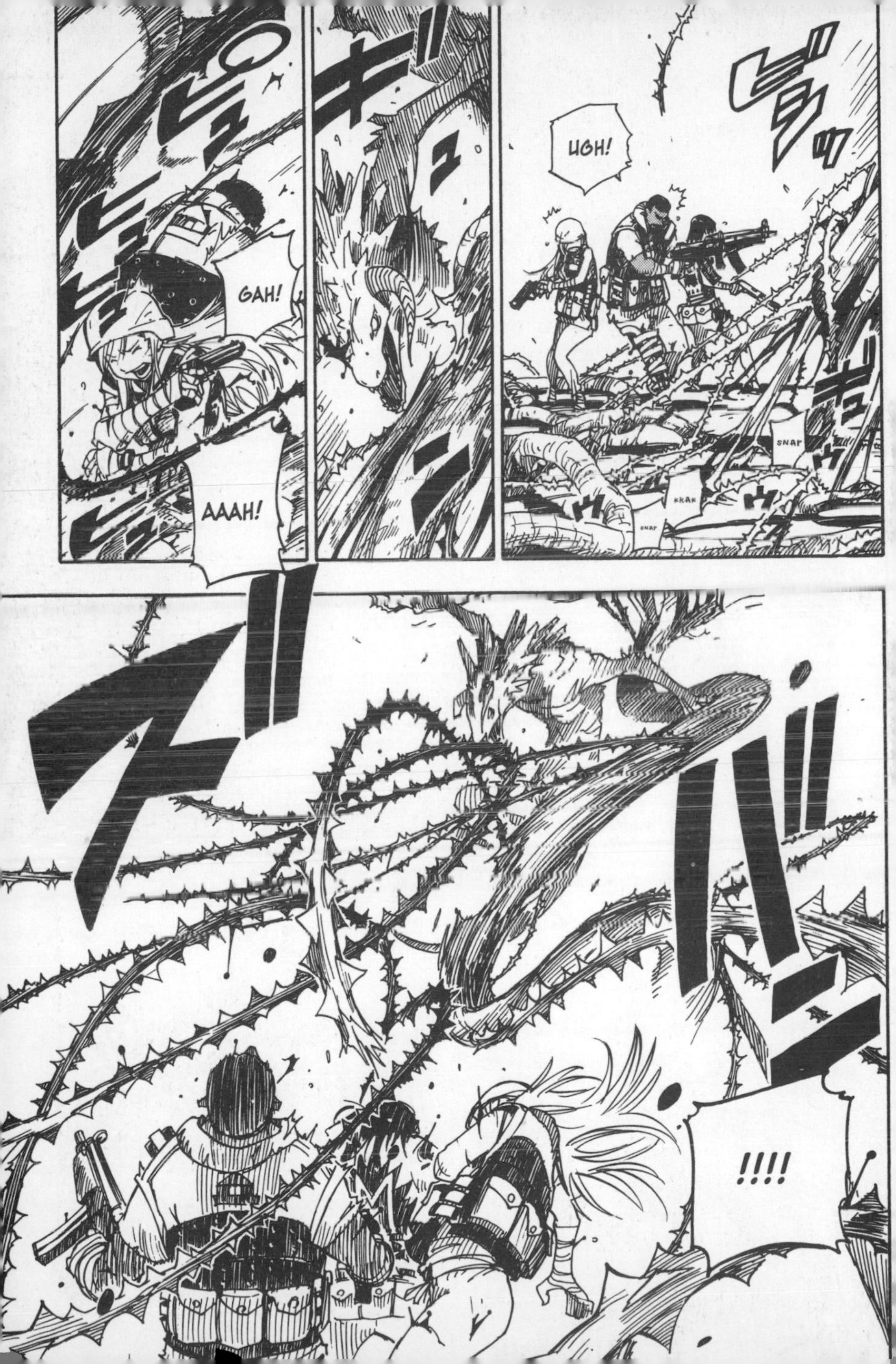
UGH!
SNAP
KRAK
SNAP
GAH!
AAAH!
!!!!

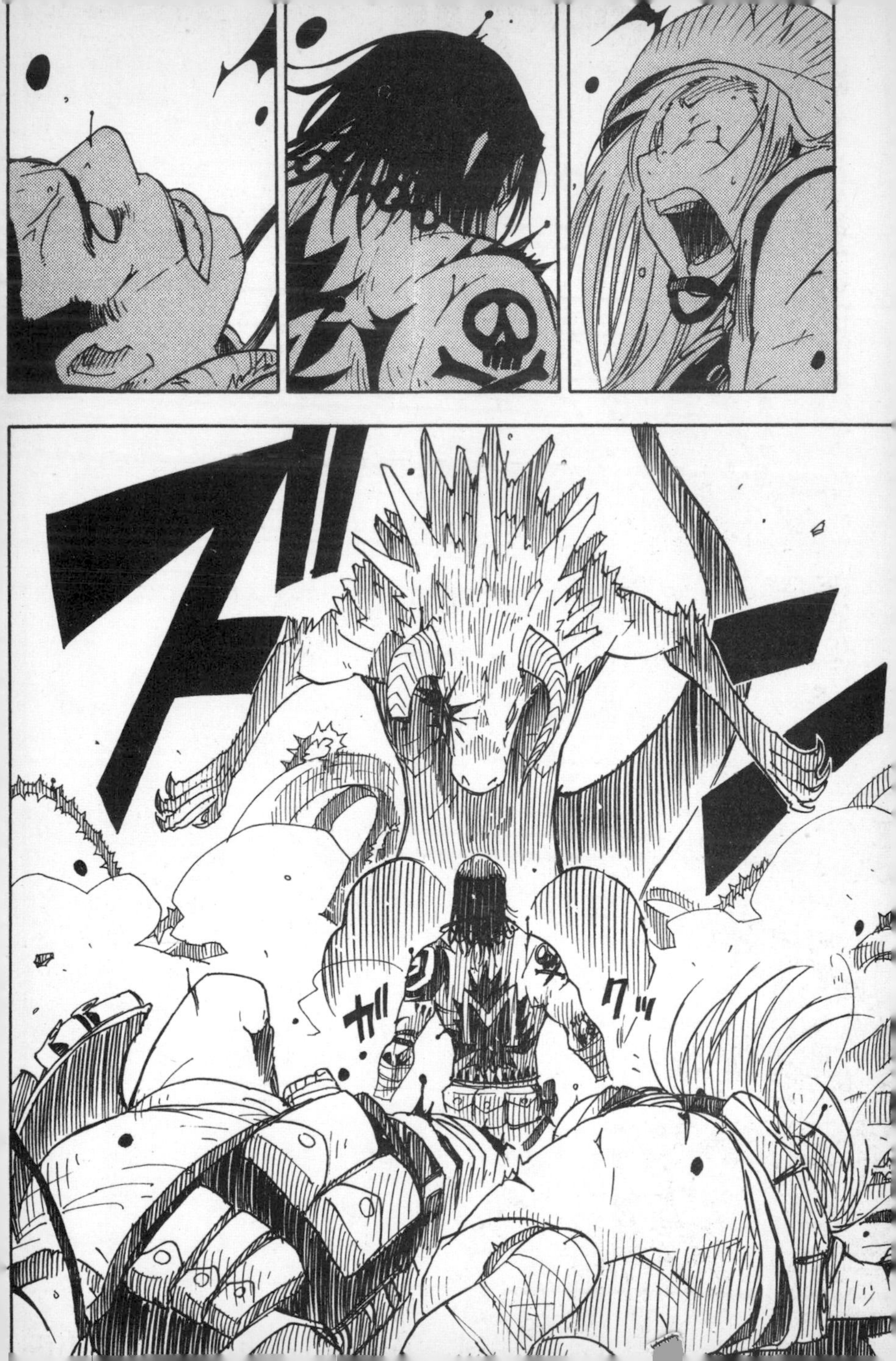
グッ
ガッ

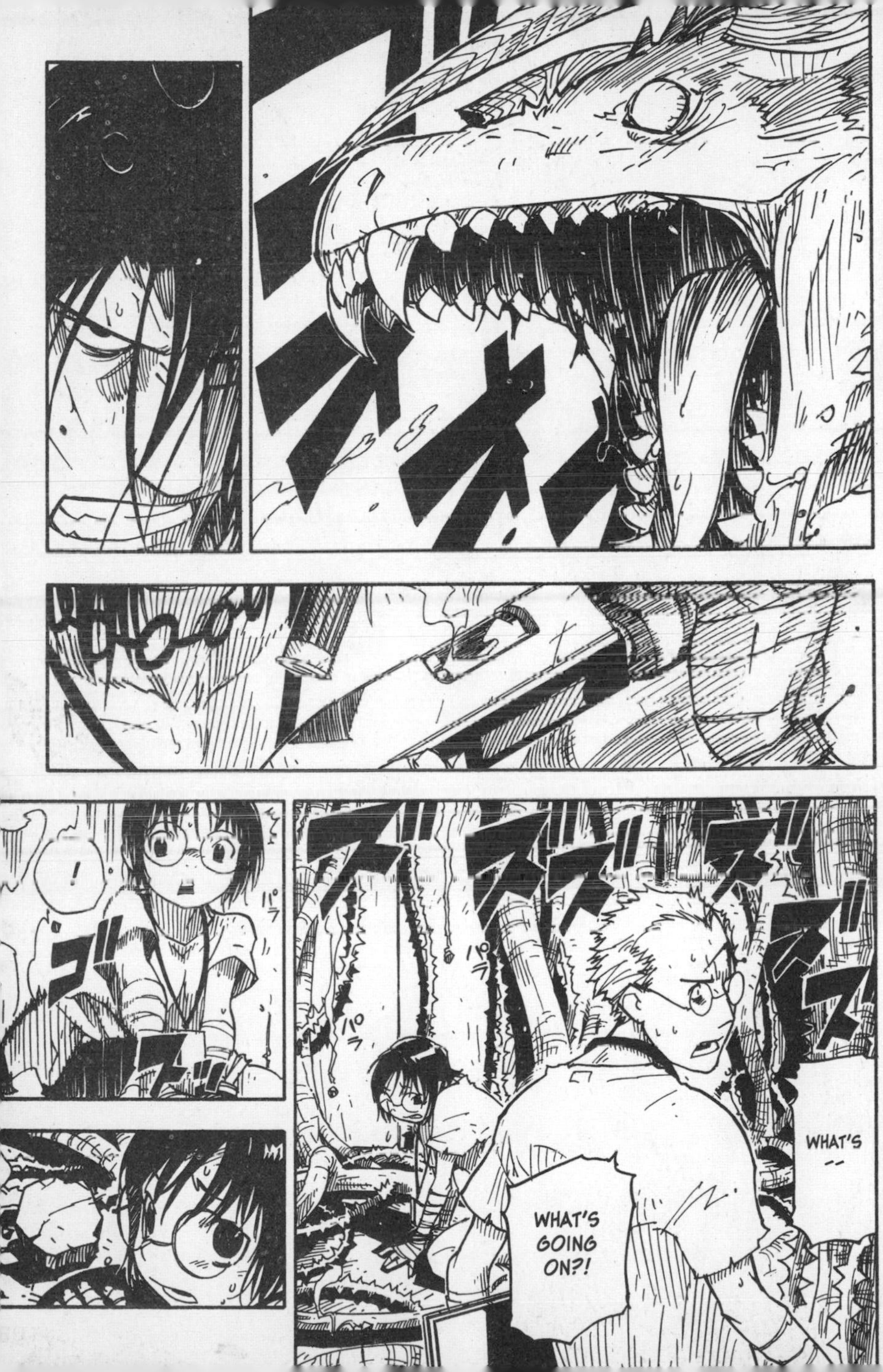
WHAT'S --
WHAT'S GOING ON?!

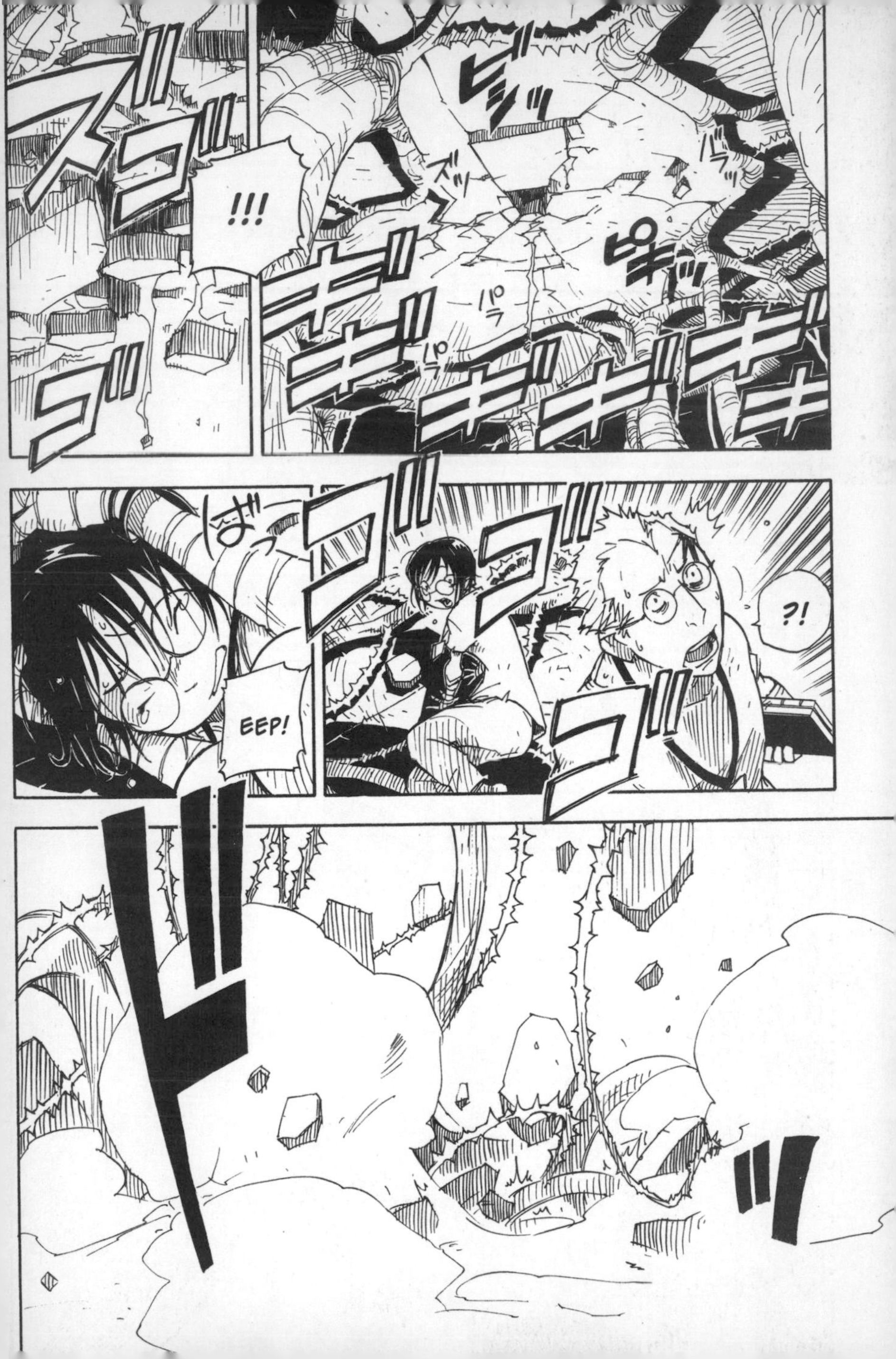
!!!
EEP!
?!

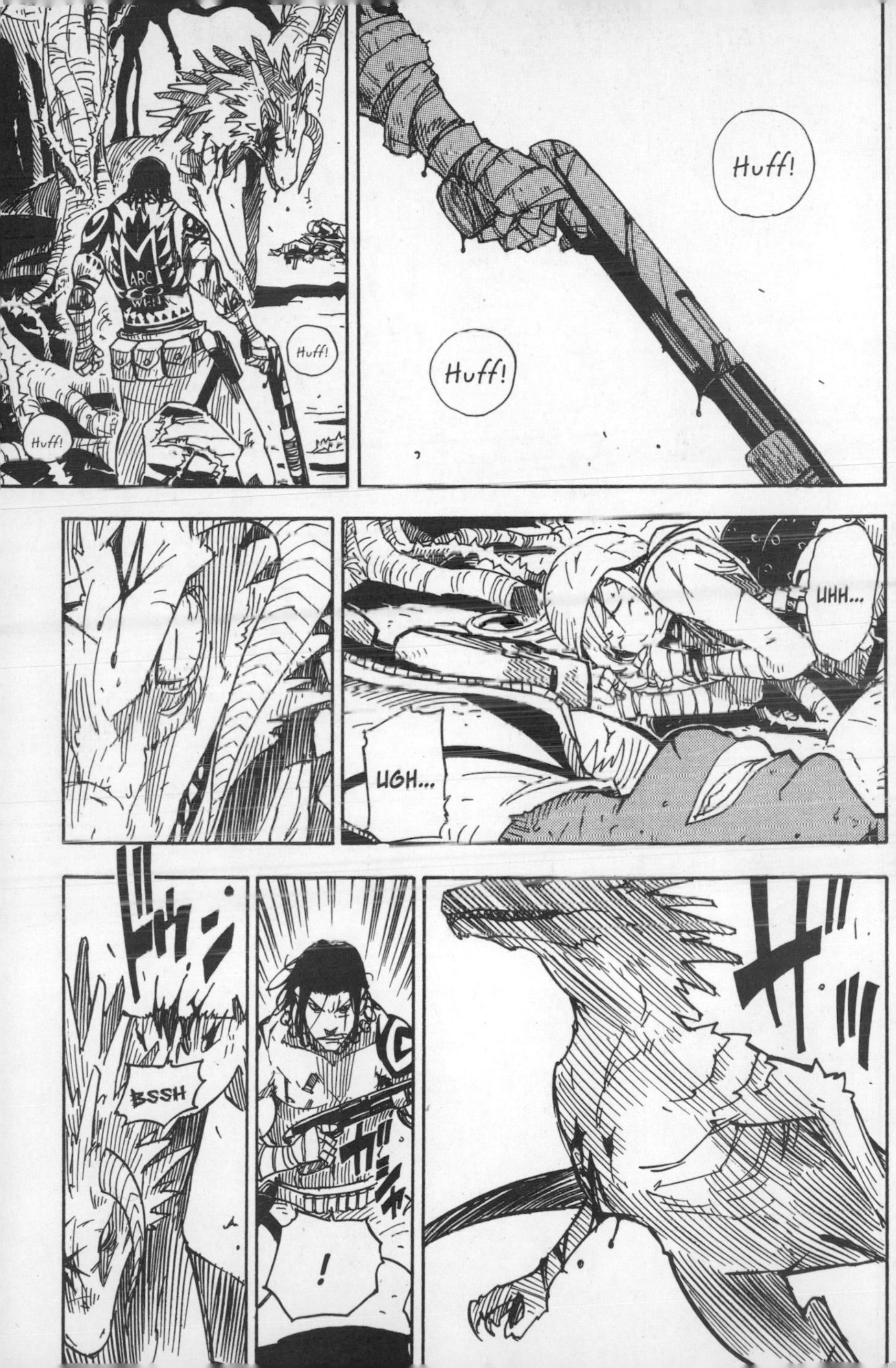
Huff!
Huff!
Huff!
Huff!
UHH...
UGH...
!
BSSH

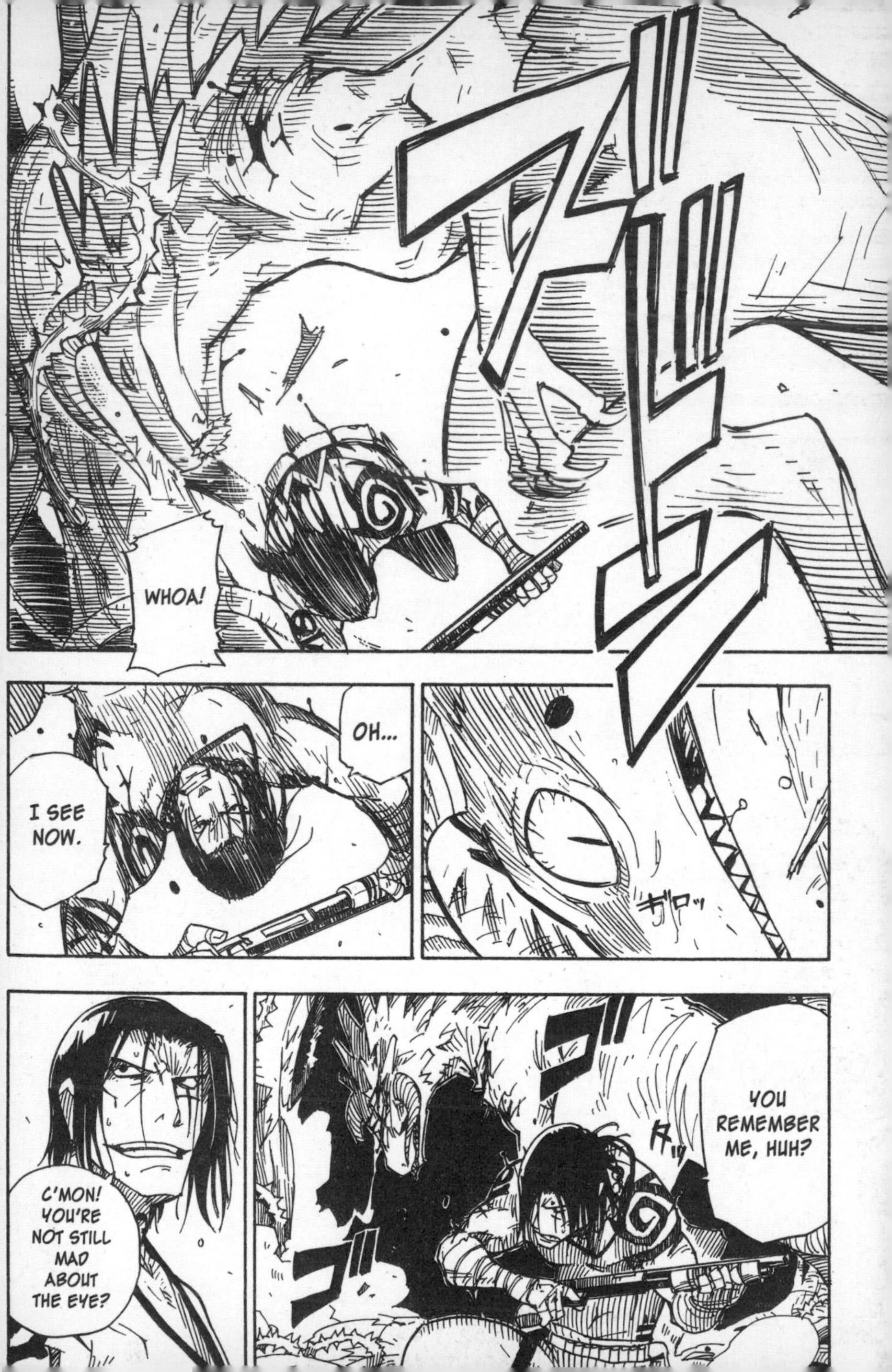
WHOA!
ギロッ
OH...
I SEE NOW.
YOU REMEMBER ME, HUH?
C'MON! YOU'RE NOT STILL MAD ABOUT THE EYE?

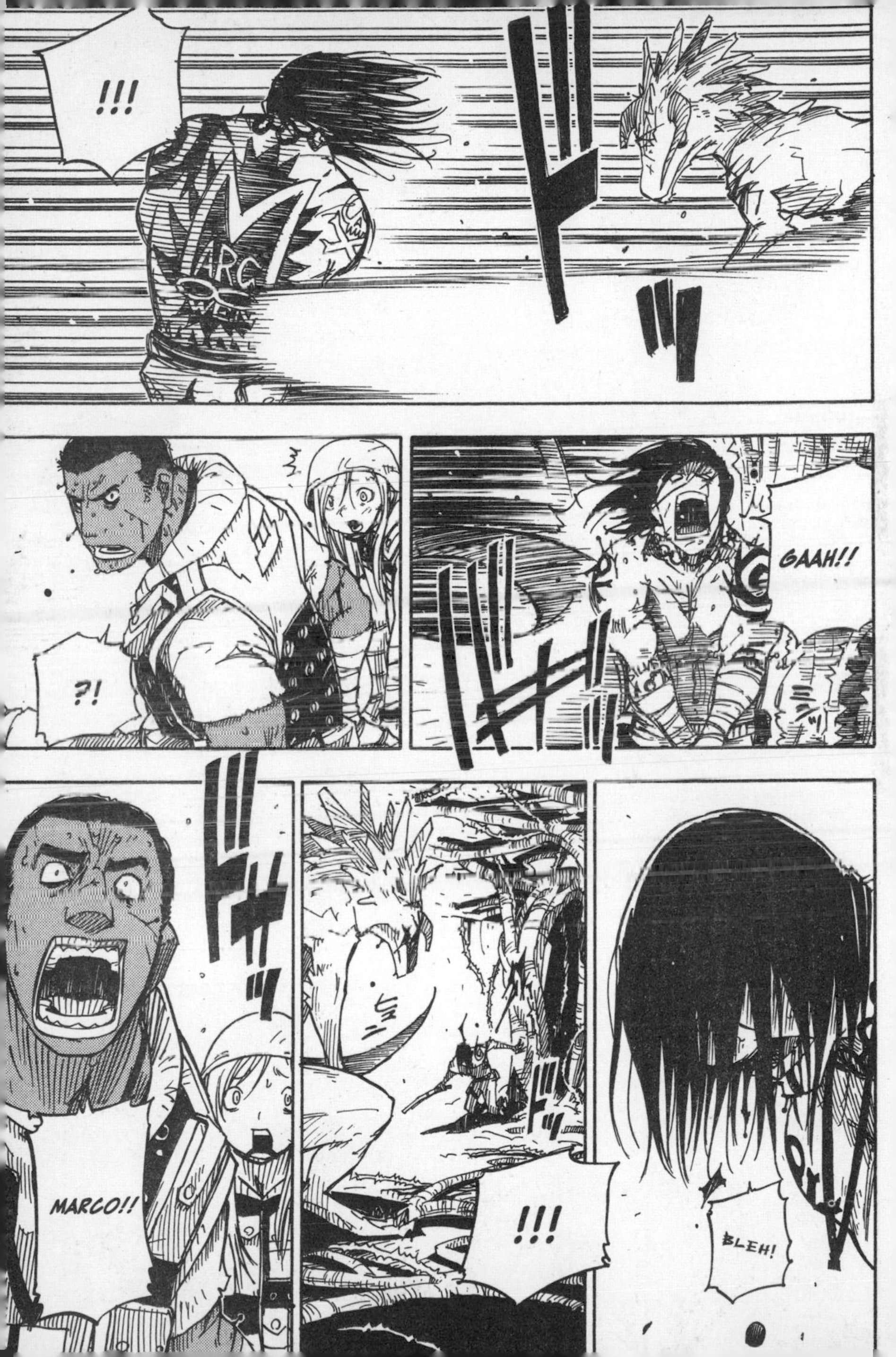
!!!
?!
GAAH!!
MARCO!!
!!!
BLEH!

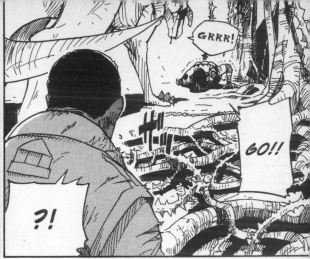

HE ONLY CARES ABOUT ME!

GET OUTTA HERE!

GRRR!

GO!!

?!

...

I'LL CATCH UP.

PIL . PIL .

BUT--

DON'T MAKE ME SAY IT AGAIN!

HE'S TOUGH.

COME ON.

HUH? BUT--

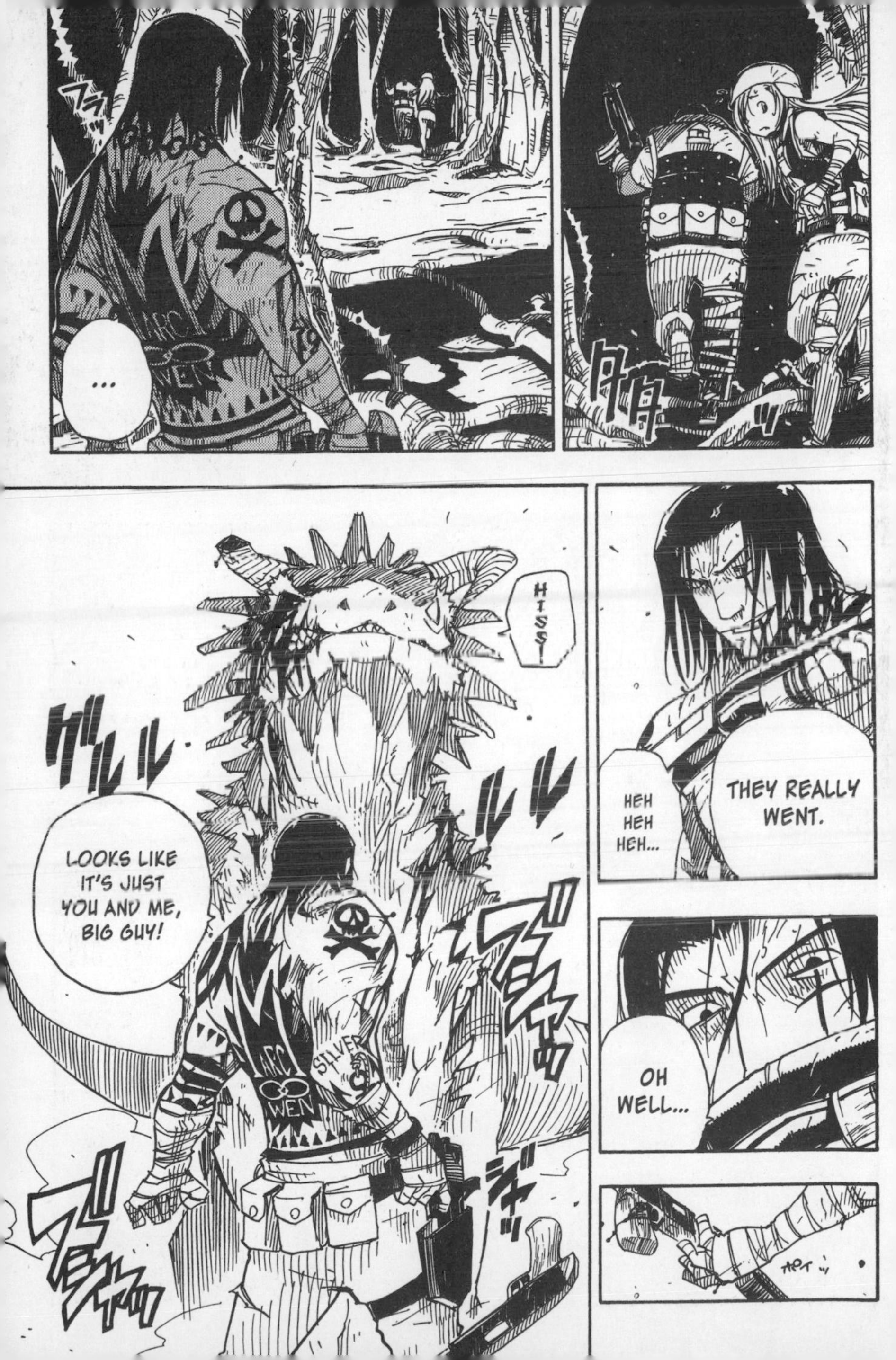
...
HEH HEH HEH...
THEY REALLY WENT.
OH WELL...
HISS!
LOOKS LIKE IT'S JUST YOU AND ME, BIG GUY!

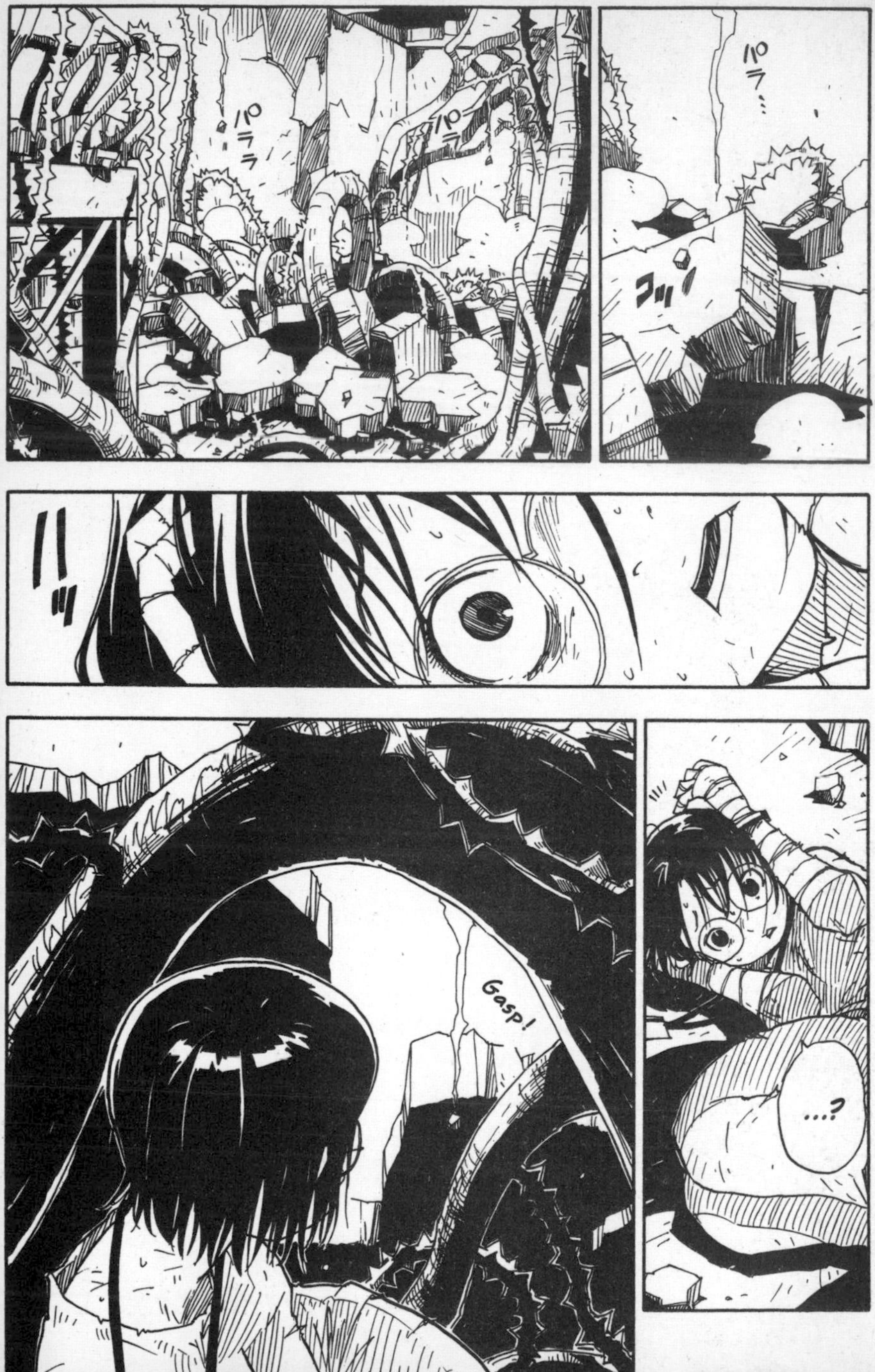
パラ…
ゴッ
パラララ
パラ
ハッ
...?
Gasp!

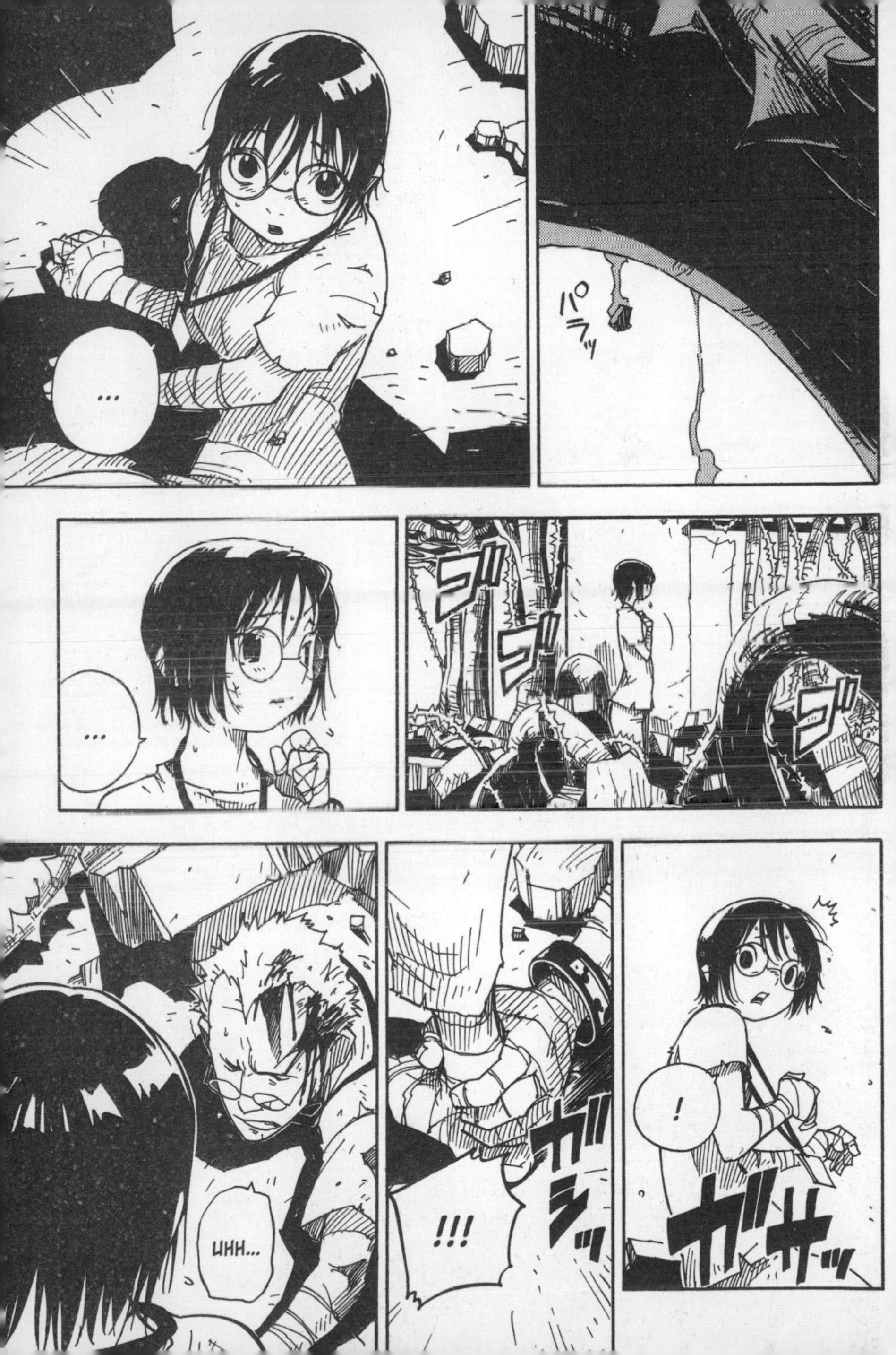
パラッ
...
...
!
ガサーッ
!!!
ガラッ
UHH...

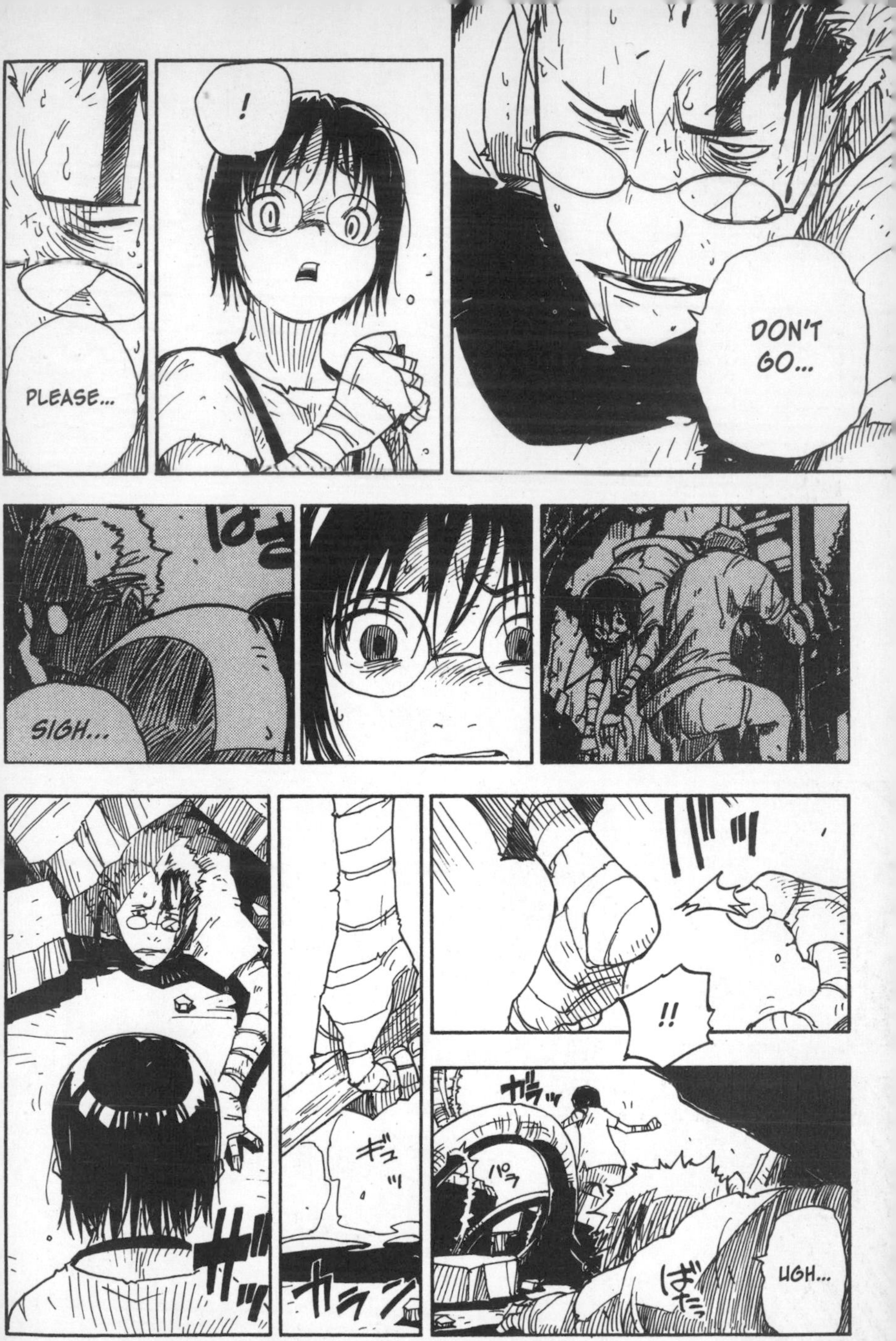
DON'T GO...
!
PLEASE...
SIGH...
!!
UGH...
ギュッ
カラン
ガッ

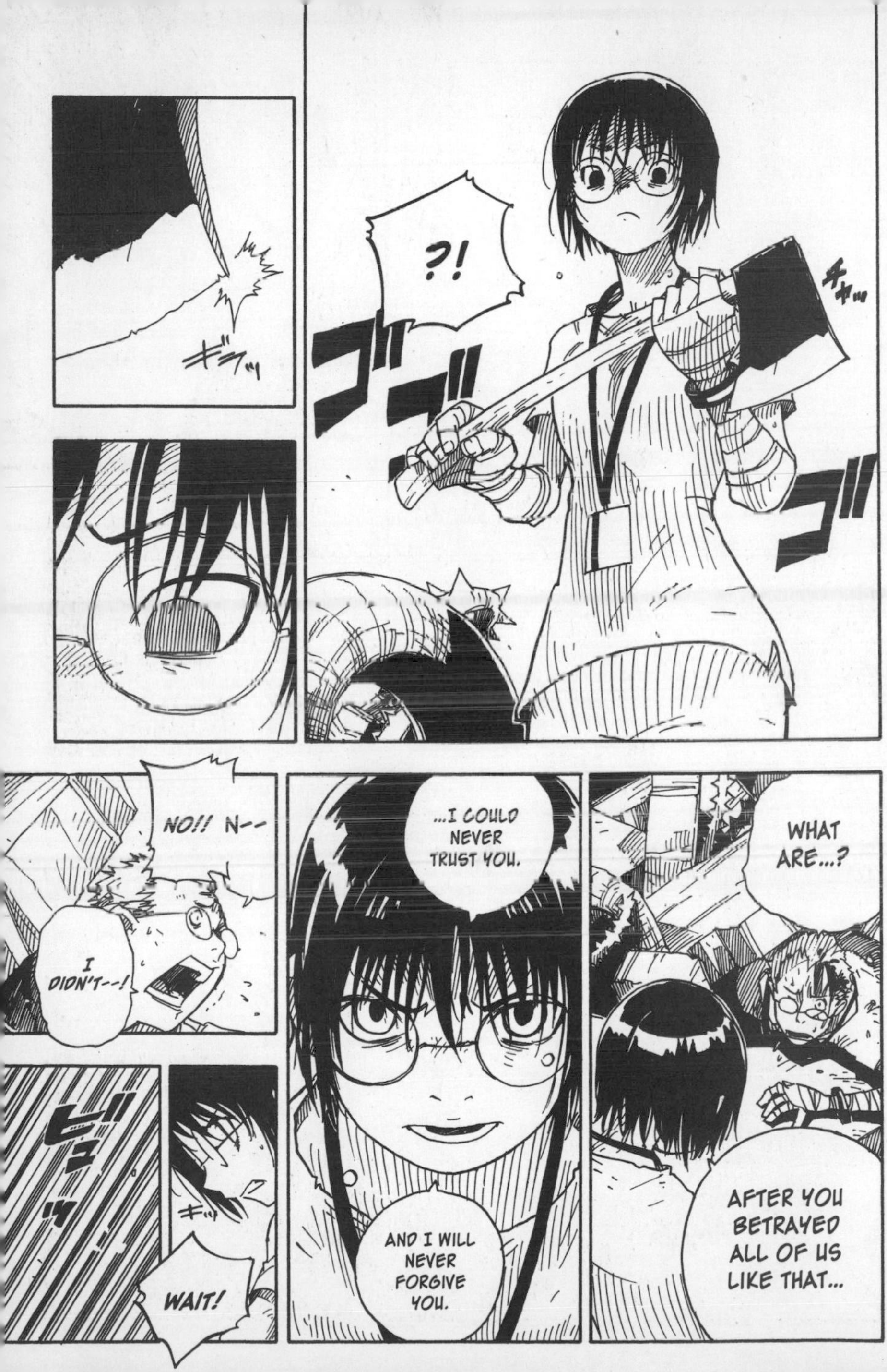
?!
WHAT ARE...?
AFTER YOU BETRAYED ALL OF US LIKE THAT...
...I COULD NEVER TRUST YOU.
AND I WILL NEVER FORGIVE YOU.
NO!! N--
I DIDN'T--!
WAIT!

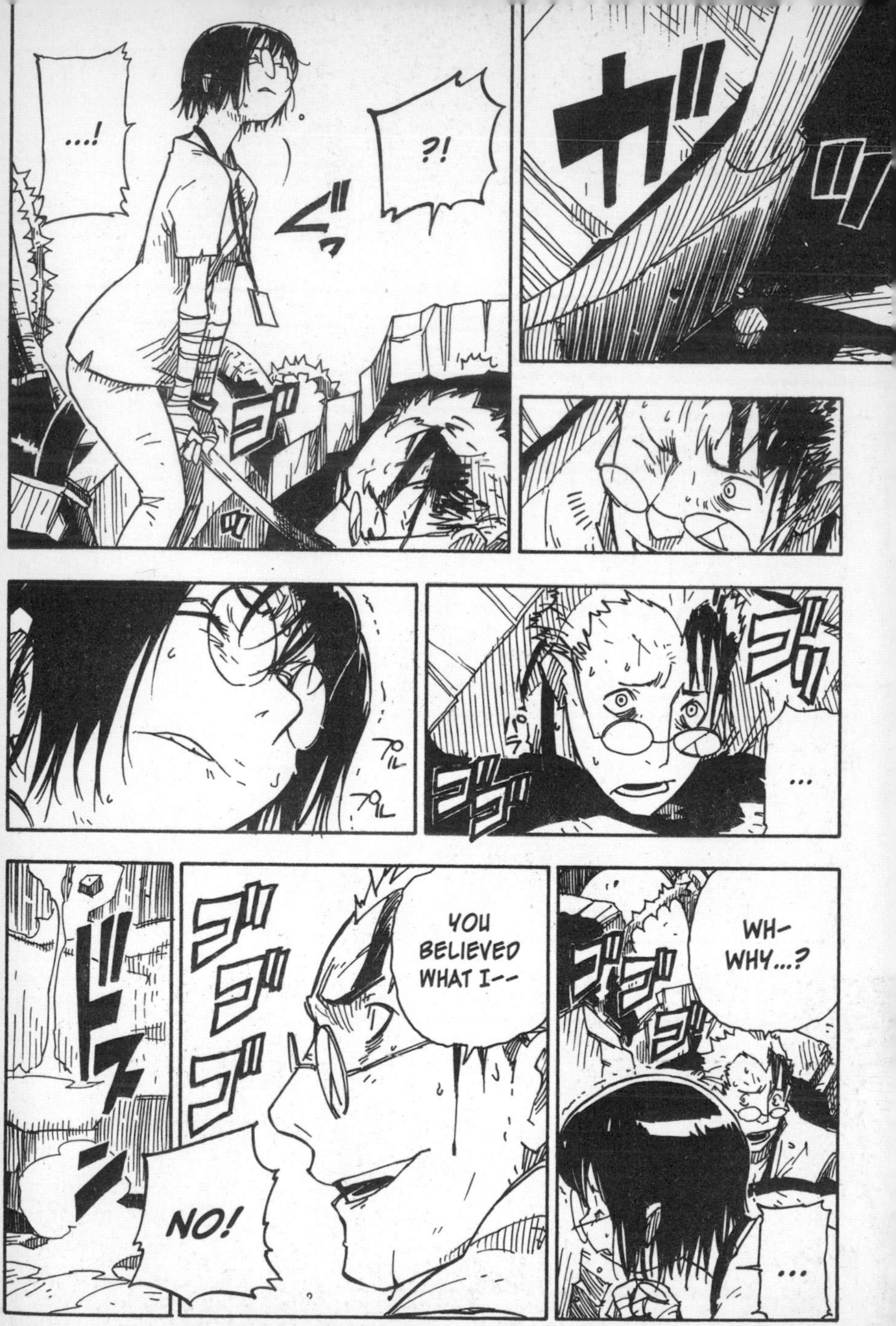
?!
...!
...
WH- WHY...?
...
YOU BELIEVED WHAT I--
NO!

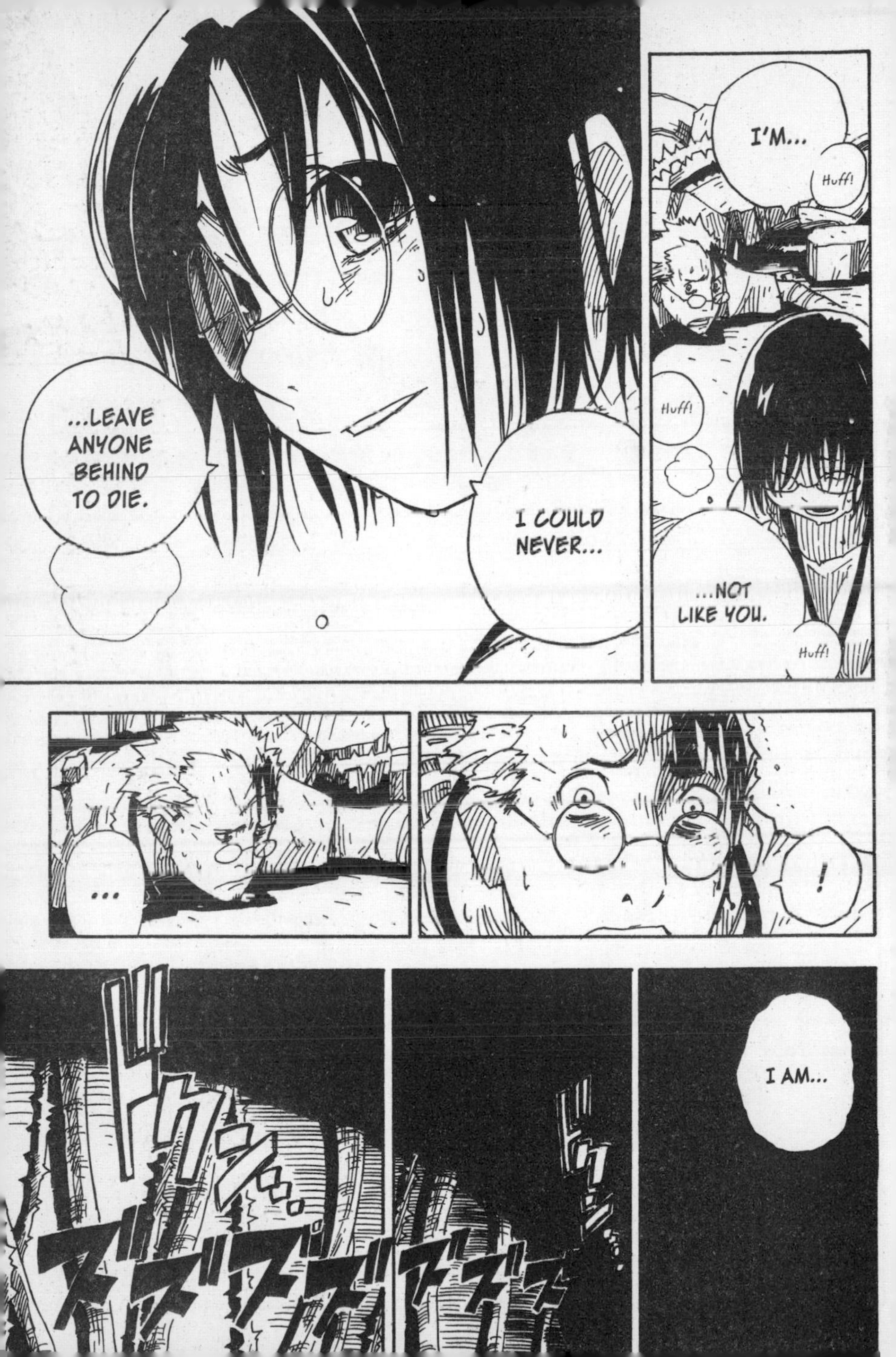
I'M...
Huff!
Huff!
...NOT LIKE YOU.
Huff!
I COULD NEVER...
...LEAVE ANYONE BEHIND TO DIE.
!
...
I AM...

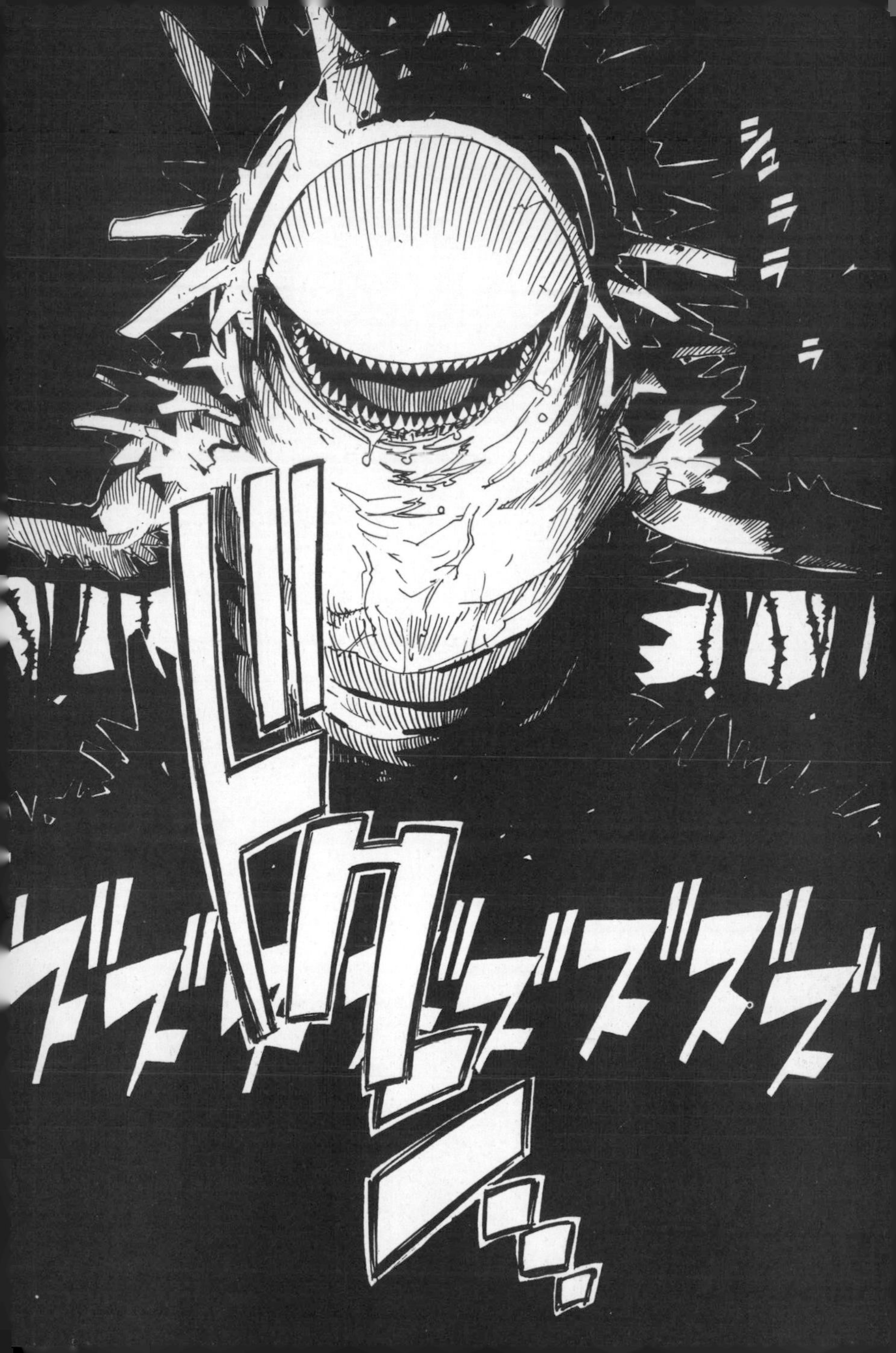

シュラララ
ドカ
ブブブブブブブ

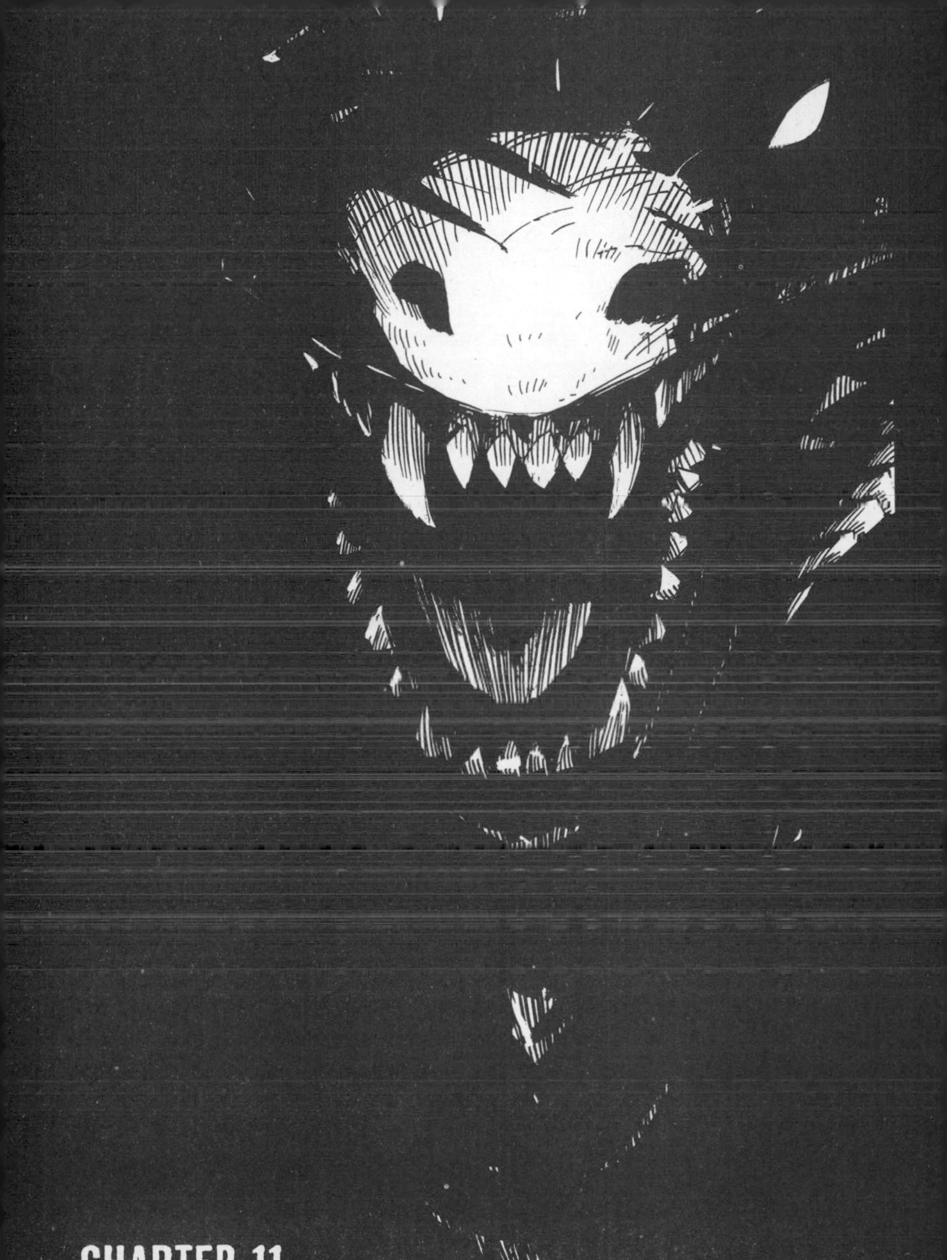

CHAPTER 11
THE CROWN OF CROSSES AND THORNS

Huff!

Huh!

COME ON, CYCLOPS.

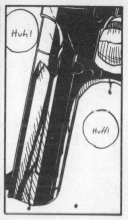

Huh!

Huff!

LET'S SETTLE THIS!

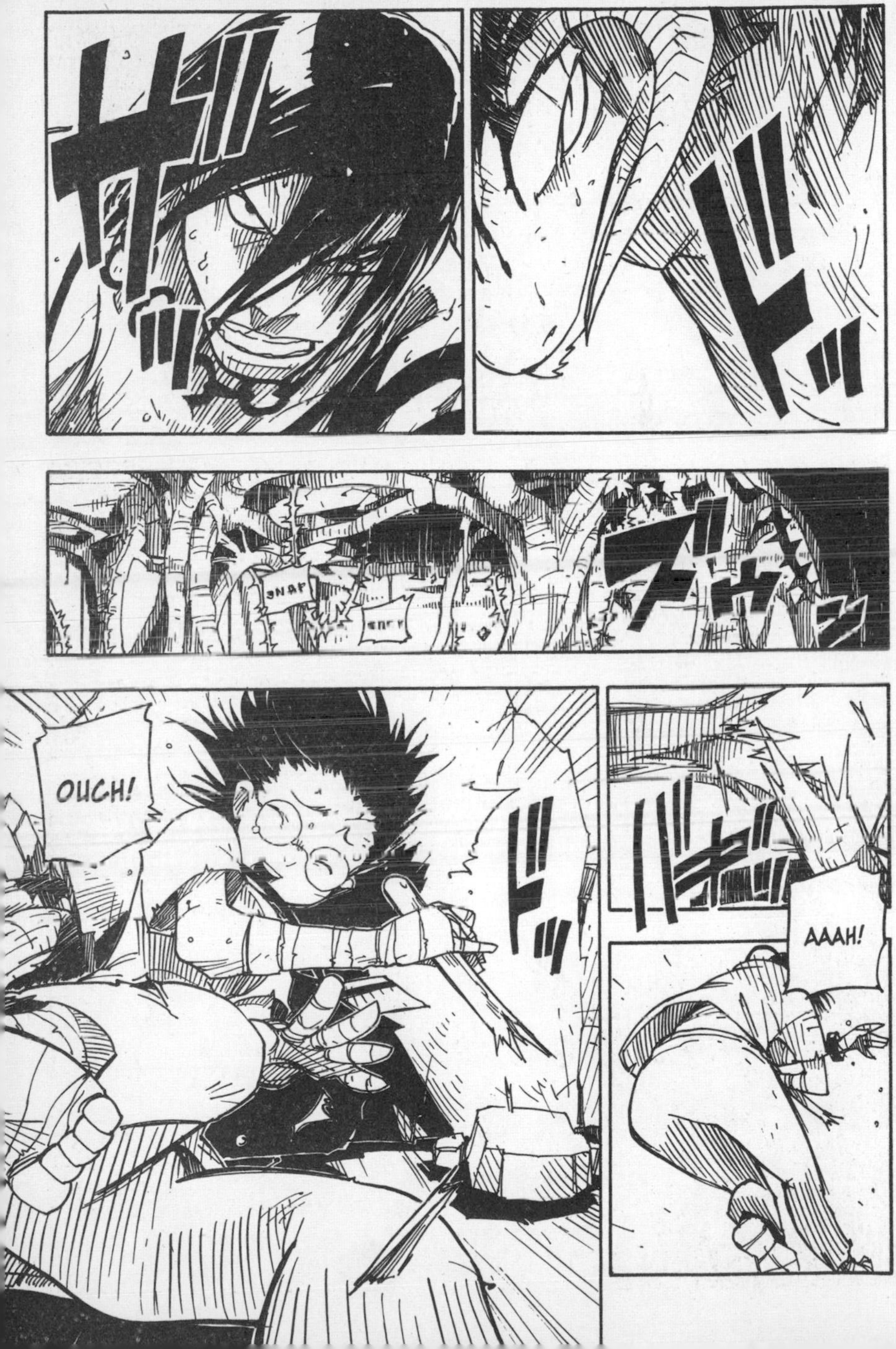
SNAP
AAAH!
OUCH!

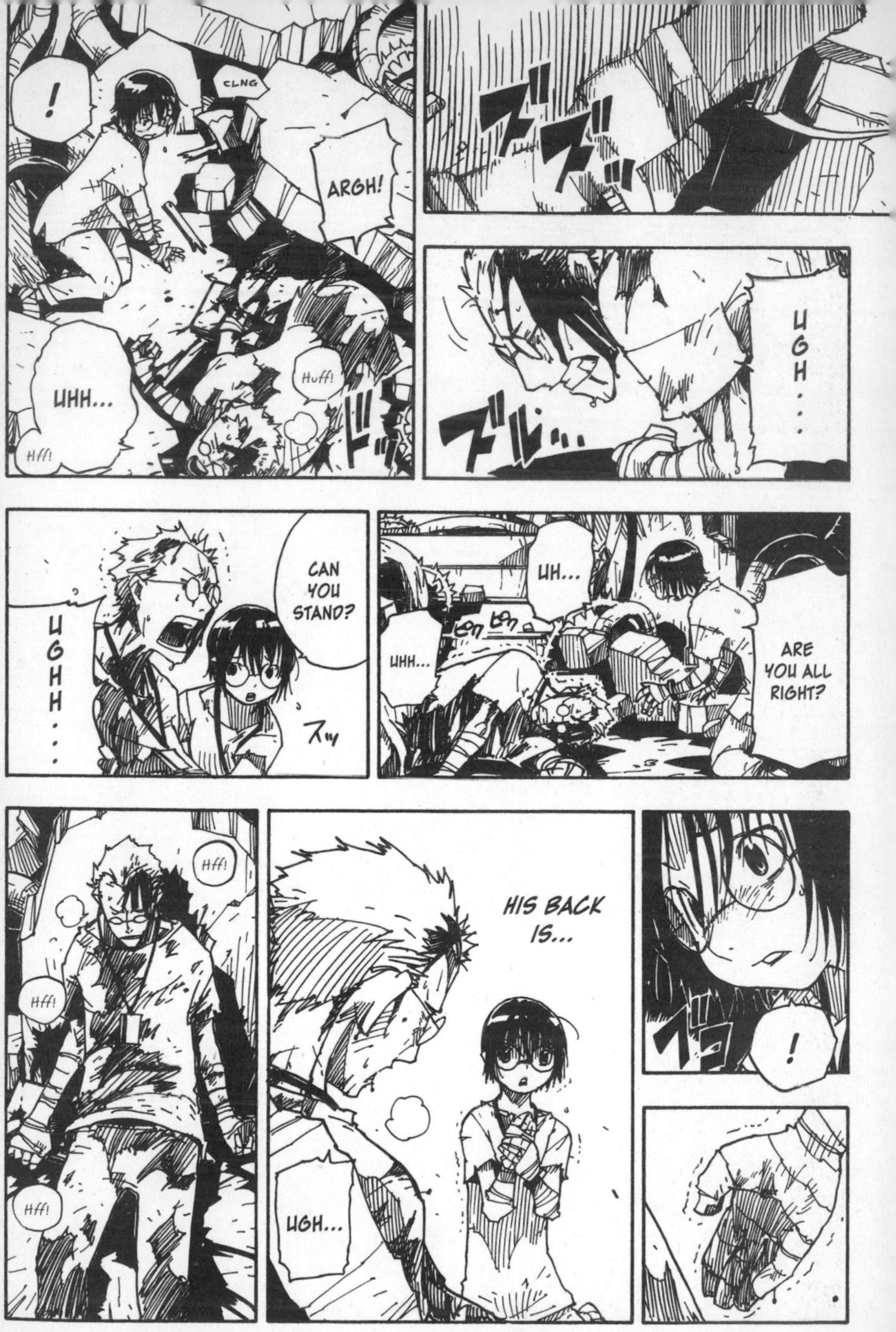
UGH...
!
CLNG
ARGH!
Huff!
UHH...
Hff!
UH...
ARE YOU ALL RIGHT?
UHH...
CAN YOU STAND?
UGHH...
!
HIS BACK IS...
UGH...
Hff!
Hff!
Hff!

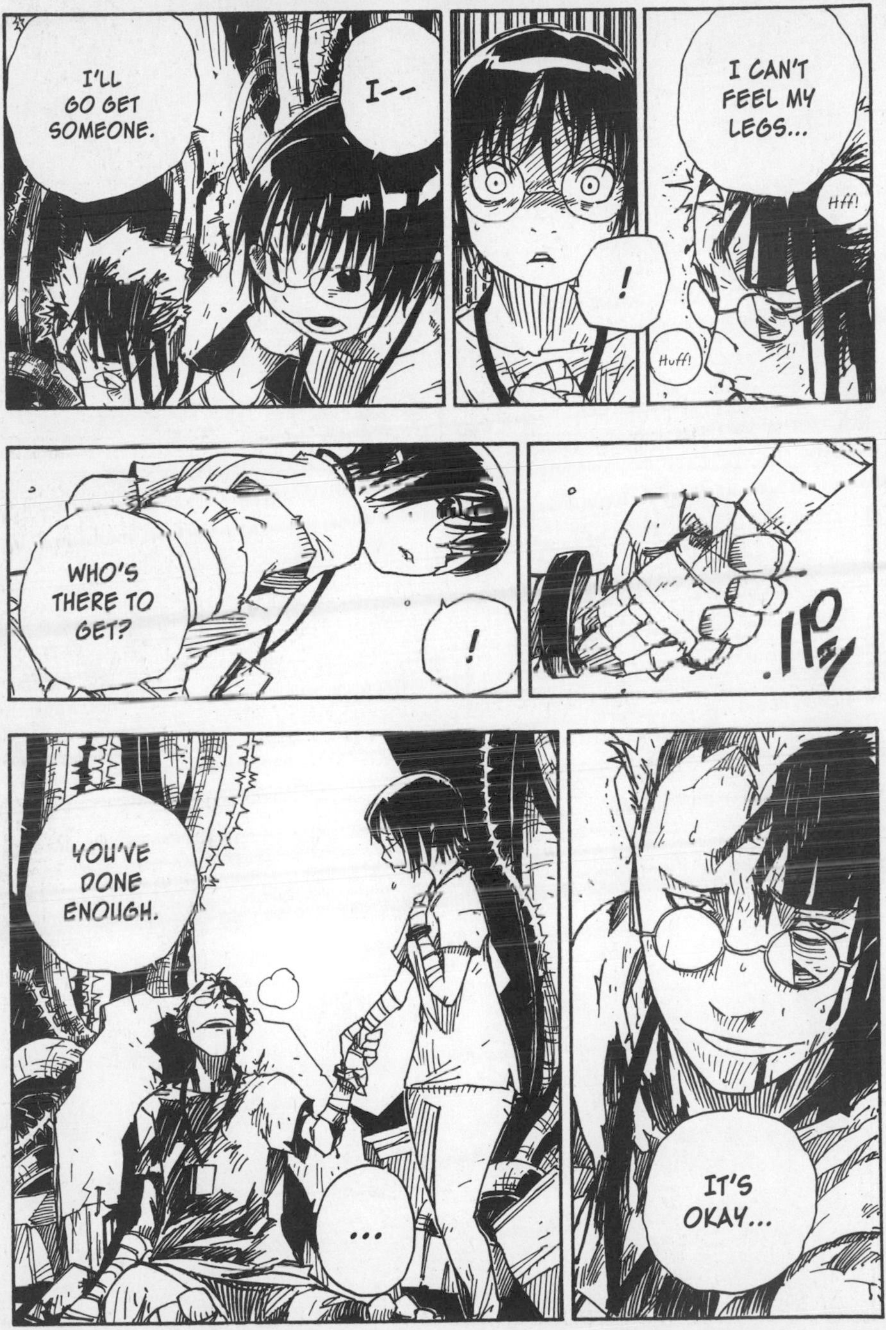
I CAN'T FEEL MY LEGS...
Hff!
Huff!
!
I--
I'LL GO GET SOMEONE.
!
WHO'S THERE TO GET?
IT'S OKAY...
YOU'VE DONE ENOUGH.
...

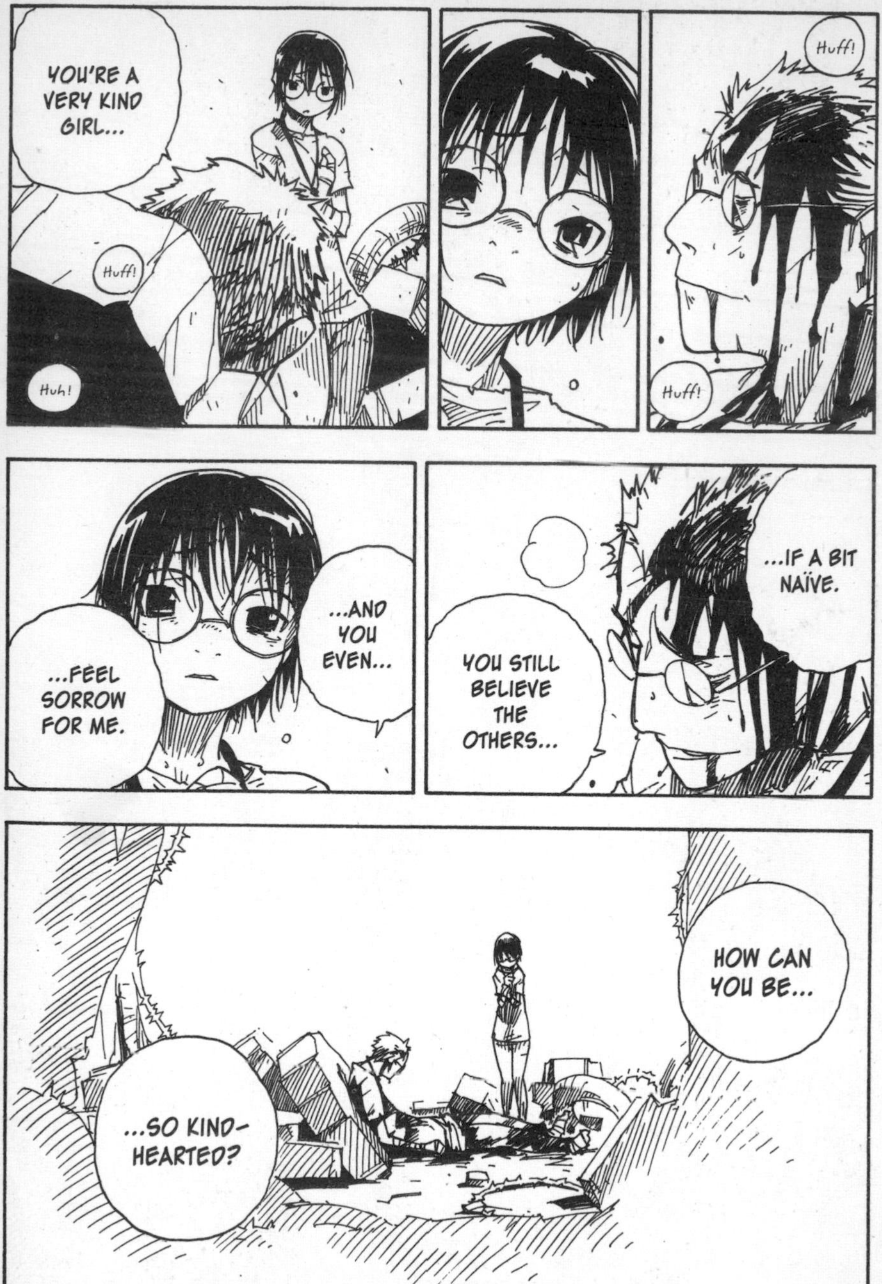

Huff!
Huff!
YOU'RE A VERY KIND GIRL...
Huff!
Huh!
...IF A BIT NAÏVE.
YOU STILL BELIEVE THE OTHERS...
...AND YOU EVEN...
...FEEL SORROW FOR ME.
HOW CAN YOU BE...
...SO KIND-HEARTED?

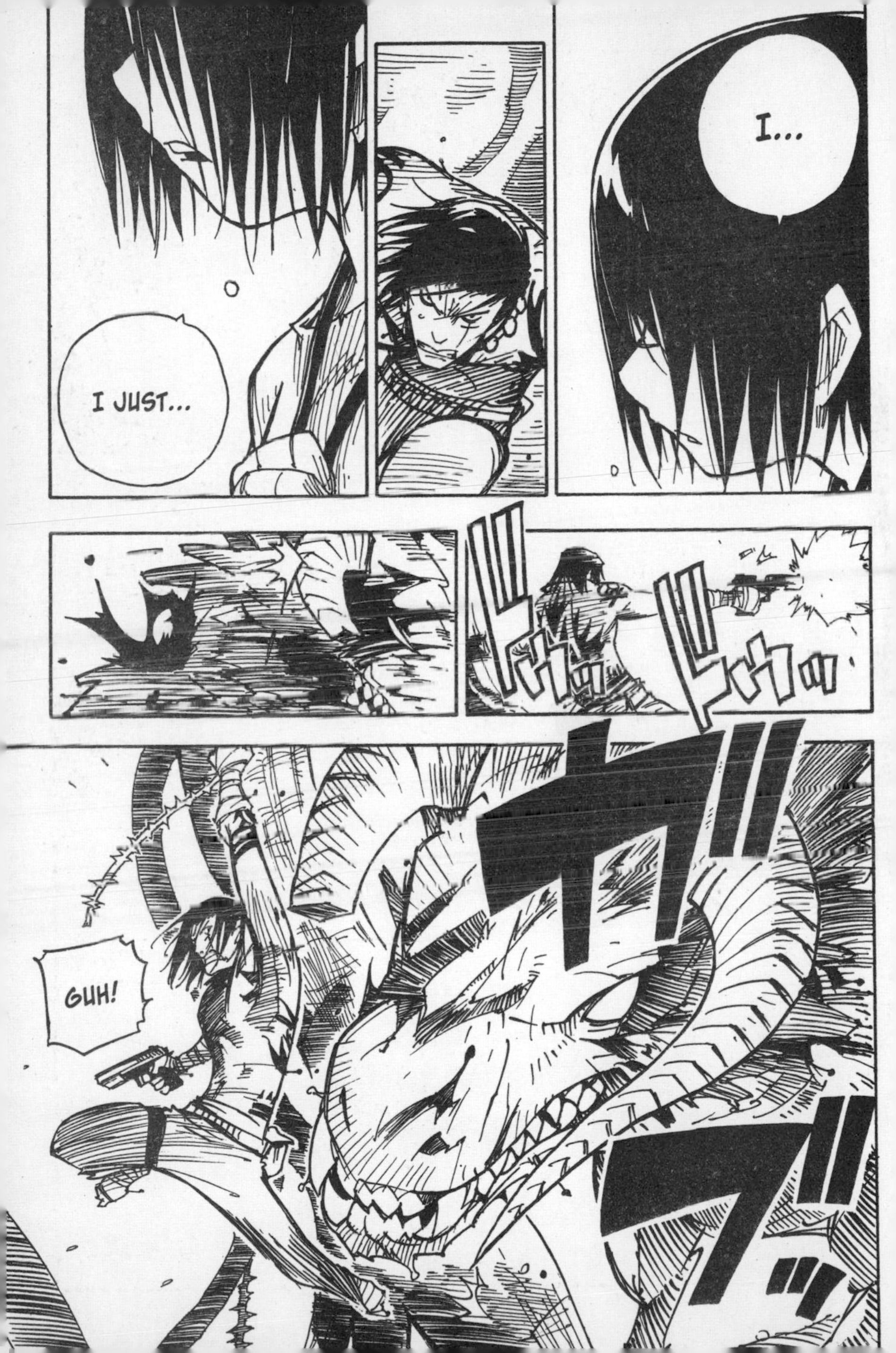
I...
I JUST...
GUH!

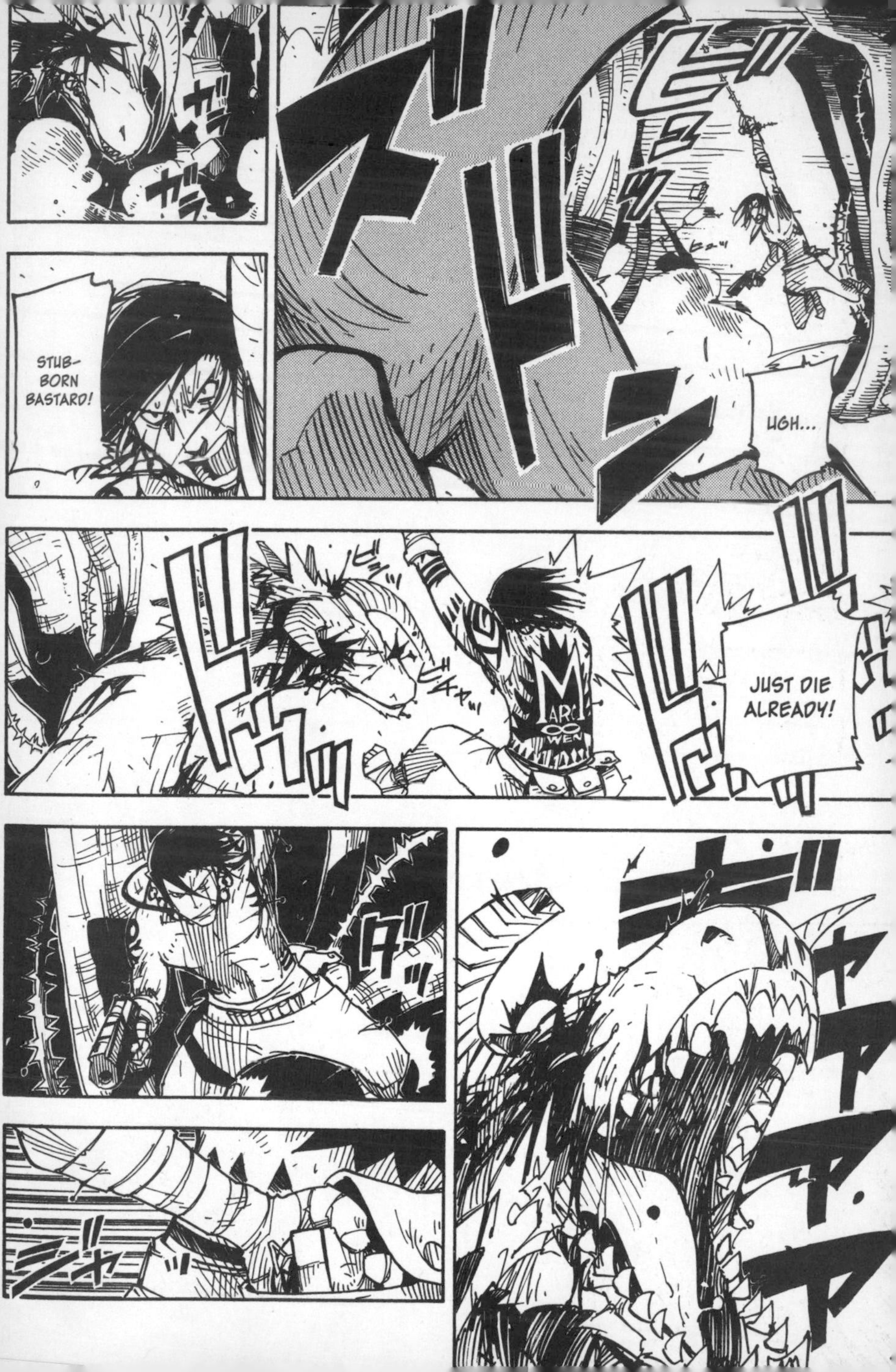

STUB-BORN BASTARD!
UGH...
JUST DIE ALREADY!

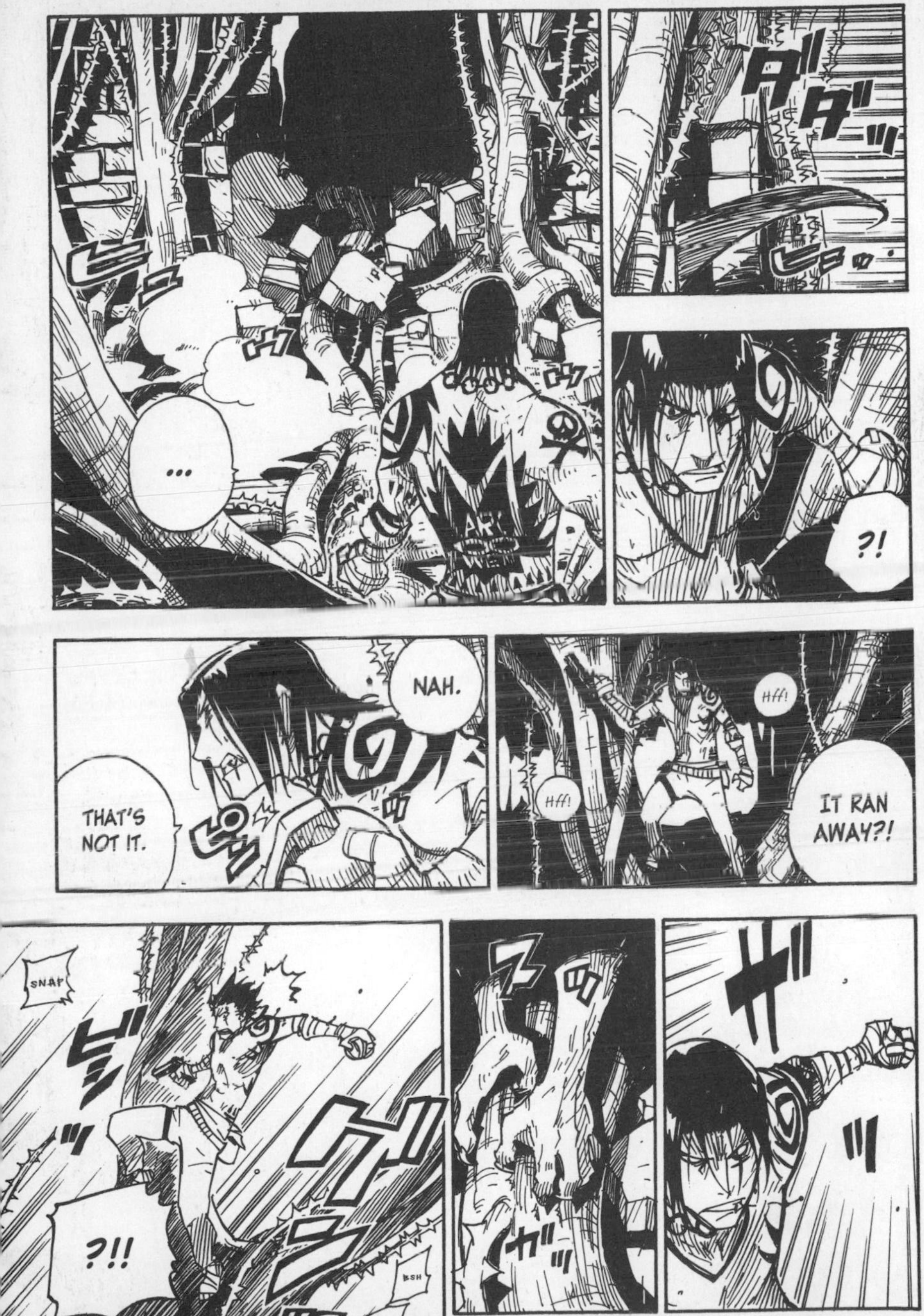

?!
...
IT RAN AWAY?!
Hff!
Hff!
NAH.
THAT'S NOT IT.
SNAP
?!!
BSH
SNAP

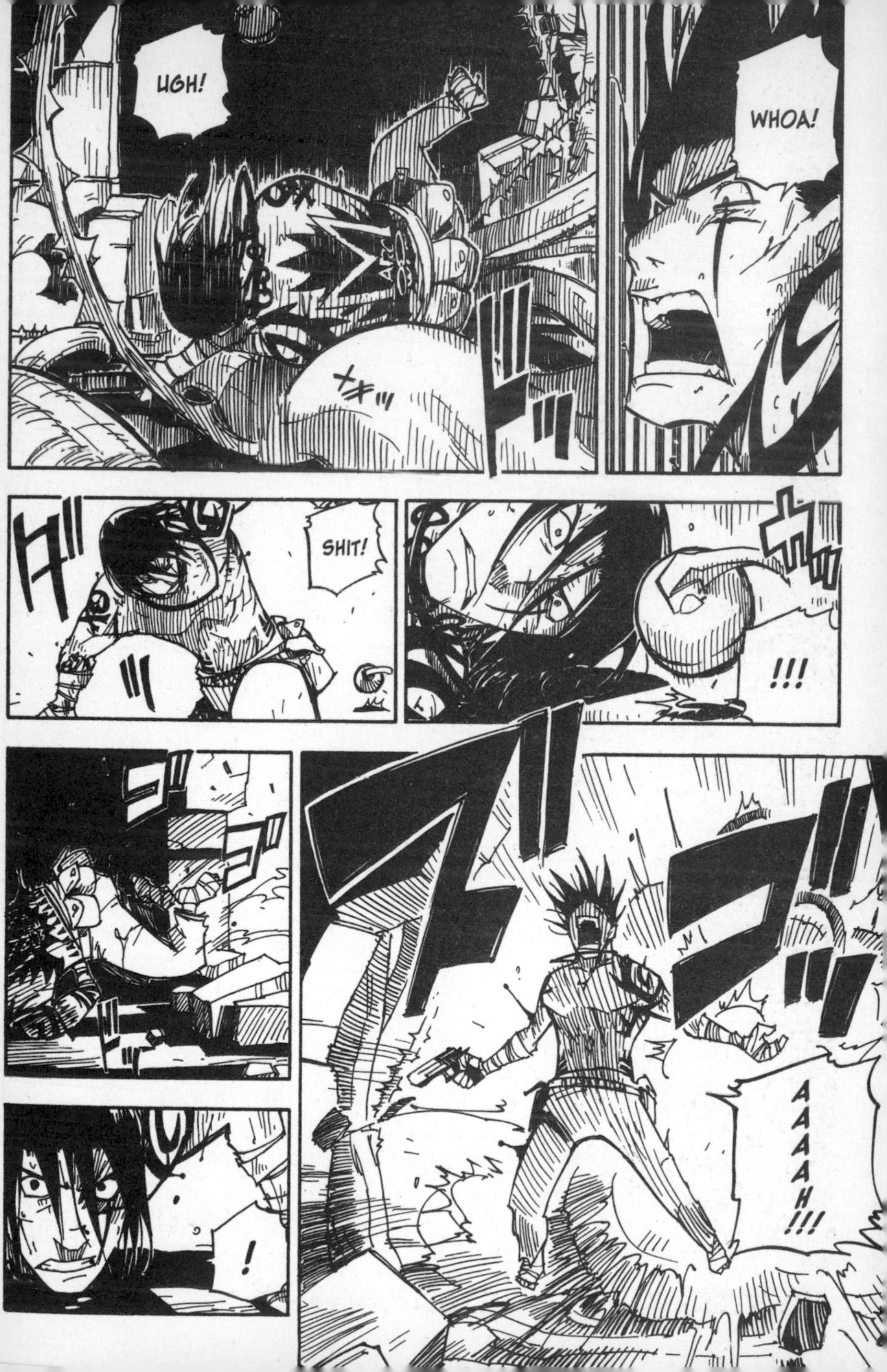
WHOA!
UGH!
SHIT!
!!!
!
AAAAAH!!!

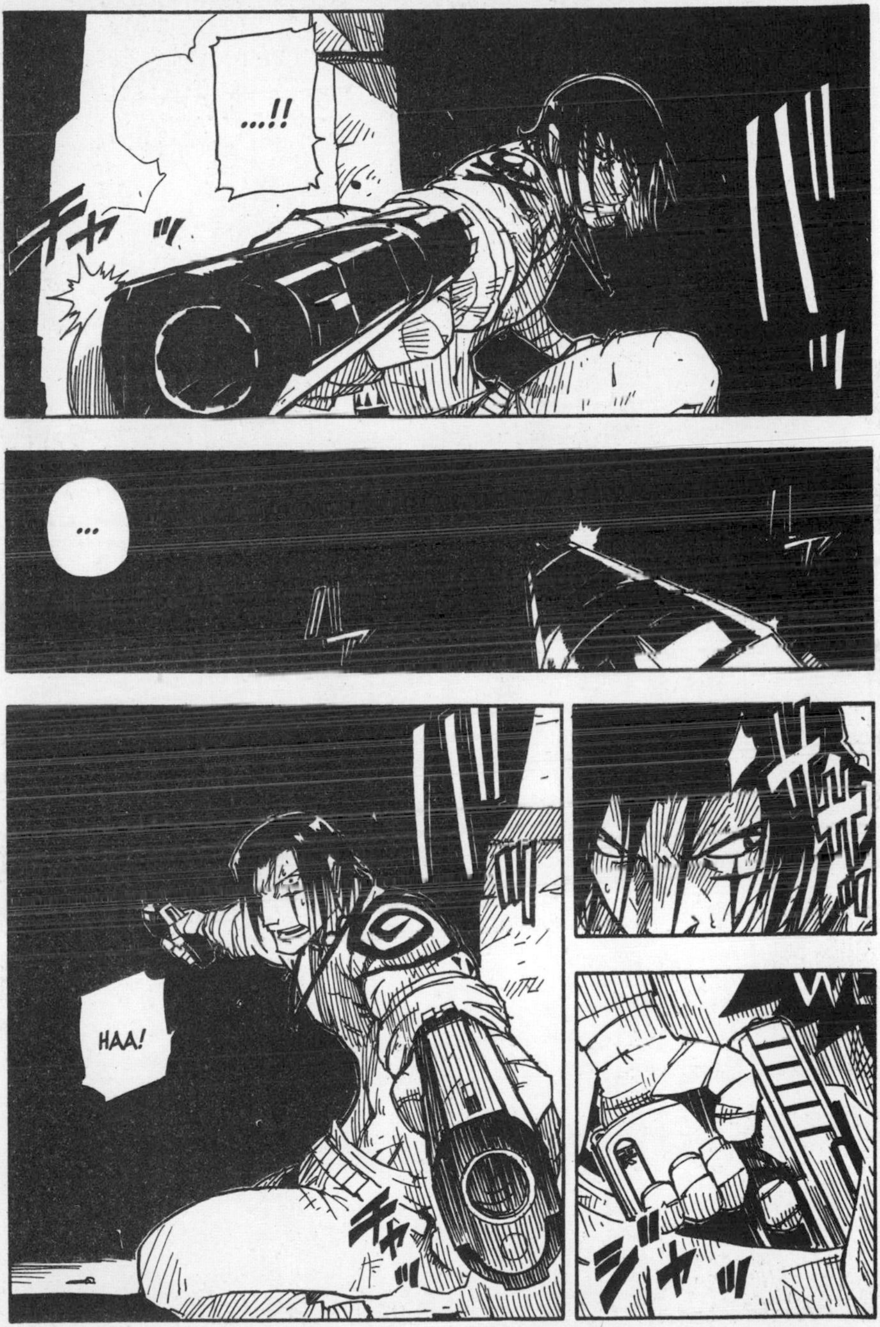
...!!
...
HAA!

WHERE'D IT GO?

Huff!

Huff!

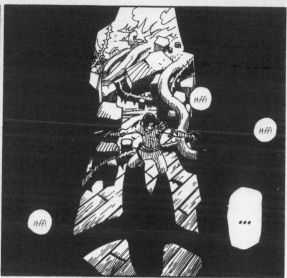

Hff!

Hff!

Hff!

...

!

THIS IS...

WOODEN FLOOR?

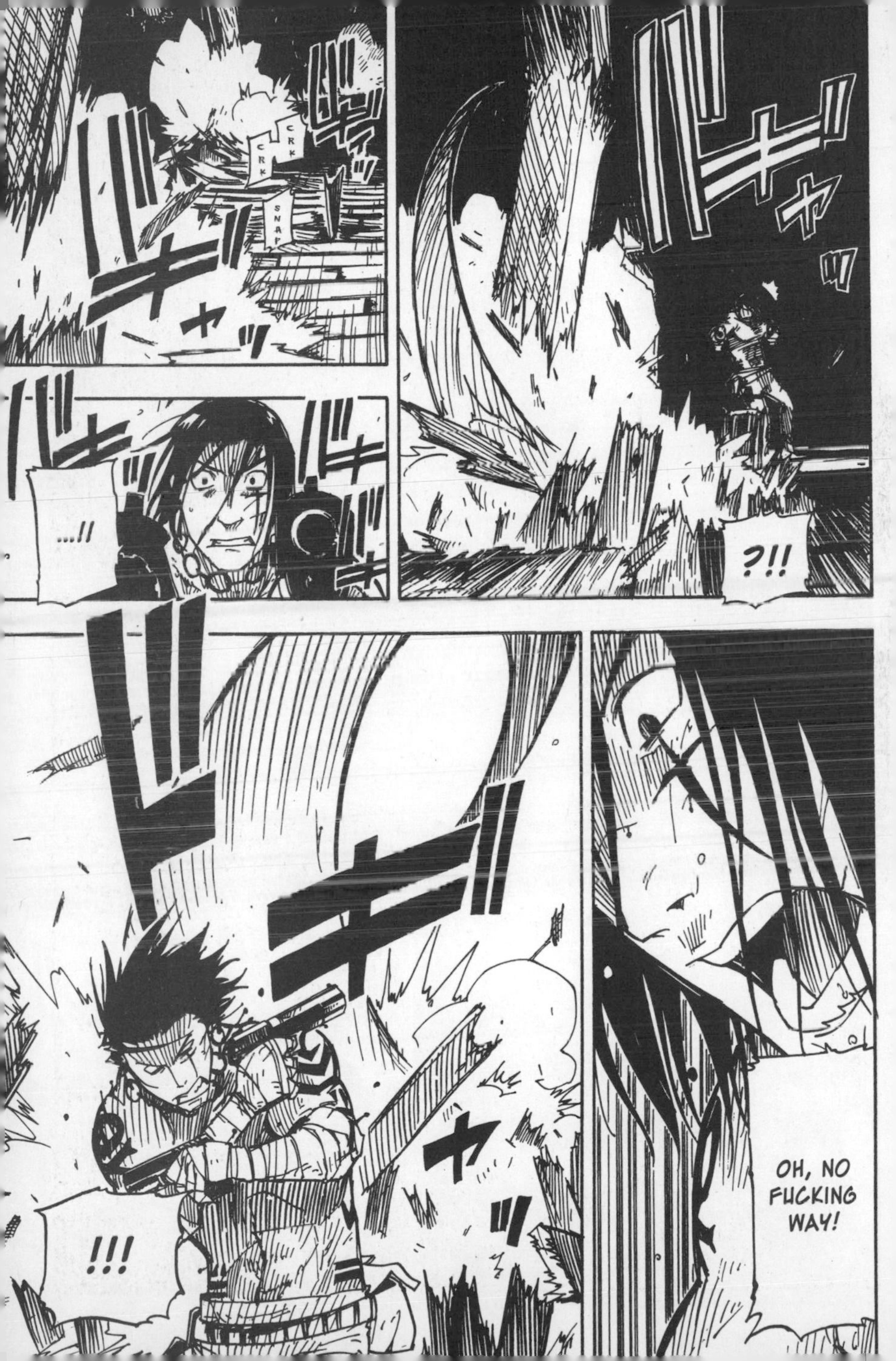
?!!
CRK CRK
SNAP
...!!
OH, NO FUCKING WAY!
!!!

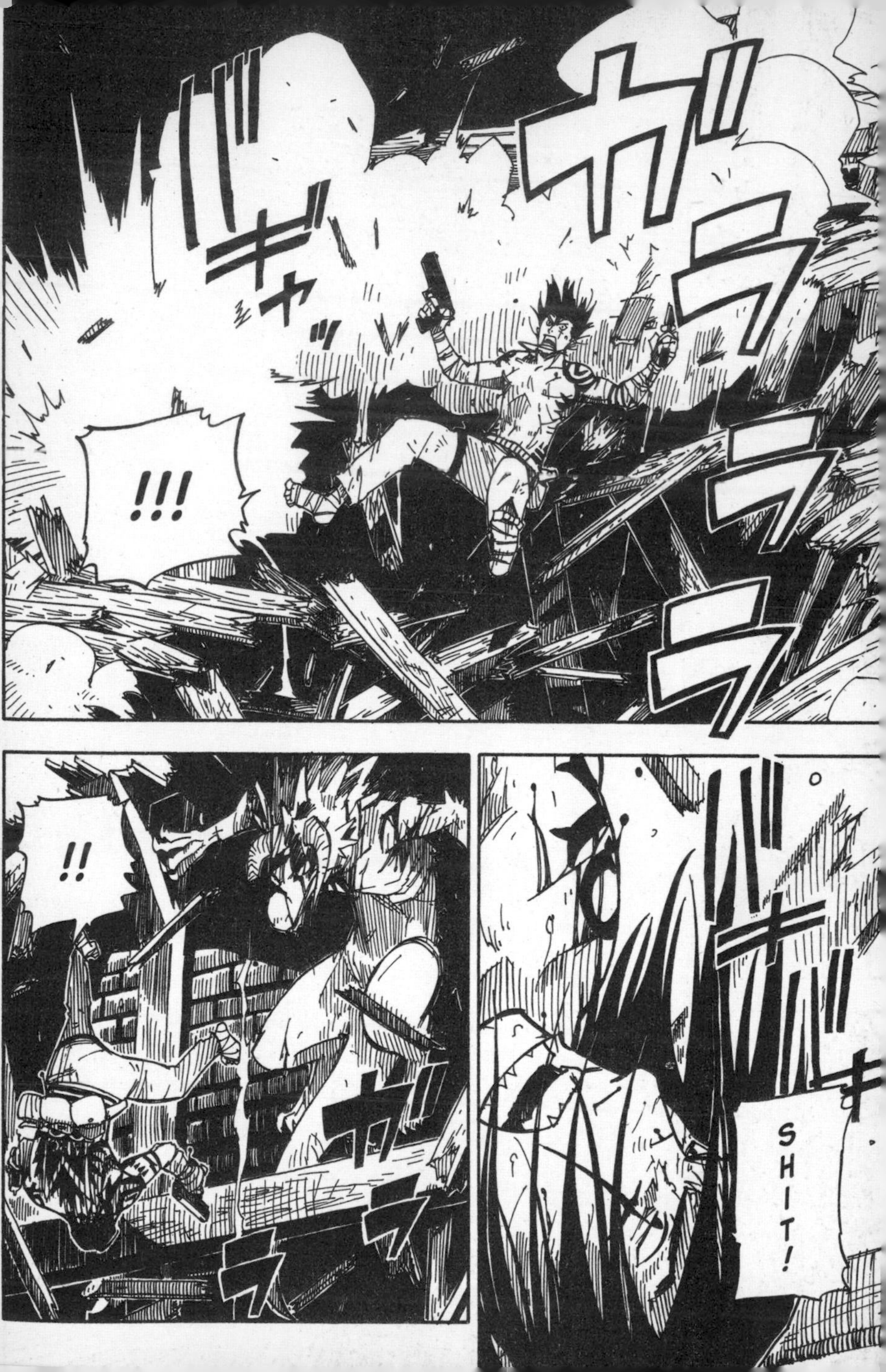
ガラララ
バギャッ
!!!
バキバキ
SHIT!
!!

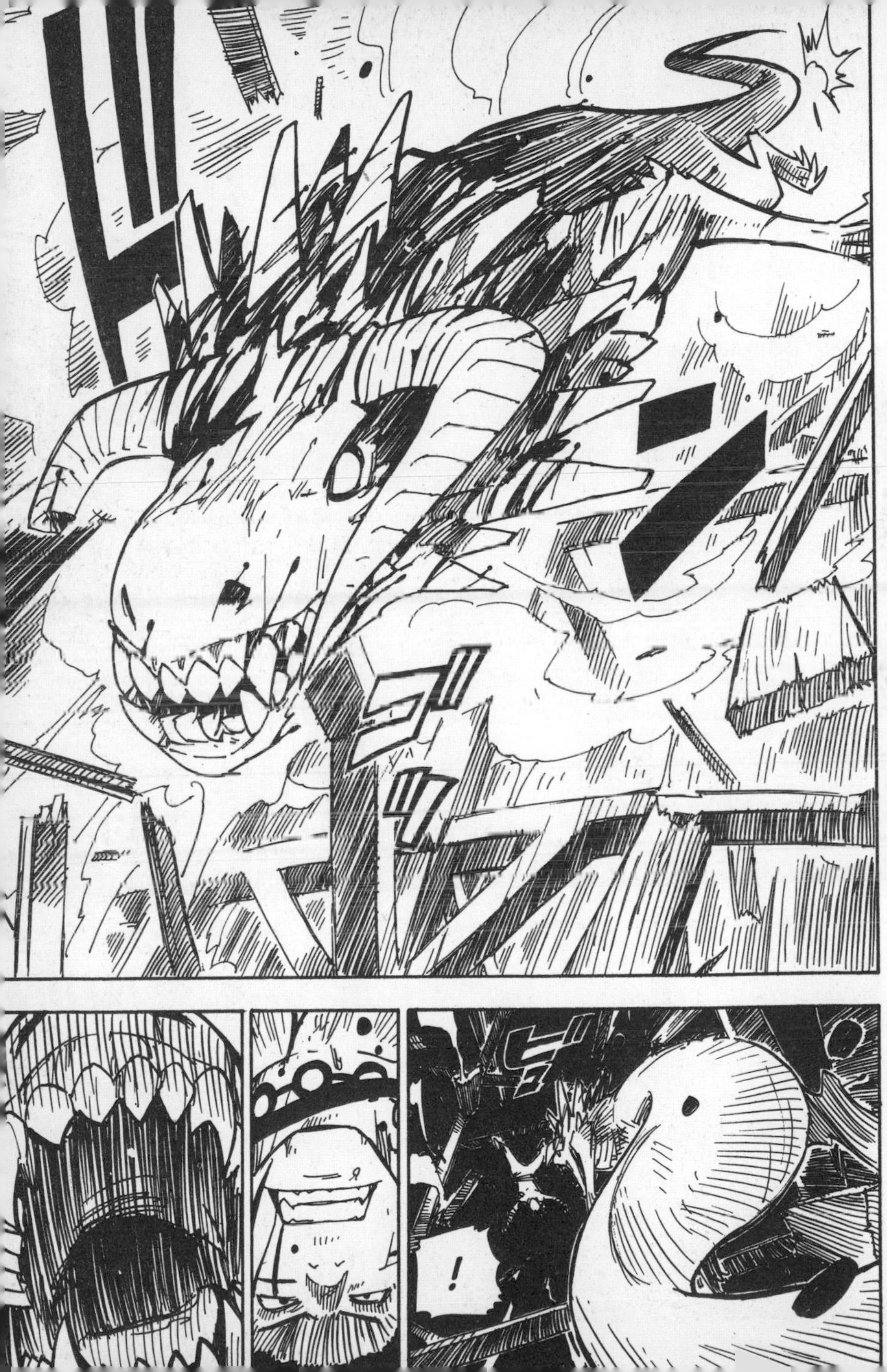
!

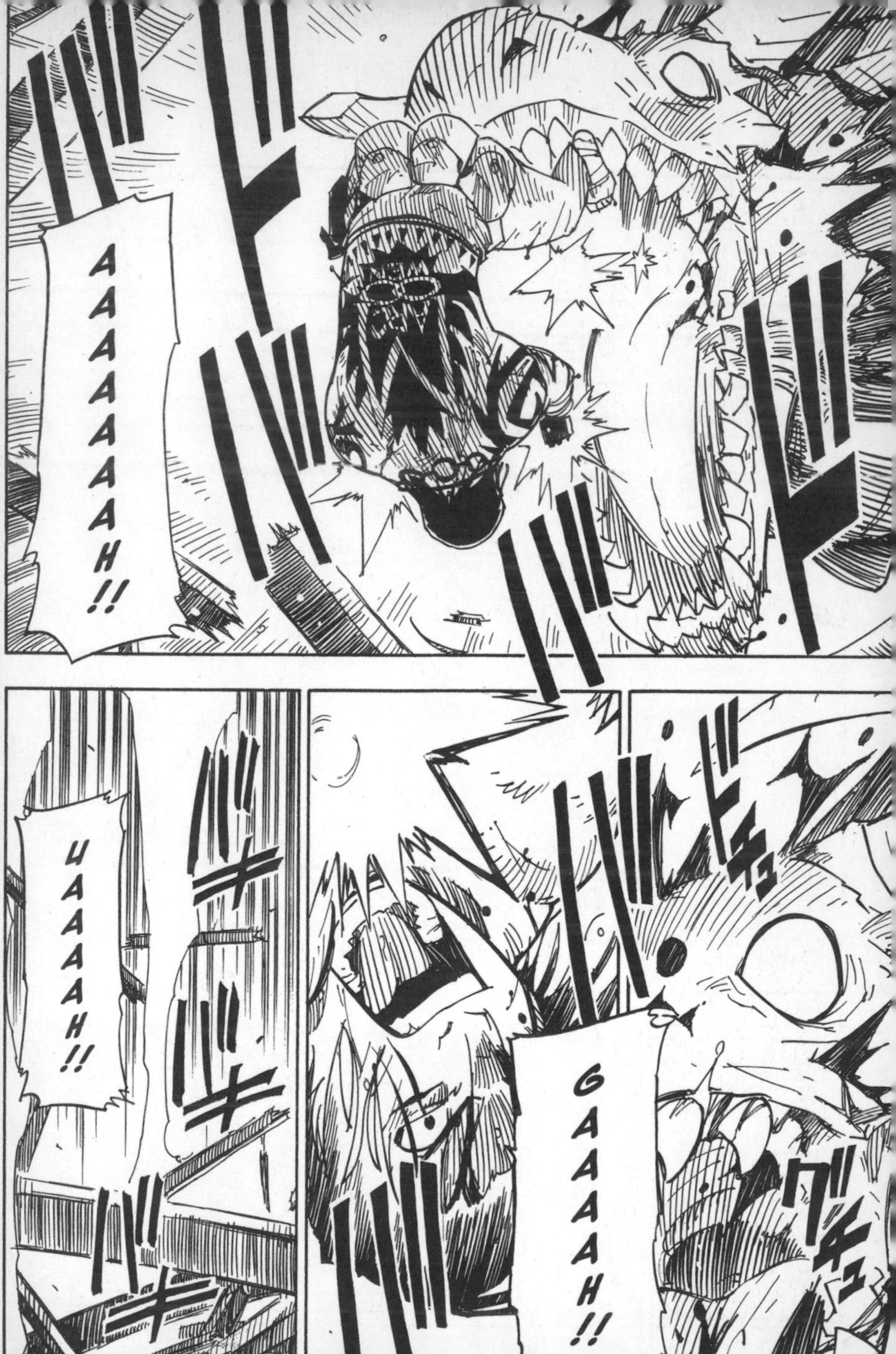
AAAAAAAH!!
GAAAAH!!
UAAAAH!!

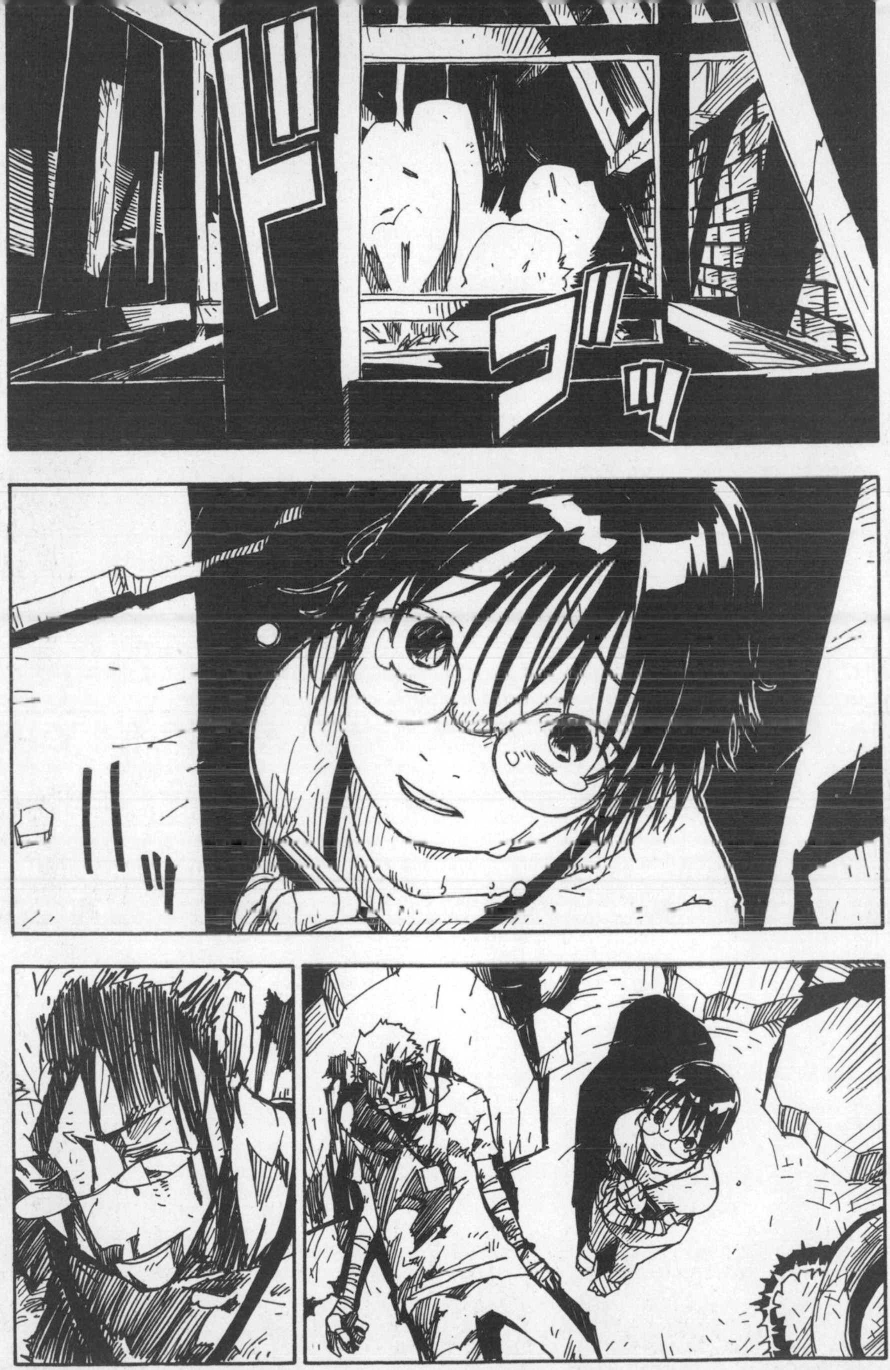

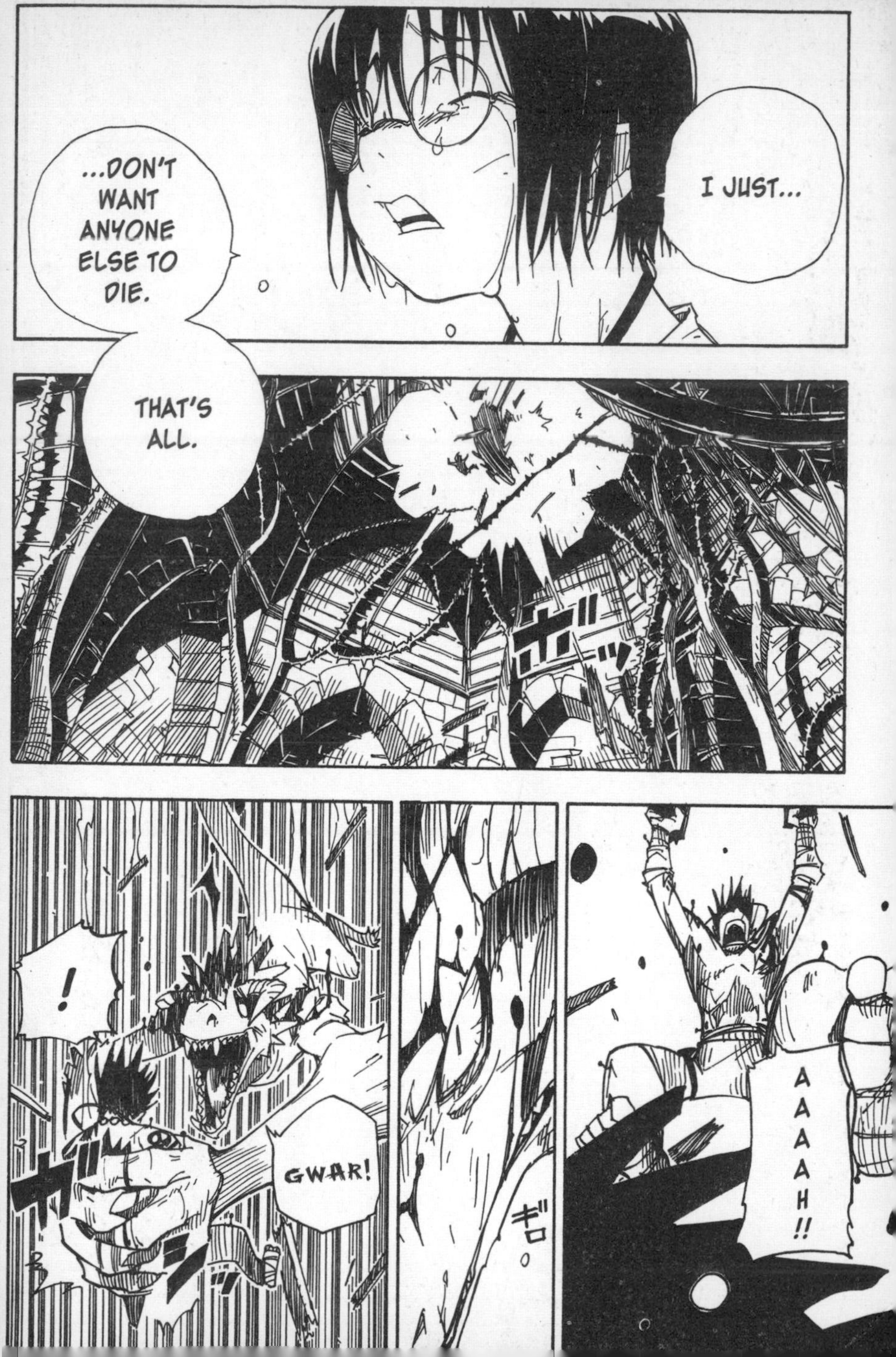

I JUST...
...DON'T WANT ANYONE ELSE TO DIE.
THAT'S ALL.
AAAAAH!!
ギロ
GWAR!
!

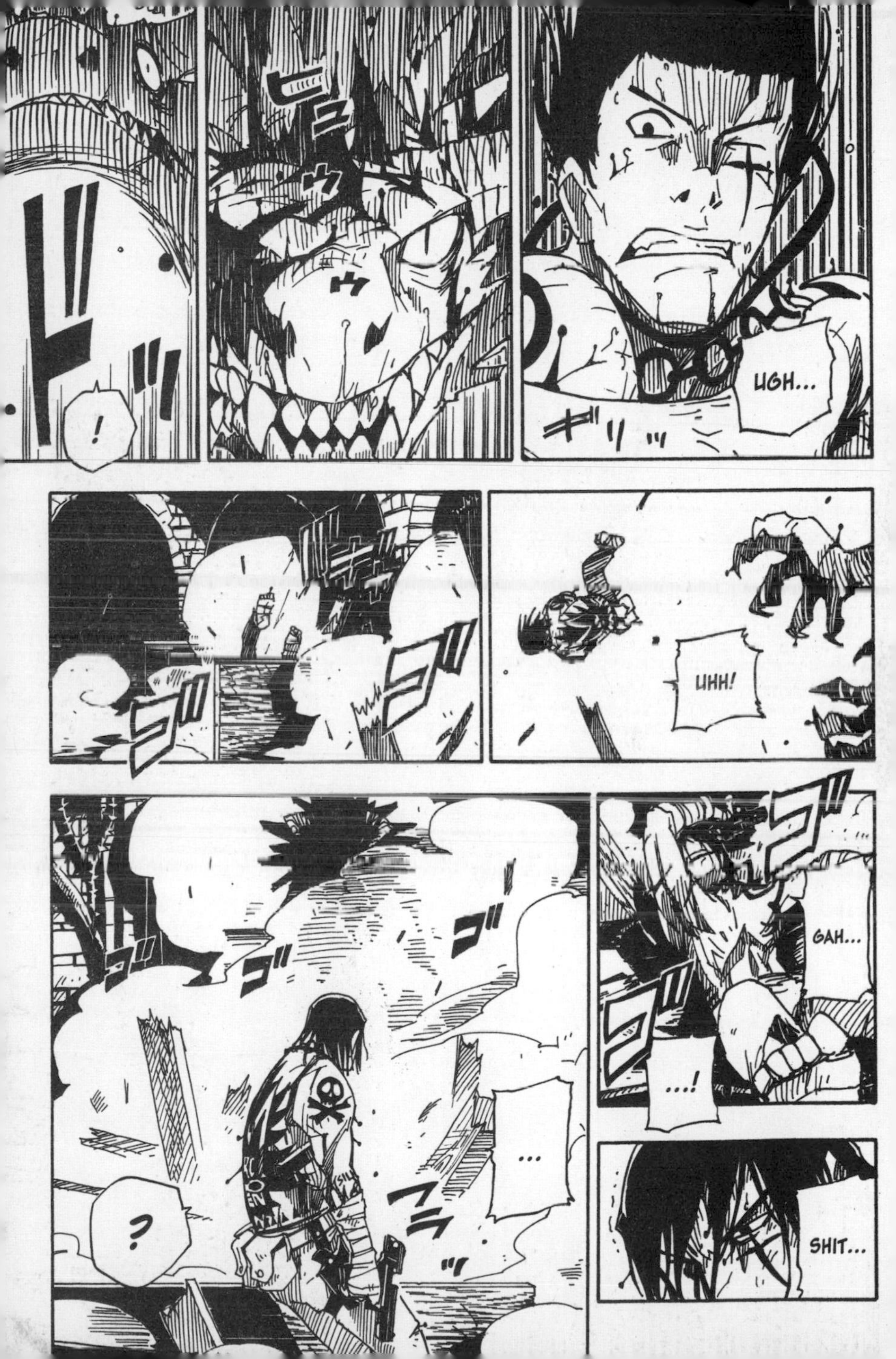
UGH...
!
UHH!
GAH...
...!
SHIT...
...
?

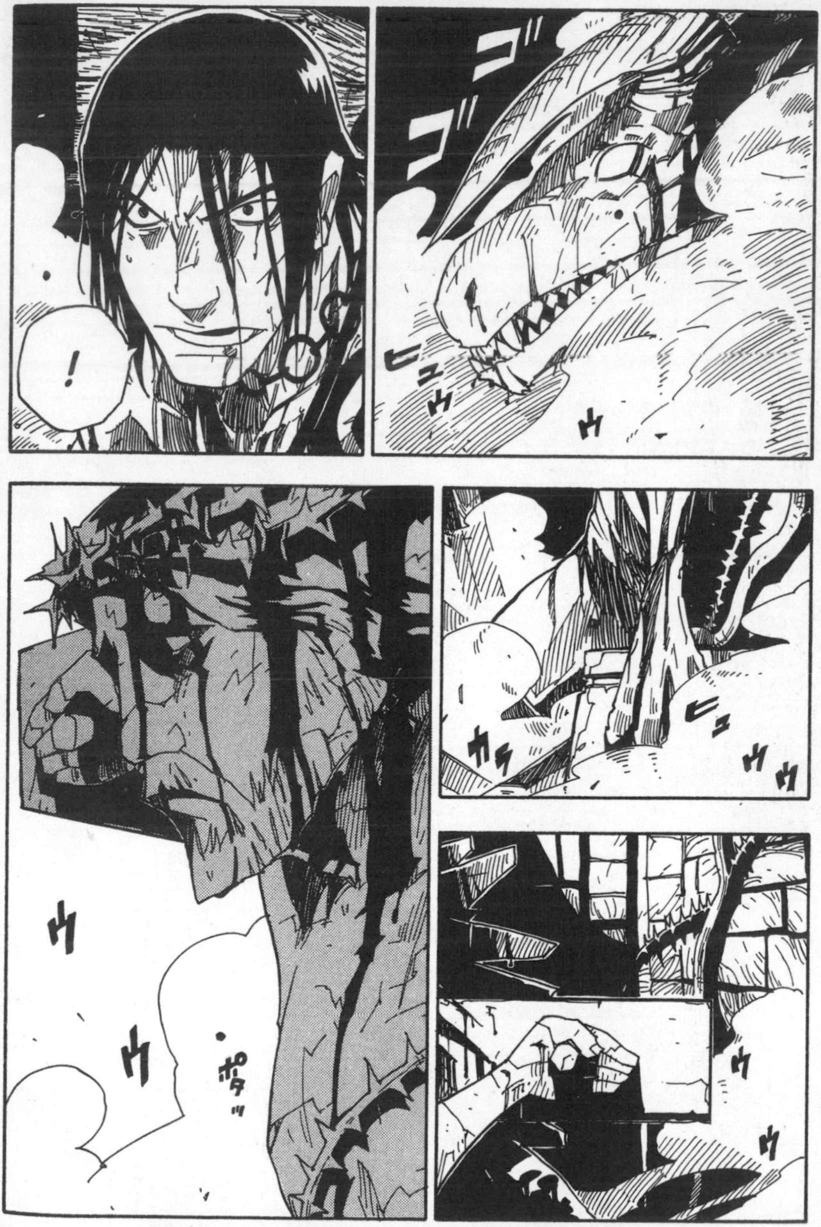
ゴゴ
ヒュウ
ウ
!
ヒュウウ
ウ
ウ
ウ
ウ
ポタッ

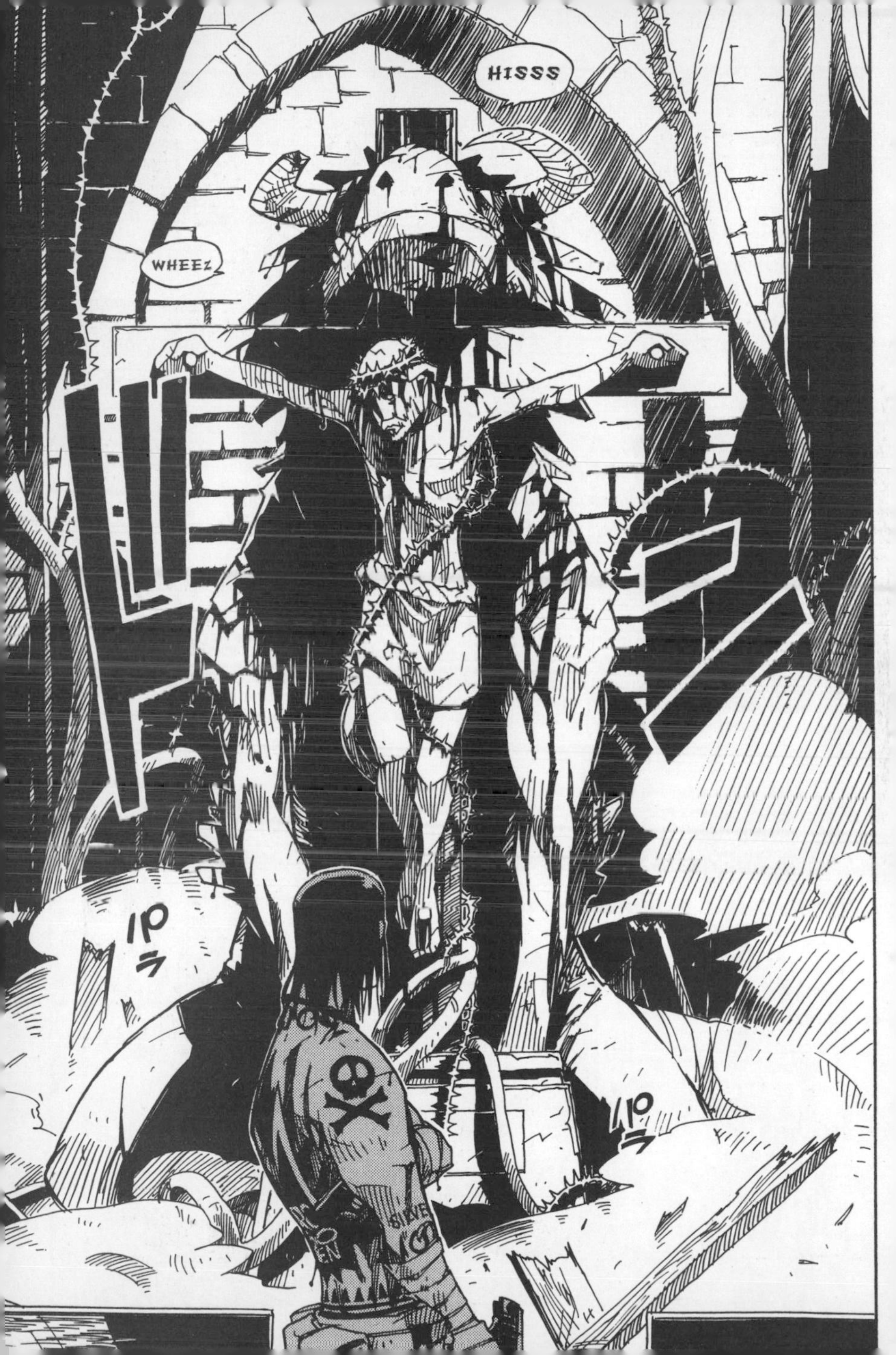
HISSS
WHEEZ
ゆラ
ゆラ

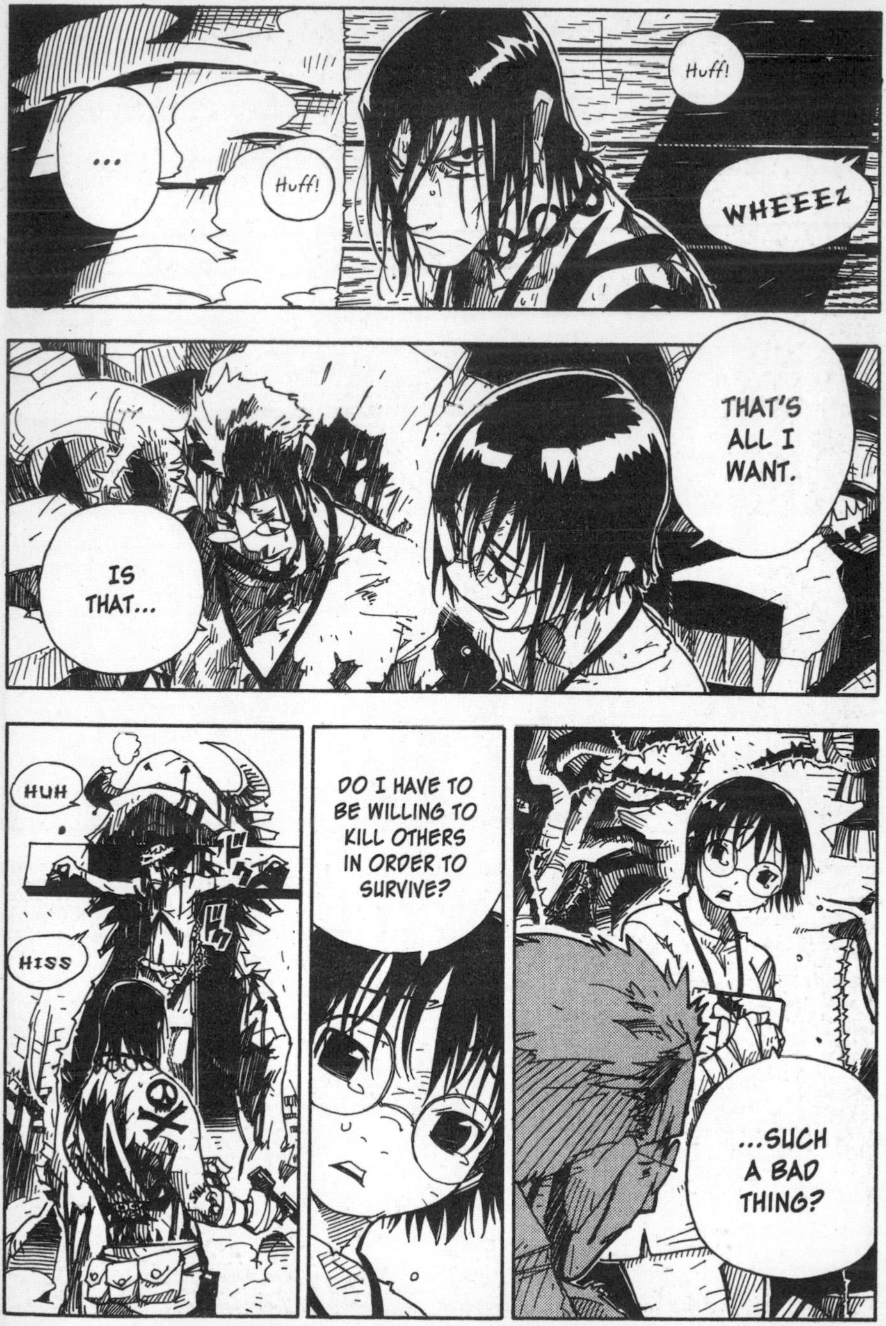
...
Huff!
Huff!
WHEEEZ
IS THAT...
THAT'S ALL I WANT.
HUH
HISS
DO I HAVE TO BE WILLING TO KILL OTHERS IN ORDER TO SURVIVE?
...SUCH A BAD THING?

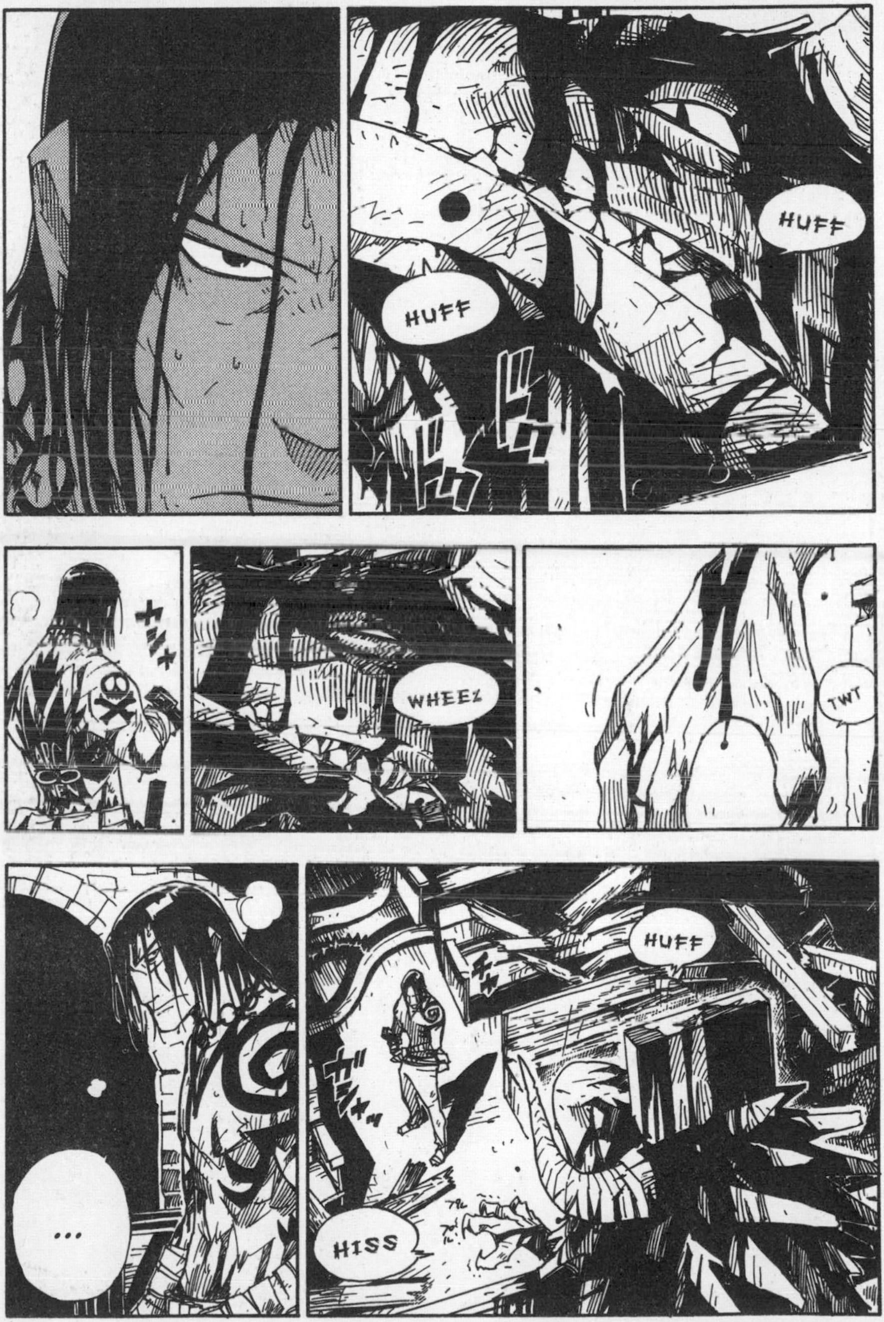
HUFF
HUFF
TWT
WHEEZ
HUFF
HISS
...

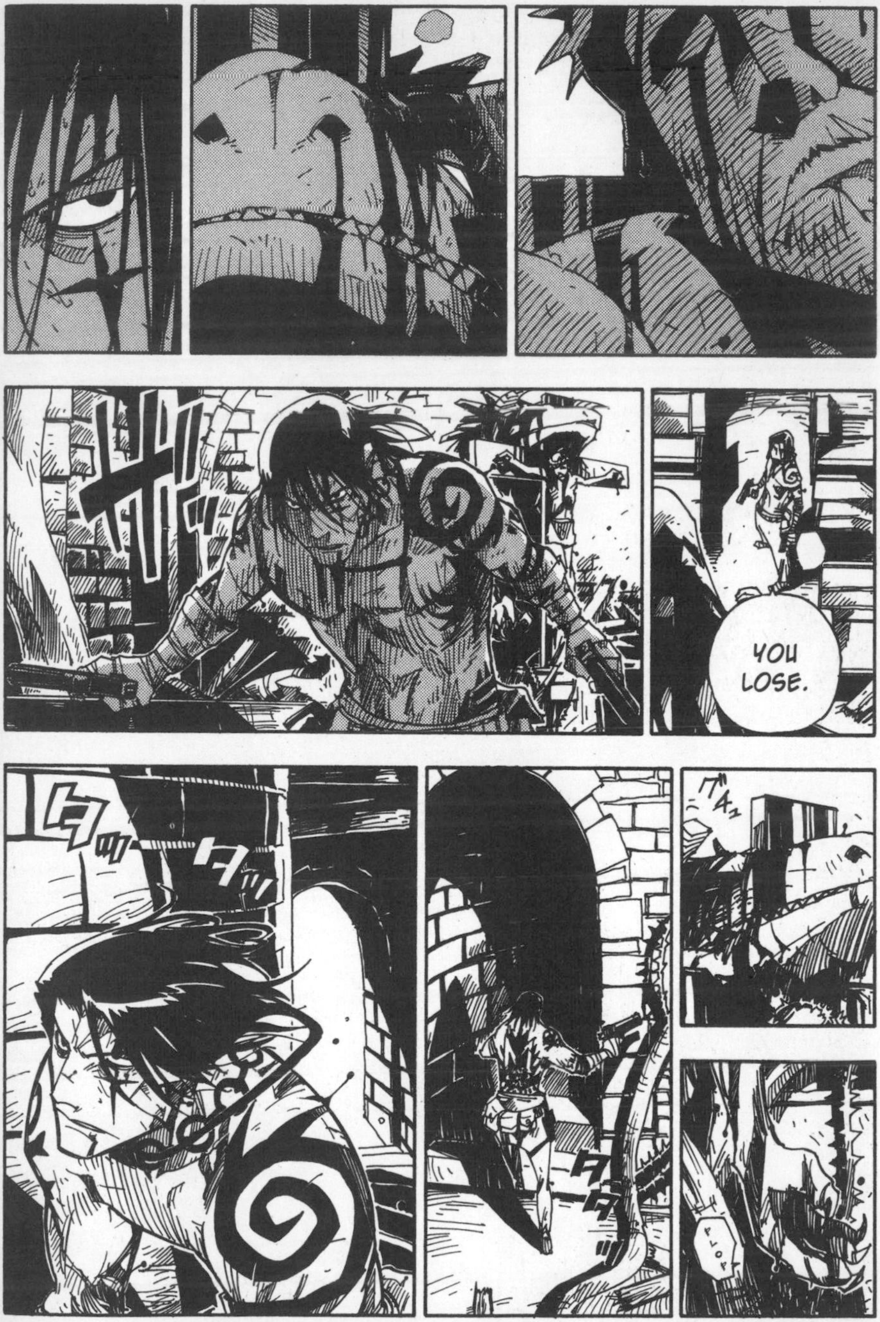
YOU LOSE.
PLOP

パリ
ピシッ
パラ
パラ
ブッ

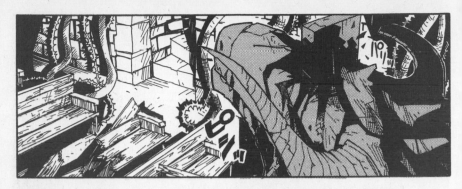

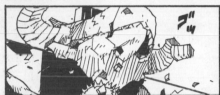

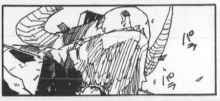

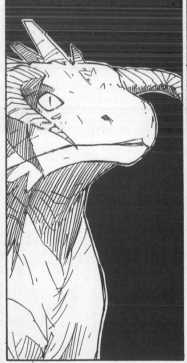

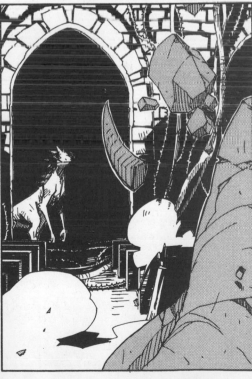

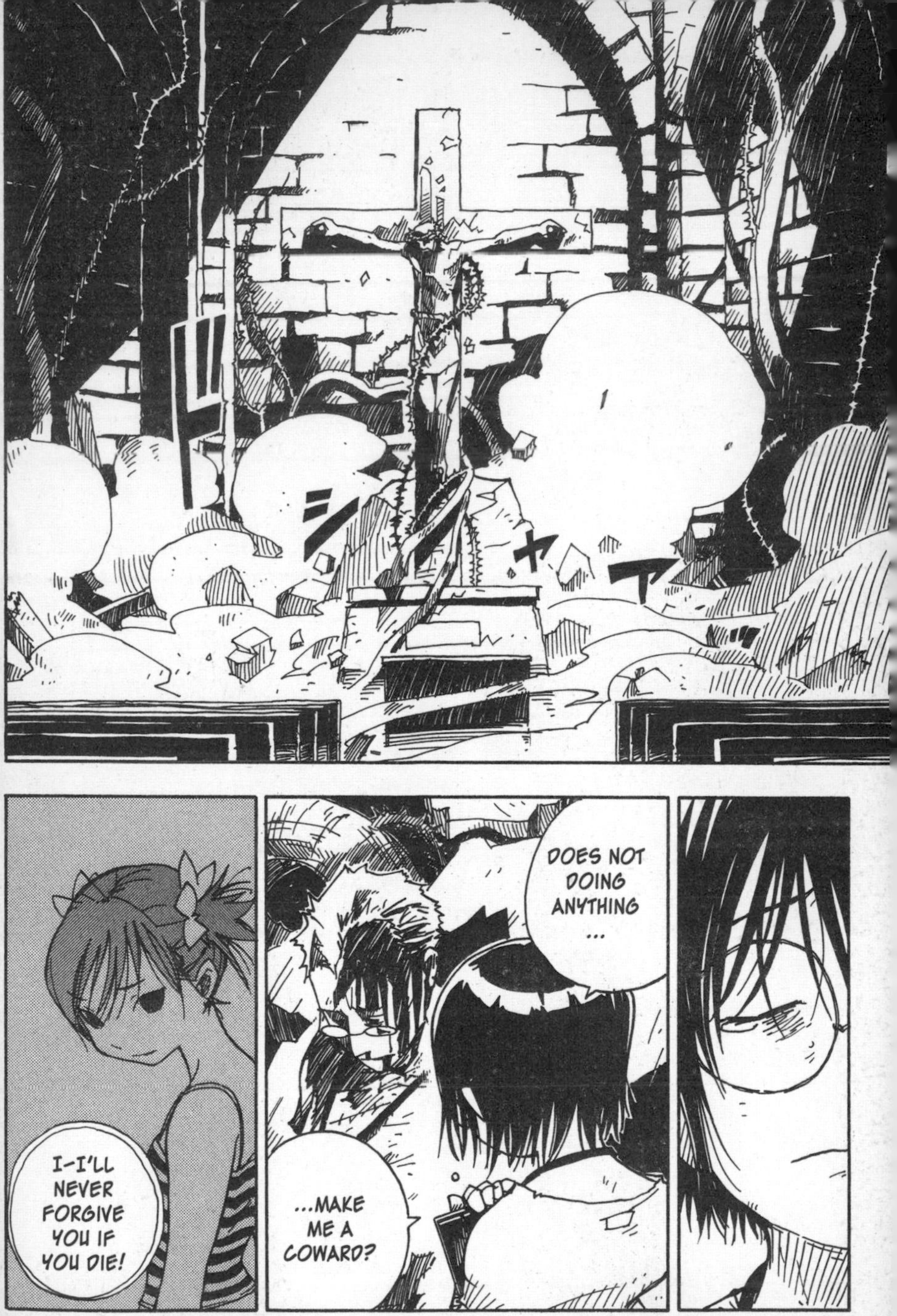
DOES NOT DOING ANYTHING ...
...MAKE ME A COWARD?
I-I'LL NEVER FORGIVE YOU IF YOU DIE!

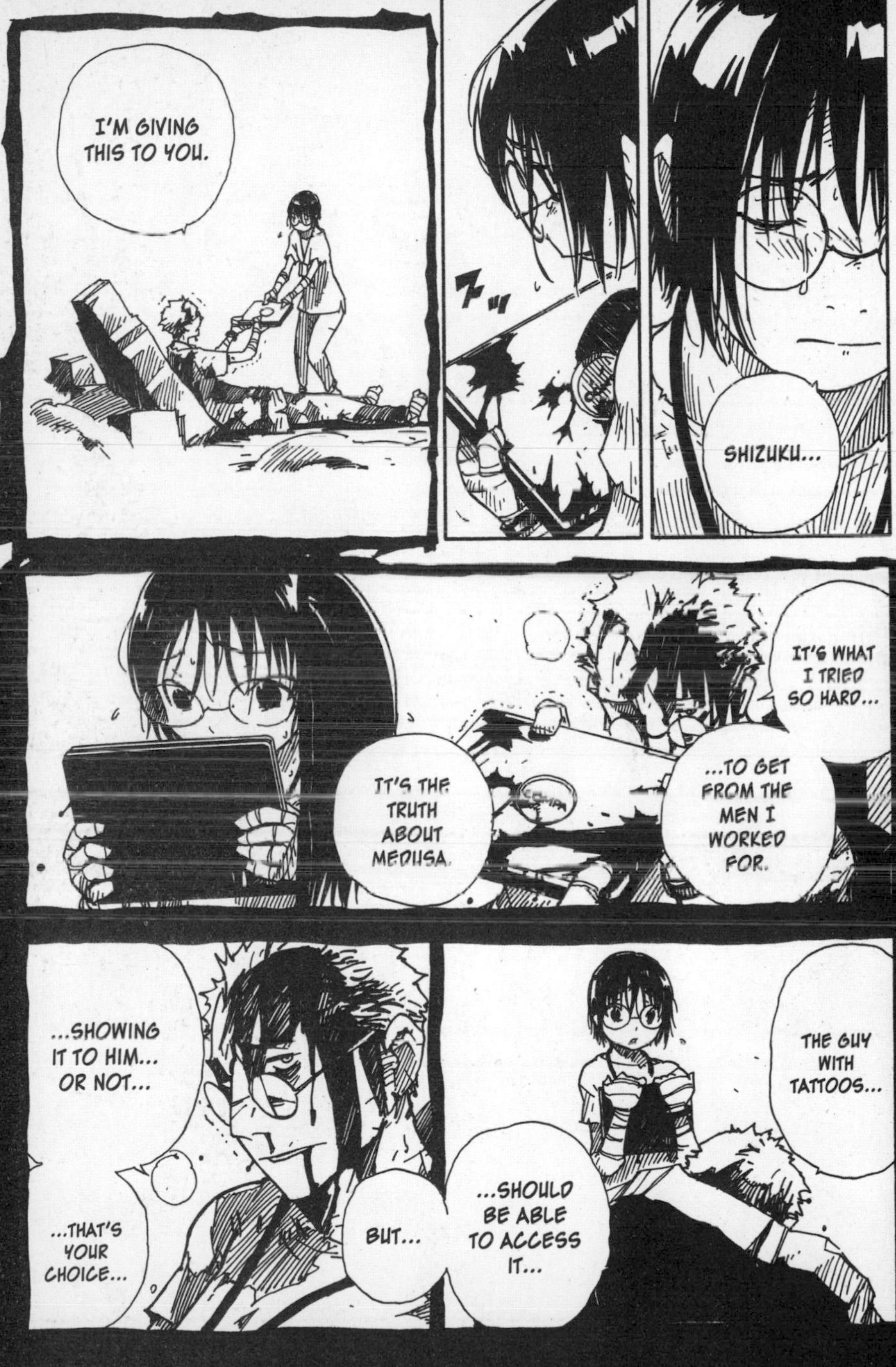
SHIZUKU...
I'M GIVING THIS TO YOU.
IT'S WHAT I TRIED SO HARD...
...TO GET FROM THE MEN I WORKED FOR.
IT'S THE TRUTH ABOUT MEDUSA.
THE GUY WITH TATTOOS...
...SHOULD BE ABLE TO ACCESS IT...
BUT...
...SHOWING IT TO HIM... OR NOT...
...THAT'S YOUR CHOICE...

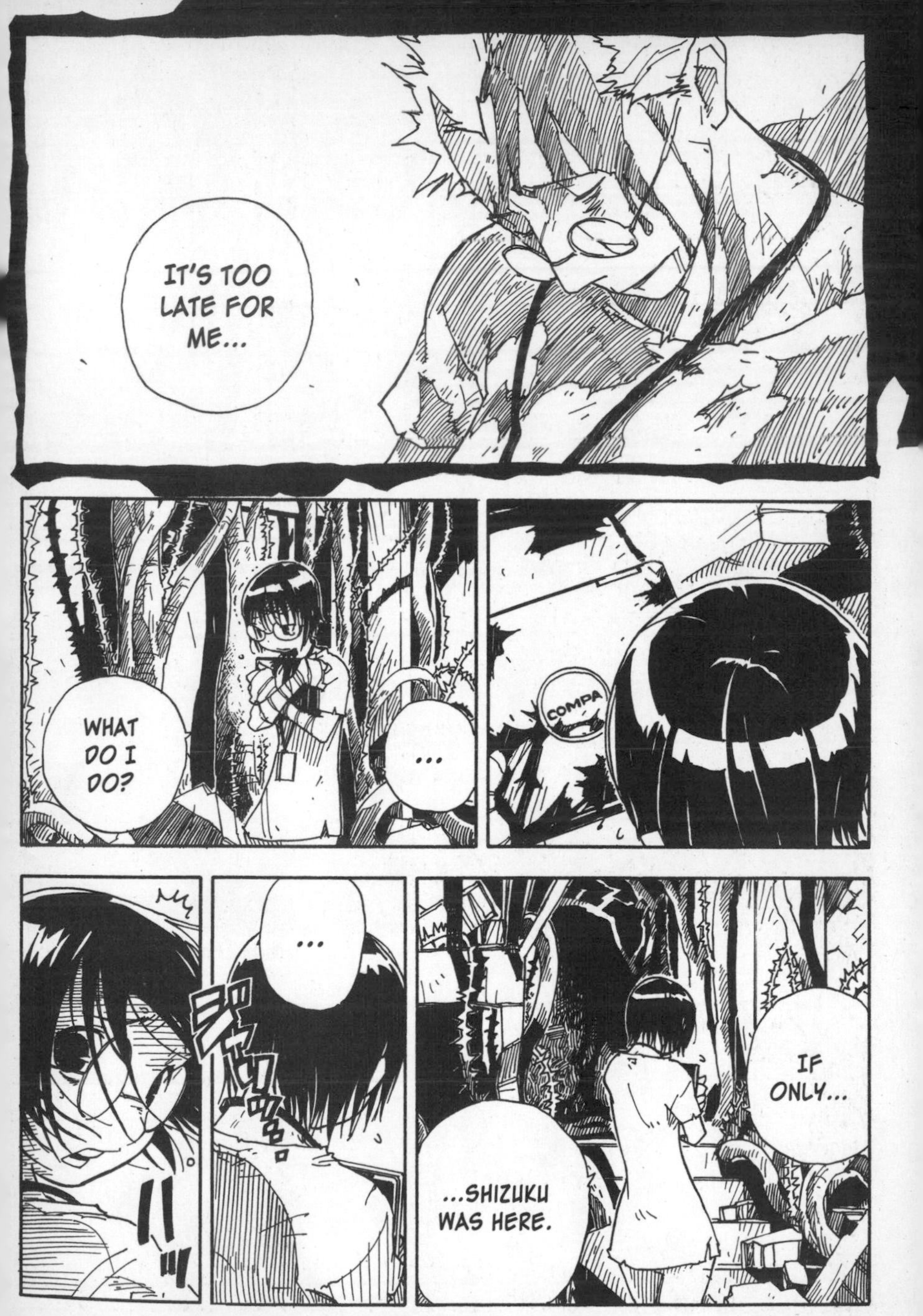
IT'S TOO LATE FOR ME...
COMPA
...
WHAT DO I DO?
IF ONLY...
...SHIZUKU WAS HERE.
...

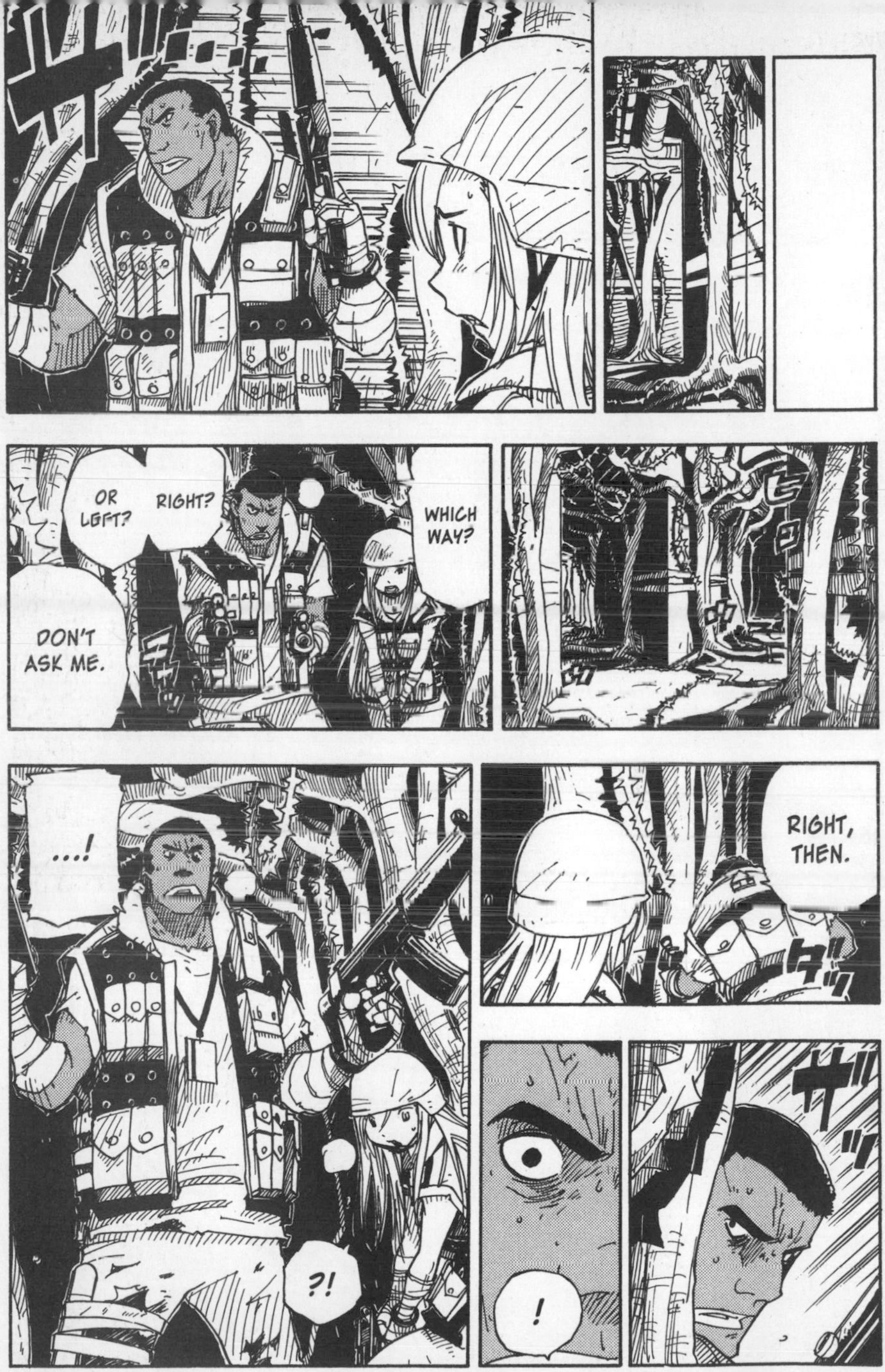
WHICH WAY?
RIGHT?
OR LEFT?
DON'T ASK ME.
RIGHT, THEN.
...!
?!
!

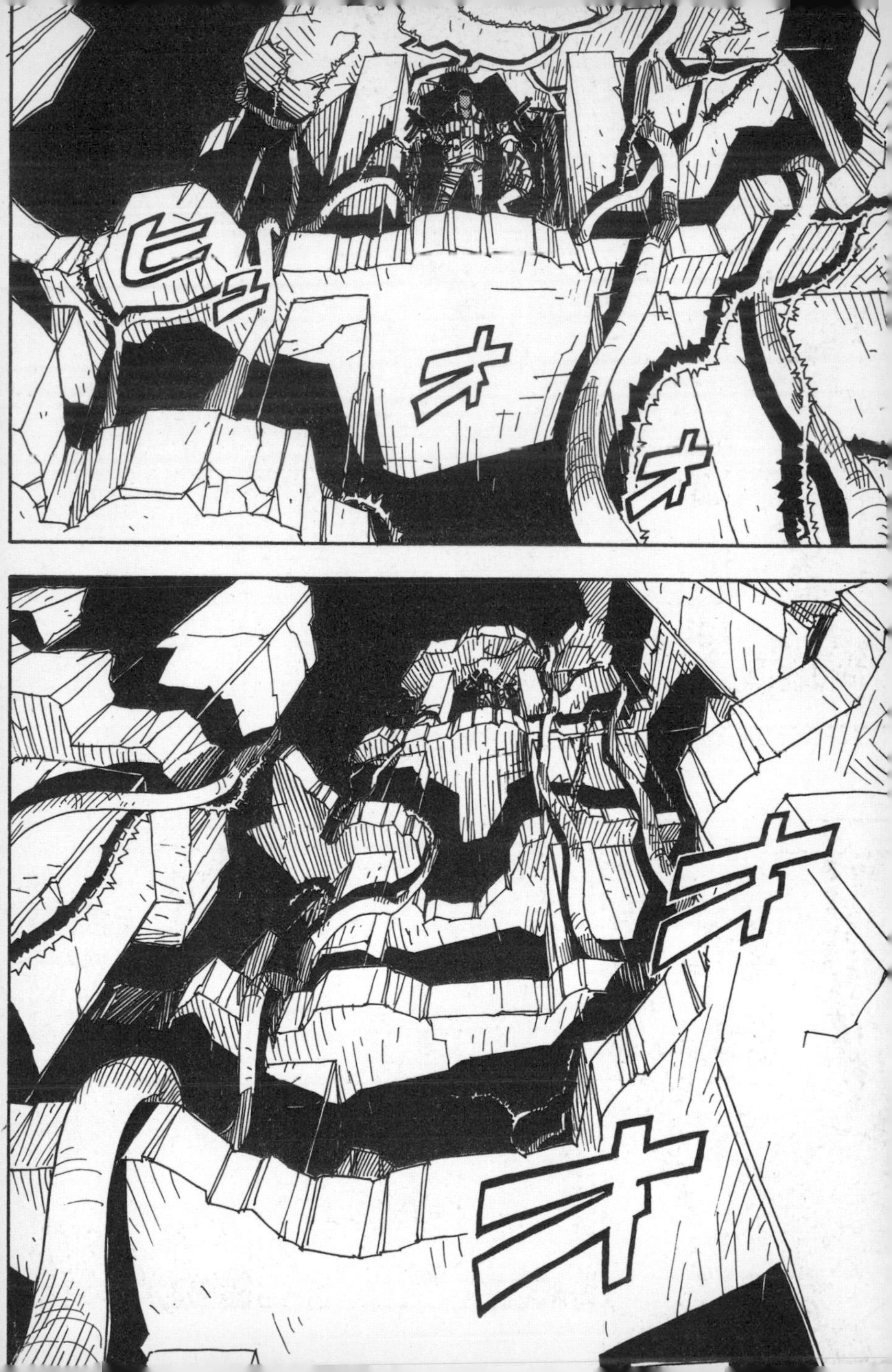
ヒュ
オ
オ
オ
オ

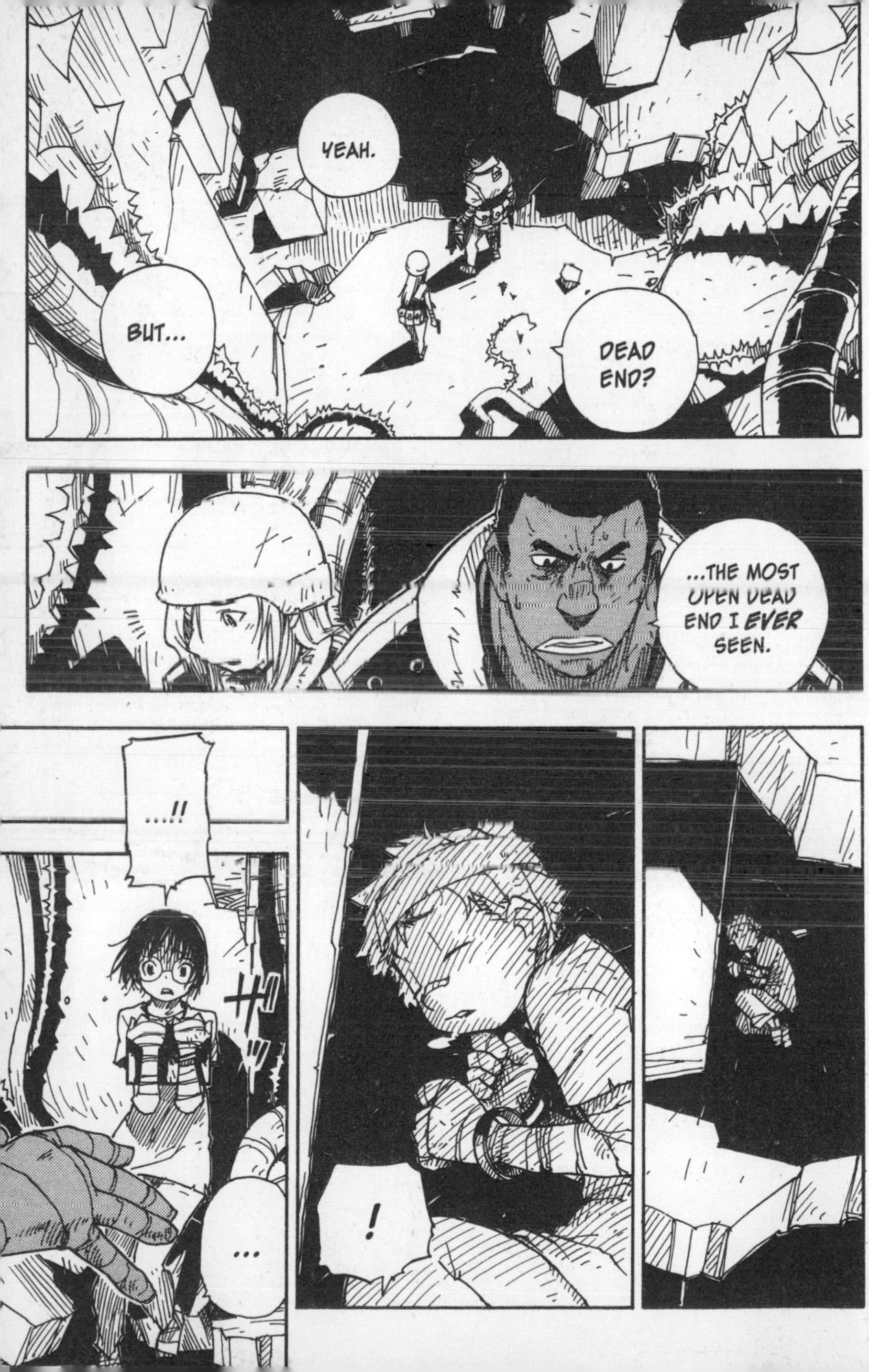
YEAH.
BUT...
DEAD END?
...THE MOST OPEN DEAD END I EVER SEEN.
...!!
...
!

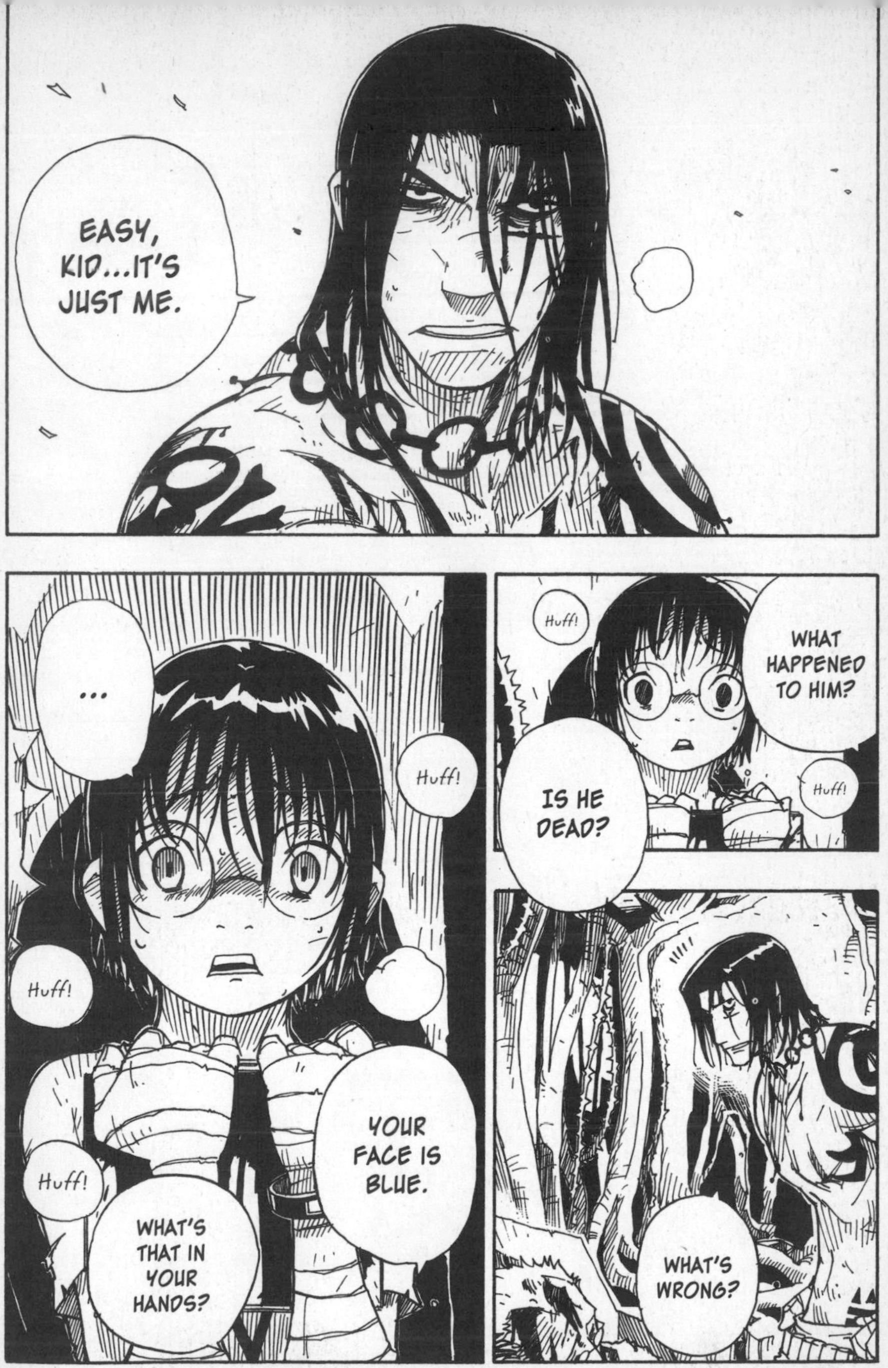
EASY, KID...IT'S JUST ME.
Huff!
WHAT HAPPENED TO HIM?
Huff!
IS HE DEAD?
WHAT'S WRONG?
...
Huff!
Huff!
YOUR FACE IS BLUE.
Huff!
WHAT'S THAT IN YOUR HANDS?

To be continued...

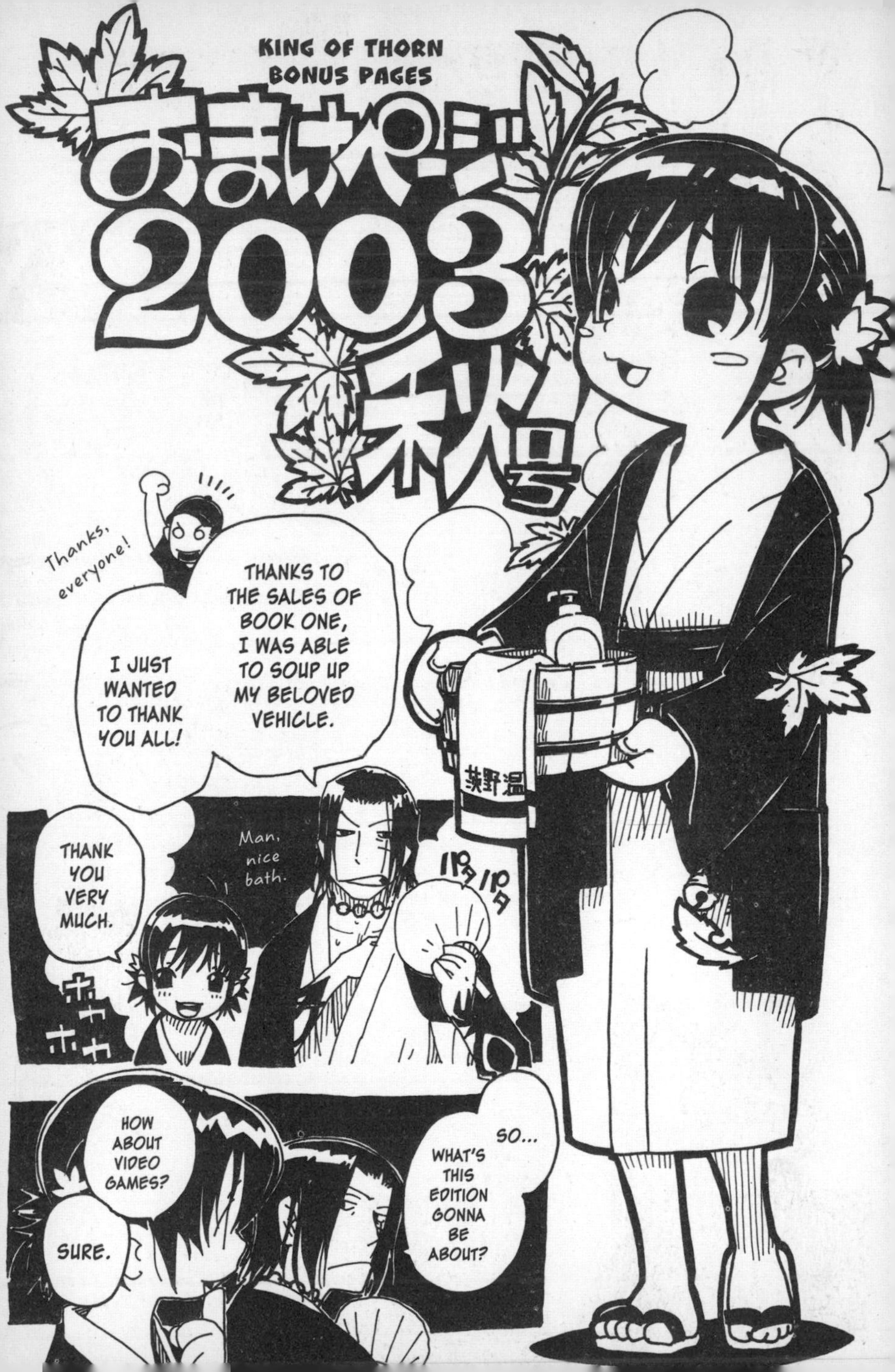

KING OF THORN
BONUS PAGES
2003
THANKS TO THE SALES OF BOOK ONE, I WAS ABLE TO SOUP UP MY BELOVED VEHICLE.
I JUST WANTED TO THANK YOU ALL!
Thanks, everyone!
Man, nice bath.
THANK YOU VERY MUCH.
SO... WHAT'S THIS EDITION GONNA BE ABOUT?
HOW ABOUT VIDEO GAMES?
SURE.

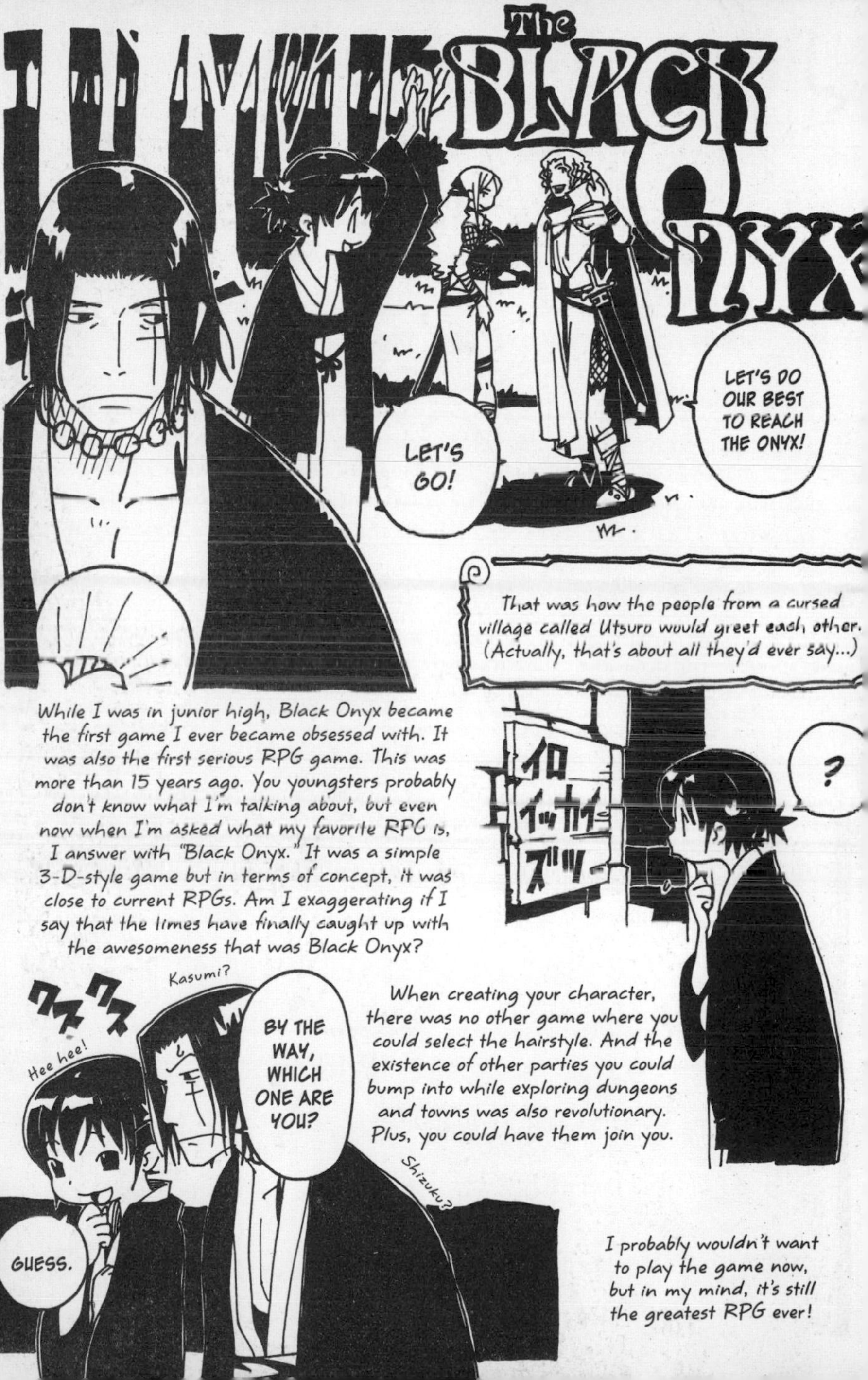
The BLACK ONYX
LET'S DO OUR BEST TO REACH THE ONYX!
LET'S GO!
That was how the people from a cursed village called Utsuro would greet each other. (Actually, that's about all they'd ever say...)
While I was in junior high, Black Onyx became the first game I ever became obsessed with. It was also the first serious RPG game. This was more than 15 years ago. You youngsters probably don't know what I'm talking about, but even now when I'm asked what my favorite RPG is, I answer with "Black Onyx." It was a simple 3-D-style game but in terms of concept, it was close to current RPGs. Am I exaggerating if I say that the times have finally caught up with the awesomeness that was Black Onyx?
?
When creating your character, there was no other game where you could select the hairstyle. And the existence of other parties you could bump into while exploring dungeons and towns was also revolutionary. Plus, you could have them join you.
Kasumi?
BY THE WAY, WHICH ONE ARE YOU?
Hee hee!
Shizuku?
GUESS.
I probably wouldn't want to play the game now, but in my mind, it's still the greatest RPG ever!

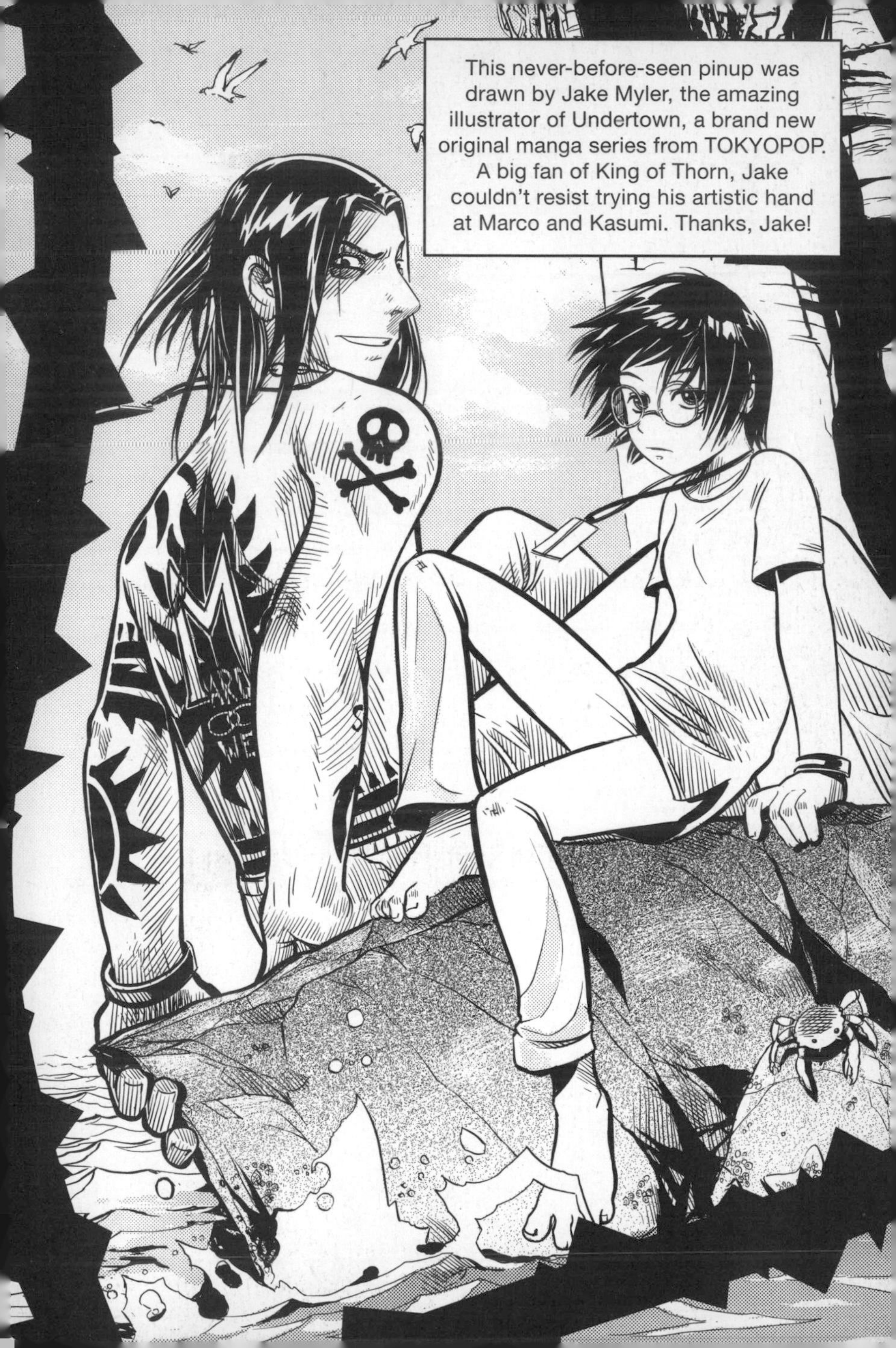
This never-before-seen pinup was drawn by Jake Myler, the amazing illustrator of Undertown, a brand new original manga series from TOKYOPOP. A big fan of King of Thorn, Jake couldn't resist trying his artistic hand at Marco and Kasumi. Thanks, Jake!

In the next...

KING of THORN ™

Having faced threats from within and without
their dwindling group, the Medusa Virus survivors
begin to probe further into what's happened.
They have Peter's hard drive, but what will
they find on it? And will they even have time
to look? A new amphibious threat emerges that
will find Marco face to frog with the slimiest
mother on this chillingly altered earth. The
former mercenary has proved to be quite adept
at staying alive, but will this confrontation
be the one that puts him in the ground?

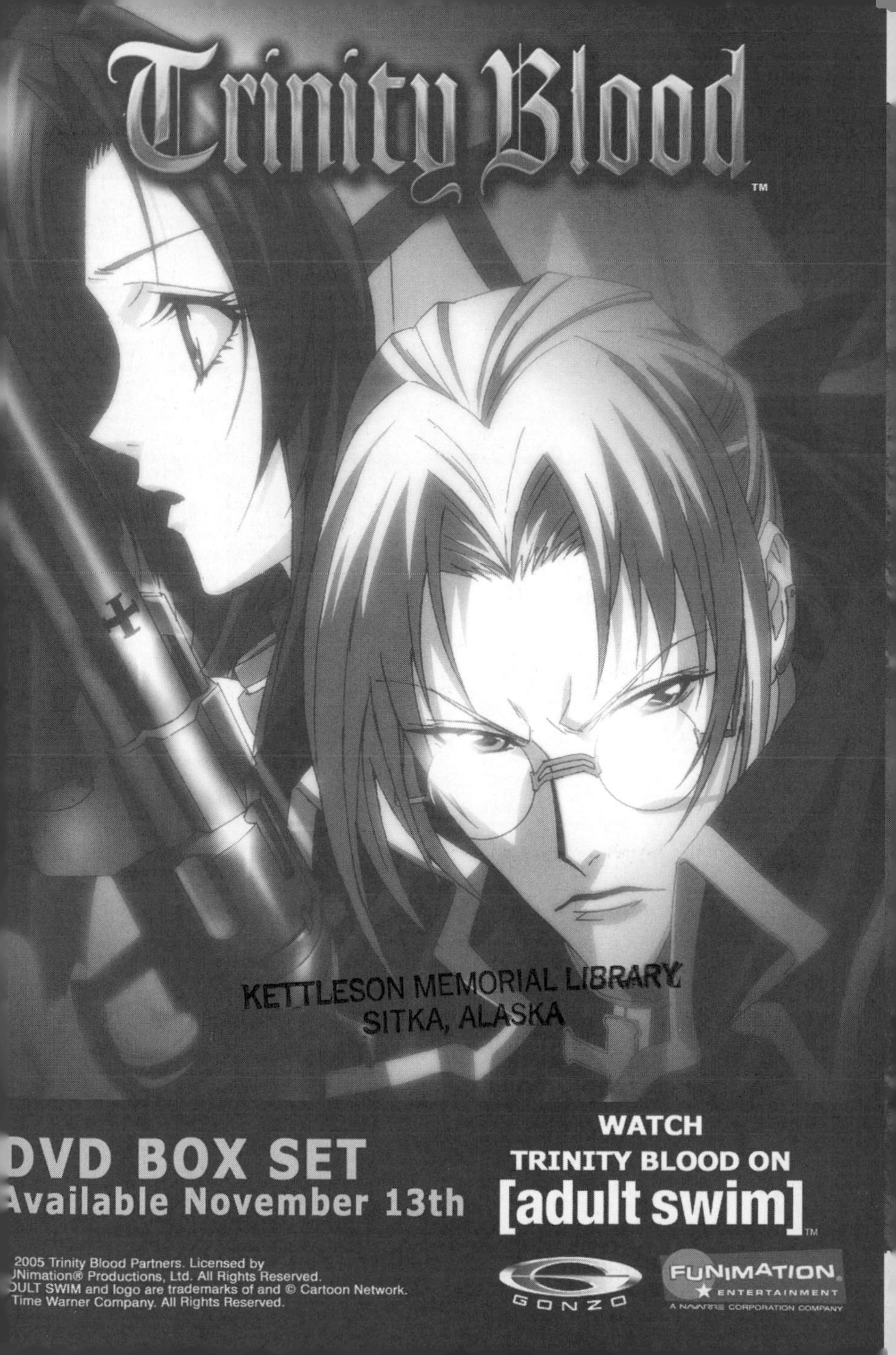
Trinity Blood
TM
DVD BOX SET
Available November 13th
WATCH
TRINITY BLOOD ON
[adult swim]
TM
2005 Trinity Blood Partners. Licensed by
UNimation® Productions, Ltd. All Rights Reserved.
DULT SWIM and logo are trademarks of and © Cartoon Network.
Time Warner Company. All Rights Reserved.
GONZO
FUNIMATION
ENTERTAINMENT
A NAVARRE CORPORATION COMPANY